COLLECTED WHEEL PUBLICATIONS

VOLUME 2

NUMBERS 16 – 30

BPE

BPS Pariyatti Editions

BPS Pariyatti Editions
An imprint of Pariyatti Publishing
www.pariyatti.org

Although this is an American edition, we have left any British spelling of words unchanged.

First BPS Pariyatti Edition, 2019
ISBN: 978-1-68172-128-6 (Print)
ISBN: 978-1-68172-129-3 (PDF)
ISBN: 978-1-68172-130-9 (ePub)
ISBN: 978-1-68172-131-6 (Mobi)
LCCN: 2018940050

Contents

WH 16 Buddhism and Christianity
Helmuth von Glasenapp ... 1

WH 17 Three Cardinal Discourses of the Buddha
Ñāṇamoli Thera ... 37

WH 18 Devotion in Buddhism ... 63

WH 19 The Foundations of Mindfulness
Nyanasatta Thera ... 85

WH 20 The Three Signata: Anicca, Dukkha, Anattā
Dr. O. H. de A. Wijesekera ... 111

WH 21 The Removal of Distracting Thoughts
Soma Thera ... 135

WH 22 Buddha the Healer
Dr. Ānanda Nimalasuria ... 159

WH 23 The Nature and Purpose of the Ascetic Ideal
Ronald Fussell ... 203

WH 24 & 25 Live Now
Ānanda Pereira ... 225

WH 26 The Five Mental Hindrances and Their Conquest
Nyanaponika Thera ... 263

WH 27 & 28 Going Forth (Pabbajjā)
Sumana Sāmaṇera ... 293

WH 29 The Light of Asia or The Great Renunciation
Edwin Arnold ... 341

WH 30 Women in Early Buddhist Literature
I. B. Horner ... 395

Key to Abbreviations

A	Aṅguttara Nikāya	Paṭis	Paṭisambhidamagga
Ap	Apadāna	Peṭ	Peṭakopadesa
Bv	Buddhavaṃsa	S	Saṃyutta Nikāya
Cp	Cariyāpiṭaka	Sn	Suttanipāta
D	Dīgha Nikāya	Th	Theragātha
Dhp	Dhammapada	Thī	Therigātha
Dhs	Dhammasaṅgaṇī	Ud	Udāna
It	Itivuttaka	Vibh	Vibhaṅga
Ja	Jātaka verses and commentary	Vin	Vinaya-piṭaka
Khp	Khuddakapāṭha	Vism	Visuddhimagga
M	Majjhima Nikāya	Vism-mhṭ	Visuddhimagga Sub-commentary
Mil	Milindapañha	Vv	Vimānavatthu
Nett	Nettipakaraṇa	Nidd	Niddesa

The above is the abbreviation scheme of the Pali Text Society (PTS) as given in the *Dictionary of Pali* by Margaret Cone.

The commentaries, *aṭṭhakathā*, are abbreviated by using a hyphen and an "a" ("-a") following the abbreviation of the text, e.g., *Dīgha Nikāya Aṭṭhakathā* = D-a. Likewise the sub-commentaries are abbreviated by a "ṭ" ("-ṭ") following the abbreviation of the text.

The sutta reference abbreviation system for the four Nikāyas, as is used in Bhikkhu Bodhi's translations is:

AN	Aṅguttara Nikāya	DN	Dīgha Nikāya
MN	Majjhima Nikāya	Sn	Saṃyutta Nikāya
J	Jātaka story	Mv	Mahāvagga (Vinaya Piṭaka)
Cv	Cullavagga (Vinaya Piṭaka)	SVibh	Suttavibhaṅga (Vinaya Piṭaka)

Buddhism and Christianity

Buddhism and the Vital Problems of our Time

by

Helmuth von Glasenapp
Professor of Indology
Tübingen (Germany)

WHEEL PUBLICATION NO. 16

Preface

We are glad to present to our readers another two essays by Prof. Dr. H. von Glasenapp, eminent Indologist of Germany, whose *Vedanta and Buddhism* we published as No. 2 of this series.

The German originals of both these essays appeared in the German magazine, *Universitas*, Vol. IV, No. 1 and V, No. 3, respectively (Stuttgart, 1949, 1950; Wissenschaftliche Verlagsgesellschaft, m.b.H.).

The English version of *Buddhism and Christianity*, translated by the Ven. Nyanaponika Mahāthera was published first in the *University of Ceylon Review*, Vol. XVI, No. 1 and 2 (Peradeniya, 1958).

The second essay, *Buddhism and the Vital Problems of Our Time*, was originally a radio talk delivered in Munich (Germany), in reply to questions formulated by that broadcasting station. It was later read and discussed at the Indian Institute of Culture, Bangalore. The English version is here reproduced, with amendments, from *The Buddhist*, Vol. XXI, No. 7 (Y.M.B.A., Colombo, 1950).

Both essays give an impartial and scholarly treatment of their respective subjects, and the publishers express the hope that especially the lucid comparison of Buddhism and Christianity will serve to the followers of both religions as a useful source of information about each other's beliefs.

Buddhist Publication Society

Buddhism and Christianity

Among the five great religions to which nearly nine-tenths of present-day humanity belong, Buddhism and Christianity have been the most frequent subjects of comparison. And rightly so. Because, together with Islam, and unlike Hinduism and Chinese Universism, they are "world religions," that is to say, forms of belief that have found followers not merely in a single though vast country, but also in wide regions of the world.

Buddhism and Christianity, however, differ from Islam in so far as, unlike the latter, they do not stress the natural aspects of world and man, but they wish to lead beyond them. A comparison between Buddhism and Christianity, however, proves so fruitful mainly because they represent, in the purest form, two great distinctive types of religion which arose East and West of the Indus valley. For two millennia, these religious systems have given the clearest expression of the metaphysical ideas prevalent in the Far East and in the Occident, respectively.

The similarities between these two religions extend, if I see it rightly, essentially over three spheres: (1) the life history of the founder, (2) ethics, and (3) church history.

1. The biographies of Buddha and Christ show many similar features. Both were born in a miraculous way. Soon after their birth, their future greatness is proclaimed by a sage (Asita, Simeon). Both astonish their teachers through the knowledge they possess, though still in their early childhood. Both are tempted by the devil before they start upon their public career. Both walk over the water (Jātaka 190; Matt. 14, 26). Both feed 500 and 5,000 persons, respectively (Jātaka 78; Mark 14, 16 ff.) by multiplying miraculously the food available. The death of both is accompanied by great natural phenomena. Also the parables ascribed to them show some similarities as, for instance, the story of the sower (SN 42:7; Matt. 13, 3), of the prodigal son (*Lotus of the Good Law*, Chap. IV; Luke, 14), of the widow's mite (*Kalpanamandiṭikā*; Mark 12).

From these parallels some writers have attempted to conclude that the Gospels have drawn from Buddhist texts. But this contention goes much too far. If there is any dependence at all of the stories in the Gospels on those of India, it could be only by oral tradition, through the migration to the West of certain themes which originated in India, and were taken over by the authors of the biblical scriptures. But that is in no way certain, because many of those similarities are not so striking as to exclude the possibility of their independent origination in different places.

2. Both Buddha and Jesus based their ethics on the "Golden Rule." Buddha told the Brahmins and householders of a certain village as follows: "A lay-follower reflects thus: How can I inflict upon others what is unpleasant to me?' On account of that reflection, he does not do any evil to others, and he also does not cause others to do so" (SN 55:7). And Jesus says in the Sermon on the Mount: "Therefore, all things whatsoever ye would that men should do to you, do so to them; for this is the law and the prophets" (Matt. 7, 12; Luke 6, 31)—this being, by the way, a teaching which, in negative formulation, was already known to the Jewish religion (Tobit 15, 4).

Also the principle "Love thy neighbour like unto yourself" (Luke 10, 27) which, in connection with Lev. 19, 18, was raised by Jesus to a maxim of ethical doctrine, is likewise found in Buddhism where it was given a philosophical foundation mainly by the thinkers of *Mahāyāna* (Śāntideva, beginning of *Sikṣāsamuccaya*). As to the injunction that love should also be extended to the enemy there is also a parallel statement by the Buddha. According to the *Majjhima Nikāya*, No. 21, he said: "If, O monks, robbers or highwaymen should with a double-handled saw cut your limbs and joints, whoso gave way to anger thereat would not be following my advice. For thus ought you train yourselves: 'Undisturbed shall our mind remain, no evil words shall escape our lips; friendly and full of sympathy shall we remain, with heart full of love, free from any hidden malice. And that person shall we suffuse with loving thoughts, and from there the whole world.'"

A practical proof of the love of enemies was given, as the report goes, by the Buddhist sage Āryadeva. After a philosophical disputation, a fanatical adversary attacked him in his cell with a sword, and Āryadeva was fatally wounded. In spite of that, he is said to have helped his murderer to escape by disguising him with his own monk's robe. Schopenhauer, and others after him, believed, in view of these ethical teachings, that the Gospels, "must somehow be of Indian origin" (*Parerga* II, § 179), and that Jesus was influenced by Buddhism with which he was said to have become acquainted in Egypt. For such a supposition, however, there is not the slightest reason, since we encounter similar noble thoughts also among Chinese and Greek sages, and, in fact, among the great minds of the whole world, without having to assume some actual interdependence.

3. Also the historical development of both religions presents several parallels. Both, setting out from the countries of their origin, have spread over large parts of the world, but in their original homelands they have scarcely any followers left. The number of Christians in Palestine is very small today, and on the whole continent of India proper, there are at present not even half a million Buddhists.[1] The brahmanical counter-reformation starting about 800 CE, and the onslaught of Islam beginning about 1000 CE, have brought about the passing of already decadent Buddhism in its fatherland, while it counts millions of devotees in Sri Lanka, Burma, Thailand, China, Japan, Tibet, Mongolia and so on. It is strange how little that fact of the disappearance of Buddhism from the land of the Ganges has been apprised by even many educated persons in the West. Some still believe that Buddhism is the dominant religion of India proper, though out of a population of 400 million, about 95 million belong to the Islam, and 270 million are Hindus (that is devotees of Vishnu and Shiva) among whom the caste system prevails, with Brahmins constituting the hereditary priestly gentry.

It is also significant that today the overwhelming majority of the followers of Buddhism and Christianity belong to a race and linguistic group different from those of their founders. Buddha was an Indo-Aryan, but, with a few exceptions, most of his devotees are found today among yellow races. Jesus and the Apostles were Jews, but the main contingent of Christians is made up of Europeans speaking Indo-Germanic languages. This shows, very strikingly, that race, language and religion are

1. Since this essay was written, the number of Buddhists in India has increased to an estimated 10–15 million in 1959, mainly due to the mass movement among the scheduled classes initiated by the late Dr. B. R. Ambedkar.—BPS Editor.

entirely different spheres. There is perhaps a deep law underlying that fact. Nations of foreign blood accept a new religion with such a great sympathy and enthusiasm probably because it offers them something which they did not possess of their own, and which, therefore, supplements their own mental heritage in an important way. This holds true also in the case of Islam, since among the nearly 300 million Mohammedans, those of the prophet's race, the Semites, are in a minority compared with the Muslims of Turkish, Persian, Indian, Malayan and African extraction.

In the course of their historical development and their dissemination among foreign nations, Buddhism as well as Christianity have absorbed much that was alien to them at the start. One may even say that, after a religion has gone through a sufficiently long period of development and has been exposed to diverse influences, more or less all phenomena will appear which the history of religion has ever produced. Buddhism and Christianity originally had strict views on all matters of sex, but in both certain sects appeared again and again which were given to moral laxity or even taught ritual sex enjoyment, as in Buddhism the Shakti cults of the "Diamond Vehicle" (*Vajrayāna*), or in Christianity certain Gnostic schools, medieval sects and modern communities. Buddha and Christ reject extreme asceticism, but there arose numerous zealots who not only advocated painful self-mortification, but even castrated (as the Skopzi) or burned themselves.

Pristine Buddhism taught self-liberation through knowledge. Later, however, a school arose which considered man too weak to win salvation by himself, and instead expected deliverance by the grace of Buddha Amitābha. These Amitābha schools have developed a theology which, to a certain extent, presents a parallel to the Protestant doctrine of salvation by faith. In Japan, the most influential of these schools, the Shin sect, has even broken with the principle of monastic celibacy, and thereby produced a sort of Buddhist clergy of the Protestant type. On the other hand, Tibetan Buddhism has created a kind of ecclesiastical state with the Dalai Lama as its supreme head.

Both Buddhism and Christianity teach the transcending of the world. And, in conformity with the ideas of the supremacy of the spiritual life over the conventions of the world, in the monastic order of the church community all class distinctions had to cease. The Buddha taught: "As the rivers lose their names when they reach the ocean, just so members of all castes lose their designations once they have gone forth into homelessness, following the teaching and the discipline of the Perfect One" (AN 8:19). And the Apostle Paul wrote (Gal. 3, 28): "There is neither Jew nor Greek, there is neither slave nor freeman, neither male nor female, for you are all one in Jesus Christ."

These postulates, however, did not change conditions prevailing in worldly life. Social reforms were entirely alien to the intentions of Buddhism and Christianity in the early days. In various Buddhist countries and up to modern times, there were not only house slaves but even temple slaves. In Christian countries, slavery was abolished only in the 19th century (Brazil, 1888).

Finally, both religions have in common certain features of cult and forms of worship. I mention here only: monasticism, tonsure of the clergy, confession, the cult of images, relic worship, ringing of bells, use of rosary and incense, and the erection of towers. There has been much controversy about the question whether, and to what extent, one may assume mutual influence with regard to these and several other similarities, but research has so far not come to an entirely satisfactory conclusion.

Though in many details there are great similarities between Buddhism and Christianity, one must not overlook the fact that in matters of doctrine they show strong contrasts, and their conceptions of salvation belong to entirely different types of religious attitude. Buddhism, in its purest form, presents a religion based on the conception of an eternal and universal law, a conception found in various forms in India, China and Japan. Christianity, on the other hand, belongs, together with the teaching of Zoroaster, the Jewish religion and Islam, to those religions that profess to have a divine revelation which is manifested in history, and these religions have conquered for themselves all parts of the world west of India. The contrast between Buddhism and Christianity will become clear by objectively placing side by side their central doctrines. I shall base that comparison on what are still today, just as nearly 2,000 years ago, the fundamental doctrinal tenets of both religions, and shall not consider here differences of detail of modern interpretations. Since I may assume an acquaintance with the teaching of Christianity, I shall begin each subsequent discussion of single points with a very brief statement of the Christian doctrine concerned, following it up with a somewhat more detailed treatment of the different teachings in Buddhism. I hope that in that way I shall be able to bring out clearly the differences between these two religions.

1. Christianity differs from all great world religions first of all in that it gives to the personality of its founder a central position in world history as well as in the doctrine of salvation. In Buddhism, Zoroastrianism, Islam, Judaism, and still more so in religions having no personal founder but being products of historical growth, like Hinduism and Chinese Universism, in all of them it is a definite metaphysical and ethical doctrine promulgated by holy men which is the very centre of their systems. For the Christian, however, it is faith in Jesus Christ that is the inner core of his religion. This evinces most clearly from the fact alone that the 22 scriptures of the New Testament contain only comparatively few sermons of Jesus concerned with doctrinal matters, while by far the greatest part of the Buddhist Canon is devoted to expositions of the Buddha's teachings. In the scriptures of the New Testament, from the Gospel of St. Matthew to the Revelation of St. John, the most important concern of the authors was to demonstrate that Christ was a supernatural figure unique in the entire history of the world. Christ's redemptory death on the cross, his resurrection, ascension, and his future advent are, therefore, the core of the Christian doctrine of salvation.

Buddha's position in Buddhist doctrine bears in no way comparison with those features of Christianity. For the historical Gotama was not the incarnation of God; he was a human being, purified through countless rebirths as animal, man or angel, until finally in his last embodiment, he attained by his own strength that liberating knowledge with enabled him to enter Nirvāna. He was one who pointed out the way to deliverance, but did not, by himself, bestow salvation on others. Though also to him a miraculous birth has been attributed, yet it was not described as a virginal birth. The whole difference, however, of the Buddha's status from that of Christ is chiefly demonstrated by the fact that a Buddha is not an isolated historical phenomenon, but that many Enlightened Ones had appeared in the past, teaching the same doctrine; and that in the future, too, Buddhas will appear in the world who will expound to erring humanity the same principles of deliverance in a new form. The latter Buddhism of the Great Vehicle (*Mahāyāna*) even teaches that many, if not all men, carry within themselves the seed of Buddhahood, so that after many rebirths they themselves will finally attain the highest truth and impart it to others.

2. The historical personalities of Jesus and the Buddha differ widely. Jesus grew up in a family of poor Jewish craftsmen. Devoting himself exclusively to religious questions, he was a successor of the Jewish prophets who enthusiastically proclaimed the divine inspirations bestowed upon them. As a noble friend of mankind, full of compassion for the poor, he preached gentleness and love for one's neighbor; but, on the other hand, he attacked abuses with a passionate zeal, for instance when he showed up as hypocrites the Scribes and Pharisees, when he drove from the Temple the traders and money-lenders, and held out the prospect of eternal damnation to those who refused to believe in him (Mark 16, 16). With the conviction of being the expected Messiah he preached the early advent of the Heavenly kingdom (Matt. 10, 23). With that promise he primarily turned to the "poor in spirit" (Matt. 5, 3), because not speculative reasoning, but pious and deep faith is the decisive factor: "What is hidden to the clever and wise, has been revealed by God to the babes" (Matt. 11, 25).

Gotama Buddha, however, stemmed from the princely house of the Sakyas that reigned on the southern slopes of the Himalaya. He lived in splendor and luxury up to his 29th year, when he left the palace and its womenfolk and went forth into homelessness as a mendicant. After a six years' vain quest for insight spent with various Brahman ascetics, he won enlightenment at Uruvelā. This transformed the Bodhisattva, i.e., an aspirant for enlightenment, into a Buddha, that is into one who has awakened to truth. From then onward, up to the eightieth year of his life, he proclaimed the path of deliverance found by him. He died at Kusināra about 480 BCE. Buddha was an aristocrat of high culture, with a very marked sense for beauty in nature and art, free from any resentment, and possessed of a deep knowledge of man's nature. He was a balanced personality, with a serene mind and winning manners, representing the type of a sage who, with firm roots within, had risen above the world. In the struggle with the systems of his spiritually dynamic time, he evolved out of his own thought a philosophical system that made high demands on the mental faculties of his listeners. As he himself said: "My doctrine is for the wise and not for the unwise." The fact that his teaching had an appeal also for the uneducated is explained by his great skill in summarizing in easily intelligible language the fundamental ideas of his philosophy.

So far we have found the following difference between Buddhism and Christianity: Christianity, from its very start was a *movement of faith* appealing to the masses; only when it won over the upper classes did a Christian philosophy evolve. Buddhism, however, was in its beginnings a *philosophical teaching of deliverance.* Its adherents were mainly from the classes of noblemen and warriors and the wealthy middle class, with a few Brahmins. Only when Buddhism reached wider circles did it become a popular religion.

3. The teachings of all great religions are laid down in holy scriptures to which an authoritative character is ascribed surpassing all other literature. Christianity regards the Bible as the "Word of God," as an infallible source of truth in which God, by inspiring the authors of these scriptures, revealed things that otherwise would have remained hidden to man. Contrary to Christianity, Islam and Hinduism, atheistic Buddhism does not know of a revelation in that sense. Nevertheless, it possesses a great number of holy texts in which the sayings of the Buddha are collected. That Canon comprises those insights which the Buddha is said to have won by his own strength through comprehending the true nature of reality. It is claimed that everyone who, in his mental development, reaches the same high stage of knowledge will find confirmed by himself the truth of the Buddha's statements. In fact, however, Buddhists ascribe to that Canon likewise a kind of revealing character, in so far as they appeal to the sayings of the "omniscient" Buddha which are regarded by them as the final authority. The interpretation of the Buddha word, however, has led among Buddhists to as many controversies as Bible exegesis among Christians.

We shall now proceed to describe the fundamental tenets of Christian and Buddhist doctrine. In doing so, we shall have to limit ourselves to the general principles which, for two thousand years, have been common to all schools or denominations of these religions. I shall first speak about the different position taken by Christians and Buddhists towards the central questions of religion—that is God, worlds and soul—and later proceed to a treatment of their teachings on salvation.

4. The central tenet of Christian doctrine is the belief in an eternal, personal, omnipotent, omniscient and all-loving God. He has created the world from nothing, sustains it, and directs its destiny; he is lawgiver, judge, the helper in distress, and the saviour of the creatures which he has brought into being. Angels serve him to carry out his will. As originally created by God, all of them were good angels. But a section of them turned disobedient, and breaking away from the heavenly hosts, formed an opposition to the other angels, a hierarchy which under its leader, Satan, strives to entice man to evil. Though the devil's power is greater than that of man, it is restricted by the power of God so that they cannot do anything without God's consent, and at the end of the days they will be subjected to divine judgement.

Buddhists, on their part, believe in a great number of deities (*devatā*) which direct the various manifestations of nature and of human life. They also know of evil demons and a kind of devil, Māra, who tries to turn the pious from the path of virtue. But all these beings are impermanent though their life span may last millions of years. In the course of their rebirths they have come to their superhuman form of existence thanks to their own deeds, but when the productive power of their deeds is exhausted, they have to be reborn on earth again, as humans. Though the world will always have a sun god or a thunder god, the occupants of these positions will change again and again, in the course of time. It is obvious that these gods with their restricted life span, range of action and power, cannot be compared with the Christian God since they cannot, be it singly or in their totality, create the world or give it its moral laws. Hence they resemble only powerful superhuman kings whom the pious devotees may well, to a certain extent, solicit for gifts and favours, but who cannot exert any influence on world events in their totality.

Many Hindus assume that above the numerous impermanent deities, exists an eternal, omniscient, all-loving and omnipotent God who creates, sustains, rules and destroys the world. But the Buddhists deny the existence of such a Lord of the Universe because, according to them, in the first place, no such original creator of the world can be proved to exist, since every cause must have another cause; and secondly, an omnipotent God will also have to be the creator of evil and this will conflict with his all-loving nature; or, alternatively, if he is to be good and benevolent, he will have to be thought of without omnipotence and omniscience, since otherwise he would not have called into existence this imperfect world of suffering or he would have eliminated evil. Buddhism, therefore, is outspokenly atheistic in that respect. The world is not governed by a personal God, but by an impersonal law which, with inexorable consistency, brings retribution for every morally good or evil deed.

The idea that there are numerous deities of limited power can be found also in other religions; and the ancient Greeks, Romans and Germans believed that, above the gods, there is Moira, Anangke, Fatum or Destiny, which eventually rules everything. For the Chinese the highest principle is the "Tao" which sustains the cosmic order and the harmony between heaven, earth and man. With the Indians there appears already in Vedic times the idea that gods and men are subject to the moral world-order, the *Ṛita*, and from about 800 BCE this idea is linked with the doctrine of *karma*, the doctrine of the after-effects of guilt and merit. According to that doctrine, every action carries in itself, seed-like, its own reward or punishment. After death, an individual, in accordance with his good or evil deeds, is reincarnated in the body of either an animal, a man, a deity or a demon, in order to reap the fruits of his previous actions. This retribution occurs automatically, as a natural, regular occurrence, without requiring a divine judge who shares out reward and punishment.

As to the differences between Buddhism and Christianity, in the present context, we may say that the same functions which in Christian doctrine are related to the concept of a personal God are in Buddhism divided among a number of different factors. The natural and moral order of the world and its periodical rise and fall are preserved by an impersonal and immanent cosmic law

(*Dharma*). The retribution for one's actions operates through the inherent efficacy of these deeds themselves. Helpers in need are the numerous but transient deities, while the truths of deliverance are revealed by human beings evolved to the perfection of Buddhas (Awakened Ones), who therefore are also made objects of cult and devotion. Saviour, however, is each man for himself, in so far as he has overcome the world through wisdom and self-control.

The homage paid to the Buddha, as it may be observed in Buddhist temples, has a meaning quite different from the worship of God in Christian Churches. The Christian worships God in reverence due to the creator of the universe and the ruler of all its destinies; or he does so in order to be granted spiritual or material boons by God's grace. The Buddhist pays homage to the Buddha without expecting that he hears him or does something for him. Since the Buddha has entered into Nirvāna he can neither hear the prayers of the pious nor can he help them. If a Buddhist turns to the Buddha as if to a personality that actually confronts him, his act has a fictive character. The devotee expects from his act only spiritual edification and a good *karma*. This theory as advocated today by orthodox Buddhism has, however, often been altered in practice and in the teachings of some of the Buddhist schools. But even those who think it possible that a Buddha may intervene in favour of a devotee regard the Buddha only as a saviour, a bringer of deliverance, and not as the creator and ruler of the universe.

5. According to the Christian doctrine, God has created the world from nothing, and he rules it according to a definite plan. The stopping of the cosmic process comprises the end of the world, the universal resurrection of the dead, the Day of Judgement, the eternal damnation of the sinners and the eternal bliss of the pious in a heavenly Jerusalem descended to earth. Until the 18th century, it was believed that the entire world history comprised only 6,000 years, though the time of the creation has been calculated differently. The Byzantines made their world era start on the 1st day of September, 5509 B.C., while Luther dated the creation at the year 3960 B.C. Although the calculations about the beginning and the end of the world—mainly based on the statements about the generations between Adam and Christ (Matt. 1, 17 and Luke 3, 21)—have been abandoned in recent times, yet for Christianity the view that the historical fact of creation and salvation constitutes a single and unrepeatable event, remains a guiding principle.

Buddhism, however, knows neither a first beginning nor a definite end of the world. Since every form of existence presupposes action in a preceding life, and since *karma* produced on one existence must find its retribution in a future one, Buddhism teaches a periodical cycle of cosmic rise and fall, evolution and dissolution. Since the number of living beings that produce *karma* is infinitely vast, and the unexhausted *karma* of beings inhabiting a world which is the process of dissolution has to find realization in a newly arising world, worldly existence will never come to an end, however large the number of human beings may be that reach deliverance. There is another essential difference between the Christian and the Buddhist conception of the world: Buddhists have always assumed an infinite number of world systems situated next to each other in space, each of them consisting of an earth, a heaven above and a hell below.

6. According to Christian views, man is composed of body and soul. While the body is formed of matter in the mother's womb, the soul is a special creation of God, from nothing. A soul is a simple, spiritual, immaterial substance. Maintained in eternal existence by God, the soul continues also after the dissolution of the body at death and receives from God the rewards of its deeds, either in heaven or hell. At the end of time, God causes a resurrection of all flesh and unites again the souls with their former bodies. By the fact that thus the whole man, i.e., not only his soul but also his body, receives reward or punishment, the bliss of the heavenly realm of the torment of eternal damnation is felt with still greater intensity. In Christianity, the significance of life on earth, and of the decisions made in it, has been enhanced to the utmost through the idea that it is man's conduct during that short life-span which determines the soul's destiny for all eternity.

Many Indian systems are based upon that anthropological dualism with the conception of an infinitely large number of eternal and purely spiritual souls linked, since beginningless time, with bodies formed by particles of primordial matter. The souls are thought to change these bodies in the course of their existences, until they become free of them on attainment of deliverance. In contrast to all Indian teachings of deliverance, and most others,

Buddhism denies the existence of eternal substances, essentially unchangeable. What appears to us as matter, actually comes into being only through the natural co-operation of a multitude of single factors like colors, sounds, odors, tactile, spatial and temporal qualities, etc. Also what we call the "soul" is only a play of ever-changing sensations, perceptions and cognitive acts, combined into an entirety, yet being devoid of any underlying entity. It is only because some of these complex phenomena seem to have a relative stability that men believe in the existence of matter or soul. But in truth, only *dharmas* exist, i.e., "factors of existence" that arise in functional dependence on each other, and cease again after a short time. This doctrine of the *dharmas* is the characteristic teaching peculiar to Buddhism. It was developed by the Buddha into a philosophy of becoming from an idea still noticeable in the *Vedic* texts ascribing positive subsistence to everything that exists including qualities, events, modal states, etc.

In that respect, Buddha is a precursor of Hume and Mach who likewise declared any substance to be a fiction. But for the Buddha, the doctrine of the *dharmas* combines with the acceptance of a moral law governing the efficacy of all actions. Just as nothing occurs without producing some effect in the physical world, so every morally good or evil act is the cause of definite effects. Though when a being dies a combination of factors is dissolved which had previously formed a personality, yet the deeds performed in the life now passed become the cause of a new and separate being's birth. The newly born is different from the being that had died, but it takes over, as it were, the latter's inheritance. Thus the stream of the factors of existence is continued also after death, and one life form follows the other without break. Since any act can have only a retribution of limited duration, Buddhists do not know eternal bliss in heaven or eternal torments in hell, but believe that the inhabitants of heaven and hell are later reborn again on earth.

7. Christianity and Buddhism agree in their strong emphasis on the impermanency of all things. In Christianity, the suffering inherent in the world is the outcome of sin, and sin is disobedience towards God's commandments. Because Adam had sinned, all his progeny is afflicted with Original Sin. Man is too weak to free himself from sin by his own strength. Therefore God in his compassion became man in Christ, and died as a vicarious redemptory sacrifice for all humanity. Through Christ's sacrificial death all men have become free from the power of sin, but that vicarious salvation from evil becomes reality only if man opens himself to divine grace through his faith in Christ.

The idea of collective guilt and collective salvation is far from the Buddhist's way of thinking. According to Buddhism, everyone accumulates his own evil and everyone has to work out his own deliverance. The entire Christian conception of sin, as a matter of fact, is alien to the Buddhist. If man has to suffer in punishment for his misdeeds, it is not on account of his disobeying divine commandments, but because his actions are in conflict with the eternal cosmic law and, therefore, produce bad *karma*. In general, the suffering which is life for a Buddhist is not stamped with the mark of sin, but carries only the character of impermanence and insubstantiality. This inherent characteristic of existence is the cause of life ever ending in death, of life with its aimless and meaningless wandering through always new forms of being. It is that which basically constitutes life's suffering. And the cause of this woeful conflict is a thirst for sense enjoyment, an attachment to existence, a will to live, a passion that either craves for possession or wants to escape.

All these propensities and impulses have their original source in ignorance, that is, in lack of insight into the true nature of reality. He who sees that neither in the internal nor in the external world can anything be found that abides, and that there is also no ego as a point of rest within the general flux of phenomena, who is aware that there is no self either as the eternal witness or temporary owner of sense perceptions and volitions—such a one, through that very knowledge, is set free of selfishness, of hate, greed and delusion. By a gradual process of purification, extending through aeons over many existences, he finally discards the illusion of self-affirmation. Through mindful observation, keen reflection and meditative calm he eliminates all selfish propensities, and sees also his own personality as a mere bundle of *dharmas*, i.e., processes of natural law that arise and vanish conditioned by functional relations. Dispassionate and without attachment, he pervades, as the Buddhist scriptures say, "the whole world with his heart filled with loving-kindness, compassion, sympathetic joy and equanimity" (DN 3). Without clinging to life and without fear of death he waits for the hour when his bodily form breaks up and he reaches final deliverance from rebirth.

8. The definite and perpetual state of salvation which is the redeemed person's share according to Christian doctrine is conceived as an eternal life in the heavenly kingdom. If, after the second advent of Christ, the resurrection of the dead and the Last Judgement, the final kingdom of God has been established, then, after the old world's destruction, on a new earth, the redeemed ones will live in an inseparable communion with God and Christ.

The Buddhist conception of Nirvāna presents the most radical contrast to Christian eschatology. The Christian hopes for infinite continuation of his entire personality, not only of his soul but also of his body resurrected from dust to a new life. The Buddhist, however, wishes to be extinguished completely, so that all mental and corporeal factors which form the individual will disappear without a remainder. Nirvāna is the direct opposite of all that constitutes earthly existence. It is a relative Naught in so far as it contains neither the consciousness nor any other factor that occurs in this world of change or could possibly contribute to its formation. Not wrongly, therefore, has Nirvāna been compared to empty space in which there are no differentiations left, and which does not cling to anything. In strongest contrast to the world which is impermanent, without an abiding self-nature and subject to suffering, Nirvāna is highest bliss, but a bliss that is not felt, i.e., is beyond the happiness of sensation (AN 9:34.1–3).

In the conception of the final goal of deliverance there is expressed the ultimate and most decisive contrast between the Christian and the Buddhist abnegation off the world. The Christian renounces the world because it is imperfect through sin, and he hopes for a personal, active and eternal life beyond, in a world which, through God's power, has been freed from sin and purified to perfection. But the Buddhist thinks that an individual existence without becoming and cessation, and hence without suffering, is unthinkable. He believes though, that in future, during the ever-recurring cyclical changes of good and bad epochs, also a happy age will dawn upon mankind again. But that happy epoch will be no less transient than earlier ones have been. Never will the cosmic process find its crowning consummation in a blessed finality. Hence there is no collective salvation, but only an individual deliverance. While the cosmic process following unalterable laws continues its course, only a saint who has become mature for Nirvāna will extinguish like a flame without fuel, in the midst of an environment that, with fuel unexhausted, is still burning.

9. The different attitude towards the world and its history tallies also with the dissimilar evaluation given to other religions by Christians and Buddhists respectively. Christianity, being convinced of the absolute superiority of its own faith, has always questioned the justification of other forms of faith. Buddhism, however, does not believe that man has to decide about it within a single life on earth. The Buddhist, therefore, regards all other religions as first steps to his own. Consequently, in the countries to which Buddhism spread, it did not fight against the original religions found there, but tried to suffuse them with its own spirit. Therefore, Buddhism has never claimed exclusive, absolute or totalitarian authority. In modern China most Buddhists are simultaneously Confucians and Taoists, and in Japan membership in a Buddhist sect does not exclude faith in the Shinto gods. This large-hearted tolerance of Buddhism is also illustrated in its history, which is almost free from religious wars and persecution of heretics.

The fundamental doctrines of Buddhism and Christianity as outlined here and accepted as concrete facts by the majority of the faithful has sometimes been interpreted by thinkers of both religions in a rationalistic or in a mystical sense, and these interpretations have modified the meaning of these doctrines considerably. In our present context, however, we cannot enter into a treatment of these transformations. By doing so, our comparative study would lack that firm ground required, which, for a historian's purpose, can be provided only by the authoritative and clearly-outlined tenets of the respective teachings.

Though Buddhism and Christianity differ from each other in their respective views about world and self, about the meaning of life and man's ultimate destiny, yet they agree again in the ultimate postulates of all religious life. For both religions proclaim man's responsibility for his actions and the freedom of moral choice; both teach retribution for all deeds, and believe in the perfectibility of the individual. "You must be perfect as your

Father in Heaven is perfect" (Matth. 5, 48), says Jesus. And the Buddha summarizes the essence of his ethics in the words: "To shun all evil, to practice what is good, to cleanse one's own heart: that is the teaching of the Enlightened Ones."

Buddhism and the Vital Problems of Our Time

Buddhism venerates as its founder the Indian Prince Siddhartha of the family of the Shakyas (circa 560–480 BCE), whom his contemporaries were accustomed to call by his surname Gotama or by the honourific "Buddha." The word Buddha means the Awakened, the Enlightened, and was applied to the Indian men of those times who were believed to have fathomed the mystery of the world and to have discovered the way to salvation by their own efforts and not through revelation. The gospel of Gotama spread quickly over the whole of India in his lifetime and after his death, but started to fall into decay by about 100 CE, and eventually had to give way, in the country of its origin, to Hinduism and Islam.

But Buddhism found ample recompense for this loss in Sri Lanka and Southeast Asia, in China, Japan, Tibet and Mongolia. The number of Buddhists in the Far East is estimated at 500 to 600 million, but this figure does not give a clear idea of its extension, since the acceptance of some of its doctrines or the observance of Buddhist customs is not incompatible with adhesion to Confucianism, Taoism, Shinto and the various popular cults. For it has always been foreign to the spirit of Buddhism to claim exclusive validity. On the contrary, in its all-embracing tolerance, it has always lived peacefully side by side with other religions, and has absorbed ideas originally foreign to it, trying to permeate them with its own spirit.

Present-day Buddhism flourishes in two different forms. In Sri Lanka and Southeast Asia the original doctrine prevails, which is called (by the *Mahāyāna* followers) the Lesser Vehicle, *Hīnayāna*, or the Vehicle of Learners, *Śrāvakayāna*. In the Far Far East and Tibetan cultural area this "simple doctrine" has undergone a significant broadening as regards philosophy and ceremonial. This is called the Great Vehicle to salvation, *Mahāyāna*, or Vehicle of Bodhisattvas, *Bodhisattvayāna*. But the basic ideas of all forms of

Buddhism have remained more or less the same, so that in our survey we need take no notice of the differences in detail.

Among world religions, Buddhism is the one whose area of influence lies furthest from the West, and also that which is most different in its doctrine from the teachings of Christianity and Islam.

God

First and foremost, Buddhism does not teach the existence of any personal god who created and rules the world. It admits the existence of many gods; but these are only transitory beings with limited powers. They are born and pass way; they can exert no influence on the world process as a whole. Also the great saints and saviours, the Buddhas and Bodhisattvas, do not have the position which the Western religions ascribe to their one God. They can enlighten individuals, and according to the Great Vehicle can lead them by their grace to the path of salvation. But they are not able to interfere with the cosmic process or change the world.

The universe follows its own unalterable natural and moral laws. The most important of these is the law of *karma*, the law of retributive moral causality. This brings it about that every ethically good or bad action inexorably finds its rewards or punishment, because the doer of the deed is born again after his death as a new being, and in that life reaps what he has sown in the previous life.

The Soul

Another point on which Buddhism differs from Christianity and Islam is this: both Western religions assume immortal souls created by God, which after death continue to exist in heaven or hell. Buddhism, however, denies that there can be anything in the world which persists unchanged. According to its theory, life is a stream of elements which are always coming into existence and ceasing to exist, which influence each other according to certain laws. The life-stream of man continues after his death as a new being which has to pursue its happy and unhappy existence, as god, man, animal or inhabitant of hell, in accordance with the good or evil nature of his deeds. A life continues until the *karma*, the power of the deeds which called the being into existence, is exhausted. Then, on the basis of the actions performed in that life, a new being comes into existence which is the heir of the previous life, and so on.

Since each life is the consequence of the actions of a previous life, no beginning of the world can be conceived. Since in each life new actions are performed which produce *karma*, there can in the natural course of things be no end of the world. A few beings, however, succeed, through knowledge of truth, in getting rid of the passions which are the root cause of the *karmic* process. They withdraw from the world, they enter into Nirvāna, into the great peace. But, however many beings may enter into Nirvāna, the cosmic process will never come to an end. For the number of beings who inhabit the infinitely vast number of worlds as animals, men, spirits, gods and inhabitants of hell, is infinitely great.

Thus as little can be said about an end of the world as about a beginning. And with this we come to a third important point where Buddhism differs from Islam and Christianity. Both of these teach that the world was created by God out of nothing, that it remains under his governance for some thousands of years and that on the Last Day it will come to a definite end, when the dead will rise again, all men will receive their eternal reward or eternal punishment, and a new earth of eternal duration and splendor will be created. The ideas of a primordial creation and a definite end of the world are as foreign to Buddhism as that of a providential direction of cosmic events in accordance with a divine plan. It will be evident that, because of these divergences from the conceptions and dogmas of theistic religions, Buddhism must strive at different answers concerning many of the questions which concern us here.

Before I proceed to discuss these questions, I must say a word about my own personal attitude towards Buddhism. I am not a Buddhist, but one engaged in Buddhist research. I have concerned myself for over thirty years with the Buddhist scriptures in the Indian languages, and have studied the principal Buddhist countries (except Tibet and Mongolia) at first-hand on three prolonged visits. In view of my knowledge of the Buddhist sacred writings, and the many discussions I have had with Buddhist monks and laymen, I believe I can answer these questions objectively and correctly in the spirit of Buddhism. I hope that in this way I shall be able to add to the understanding of a doctrine the study of which has been my life's work, and a knowledge of which, in my opinion, is necessary for anybody who seriously concerns himself with the various solutions which the riddle of existence puts before us.

Question 1: The Meaning of Life

The first question which has been addressed to me is:

"So far as we can see, both the life of the individual, and the history of mankind, as a whole, proceed according to definite laws and in definite phases. Apart from such causal regularities, has life any *meaning* which is comprehensible to us? Has man any definite task within this world? Or does this task merely consist in preparing himself to leave the world?

"Regarded from the religious standpoint, is it ultimately unimportant how man behaves in this world? If not, where can he find directions as to his behaviour, and how can he know the validity of these directions? If the world has a comprehensible meaning, how is the suffering of innocent people to be explained?"

As I see it, there are no fewer than six separate questions here. I shall answer them one by one.

Cosmology

(a) What is the goal of the cosmic process? According to the Buddhist view, which I have already outlined, this question cannot be answered. For Buddhism does not believe in a final state of things towards which history progresses. The cosmos is in eternal movement, and the numerous world systems of which it consists pass periodically through the four phases of coming into being, existence, dissolution and non-existence.

Buddhist cosmology usually starts by describing how an existing world which is ripe for dissolution is emptied of its inhabitants. These beings, after their death, are born again in another world, and the uninhabited world is destroyed completely by fire, water or wind. The world thus destroyed disappears for an enormous period of time, and there exists in its place only empty space. When the lawfully fixed period of non-existence comes to an end, there arises a new world system by virtue of the latent *karmic* power of the beings of the world which was destroyed. In empty space there first springs up a faint breeze which grows ever stronger and finally the heaven worlds, earth, and hell are formed. These are then populated with the beings who have had to live through the intervening period in other worlds.

At the beginning of such a newly arisen world, men are without sex. They are endowed with a radiant body, they hover over the earth's surface, and they need no physical nourishment. But because out of curiosity they feed on the finer substance of the earth, they become earth-bound creatures with gross and perishable bodies. Desire which grows ever stronger in them causes them gradually to lose their original purity and virtue; they give themselves to bodily pleasures and quarrel with each other over their possessions which had so far been held in common. So that order may be re-established, property is introduced, and one man is installed as king. The need for a division of labour then leads to the formation of special callings and castes.

Over a period of millions of years, the natural and moral condition of the world deteriorates from generation to generation, so that human beings who in the beginning had an unimaginably long life, now never live beyond a hundred years. This position in which we find ourselves now will in the future become still worse. At last Armageddon, "the time of the swords," breaks out, which lasts for seven days, during which the greater part of mankind is killed.

During this period of horror a few men have gone back to live in the forest and subsist peacefully on fruit and roots. Taught by the catastrophe, they determine for the future to live a peaceful, moral life. Henceforth conditions improve so that men become good and happy. This better state of things again lasts only for a time, and then decline sets in. Twenty periods of this kind of falling and rising culture, follow in succession. When in the last, the twentieth period, the optimal point is reached, an emptying of the world from all living beings takes place, and finally its destruction, as described before. In this manner the cosmos undergoes continuous change, as in accordance with eternal laws, many worlds, one after another, come into existence and pass away.

(b) Thus Buddhism knows no ultimate goal of world evolution. Nevertheless, the world has a meaning. It is the ever-changing scene of the retribution of good and evil deeds (*karma*).

(c) The duty of man consists, in the first place, to see to it that through leading a moral life he is reborn in a good environment, with a happy future. As a distant and supreme goal Nirvāna beckons to the religious man, but it can be attained only after long purification. Hence the final task of man is to prepare himself to leave the world.

(d) From the foregoing it follows that according to the Buddhist view the present conduct of man is of fundamental importance for his future fate. The entire Buddhist teaching is based on a belief in the moral structure of the universe. Such a belief rests not only on the conviction that everything good and evil will have its retribution and that it is possible for man continually to perfect himself, it also presupposes that there exists an objective criterion of what helps man on the way to perfection and of what obstructs his progress.

The Buddha proclaimed an ethics of intention. What decides whether an action produces good or bad *karma* is the intention with which it is performed. Therefore, actions which are not performed as the result of a moral decision, positive or negative, have no *karmic* results.

It is understandable that this lofty philosophical view was not preserved for long. In the course of its history Buddhism has developed, in many different forms, the theory that the giving of gifts to monks, and the performance of certain sacred rites, produce a store of meritorious works. Indeed, in many of the schools of the Great Vehicle, ritualism has obtained such importance that the performance of magical rites, like the mechanical turning of prayer-wheels or the muttering of certain sacred formulae, has become a principal activity of the devotees. This is a regrettable though understandable degeneration, which, indeed, is not unknown in other religions.

Rebirth

(e) For the doctrine that good or evil deeds receive their reward or punishment in a new existence, Buddhists find empirical confirmation of this in, according to their opinion, men who have reached a certain height of spiritual development are able to look back upon their own previous lives and the rebirths of other beings. Since only a few individuals have reached so high a stage of spiritual maturity, the rest of us must rely on the testimony of these saints, just as those who have not visited a foreign country have to put their trust in the statement of reliable travelers.

First among possessors of such knowledge come the Buddhas, i.e., men to whom, by virtue of the enlightenment they have attained, the connection between natural events and the moral realm has become evident. The word of a Buddha, therefore, ranks as the highest authority for all conduct; and from the sayings of Gotama preserved in the holy scriptures, a Buddhist derives guidance for his life.

(f) The doctrine of moral causality offers the Buddhists an explanation of why one man is distinguished, rich and happy, and the other lowly, poor and miserable. The fact that good men often fare badly, while evil men are happy, is explained according to this doctrine by assuming that the good men have still to expiate in this life the sins of a previous existence while a bad man who has done good deeds in his previous life is now getting the reward for them. The whole of the circumstances in which anyone now lives is a consequence of the actions of his previous existence, while on the other hand, what he does now is done by the free decision of his will.

This theory can be objected to in that, his behaviour, man is very largely determined by his predispositions, and that it is therefore difficult to establish the freedom of his moral decisions. Buddhism replies on this point that, against the fatalistic teachings of his time, the Buddha always emphasized: "I teach (the efficacy of) action and energy," and that the workings of the law of *karma* are beyond the grasp of the ordinary man.

Question 2

The second question which I have to answer from the standpoint of Buddhism runs thus:

"If man has a normative ideal to which he has to conform, what are the conditions of life which guarantee him the quickest fulfillment of this task?"

According to the Buddhist view, man occupies an exceptional position among living beings. He alone is in a position to question life itself and to achieve a transcending of it. Animals cannot do so, since they are wholly absorbed by the life of the senses. The heavenly beings also cannot do so, since because of their long life and the happiness they enjoy, the idea never occurs to them that life is transient and, therefore, insubstantial and unsatisfactory.

In consequence of this middle position in the hierarchy of living forms which man occupies, existence as a man is always praised as a rare piece of good fortune. On this point it is said: "The chance is as small as that a blind turtle, emerging from the sea once in a hundred years, should put its head straight into a single-necked yoke—so small is the chance that a being in the course of his repeated rebirth should once become a man" (MN 129).

Man should, therefore, make use of the precious boon which has fallen to his lot, and take care that he improves himself morally, in order gradually to attain perfection. A famous saying in the *Dhammapada* (v. 183) shows the way to the fulfillment of this task: "Shun all evil, do good, and purify your own heart: that is the teaching of the Buddhas." The avoidance of evil consists in not killing, not stealing, not lying, not committing fornication and not using intoxicating drinks, which reduce man's mental capacity or deaden his sense of responsibility. He should, therefore, follow no calling in which he is bound to come into conflict with these postulates; he cannot be a hunter, a butcher, an executioner, a publican, and so on. It is easiest for him if he detaches himself from the world, and thus avoids its temptations. But only a few are mature enough to enter the monastery or live as pious hermits.

Thus the Buddhist ought not to be content with conditions as he finds them; he must try, wherever he can, to change them in accordance with Buddhist principles. Where that is not possible, his effort must be to make himself inwardly free from his environment so that he may detach himself from it and rise above it.

Question 3

We now come to the third question which raises the following problem:

"Are all men equal? If not, in what do they differ? In what respects is equality of all men desirable, and how far should existing differences be preserved?"

Since not even twins are completely alike in their abilities and their destiny, there can be in practice no complete equality of all men. Buddhism has, therefore, never tried to make all men alike. According to Buddhism mankind as a whole resembles to a certain extent a great pyramid, the broad base of which consists of the crude worldlings who are still far removed from the light of truth, while the narrow summit comprises only the few perfected ones. And between these two extremes, men are ranged in infinitely many degrees of virtue and knowledge. But for all of them, Buddhism tries to show the way to spiritual progress, by prescribing for them a spiritual diet suited to their individual needs. And just as it answers to many different levels of comprehension of men, it also tries to adapt itself to the peculiarities of various cultures and races.

The Amitābha Cult

In its eagerness to satisfy the most varied needs of people, the Great Vehicle in particular has taken over many features and conceptions which were originally foreign to Buddhism. Thus in East Asia today, the cult of Buddha Amitābha is very widespread. This mythical saviour calls to his heavenly paradise all those who in their hour of death in faith seek refuge in him; so that, being protected there from all evil influences, they can prepare themselves for Nirvāna. Here Buddhism has adopted modes of thought from the theistic religions of divine grace. But in doing so it has not abandoned its principle of an eternal cosmic law which governs everything, for Amitābha is only the bringer of good tidings into this sorrowful world. He has no part in creating or ruling it, for how could an omniscient spiritual being bring into existence this world full of pain, or hurl the wicked down into the abyss of hell for their misdeeds, or condemn them to reincarnation in miserable forms of life?

Thus Buddhism acknowledges the differences among men in spiritual religious matters, and has, therefore, presented its doctrine of salvation in the most variegated forms. On the other hand, it attaches no weight to differences of race, nationality, class or creed. In contrast to Brahmanism it has not excluded wide sections of the people from its gospel of salvation, and entry into its order is open to all strata of society.

Question 4

The fourth question which has been put to me is this:

"Which social institutions belong to the foundations of mankind and which are susceptible of alteration and development without harm to what is truly human? How does it stand in this regard with marriage, the family, the State, property, the right of self-determination of the individual, and so on?"

According to its doctrine that all things are in a continual process of change, Buddhism recognizes no social institution as eternal or unalterable. While the Chinese consider the State an institution belonging to mankind from its earliest times, Buddhism holds that it arose at a definite period of the cosmic process and will later disappear. Caste, which for the Hindus rests on God-given foundations, is for Buddhism a system arising from needs of the time, and having value only for India. Likewise marriage, the family and property are obligatory only for worldly men of a limited historical period. With the giving up of the worldly life all these institutions lose their significance. The monk, who has renounced worldly life, has, at least in theory, risen above these obligations.

It is not surprising that this standpoint, adopted by the Buddha and by the authoritative fathers of the Buddhist church, has been much modified in the course of history. Under the pressure of outside forces, Buddhism had to make concessions to the State in several countries, and the prevailing ideal of nationalism is not without influence on the thought of many Buddhists. It is well known that in Japan among many sects loyalty to the monarch and patriotism have become articles of religious faith, and that in Tibet a kind of theocratic state has arisen in the past.

No Central Authority

All these facts in no way alter the basic position which Buddhism adopts in relation to all earthly institutions. They have their value and their sphere of application at a certain stage; but for those who can see everything from a higher plane, they are in themselves only temporary means whereby order is maintained in the world.

As I understand it, Buddhism is all throughout a doctrine of salvation for the individual; the idea of a human collectivity, which has sinned and can be redeemed, is alien to it. Therefore, it has no central authority which claims the right of issuing orders or proclaiming dogmas binding on all the Buddhists of the world. When the Buddha lay on his death-bed and was asked who henceforth would lead the community, he said, "In future the Dharma will be your master."

It is clear that this pronouncement of the Exalted One had various unfortunate consequences for the community. For the absence of a generally acknowledged supreme spiritual authority had the result that very soon after the Nirvāna of the Perfect One dissensions arose over the interpretation of controversial points in the doctrine or over individual cases of monastic discipline, and that again and again new sects appeared.

Buddhism has accepted this with open eyes, for the right of self-determination of the individual and of the local congregation represented by the monastic chapter has always seemed to it to outweigh these disadvantages. How far-reaching this right of self-determination is can be seen from the fact that it not only was and is open to the layman, under certain conditions, to enter at any time into the circle of devotees of the Exalted One, and to leave it again, but it was and is even possible to belong at the same time to other religious communities and cults. The monk was always free to leave the order, and it often happened that people repeatedly during their lives became monks and returned to the world again.

In the twenty-five centuries of the history of Buddhism one naturally comes across instances in which the conditions described here have undergone modification for a time. But in general both the Lesser and the Great Vehicle have maintained the basic principle of the right of self-determination.

Question 5: Buddhism and Politics

The fifth question addressed to me runs as follows:

"As far as it appears possible and necessary to alter social institutions, how far and by what means is it permissible to act against the existing system and its defenders? When may cooperation be refused in the undertakings carried on by the current holders of power? When is obedience to the conventions of the society in which one was born obligatory?"

The answer to this can be given briefly. Since Buddhism tried to establish a spiritual order which is not for this world, it does not claim to be a protagonist of social reforms. It is a common error to believe that the Buddha wished to destroy the caste system in India; he did not interfere with the social order as it existed when he laid down that caste differences should no longer be observed within his order. This was no innovation, for this principle was observed among other Indian ascetics.

To change existing conditions by violence must appear to all Buddhists completely opposed to the teaching of the Master. For any exercise of brute force is alien to the merciful spirit of the pure doctrine. The Buddha condemned any thought of hate-inspired retaliation (Dhp 3–5).

Certainly, departures from this hallowed principle occurred, but in the whole course of Buddhist history they play no important part. It has, therefore, never known either a social revolution, nor crusades, nor wars of religion. The struggle against conditions which were found to be oppressive, and against the unrighteous claims of the mighty, was, therefore, mostly conducted in a peaceful manner by way of passive resistance.

Question 6: The Perfectibility of Man

The answer to the sixth question will also not occupy us long. It is as follows:

"Is man capable of changing, transforming himself, induced by instruction or revelation, and has he perhaps that capacity even to an unlimited extent? And what are the limits of his capacity to become good and wise?"

Buddhism does not recognize any fundamental difference between the children of light and the children of darkness, foreordained to eternal bliss or to eternal damnation. On the contrary, it assumes that there are infinitely many stages in spiritual development, and in the achievement of them, beings rise or fall in accordance with their actions performed in the course of their rebirths. The story of the robber-chief, Aṅgulimāla, who had committed many murders, shows that a man may by virtue of right instruction, evolve from a criminal to a saint in the course of one existence. Converted by the Buddha, Aṅgulimāla became an Arahat, and entered into Nirvāna.

That even the worst sinner can finally attain perfection is also shown by the story of the Buddha's cousin, Devadatta. This man committed the two worst sins known to Buddhism: he had sought, inspired by ambition, to murder the Buddha, and he had brought about a schism in the order. As punishment he died of a hemorrhage and went to hell. When he will have atoned for his misdeeds by staying in hell for a hundred thousand eons, he will be purified of evil, and finally attain enlightenment and become a Pacceka-Buddha. The belief in man's unlimited capacity for change could hardly go farther than that.

The related question, whether all beings have the capacity, in the course of their rebirths, to become wise and good and thereby finally attain deliverance, was not answered by the Buddha. Later teachers expressed themselves on this subject in various ways. While many seem to have accepted such a belief, others[2] thought that there are beings who are by nature incapable of assimilating the highest knowledge, and, therefore, must remain forever subject to the cycle of rebirths.

Question 7: Buddhism and Modern Science

I now turn to the seventh and last question. It runs:

"How far is what contemporary science has to say about man and the world in harmony with the teachings of Buddhism, or in contradiction of it?"

Buddhism originated 2,500 years ago in India, and until the beginning of the 19th century it was confined to countries which were entirely untouched by modern Western science. It therefore goes without saying that many of its doctrines, so far as they touch upon scientific, cosmological and geographical matters, are irreconcilable with the results of modern Western science. It was born and grew in an era when unlimited credulity prevailed; if we read the holy scriptures as we should read works of later times, in the spirit of literal history, we shall find things which do not fit into our modern picture of the world. We read that the Buddha was conceived by his mother miraculously, that he was able to fly through the air to Ceylon three times, that he increased food by magic, walked on water, and so on. And similar miracles are reported of his followers and of later saints; visions, magical cures, fantasies and the like, in short almost all those things which were

2. This refers to certain Mahayana Schools.—BPS Editor.

natural to the mode of thought of antiquity and medieval times in all parts of the world.

A Law-Governed Universe

Notwithstanding many such features, so strange to us, which like a thick undergrowth overspread more especially the later literature, we do, on the other hand, find much, even in the old texts, which strikes us as quite modern.

(a) First and above all is to be noted the principle of general and thoroughgoing conformity to natural law which rules the whole Buddhist system. Again and again it is said: "This basic principle stands firm, this universal conformity to law, the conditions of one thing by another" (SN 12:20.4). "Profound is the law of dependent origination. Since it does not know, understand or grasp this law, this generation has become confused, like a ball of thread" (ibid. 12:4). But a well-trained disciple ponders thoroughly the dependent origination, for he knows thus: "When that is, this comes into being; through the destruction of that, this is destroyed" (ibid. 12:41–51, etc.).

(b) A further point of agreement is its positivistic character. For the Buddhist doctrine denies the existence of eternal substances: matter and spirit are false abstractions; in reality there are only changing factors (*dharmas*) which are lawfully connected and arise in functional dependence on each other. Like Ernst Mach, the Buddha therefore resolves the ego into a stream of lawfully cooperating elements, and can say with him: "The ego is as little an absolute permanent entity as the body. The apparent permanence of the ego consists only in its continuity."

In the philosophy of the Great Vehicle, Buddhism goes to the point of denying the reality of the external world. It is characteristic of the philosophical spirit of Asia that such epistemological doctrines do not, as with us, remain without close relation to the true religious life, but enter deeply into it and occupy the thought of wide circles. The consistent idealism of the theory of "Consciousness only" forms the basis of the Zen sect, widespread in China and Japan, which tries through meditation to realize the "void" which is above contradictions; and it is also the basis of the priestly magic and mysticism of Tibet.

(c) It resembles modern modes of thought when the Buddha teaches that there are many problems that man, with his limited intellectual capacity, will never be able to solve, but in his cogitations about them entangles himself again and again in contradictions concerning problems such as the workings of *karma*, the nature of the world, the question whether the world is eternal or not, finite or infinite, how the vital principle connects with the body, and what is the state of the saint who has entered into Nirvāna.

(d) Buddhism also agrees with modern science in its picture of a universe of a vast spatial extent and unending time. The Buddha taught that there exist side by side infinitely many world systems which continually come into existence and perish again. It is not that he anticipated Copernicus; for each world system has an earth at the centre, and sun, moon and stars revolve round it. It is rather that the conception of a multiplicity of worlds appears in his teaching as the natural consequence of the principle of retributive causality of actions. The number of actions which have to find reward or punishment is so infinitely great, that the appropriate retribution could not be comprised within one world, with its regular alternation of rising and falling cultural levels.

(e) Buddhism finds itself again in agreement with modern biology in that it acknowledges no essential difference, but only a difference of degree, between man and animal. However, it is far from the Darwinian line of thought.

(f) Finally, it can also be said that the Indians discovered the unconscious earlier than the Western psychologists. For them the unconscious consists in the totality of the impressions which slumber in the individual as the inheritance from his previous existence. The Buddhist technique of meditation, which is concerned with these latent forces, is thus a forerunner of modern psychoanalysis, of autogenic mental training, etc.

The attitudes of present-day Buddhists towards modern science vary. So far as I can see, three attitudes can be distinguished:

(1) The great mass of Buddhist laymen and monks in Asia are still untouched by the modern natural sciences. For them the words of the Buddha and the commentaries on them are still the infallible source of all knowledge of the universe and its phenomena.

(2) Many Buddhists try to prove that the cosmological ideas and miraculous stories of the Canon conform to fact, and for this purpose interpret the texts in an artificial sense or draw upon the assertions of modern occultism as proofs. It is noteworthy that they do not consider miracles to be violations of the law of nature brought about by a supernatural power, but assume that there are unknown forces and laws which cause events that to us appear as miracles but are really not.

(3) Other Buddhists, however, regard the statements of the texts on natural phenomena as conditioned by the ideas prevailing in those times and, therefore, no longer authoritative. They say that the Buddha was not concerned to put forward a scientific world view valid for all time, but that the essential core of Buddhism is rather its practical doctrine of salvation. The Buddha always maintained that everything of this earth is transitory, unreal and, therefore, unsatisfactory, and that so long as man is still under the subjection of the three cardinal vices of hatred, greed and ignorance he will never attain to inner peace and serene clarity of vision. Only through the purification from all desires and the complete realization of absolute selflessness, through a moral conduct of life and constant practice of meditation, can he approach a state in which he lives in peace with himself and with the world. Man can elevate himself and raise his stature by emulating the great example of the Buddha seated in calm meditation, whose face shines in triumphant peace. Then can man lift himself above the fierce current of time, up to the imperishable state that is beyond all the unrest of the inexorable nexus of becoming and suffering. And the ideal that presents itself here is that unshakable composure of mind which a Buddhist verse describes:

> He whose mind is like a rock,
> Firmly anchored, shakes no more;
> Who has escaped from all passion,
> Is no more angry and no more afraid;
> He whose mind is thus without equal,
> How can sorrow defeat him?

Udāna 4.4

Three Cardinal Discourses of the Buddha

Setting Rolling the Wheel of Truth
The Not-self Characteristic
The Fire Sermon

Translated by

Ñāṇamoli Thera

WHEEL PUBLICATION NO. 17

Introduction

Not doing any kind of evil,
Perfecting profitable skill,
And purifying one's own heart:
This is the Buddha's dispensation.

Dhammapada 183

The message of the Awakened Ones, so stated as it is in the *Dhammapada* in the plain terms of good and evil, upholds the same values that every great compassionate religion shares. But the seed of good has to grow in the soil of truth; and how the tree grows depends upon the nature of the soil in which it is planted, and whence it draws its nourishment. With men as the custodians of the true, the fulfilment of the good depends upon how truth is conceived by men to be. By their acts they verify it.

"A monk called Gotama, it seems, a son of the Sakyans who went forth into homelessness from a Sakyan clan, has come... Now a good report of Master Gotama has been spread to this effect: 'That Blessed One is such since he is accomplished and fully awakened, perfect in true knowledge and conduct, sublime, knower of worlds, incomparable leader of men to be tamed, teacher of gods and men, awakened and blessed... He teaches a Teaching (Dhamma) that is good in the beginning, good in the middle, and good in the end, with its own special meaning and phrasing; he exhibits a holy life that is utterly perfect and pure.' Now it is good to see such Accomplished Ones." (MN 41)

So it was said of him at the time. But what, then, was the fundamental ground of that teaching? Of the many ways that such a question might be answered, perhaps the simplest and best is this: "He expounded the teaching that is peculiar to Buddhas: suffering, origin, cessation and a path" (MN 56). These four are known otherwise as the *Four Noble Truths.* This, with the cognate teaching of no self, may be said to constitute the fundamental ground of the teaching of Buddhas; this is what marks them, sets them apart and entitles them to the unique epithet "Buddha."

The three discourses here presented display precisely, in all its incomparably serene simplicity, without assumptions, that special fundamental teaching, from which all Buddhism branches, and to which it all points back. The first discourse displays this fourfold Truth as something to be realized and verified for oneself here and now; the second discloses the contradictions which infect all "self" conceits; the third echoes the second from another angle.

The circumstances that led up to the discovery of these four Truths, and to the delivery of these three discourses, were briefly as follows. The Bodhisatta—as he then was, before his awakening—was twenty-nine when he left the house life, where he enjoyed the extreme of luxury. He went into "exile" in order to find not a palliative but the true and incontrovertible way out from suffering.

> This world has surely happened upon woe, since it is born and ages and dies but to fall from one kind of existence and reappear in another. Yet it knows no escape from this suffering, from ageing and death; surely there is an escape from this suffering, from ageing and death? (SN 12:65)

He studied and practised under two of the foremost teachers of *samādhi* (concentration, or quiet), and reached the highest meditative attainments possible thereby. But that was not enough ("I was not satisfied with that teaching; I left it and went away." MN 36) He then spent the best part of the next six years in the practice of asceticism, trying every sort of extreme self-mortification. During this time he was waited on by five ascetics, who hoped that if he discovered the "deathless state" he would be able to communicate his discovery to them. This too failed.

> By this gruelling penance I have attained no distinction higher than the human ideal worthy of a noble one's knowing and seeing. Might there be another way to awakening? (MN 36)

He decided to try once more the path of concentration, attained through mindfulness of breathing, though this time not pushed to the extremity of quiet, but guided instead by ordered consideration.

> I thought: "While my Sakyan father was busy and I (as a child) was sitting in the shade of a rose-apple tree, then quite secluded from sensual desires, secluded from unprofitable

ideas, I had direct acquaintance of entering upon and abiding in the first *jhāna*—meditation, which is accompanied by thinking and exploring, with happiness and pleasure born of seclusion. Might that be the way to enlightenment?" And following upon that memory came the recognition: "That is the only way to enlightenment." (MN 36)

He now gave up self-mortification and took normal food again in order to restore to his emaciated body strength sufficient for his purpose. Then the five ascetics left him in disgust, judging that he had failed, and was merely reverting to what he had forsaken. But now in solitude, his new balanced effort in the harmony of virtue, unified in concentration, and guided by the ordered consideration of insight with mindfulness, at length brought success in discovery of the way to the goal he had sought for so long. "So I too found the ancient path, the ancient trail, travelled by the Awakened Ones of old." (SN 12:65) Five faculties in perfect balance had brought him to his goal: they were the four, namely energy, mindfulness, concentration, and understanding, with faith in the efficacy of the other four—the five that "merge into the Deathless." (SN 48:57) According to tradition, the "Awakening" took place on the night of the Vesākha full moon in the fruitful month of May.

It was upon invitation that he resolved to communicate his discovery to others. For his first audience to whom to divulge it he chose the five ascetics who had shared his self-mortification, but had later left him. They were now at Benares—India's "eternal city"—and so in due course he went there to rejoin them. Just two months after his awakening he preached his first sermon—the "Setting Rolling of the Wheel of Truth" or "Bringing into Existence the Blessing of the True Ideal"—with the five ascetics for his hearers. The tradition says it was the evening of the Āsāỹha full moon in July, the day before the rainy season begins, and he began to speak at the moment when the sun was dipping, and the full moon simultaneously rising.

This, his first sermon, made one of his listeners, the ascetic Koṇḍañña, a "stream-enterer," with his attainment of the first of the four progressive stages of realization. The other four soon followed in his footsteps. The second sermon, on the characteristic of not-self, was preached to the same five, and it brought them to the fourth and final stage, that of arahatship: "and then" as it is said, "there were six arahats in the world." (Vinaya Mahāvagga I)

These are the first two discourses presented here, and they were the first two sermons ever uttered by the Buddha. The third, the "Fire Sermon," was delivered some months later to an audience of a thousand ascetics converted from the heaven-bent practice of fire-worship.

All three discourses deal only with understanding (*paññā*), among the faculties mentioned above as required to be balanced. But understanding, in order to reach perfection, has indeed to be aided by the others, or in other words to be founded upon virtue ("habit without conflict"), and to be fortified by concentration (though not necessarily developed to the fullness of quietism). Thus and no otherwise can it reach its goal of unshakable liberation. Virtue and concentration alone without the guidance of understanding can do no more than suppress, but they cannot of themselves alone give unshakable liberation. Now the hearers of all these three discourses were, like the Buddha himself, all ascetics already expert in the techniques and refinements of both virtue (*sīla*) and concentration (*samādhi*). So the Buddha had thus no need to tell them about what they already knew very well. Similarly he had no need to expound the doctrine of action (*kamma*) and its ripening (*vipāka*), with which they were already thoroughly acquainted through the ancient teachings. What he had to do was first to show how it is possible to go astray towards the opposite extremes of sensual indulgence and self-torment; and second to describe the facts, to show how things are, clearly and succinctly enough to stir his hearers to the additional spontaneous movement of understanding essential and indispensable for the final discovery of deliverance, each for himself. "A 'Perfect One' is one who shows the way." (MN 70)

Now let the discourses speak for themselves. Their incalculable strength lies in their simplicity, and in their actuality. The profound truth is there, discoverable even through the misty medium of translation!

Setting Rolling the Wheel of Truth
(Dhamma-cakka-pavattana-sutta)

Thus I heard.[1] On one occasion the Blessed One was living at Benares in the Deer Park at Isipatana (the Resort of Seers). There he addressed the bhikkhus of the group of five.

"Bhikkhus, these two extremes ought not to be cultivated by one gone forth from the house-life. What are the two? There is devotion to indulgence of pleasure in the objects of sensual desire, which is inferior, low, vulgar, ignoble, and leads to no good; and there is devotion to self-torment, which is painful, ignoble and leads to no good.

"The middle way discovered by a Perfect One[2] avoids both these extremes; it gives vision, it gives knowledge, and it leads to peace, to direct acquaintance, to discovery, to Nibbāna[3]. And what is that middle way? It is simply the noble eightfold path, that is to say, right view, right intention; right speech, right action, right livelihood; right effort, right mindfulness, right concentration[4]. That is the middle way discovered by a Perfect One, which gives vision, which gives knowledge, and which leads to peace, to direct acquaintance, to discovery, to Nibbāna.

"Suffering[5], as a noble truth[6], is this: Birth is suffering, ageing is suffering, sickness is suffering, death is suffering, sorrow and lamentation, pain, grief and despair are suffering; association with the loathed is suffering, dissociation from the loved is suffering, not to get what one wants is suffering—in short, suffering is the five categories[7] of clinging[8] objects.

"Thus origin of suffering, as a noble truth, is this: It is the craving[9] that produces renewal of being accompanied by enjoyment and lust, and enjoying this and that; in other words, craving for sensual desires, craving for being, craving for non-being.

"Cessation[10] of suffering, as a noble truth, is this: It is remainderless fading and ceasing, giving up, relinquishing, letting go and rejecting, of that same craving.

"The way leading to cessation of suffering, as a noble truth, is this: It is simply the noble eightfold path, that is to say, right view, right intention; right speech, right action, right livelihood; right effort, right mindfulness, right concentration.

"'Suffering, as a noble truth, is this.' Such was the vision, the knowledge, the understanding, the finding, the light, that arose in regard to ideas not heard by me before. 'This suffering, as a noble truth, can be diagnosed.' Such was the vision, the knowledge, the understanding, the finding, the light, that arose in regard to ideas not heard by me before. 'This suffering, as a noble truth, has been diagnosed.' Such was the vision, the knowledge, the understanding, the finding, the light, that arose in regard to ideas not heard by me before.

"'The origin of suffering, as a noble truth, is this.' Such was the vision... 'This origin of suffering, as a noble truth, can be abandoned.' Such was the vision... 'This origin of suffering, as a noble truth, has been abandoned.' Such was the vision... in regard to ideas not heard by me before.

"'Cessation of suffering, as a noble truth, is this.' Such was the vision... 'This cessation of suffering, as a noble truth, can be verified.' Such was the vision... 'This cessation of suffering, as a noble truth, has been verified.' Such was the vision... in regard to ideas not heard by me before.

"'The way leading to cessation of suffering, as a noble truth, is this.' Such was the vision... 'This way leading to cessation of suffering, as a noble truth, can be developed.' Such was the vision... 'This way leading to cessation of suffering, as a noble truth, has been developed.' Such was the vision, the knowledge, the understanding, the finding, the light, that arose in regard to ideas not heard by me before.

"As long as my knowing and seeing how things are[11], was not quite purified in these twelve aspects, in these three phases of each of the four noble truths, I did not claim in the world with its gods, its Māras and high divinities, in this generation with its monks and brahmans, with its princes and men to have discovered the full awakening that is supreme. But as soon as my knowing and seeing how things are, was quite purified in these twelve aspects, in these three phases of each of the four noble truths, then I claimed in the world with its gods, its Māras and high divinities, in this generation with its monks and brahmans, its princes and men to have discovered the full awakening that is supreme. Knowing and seeing arose in me thus: 'My heart's deliverance is unassailable. This is the last birth. Now there is no renewal of being.'"

That is what the Blessed One said. The bhikkhus of the group of five were glad, and they approved his words.

Now during this utterance, there arose in the venerable Koṇḍañña[12] the spotless, immaculate vision of the Teaching (Dhamma): "Whatever is subject to arising is all subject to cessation."

When the Wheel of Truth had thus been set rolling by the Blessed One the earthgods raised the cry: "At Benares, in the Deer Park at Isipatana, the matchless Wheel of Truth has been set rolling by the Blessed One, not to be stopped by monk or divine or god or death-angel or high divinity or anyone in the world."

On hearing the earthgods' cry, all the gods in turn in the six paradises of the sensual sphere took up the cry till it reached beyond to the Retinue of High Divinity in the sphere of pure form. And so indeed in that hour, at the moment the cry soared up to the World of High Divinity, this ten-thousandfold world-element shook and rocked and quaked, and a great measureless radiance surpassing the very nature of the gods was displayed in the world.

Then the Blessed One uttered the exclamation: "Koṇḍañña knows! Koṇḍañña knows!" And that is how that venerable one acquired the name, Añña-Koṇḍañña—Koṇḍañña who knows.

SN 56:11

The Not-self Characteristic
(Anatta-lakkhaṇa-sutta)

Thus I heard. On one occasion the Blessed One was living at Benares, in the Deer Park at Isipatana (the Resort of Seers). There he addressed the bhikkhus of the group of five: "Bhikkhus."—"Venerable sir," they replied. The Blessed One said this.

"Bhikkhus, form[13] is not-self[14]. Were form self, then this form would not lead to affliction, and one could have it of form: 'Let my form be thus, let my form be not thus.' And since form is not-self, so it leads to affliction, and none can have it of form: 'Let my form be thus, let my form be not thus.'

"Bhikkhus, feeling[15] is not-self...

"Bhikkhus, perception[16] is not-self...

"Bhikkhus, determinations[17] are not-self...

"Bhikkhus, consciousness[18] is not self. Were consciousness self, then this consciousness would not lead to affliction, and one could have it of consciousness: 'Let my consciousness be thus, let my consciousness be not thus.' And since consciousness is not-self, so it leads to affliction, and none can have it of consciousness: 'Let my consciousness be thus, let my consciousness be not thus.'

"Bhikkhus, how do you conceive it: is form permanent or impermanent?"—"Impermanent, venerable Sir."—"Now is what is impermanent painful or pleasant?"—"Painful, venerable Sir."—"Now is what is impermanent, what is painful since subject to change, fit to be regarded thus: 'This is mine, this is I, this is my self'"?—"No, venerable sir."

"Is feeling permanent or impermanent?...

"Is perception permanent or impermanent?...

"Are determinations permanent or impermanent?...

"Is consciousness permanent or impermanent?"—"Impermanent, venerable sir."—"Now is what is impermanent pleasant or painful?"—"Painful, venerable sir."—"Now is what is impermanent, what is painful since subject to change, fit to be regarded thus: 'This is mine, this is I, this is my self'"?—"No, venerable sir."

"So, bhikkhus any kind of form whatever, whether past, future or presently arisen, whether gross or subtle, whether in oneself or external, whether inferior or superior, whether far or near, must with right understanding how it is, be regarded thus: 'This is not mine, this is not I, this is not myself.'

"Any kind of feeling whatever...

"Any kind of perception whatever...

"Any kind of determination whatever...

"Any kind of consciousness whatever, whether past, future or presently arisen, whether gross or subtle, whether in oneself or external, whether inferior or superior, whether far or near must, with right understanding how it is, be regarded thus: 'This is not mine, this is not I, this is not my self.'

"Bhikkhus, when a noble follower who has heard (the truth) sees thus, he finds estrangement[19] in form, he finds estrangement in feeling, he finds estrangement in perception, he finds estrangement in determinations, he finds estrangement in consciousness.

"When he finds estrangement, passion fades out. With the fading of passion, he is liberated. When liberated, there is knowledge that he is liberated. He understands: 'Birth is exhausted, the holy life has been lived out, what can be done is done, of this there is no more beyond.'"

That is what the Blessed One said. The bhikkhus were glad, and they approved his words.

Now during this utterance, the hearts of the bhikkhus of the group of five were liberated from taints through clinging no more.

SN 22:59

The Fire Sermon
(Āditta-pariyāya-sutta)

Thus I heard. On one occasion the Blessed One was living at Gayā, at Gayāsīsa, together with a thousand bhikkhus. There he addressed the bhikkhus.

"Bhikkhus, all is burning. And what is the all that is burning?

"The eye[20] is burning, forms[21] are burning, eye-consciousness is burning, eye-contact[22] is burning, also whatever is felt as pleasant or painful or neither-painful-nor-pleasant that arises with eye-contact for its indispensable condition, that too is burning. Burning with what? Burning with the fire of lust, with the fire of hate, with the fire of delusion. I say it is burning with birth, ageing and death, with sorrows, with lamentations, with pains, with griefs, with despairs.

"The ear is burning, sounds are burning...

"The nose is burning, odours are burning...

"The tongue is burning, flavours are burning...

"The body[23] is burning, tangibles are burning...

"The mind[24] is burning, ideas[25] are burning, mind-consciousness[26] is burning, mind-contact is burning, also whatever is felt as pleasant or painful or neither-painful-nor-pleasant that arises with mind-contact for its indispensable condition, that too is burning. Burning with what? Burning with the fire of lust, with the fire of hate, with the fire of delusion. I say it is burning with birth, ageing and death, with sorrows, with lamentations, with pains, with griefs, with despairs.

"Bhikkhus, when a noble follower who has heard (the truth) sees thus, he finds estrangement in the eye, finds estrangement in forms, finds estrangement in eye-consciousness, finds estrangement in eye-contact, and whatever is felt as pleasant or painful or neither-painful-nor-pleasant that arises with eye-contact for its indispensable condition, in that too he finds estrangement.

"He finds estrangement in the ear... in sounds...

"He finds estrangement in the nose... in odours...

"He finds estrangement in the tongue... in flavours...

"He finds estrangement in the body... in tangibles...

"He finds estrangement in the mind, finds estrangement in ideas, finds estrangement in mind-consciousness, finds estrangement in mind-contact, and whatever is felt as pleasant or painful or neither-painful-nor-pleasant that arises with mind-contact for its indispensable condition, in that too he finds estrangement.

"When he finds estrangement, passion fades out. With the fading of passion, he is liberated. When liberated, there is knowledge that he is liberated. He understands: 'Birth is exhausted, the holy life has been lived out, what can be done is done, of this there is no more beyond.'"

That is what the Blessed One said. The bhikkhus were glad, and they approved his words.

Now during this utterance, the hearts of those thousand bhikkhus were liberated from taints through clinging no more.

SN 35:28

Notes

First Sutta

1. THUS I HEARD: Words spoken by Ānanda Thera at the First Council when all the Discourses were recited, three months after the Buddha's *Parinibbāna.*

2. PERFECT ONE: The Pali word *Tathāgata* has several alternative explanations, including *tathā āgato* ("thus come," i.e., by the way followed by all Buddhas), *tathā gato* ("thus gone," i.e., to the discovery of the Four Truths), and *tathālakkhaṇaṃ āgato* ("come to the characteristic of the 'real' or the 'such,' namely the undeceptive truth").

3. NIBBĀNA: Pali *nibbāna,* Sanskrit *nirvāna.* The meaning is "extinction," that is, of the "fires" of lust, hate, and delusion, or, more briefly, of craving and ignorance, and so *nibbāna* is a name for the third Truth as liberation. The word is made up of the prefix *nir* (not) and *vana* (effort of blowing; figuratively, craving); probably the origin was a smith's fire, which goes out or becomes extinguished (*nibbāyati*) if no longer blown on by the bellows; but the simile most used is that of a lamp's extinguishment (*nibbāna*) through exhaustion of wick and oil.

4. Noble Eightfold Path: The members of the path are defined in the *Maha-satipaṭṭhāna Sutta* and elsewhere as follows:

Right View of the Four Truths;
Right Intention governed by renunciation (non-sensuality), non-ill-will, and non-cruelty (harmlessness);
Right Speech in abstention from lying, slander, abuse and gossip;
Right Action in abstention from killing, stealing, and sexual misconduct;
Right Livelihood for bhikkhus as that allowed by the Rules of the Discipline, and for laymen as avoidance of trading in weapons, living beings, meat, intoxicants, and poisons (AN V);
Right Effort to avoid unarisen and to abandon arisen evil, and to arouse unarisen and to develop arisen good;
Right Mindfulness of the Four Foundations of Mindfulness as given in the *Mahā-satipaṭṭhāna Sutta*—that is, contemplation of the body as a body, of feelings as feelings, of states of consciousness as states of consciousness, and of ideas as ideas;
Right Concentration as (any of) the four *jhāna* meditations.

Collectively the first two members are called understanding (*paññā*), the next three virtue (*sīla*), and the last three concentration (*samādhi*). The Noble Eightfold Path is developed in four progressive stages, namely those of Stream-Entry (where wrong view, ritualism and doubt are ended), Once-Return (where sensuality and ill will are weakened), Non-Return (where these two are ended) and Arahatship (where lust for form, lust for the formless, conceit, agitation and ignorance are ended), this being the end of craving which causes suffering.

5. Suffering: the Pali word *dukkha,* made up of *dur* (bad, unsatisfactory) and *kha* (state, "-ness"), extends its meaning from the actual suffering present in physical pain or mental grief to any unwelcome state of insecurity, no matter how vague.

6. Truth: Pali *sacca* (compare Sanskrit *satya*), from the root *sat* (to be there, to be existent, to have reality, etc.) and so literally a "there-is-ness" in the sense of a state that, unlike a mirage, does not deceive or disappoint. The common sense use of truth is by no means always consistent, and the word and the notion must

therefore be handled with some care, taking it here only as treated by the Buddha.

As to individual philosophers' and divines' individual factional truths—that is to say, "The world is eternal" or "The world is not eternal"; or "The world is finite or the world is infinite"; "The soul is what the body is" or "The soul is one, the body is another"; "After death a Perfect One is" or "After death a Perfect One is not" or "After death a Perfect One both is and is not" or "After death a Perfect One neither is nor is not"—when a bhikkhu has cast off all these, has renounced and rejected, banished, abandoned, and relinquished them all, he thus becomes one who has cast off factional truths. (AN 4:38)

But how is truth to be found which is not factional?

There are five ideas that ripen here and now in two ways. What five? Faith, preference, hearsay-learning, arguing upon evidence, and liking through pondering a view. Now something may have faith well placed in it and yet be hollow, empty, and false; and again something may have no faith placed in it and yet be factual, true, and no other than it seems; and so with preference and the rest. If a man has faith, then he guards truth when he says, "My faith is thus," but on that account draws no unreserved conclusion, "Only this is true, the other is wrong." In this way he guards truth; but there is as yet no discovery of truth. (And so with preference and the rest.)

How is truth discovered? Here a bhikkhu lives near some village or town. Then a householder or his son goes to him in order to test him in three kinds of ideas, in ideas provocative of greed, of hate, and of delusion, wondering, "Are there in this venerable one any such ideas, whereby his mind being obsessed he might not knowing, say 'I know,' unseeing, say 'I see,' or get others to do likewise, which would be long for their harm and suffering?" While thus testing him he comes to find that there are no such ideas in him, and he finds that, "The bodily and verbal behaviour of that venerable one are not those of one affected by lust or hate or delusion. But the Teaching (Dhamma) that this venerable one teaches is profound, hard to see and discover; yet it is the most peaceful and superior of all, out of reach of logical ratiocination, subtle, for the wise to experience; such a Teaching cannot be taught by one affected by lust or hate or delusion."

It is as soon as by testing him, he comes to see that he is purified from ideas provocative of lust, hate, and delusion, that he then plants his faith in him. When he visits him he respects him, when he respects him he gives ear, one who gives ear hears the Teaching with attentiveness. Having heard the Teaching, he remembers it, he investigates the meaning of ideas remembered. When he does that he acquires a preference by pondering the ideas. That produces interest. One interested is actively committed. So committed he makes a judgment. According to his judgment he exerts himself. When he exerts himself he comes to realize with the body the ultimate truth, and he sees it by the penetrating of it with understanding. That is how there is discovery of truth. But there is as yet no final arrival at truth. How is truth finally arrived at? Final arrival at truth is the repetition, the keeping in being, the development, of those same ideas. That is how there is final arrival at truth. (MN 95, abbreviated)

This undeceptive truth so arrived at is the Four Noble Truths, of which it is said:

> These four noble truths are what is real, not unreal, not other (than they seem), that is why they are called Noble Truths. (Sacca-Saṃyutta)

Besides this essential static unity of the four truths as undeceptiveness, the dynamic structure of the transfiguration which they operate in combination is expressed as follows:

> Who sees suffering sees also the origin of suffering and the cessation of suffering and the way leading to cessation of suffering (and whichever of the four truths he sees, he sees the other three therewith). (Sacca Saṃyutta)

and:

> Of these four noble truths, there is noble truth to be diagnosed, there is noble truth to be abandoned, there is noble truth to be verified, and there is noble truth to be developed (kept in being). (Sacca Saṃyutta)

7. Categories: this represents the Pali word *khandha* (Sanskrit *skandha*), which is often rendered by "aggregate." The five are as given in the second Discourse. They are headings that comprise

all that can be said to arise and that forms the object of clinging. "The clinging is neither the same as these five categories which are its objects, nor is it something apart from them; it is will and lust in regard to these five categories of clinging's objects that is the clinging there." (MN 109) The five are respectively compared to a lump of froth, a bubble, a mirage, a coreless plantain-stem, and a conjuring trick.

8. CLINGING: an unsatisfactory and inadequate, but accepted rendering for the Pali *upādāna.* The word means literally "taking up" (*upa* plus *ādāna;* compare the Latin *assumere* from *ad* plus *sumere*). By a first metaphor it means a fire's fuel, i.e., what a fire takes upon itself and consumes. By a second metaphor it is used for the assumption and consumption that satisfies craving and produces existence. As such it is the condition *sine qua non* for being. What is consumed (or assumed) is the categories (q.v.). The word "clinging" has to represent this meaning. Clinging's ending is Nibbāna.

9. CRAVING: though the word *taṇhā* doubtless once meant "thirst" (compare Sanskrit *tṝṣṇa*) it is never used in Pali in that sense. With ignorance it is regarded as a basic factor in the continuity of existence. Craving draws creatures on through greed, and drives them on through hate, while ignorance prevents their seeing the truth of how things are or where they are going. Denial is as much an activity of craving as assertion is. Denial maintains the denied.

10. CESSATION: *nirodha,* meaning the cessation of suffering through the cessation of craving, is regardable as the removal of a poison, the curing of a disease, not as the mere denial of it opposed to the assertion of it, or the obstruction (*paṭivirodha*) of it in conflict with the favouring (*anurodha*) of it (see under CRAVING), since both assertion and denial confirm and maintain alike the basic idea or state that is required to be cured. Cessation, therefore, is not to be confounded with mere negativism or nihilism. "Any pleasure and joy that arise in dependence on the world is *gratification*: that the world is impermanent, pain-haunted and inseparable from the idea of change is the *disappointment* in the world; the removal of desire and lust is the *cure* (the *escape*) in the world." (AN 3) The cure or escape is Cessation: the Buddha would not claim awakening till he had diagnosed how these three things came to be.

11. Knowing and Seeing How Things Are: the force of the Pali word *yathābhūta,* literally how (it has) come to be, how (it) is, how (things) exist lies in the direct allusion to the absolutely relative conditionedness of all being. It is given specially thus: "Seeing 'such is form, such its origin, such its going out,'" and so with the other four categories.

12. The Venerable Koṇḍañña: one of the five bhikkhus. See Introduction.

Second Sutta

13. Form: Pali *rupa* (what appears, appearance). As the first of five categories (q.v.) it is defined in terms of the four Great entities, namely earth (hardness), water (cohesion), fire (temperature), and air (distension and motion), along with the negative aspect of space (what does not appear), from all of which are derived the secondary phenomena such as persons, features, shapes, etc.: these are regarded as secondary because while form can appear without them they cannot appear without form. It is also defined as "that which is being worn away" (*ruppati*), thus underlining its general characteristic of instability.

14. Not-Self: Together with the four truths, this is taught only by Buddhas. *Anattā* (not-self) is shown as a general characteristic without exception.

> The characteristic of impermanence does not become apparent because, when rise and fall are not given attention, it is concealed by continuity; the characteristic of pain does not become apparent because, when continuous oppression is not given attention, it is concealed by the postures (changing from one posture to another, waking and sleeping); the characteristic of not-self does not become apparent because, when resolution into the various elements (that compose whatever is) is not given attention, it is concealed by compactness. (*Visuddhimagga* Ch. XXI)

Self-identification and hunger for permanence and bliss form the principal manifestations of craving, guided by view that is wrong because it is not in conformity with undeceptive truth. When confronted with the contradictions and the impossibility of self-identification with any of the five categories of clinging's objects (q.v.) craving seeks to satisfy this need by imagining a soul (individual or universal); but since no such soul, however conceived, can escape falling within the five categories of clinging's objects, this solution is always foredoomed to failure. Similarly any attempt to identify self with Nibbāna must always fail for the same reason. Nibbāna conceived as identical (with self) or (self) as apart from it (emanence) or inside it (immanence), or Nibbāna conceived as "mine" is misconceived. (MN 1). This does not prevent a Perfect One from using the speech that is current in the world in order to communicate, though he does so without misapprehending it, as is shown in the Dhammapada:

Self is saviour of self;
what other saviour could there be?
For only with (one-) self well tamed
one finds the saviour, hard to find.
Only by self is evil done,
self born and given being by self,
oppressing him who knowledge lacks
as grinding diamond does the stone.

Dhammapada 160–161

Similarly with the expression "in oneself" (*ajjhattaṃ*) in the Second Discourse, this is simply a convenient convention for the focus of the individual viewpoint, not to be misapprehended. A bhikkhu heard the Buddha saying, as in the Second Discourse here, that the five categories are "not mine," etc., and he wondered; "So it seems form is not-self; feeling, perception, determinations, and consciousness are not-self. What self, then, will the action done by the not-self affect?" He was severely rebuked by the Buddha for forgetting the conditionedness of all arisen things. (MN 109) "It is impossible that anyone with right view should see any idea as self." (MN 115) and "Whatever philosophers and divines see self in its various forms, they see only the five categories, or one or other of them." (SN 12:47)

15. Feeling: (*vedanā*) this is always confined strictly to the affective feelings of (bodily or mental) pleasure and pain with the normally ignored neutral feeling of "neither-pain-nor pleasure." These can be subdivided in various ways.

16. PERCEPTION: (*saññā*) means simply recognition.

17. DETERMINATIONS: a great many different renderings of this term are current, the next best of which is certainly "formations." The Pali word *saṅkhāra* (Sanskrit *saṃskāra*) means literally "a construction," and is derived from the prefix *saṃ* (con) plus the verb *karoti* (to do, to make); compare the Latin *conficere* from *con* plus *facere* (to do), which gives the French *confection* (a construction). The Sanskrit meant ritual acts with the purpose of bringing about a good rebirth. As used in Pali by the Buddha it covers any aspects having to do with action, willing, making, planning, using, choice, etc. (anything teleological); and contact (q.v.) is often placed at the head of lists defining it. Otherwise defined as bodily, verbal, and mental action.

18. CONSCIOUSNESS: (*viññāṇa*) is here the bare "being conscious" left for consideration when the other four categories have been dealt with. It is only describable in individual plurality in terms of the other four categories, as fire is individualized only by the fuel it burns (see MN 38 & 109). Otherwise it is regardable as an infiniteness (MN 111) dependent upon the contemplation of it as such. It is impermanent, etc., because however it arises, it can only do so in dependence on the other categories, that is, on conditions themselves impermanent, painful and not-self. It never arises unless accompanied by co-nascent *perception* (q.v.) and *feeling* (q.v.). It has six "doors" (see under EYE and MIND) for cognizing its objective fields, but no more.

19. ESTRANGEMENT: the Pali noun *nibbidā* and its verb *nibbindati* are made up from the prefix *nir* in its negative sense of "out," and the root *vid* (to find, to feel, to know intimately). *Nibbidā* is thus a finding out. What is thus found out is the intimate hidden contradictoriness in any kind of self-identification based in any way on these things (and there is no way of determining self-identification apart from them—see under NOT-SELF). Elsewhere the Buddha says:

> Whatever there is there of form, feeling, perception, determinations, or consciousness, such ideas he sees as impermanent, as subject to pain, as a sickness, as a tumour, as a barb, as a calamity, as an affliction, as an alienation, as a disintegration, as void, as not-self. He averts his heart from

> those ideas, and for the most peaceful, the supreme goal, he turns his heart to the deathless element, that is to say, the stilling of all determinations, the relinquishment of all substance, the exhaustion of craving, the fading of passion, cessation, extinction. (MN 64)

The "stuff" of life can also be seen thus. Normally the discovery of a contradiction is for the unliberated mind a disagreeable one. Several courses are then open. It can refuse to face it, pretending to itself to the point of full persuasion and belief that no contradiction is there; or one side of the contradiction may be unilaterally affirmed and the other repressed and forgotten; or a temporary compromise may be found (all of which expedients are haunted by insecurity); or else the contradiction may be faced in its truth and made the basis for a movement towards liberation. So too, on finding estrangement thus, two main courses are open: either the search, leaving "craving for self-identification" intact, can be continued for sops to allay the symptoms of the sickness; or else a movement can be started in the direction of a cure for the underlying sickness of craving, and liberation from the everlasting hunt for palliatives, whether for oneself or others. In this sense alone, "Self protection is the protection of others, and protection of others self-protection" (*Satipaṭṭhāna Saṃyutta*).

Third Sutta

20. Eye, etc.: the six, beginning with the eye and ending with the mind (q.v.), are called the six "bases for contact (see Contact) in oneself," and are also known as the six "doors" for perception. Their corresponding objects are called "external bases," ("sense-organ" is both too material and too objective), since the emphasis here is on the subjective faculty of *seeing*, etc., not the associated piece of flesh *seen* in someone else or in the looking-glass, which, in so far as it is visible, is not "seeing" but "form" as the "external" object of the seeing "eye in oneself," and insofar as it is tangible is the object of the body-base in oneself, and insofar as it is apprehended as a "bodily feature" is the object of the mind-base in oneself. Here the eye should be taken simply as the perspective-pointing-inward-to-a-centre in the otherwise uncoordinated visual field consisting of colours, which makes them cognizable by eye-

consciousness, and which is misconceivable as "I." The six bases in oneself are compared to an empty village, and the six external bases to village-raiding robbers.

21. FORMS: the first of the six external bases, respective objective fields or objects of the six bases in oneself (see EYE). The same Pali word *rūpa* is used for the eye's object as for the first of the five categories, but here in the plural. Colours, the basis for the visual perspective of the eye (q.v.), are intended primarily (see also under FORM above).

22. CONTACT: the Pali word *phassa* comes from the verb *phusati* (to touch, sometimes used in the sense of to arrive at, or to realize), from which also comes the word *phoṭṭhabba* (tangible, the object of the fifth base in oneself, namely, body-sensitivity). But here it is generalized to mean contact in the sense of presence of object to subject, or presence of cognized to consciousness, in all forms of consciousness. It is defined as follows: "Eye-consciousness arises dependent on eye and on forms; the coincidence of the three is contact (presence), and likewise in the cases of the ear, nose, tongue, body and mind. Failing it, no knowledge, no consciousness of any sort whatever, can arise at all." This fundamental idea is sometimes placed at the head of lists of things defining Determinations (q.v.).

23. BODY: the Pali word *kāya* is used both for the physical body and for any group, as the English word "body" is. In Pali it is also used in the sense (a) for the physical frame, namely "this body with its consciousness" in a general sense, sometimes called "old action," and then it forms the subject of body contemplation as set forth in the *Satipaṭṭhāna Sutta,* the aim of which is to analyse this "conglomeration" into its motley constituents. Or else it is used in a strict sense, as here, namely (b) that "door" of the subjective body-sensitivity or tactile sense, the perspective-pointing-inwards-to-a-centre in the otherwise uncoordinated tactile field of tangibles consisting of the hard, the hot-or-cold, and the distended-and-movable (see also under EYE).

24. MIND: the Pali word *mano* belongs to a root meaning to measure, compare, coordinate. Here it is intended as that special "door" in which the five kinds of consciousness, arising in the other five doors (see under EYE), combine themselves with their objective fields into a unitive *perspective-pointing-inwards-to-a-centre,* together with certain objects apprehendable in this mind-

door, such as infiniteness of space, etc. (and names, fictions, etc.). Whatever is cognized in this door (see under CONSCIOUSNESS) is cognized as an *idea* (q.v.) as opposed to the bare objects of the eye uncognized by it as well. Here it makes this otherwise uncoordinated field of ideas cognizable by mind-consciousness (q.v.). And in the presence (with the contact) of ignorance (of the four truths) it is misconceived as "I." It is thus the fusing of this heterogeneous stuff of experience into a coherent pattern, when it also has the function of giving temporal succession and flow to that pattern by its presenting all ideas for cognition as "preceded." In the Abhidhamma, but not in the Suttas, "the (material) form which is the support for mind" is mentioned (implying perhaps the whole "body with its consciousness"), but not further specified. This would place mind on a somewhat similar basis to the eye-seeing, as meant here in its relation to the objective piece of flesh (see under EYE). Later notions coupled it with the heart. Now fashion identifies it with the brain; but such identifications are not easy to justify unilaterally; and if they in any way depend upon a prior and always philosophically questionable assumption of a separate body-substance and a mind-substance, they will find no footing in the Buddha's teaching where substances are not assumed.

25. IDEA: the word *dhamma* is gerundive from the verb *dharati* (to carry, to remember), thus it means literally a "carryable, a rememberable." In this context of the six pairs of Bases it means the rememberables which form the mind's special object; as distinct from the forms seen only with the eye, the sounds heard with the ear, the odours smelt with the nose, the flavours tasted with the tongue, and the tangibles touched with the body, ideas are what are apprehended through the mind-door (see under EYE, FORMS and MIND, and also CONTACT). These six cover all that can be known. But while the first (see FORMS) are uncoordinated *between themselves* and have no direct access to each other, in the mind-door the five find a common denominator and are given a coordinating perspective, together with the mind's own special objects. So the *idea* as a rememberable, is the aspect of the known apprehended by the mind, whether coordinating the five kinds of consciousness, or apprehending the ideas peculiar to it (see MIND), or whether apprehending its own special objects. This must

include all the many other meanings of the word *dhamma* (Sanskrit *dharma*). Nibbāna, in so far as it is knowable—describable—is an object of the mind, and is thus an idea. "All ideas are not-self." What is inherently unknowable has no place in the Teaching

26. MIND-CONSCIOUSNESS: if it is remembered that each of the six pairs of bases, the five consisting of eye, ear, nose, tongue, and body, being coordinated by mind, are open to any one's self-inspection; and that consciousness is considered here as arising dependently upon each of these six pairs of bases and in no other way whatsoever (since no other description rejecting all six is possible without self-contradiction); then this notion of mind-consciousness should present no special difficulty.

The Three Suttas and Their Relationship

The first of these three discourses sets out the vision of the truth peculiar to Buddhas, with its foundation of suffering ("I teach only suffering, and the liberation from suffering"). The second then takes the five categories given in the definition of suffering in the first, and it shows how, in this comprehensive analysis every component can be diagnosed rightly, that is to say in conformity with truth. It is this treatment that elicits the characteristic of not-self. The two characteristics of Impermanence and Suffering in the world were well recognized in ancient Indian philosophies and have never been peculiar to Buddhism. This exposure of the inherent contradiction in the very nature of the idea of self-identity, to which craving cleaves with the would-be self-preserving stranglehold of a drowning man upon his rescuer, is here made the very basis for the movement to liberation. Craving is cured through coming to understand how things are while truth is being guarded (see under TRUTH above). The consequent fading of lust is brought about by the discovery of truth, and the understanding that there is no more of this beyond is the result of the final arrival at Truth by keeping it in being through development. In the third discourse the very same ground is gone over but described in different terms. The comprehensive analysis in terms of the five categories with their general rather than individual emphasis, is replaced by the equally comprehensive and complementary analysis in terms of the six pairs of bases, which analyse the individual viewpoint, without which no consciousness can arise. And instead of the dispassionate term "not-self," everything that could possibly be identified as self is, without mentioning the term, presented to the same effect in the colours of a conflagration of passion behind a mirage of deception. Only a Buddha "whose heart is cooled by compassion" can have the courage to venture so far in the search for truth and discover thereby the true state of peace.

Questions

Is not seeking one's own salvation a selfish aim?

If the aim prescribed were a heavenly personal existence forever with self-preservation (whether through selfishness as such, or disguised as altruism), then the answer could hardly but be Yes. But with the aim as the removal of self-insistence in every form (not excluding ultimately self-denial, which like any negation, is just another affirmation of the basic idea so strenuously denied)—the cure of the infectious sickness that leads to untold suffering—does the question arise at all? But even granting that it did, would not the Arahat disciple display, after the Buddha, the highest altruism by showing how the aspiration to health is not a deception, since by his success he bears witness that it can be achieved and that no one is forever excluded from following his example?

But this description in terms of suffering, is it not pessimistic?

Is it not rather the very reverse? For true optimism is surely shown by having the courage and energy to see how things are, and where liberation lies; and would it not be true pessimism to be satisfied to try and make existence out to be pleasanter or safer, and liberation easier, than is in conformity with the truth? Must not true liberation lie beyond the dialectic of pessimism and optimism, beyond alternatives of selfishness and altruism, as Truth (not factional truths) lies beyond that of being and non-being?

Does not the teaching of "not-self" imply that there is in fact no action; that, for instance, there are no living beings to kill?

The answer is certainly "No." The reasons would be too lengthy to go into here in detail. But it is said by the Buddha:

"The Buddhas in the past, accomplished and fully awakened, those Blessed Ones maintained the efficacy of action and of certain action to be done, and so will those do in the future, and so do I now." (AN 3:136)

Devotion in Buddhism

Three Essays

WHEEL PUBLICATION NO. 18

Homage to the Buddha by Sabhiya
on his Acceptance of the Doctrine

Ending, transcending ills
Cankerless Arahat,
thy insight, light, and lore,
have brought me safe across!

For marking my distress,
for freeing me from doubt,
I laud thee, sage benign,
consummate master-mind,
great Kinsman of the Sun!

The doubts I had are solved by thee,
O Seer, O All-Enlightened Sage Immaculate!

With every perturbation rooted up
unfevered tranquil, strong in Truth art thou!

Great Victor! Paragon! Thy words rejoice
all gods, all Nāradas, all Pabbatas.

I hail thee noblest, foremost of mankind;
nor earth nor heaven holds thy counterpart!

Enlightened Master! Over Māra's hosts
triumphant! Sage, who, wrong propensities
uprooting, for thyself salvation found
and taught mankind to find salvation too!

Thou hast surmounted all that breeds rebirth
and extirpated canker-growths within!
With naught to bind thee thrall to life, thou'rt free
as forest lion from all fears and dread.

Even as a lotus fair to water gives
no lodgement, thou by good and bad alike
art unaffected. Stretch thou forth thy feet,
O Victor! I salute my Master's feet!

From *Buddhas Teachings* (*Suttanipāta*)
translated by Lord Chalmers (Harvard Oriental Series)

Devotion in Buddhism I

by Nyanaponika Thera

The Buddha repeatedly discouraged any excessive veneration paid to him personally. He knew that an excess of purely emotional devotion can obstruct or disturb the development of a balanced character, and thus may become a serious obstacle to progress on the path to deliverance. The history of religion has since proved him right, as illustrated by the extravagancies of emotional mysticism in East and West.

The suttas relate the story of the monk Vakkali, who full of devotion and love for the Buddha, was ever desirous to behold him bodily. To him the Buddha said: "What shall it profit you to see this impure body? He who sees the Dhamma sees me."

Shortly before the Buddha passed away, he said: "If a monk or a nun, a devout man or a devout woman, lives in accordance with the Dhamma, is correct in his life, walks in conformity with the Dhamma—it is he who rightly honours, reverences, venerates, holds sacred and reveres the Perfect One (*Tathāgata*) with the worthiest homage."

A true and deep understanding of the Dhamma, together with conduct in conformity with that understanding—these are vastly superior to any external homage or mere emotional devotion. That is the instruction conveyed by these two teachings of the Master.

It would be a mistake, however, to conclude that the Buddha disparaged a reverential and devotional attitude of mind when it is the natural outflow of a true understanding and a deep admiration of what is great and noble. It would also be a grievous error to believe that the "seeing of the Dhamma" (spoken of in the first saying) is identical with a mere intellectual appreciation and purely conceptual grasp of the doctrine. Such a one-sided abstract approach to the very concrete message of the Buddha all too often leads to intellectual smugness. In its barrenness it will certainly not be a substitute for the strong and enlivening impulse imparted by a deep-felt devotion to what is known as great, noble and exemplary. Devotion, being a facet and natural accompaniment of confidence (*saddhā*), is a necessary factor in the "balance of faculties" (*indriya-samatā*) required for final deliverance. Confidence, in all its aspects, including the devotional, is needed to resolve any stagnation and other shortcomings resulting from a one-sided development of the intellectual faculties. Such development often tends to turn around in circles endlessly, without being able to effect a break-through. Here, devotion, confidence and faith—all aspects of the Pali term *saddhā*—may be able to give quick and effective help.

Though the Buddha refused to be made the object of an emotional "personality cult," he also knew that "respect and homage paid to those who are worthy of it is a great blessing." The Buddha made this statement in the very first stanza of one of his principal ethical injunctions, the Discourse on Blessings (*Mahāmaṅgala Sutta*).[1] Mentioning the value of a respectful, reverential attitude together with the blessings of "avoiding fools and associating with the wise," the Buddha obviously regarded such an attitude as fundamental for individual and social progress and for the acquisition of any further higher benefits. One who is incapable of a reverential attitude will also be incapable of spiritual progress beyond the narrow limits of his present mental condition. One who is so blind as not to see or recognize anything higher and better than the little mud-pool of his petty self and environment will suffer for a long time from retarded growth. And one who, out of a demonstrative self-assertion, scorns a reverential attitude in himself and in others will remain imprisoned in his self-conceit—a most formidable bar to a true maturity of character and to spiritual growth. It is by recognizing and honouring someone or something higher that one honours and enhances one's own inner potentialities.

When the high heart we magnify,
And the sure vision celebrate,
And worship greatness passing by,
Ourselves are great.

Since respect, reverence and devotion are partial aspects of the Buddhist concept of confidence, one will now understand why confidence has been called the seed of all other beneficial qualities.

1. See The Wheel No. 14 *Everyman's Ethics.*

The nobler the object of reverence of devotion, the higher is the blessing bestowed by it. "Those who have joyous confidence in the highest, the highest fruit will be theirs" (AN 4:34). The supreme objects of a Buddhist's reverence and devotion are his Three Refuges, also called the Three Jewels or Ideals: the Buddha, his Teaching (*Dhamma*) and the Community of saintly monks and nuns (*Sangha*).[2] Here, too, the Buddha is revered not as a personality of such a name, nor as a deity, but as the embodiment of Enlightenment.

A text often recurring in the Buddhist scriptures says that a devout lay disciple "has confidence, he believes in the Enlightenment of the Perfect One." This confidence, however, is not the outcome of blind faith based on hearsay, but is derived from the devotee's reasoned conviction based on his own understanding of the Buddha Word, which speaks to him clearly with a voice of unmistakable Enlightenment. This derivation of his assurance is emphasized by the fact that, along with confidence, wisdom also is mentioned among the qualities of an ideal lay follower.

We may now ask: Is it not quite natural that feelings of love, gratitude, reverence and devotion seek expression through the entire personality, through acts of body and speech as well as through our thoughts and unexpressed sentiments? Will one, for instance, hide one's feelings towards parents and other loved ones? Will one not rather express them by loving words and deeds? Will one not cherish their memory in suitable ways, as for instance, by preserving their pictures in one's home, by placing flowers on their graves, by recalling their noble qualities? In such a way, one who has become critical of the devotional aspects of religion may seek to understand the outward acts of homage customary in Buddhist lands when, with reverential gesture, flowers and incense are placed before a Buddha image and devotional texts are recited not as prayers but as meditation. Provided that such practice does not deteriorate into a thoughtless routine, a follower of the Dhamma will derive benefit if he takes up some form of a devotional practice, adapting it to his personal temperament and to the social customs of his environment. Buddhism, however, does not in the least impose upon its

2. See Bodhi Leaves No. 5, *The Three Refuges*, by Bhikkhu Ñāṇamoli.

followers a *demand* to observe any outward form of devotion or worship. This is entirely left to the choice of individuals whose emotional, devotional and intellectual needs are bound to differ greatly. No Buddhist should feel himself forced into an iron-cast mould, be it of a devotional or a rationalistic shape. As a follower of the middle way, he should, however, also avoid one-sided judgement of others, and try to appreciate that their individual needs and preferences may differ from his own.

More important and of greater validity than outward forms of devotion is the basic capacity for respect and reverence discussed at the beginning of this essay, and also the practice of meditations or contemplations of a devotional character. Many benefits accrue from these, and hence it was for good reasons that the Enlightened One strongly and repeatedly recommended the meditative recollection of the Buddha (*buddhānussati*), along with other devotional recollections.[3] Here again, the reference is to the embodied ideal; thus the Buddha, as a being freed from all traces of vanity and egotism, could venture to recommend to his disciples a meditation on the Buddha.

What, then, are the benefits of such devotional meditations? Their first benefit is *mental purification*. They have been called by the Buddha "efficacious procedures for purifying a defiled mind" (AN 3:71). "When a noble disciple contemplates upon the Enlightened One, at that time his mind is not enwrapped in lust, nor in hatred, nor in delusion. At such time his mind is rightly directed: it has got rid of lust, is aloof from it, is freed from it. Lust is here a name for the five sense desires. By cultivating this contemplation, many beings become purified" (AN 6:25).

If, by practising that devotional meditation, one endeavours to live, as it were, "in the Master's presence" (*satthā sammukhībhūta*), one will feel ashamed to do, speak or think anything unworthy; one will shrink back from evil; and as a positive reaction, one will feel inspired to high endeavour in emulation of the Master's great example.

Images, and not abstract concepts, are the language of the subconscious. If, therefore, the image of the Enlightened One

---

3. See *The Path of Purification* (*Visuddhimagga*), translated by Bhikkhu Ñāṇamoli, Chapter VII.

is often created within one's mind as the embodiment of man perfected, it will penetrate deeply into the subconscious, and if sufficiently strong, will act as an automatic brake against evil impulses. In such a way the subconscious, normally so often the hidden enemy in gaining self-mastery, may become a powerful ally of such an endeavour. For the purpose of *educating the subconscious*, it will be helpful to use a Buddha image or picture as an aid in visualization. In that way concentration of mind may be attained fairly soon. For evoking and deeply absorbing some features of the Buddha's personality, his qualities should be contemplated, for instance in the way described in the *Visuddhimagga*.

The recollection of the Buddha, being productive of joy (*pīti*), is an effective way of *invigorating the mind*, of lifting it up from the states of listlessness, tension, fatigue and frustration, which occur during meditation as well as in ordinary life. The Buddha himself advised: "If (in the strenuous practice of meditation, for instance) in contemplation of the body, bodily agitation, including sense desires, or mental lassitude or distraction should arise, then the meditator should turn his mind to a gladdening, elevating subject" (SN 47:10). And here the teachers of old recommend especially the recollection of the Buddha. When those hindrances to concentration vanish under its influence, the meditator will be able to return to his original meditation subject.

For a beginner especially, attempts at gaining concentration are often frustrated by an uneasy self-consciousness; the meditator, as it were, squints back upon himself. He becomes disturbingly aware of his body with its little discomforts, and of his mind struggling against obstacles which only grow stronger the more he struggles. This may happen when the subject of meditation is one's own physical or mental processes, but it may also occur with other subjects. In such a situation, it will be profitable to follow the advice given earlier and to turn one's attention from one's own personality to the inspiring visualization of the Buddha and the contemplation of his qualities. The joyful interest thus produced may bring about that self-forgetfulness which is such an important factor for gaining concentration. Joy produces calm (*passaddhi*), calm leads to ease (*sukha*), and ease to concentration (*samādhi*). Thus devotional meditation can serve as a valuable *aid in attaining mental concentration* which is the basis of liberating insight. This function of devotional meditation cannot be better described than in the words of the Master:

> "When a noble disciple contemplates upon the Enlightened One, at that time his mind is not enwrapped in lust, nor in hatred, nor in delusion. At such a time his mind is rightly directed towards the Perfect One (*Tathāgata*). And with a rightly directed mind the noble disciple gains enthusiasm for the goal, enthusiasm for the Dhamma, gains the delight derived from the Dhamma. In him thus delighted, joy arises; to one who is joyful, body and mind become calm; calmed in body and mind, he feels at ease; and if at ease, the mind finds concentration. Such a one is called a noble disciple who among humanity gone wrong, has attained to what is right; who among a humanity beset by troubles, dwells free of troubles." (Mahānāmasutta, AN 6:10)

Devotion in Buddhism II

By Ācārya Buddharakkhita

Religion and devotion are inseparable, and Buddhism is no exception to this rule. Theravada or Buddhism based on the Pali Tipiṭaka, the original Teachings of the Buddha (sometimes called Hīnayāna), is alleged by some to be dry and intellectual, to have no devotion or higher emotional content in it. There may be some truth in this allegation when it concerns those people who only superficially profess adherence to the Teaching (*Dhamma*) or who limit themselves only to an intellectual study and appreciation of the Dhamma without applying its tenets to their everyday life. For the true follower of Theravada, however, devotion is an indispensable aid on the way to Deliverance. For him even the word "Buddha" can produce the deepest emotional stirring and rapture.

Dhamma, said the Buddha, may be compared to a snake which if caught by the head is brought under control but if seized by the tail, carries death. Similarly the Dhamma rightly understood and lived, leads to the extinction of all suffering, but will cause harm if misunderstood and misapplied.[4] If we are to accept that Buddhism starves emotion and lays emphasis on reason alone then it would have been impossible for Buddhism to flourish for more than 2500 years as a living religion providing the spiritual and cultural requirements of millions. Countries like Burma, Thailand, Ceylon, Cambodia, Laos, Vietnam cannot conceivably be supposed to have quenched their spiritual thirst with mere dry abstractions. Further, emotion, as a distinct mental factor, cannot be suppressed; it is bound to express itself. In point of fact, the balancing of these two mental faculties, emotion and reason, is considered in Buddhism most essential for a harmonious spiritual development. Harmony, moderation and gradual development are features that run through the entire system of Buddhism like a scarlet thread.

In the theistic conception of *bhakti* or faith, devotion is always accompanied by practices like prayers, rituals, vows, and an unquestioned obedience to a Creator God, his earthly incarnation or some deity. There is fear of being punished if the command of God is either questioned or not followed with submission. And wherever there is fear there will arise blind faith, dogmatism, superstition, ritualism, intolerance and such other evil consequences, because fear restricts mental growth, traps the mind and makes it insular. Prayers, rituals and vows lead men to ask and crave for worldly boons and pleasures while alive, and for happy states on earth or in heavenly worlds, after death. Love taking the form of an uncontrolled emotional devotion may, and often does, create selfish affection (*sneha*) and a physical relationship between the devotee and his or her lord which in many cases may turn carnal. Being associated with religion, such indulgences may remain undetected and even become a holy practice which could be conducted unhindered. This would give one a free licence to roam in the wilderness of vague imaginations. One waits for the saving grace of the God in all activities and thereby loses self-confidence and becomes indolent and a slave to superstitions. Devotion should not be wholly emotional, for it may grow positively harmful in that the devotee may become

4. See *The Discourse on the Simile of the Serpent* (Majjhima Nikāya No. 22. Alagaddūpama Sutta).

fanatical or, having become too sensitive emotionally, get upset by little mishaps or gains.

Against such one-sided emphasis, the concept of devotion in Theravada Buddhism is distinctly different. Devotion from this stand-point is *ñāṇasampayutta;* i.e. accompanied by Knowledge, so that it presents, on both the philosophical and emotional level, a strong contrast to those religions which lay emphasis on emotion alone. The philosophical aspect calls into play two important mental faculties, viz., the rational and the volitional. The emotional aspect has, as it were, many facets, bringing together several mental factors, such as gratitude, reverence, love, faith or confidence, and joy. For as much as devotion is a culture of mind, it sets on foot a harmonious development of all the mental faculties bringing about integration and wholeness of character required for the attainment of Nibbāna. What part each of these different faculties play in the act of devotion, will be discussed later.

The object of devotion in Buddhism is what is known as the "Triple Gem" (*ratanattāya*) or the "Threefold Refuge" (*saraṇattaya*), comprising the Buddha, the Dhamma and the Sangha; that is, the Enlightened One, his doctrine and the order of his noble disciples, i.e. the *ariyas* or saints. The Three Gems are so called because nothing can be more precious and worthy of bestowing incomparable and unalloyed peace and happiness than these; hence they are also the highest refuge, the peerless source of security and protection.

The practice of devotion consists of reflecting or meditating (*anussati*) on the qualities or attributes of that Triple Gem. These qualities are embodied in the most simple yet profound formula known as *Ratanattāya Vandanā Gāthā*—the Verses of Homage to the Triple Gem—familiar to all Buddhists from the time they learn to speak, which they recite on all occasions of worship.

> *Iti pi so Bhagava, Arahaṃ, Sammāsambuddho, vijjācaraṇasampanno, sugato, lokavidū, anuttaro purisadammasārathi, satthā, devamanussānaṃ, Buddho, Bhagavā-ti.*

> "Thus, indeed, is that Blessed One, he is the Holy One, fully enlightened, endowed with vision and conduct, sublime, the knower of worlds, the incomparable leader of men to be tamed, the teacher of gods, and men, enlightened and blessed."

Svākkhāto Bhagavatā dhammo, sandiṭṭhiko, akāliko, ehipassiko, opanayiko, paccattaṃ veditabbo viññūhī-ti.

"Well-expounded is the Dhamma (teaching) by the Blessed One, verifiable here and now, with immediate fruit, inviting all to test for themselves, leading on to Nibbāna, to be comprehended by the wise, each for himself."

Supaṭipanno bhagavato sāvaka-saṅgho, ujupaṭipanno bhagavato sāvakasaṅgho, ñāyapaṭipanno bhagavato sāvakasaṅgho sāmicipaṭipanno bhagavato sāvakasaṅgho; yadidaṃ cattāri purisayugāni aṭṭhapurisapuggalā, esa bhagavato sāvakasaṅgho, āhuneyyo, pāhuneyyo, dakkhiṇeyyo añjalikaraṇīyo, anuttaraṃ puññakkhettaṃ lokassā-ti.

"Of perfect conduct is the Order of the Lord's Disciples, of wise conduct is the Order of the Lord's Disciples, of dutiful conduct is the Order of the Lord's Disciples; that is to say, the Four Pairs of men,[5] the Eight persons. This Order of the Lord's Disciples is worthy of offerings, worthy of hospitality, worthy of gifts, worthy of reverential salutation, as an incomparable field of merit to the world."

Space does not permit to go here into the details of the practice of devotional meditations. Briefly, it is meditating on the true significance of these attributes—nine of the Buddha, six of the Dhamma, ten of the Sangha—and accomplishing an inner transformation by implanting them, as it were, within.

Buddha is venerated and followed as the Great Teacher, the spiritual Master. The term Buddha is an honorific expression implying the attainment of Supreme Enlightenment; that is to say, it is not a personal name but an indication of a state of perfection. It is also an attribute of a perfect and holy guide who, by virtue of having discovered a truth unaided and through long and painful struggle, guides, points out and makes known to beings, out of great compassion, the nature of reality otherwise called the Four Noble Truths—*cattāri ariya-saccāni.* These are embodied in this

5. The Four Pairs and Eight Persons refer to the four stages of Sainthood endowed with the eightfold Supramundane Knowledge of Path (*magga*) and Fruition (*phala*).

succinct and profound saying of the Master: "Sorrow I point out and sorrow's end".

Hence, to the Buddhists the Buddha is not a God or an incarnation of a God (*avatāra*), nor is he an ever abiding universal principle; and the Buddha has no commandments to give which need be accepted with unquestioning obedience. Prayers to him, or rituals and vows, and blind faith in him have no meaning whatsoever.

Dhamma here constitutes the transcendental truths of Nibbāna as well as the Eightfold Path leading to Nibbāna as discovered and proclaimed by the Buddha. Here reflection (*anussati*) is meditation on the Dhamma's transcendental qualities, that is to say, meditation on that perfect state of deliverance which is freed from greed, hate and delusion—the sources of all saṃsāric turmoil—and a condition of peace and bliss that terminates death and rebirth for all time. It is also meditation on that perfect path which leads to this perfect goal, namely, on Right Understanding, Right Intention, Right Speech, Right Action, Right Livelihood, Right Effort, Right Mindfulness, and Right Concentration.

Sangha is the Order or Community of Noble Disciples (*ariyas*) established in the goal or on the path that leads to the goal; thus forming the 'living example' to those still striving.

Briefly, Buddha is the Way-finder, the Supreme Teacher, the Unmatched Guide; Dhamma is the incomparable Way, the Perfect Teaching; the Sangha refers to those who, dedicating themselves to the full realisation of the Dhamma and earnestly striving, have entered upon the Paths of Sanctitude.

In the course of the actual practice of devotion, these three, however, embody and culminate in one idea, one Truth. Hence it is said:

Dhammakāyo yato satthā,
Dhammo satthā tato mato;
Dhamme ṭhito so saṅgho ca
satthu saṅkhaṃ nigacchati.

Since the Teacher is the Truth-embodiment,
so is the Truth the very Teacher,
and the Noble Order being established on the Truth,
Also goes by the name of the Teacher.

Thus the act of devotion is directed to one single object which forms the Guide as well as the Goal, independent of, and unmixed with, the notion of any personality or incarnation, a God or *Paramātman*, but purely as an aspiration for an ideal of absolute perfection and purity, attainable through self-control, discipline and mental development.

Devotional acts with such background and based on the realisation of these great attributes, set going mental dispositions favourable to the attainment of similar qualities in one's own mind, be it even to a small degree. At first, they appear as a rather unimportant contribution to the attainment of the lofty goal, but the cumulative effect of a series of such devotional acts later grows and transforms itself until it becomes of the same stuff—*evaṃ dhammo*—as these great attributes, i.e., of the very truth. Further, this form of devotion with mental faculties well-balanced, maintains itself as a habitual frame of mind and not as an isolated act spasmodically indulged in, thus ensuring a steady progress. When devotion reaches a very high point, the distinction of subject, i. e. the self-notion, disappears and what is realised is the very 'stuff', nature or substance of the Triple Gem. Hence devotion is directed towards an ever-present reality and not merely towards a dead teacher or empty abstractions.

As mentioned earlier, a devotional act calls into play many forces and faculties of the mind. The most important of these is faith (*saddhā*) in the Triple Gem, which, in Buddhism, means conviction and confidence born of knowledge. Faith is associated with other factors such as gratitude, love, joy and deep reverence, forming as a whole, what may be called here, the emotional aspect. In as much as this *saddhā* or conviction born of knowledge contains no element of selfish affection (*sineha*) nor personal relationship nor blind faith, it differs essentially from the theistic concept of faith and devotion. The basis of *saddhā* is wise understanding of the true significance of the Triple Gem with respect to the problem of suffering and the deliverance from it. At least it must be accompanied by a deep conviction in the 'Law of Kamma' as a factor that sustains and perpetuates this endless course of birth and death, and the suffering associated with life.

Since *saddhā* is the one indispensable factor that governs all spiritual endeavour, it is called the seed (*bīja*) from which is born the 'tree of wisdom' that bears the 'fruit of deliverance'. There are five mental powers (*bala*), also called spiritual faculties (*indriya*), namely: *saddhā*—faith; *viriya*—energy; *sāti*—mindfulness; *samādhi*—concentration; *paññā*—intuitive insight or wisdom. Of these the primary factor is *saddhā* which, if properly cultivated, conditions the development of the rest. In its highest, i.e., supramundane sense, *saddhā* is *aveccapasāda*, unshakable faith in the Triple Gem—achievable through the attainment of the Noble Path (*ariya magga*). And only in this sense is it true 'self-surrender' which is the culmination of devotion. Self-surrender, in the Buddhist sense, is not a spiritual unification with some other entity or merging with some universal principle nor the sacrifice of one's will at the feet of someone else, a God, deity or teacher. But it is the entire abandonment, down to the last vestige, of all 'self-notion', of 'personality-belief' (belief in an immortal self)—*sakkāyadiṭṭhi.* When accomplished, this brings to pass the overcoming of at least two other mental fetters (*saṃyojana*), namely, sceptical doubt (*vicikicchā*) and clinging to rites and rituals (*sīlabbata-parāmāsa*). Lastly since *saddhā* rouses other concomitant factors, such as assurance, joy, gratitude and reverence, one will realise the tremendous significance of the Triple Gem as the true refuge from the toils and tumults of saṃsāra. A deliberate and conscious cultivation of this one factor, therefore, means the development of the entire emotional aspect which forms the source of all mental energy.

This brings us to the philosophical side with its two faculties, the rational and the volitional. The function of the rational faculty is to investigate and probe into the nature of existence in order to understand, at least intellectually, its reality in the true perspective. It is the dispassionate and objective study and scrutiny of things. When one removes the lid of 'self' or 'ego-centric consciousness' from the jar of life and lays it bare for objective analysis and observation, only then does true understanding spring up in the mind. It must be agreed that understanding is manifold and of various kinds, so that one particular object may also be explained in quite the opposite way, perhaps reasonably too! Hence, what is intended here is understanding in terms of the Noble Truths, according to which existence is regarded not as something permanent, pleasurable and endowed with a self or ego, but as an impersonal process, arising and passing away dependent on conditions; that is to say, as impermanent, subject to suffering and unsubstantial (*anicca, dukkha, anattā*).

It is a proven fact that the basic instinct in all beings is the search for happiness and pleasure, and security or safety against death, disease and danger, although it is quite obvious that death is more certain than life. If life were not impermanent then there would be no need to crave for security and protection; likewise, the search for happiness and pleasure is another proof of the intrinsic suffering in life. The same is true of the self delusion; for, if there were such a thing as an abiding self then it would mean that we would be free from the clutches of death and from all misery. 'Self' as an independent entity, unaffected by all empirical fetters and limitations, presupposes 'ownership', and the status of being the 'master' and 'possessor' of this life. Nobody ever wishes to suffer or to die. If there were an eternal or divine self, then it would prevent all forms of suffering, death, etc. But that does not happen. Why would such a freed, happy and permanent self need to strive for freedom, happiness and security? And where is the need for religion which aims at these attainments? The reality, however, is that there is only a self-delusion which is the root of all suffering and the cause of all limitation. Conditioned by this delusion, known to Buddhists as *avijjā*, beings engage themselves in this mad rush of activities driven all the time by manifold cravings. Actions must produce reactions and these acts of craving that we always and almost helplessly perform cannot escape from producing results, namely the continuity of this stream of life, this cycle of births and deaths. But this inherent unsatisfactoriness in saṃsāric existence need not create undue anxiety, frustration or pessimism; in fact, it should be the greatest incentive to hope, assurance and optimism. For the opposite of suffering too must exist. If only these actions are free from craving—the root cause of suffering—there is no reason why lasting happiness and peace could not be achieved. This, a deathless state of supramundane happiness called "Nibbāna," is the goal of Buddhism.

With this background, it may be noticed the rational faculty is not limited to a barren intellectualism; besides causing a definite enrichment of the emotional faculty, it arouses the volition to transform knowledge into a living truth. Such understanding may arise as a result of study and hearing of the Dhamma (*sutamaya-ñāṇa*), or through deep thinking and observation of things as they really are (*cintāmaya-ñāṇa*), or again through meditation (*bhāvanāmaya-ñāṇa*). While *saddhā* should have firm roots in right understanding, also true understanding on its part should not be devoid of faith or confidence in order to avoid the futility and dryness of remaining merely theoretical. The same is true in the case of will or determination. It must likewise be based on *saddhā* in order to maintain the firmness and vigour by which theory is translated into practice.

This brings us to the function of the volitional faculty as purposive will, resoluteness or determination. It is the drive, the propulsive agency, that transforms knowledge into action. It functions on the basis of understanding, as a factor that harnesses mental energy for one-pointed application, for singleness of aim. It frees intellect from dryness and prevents emotion from indulgence and overactivity, that is, from undue dissipation of mental energy, thereby mobilizing purpose and concentrated effort. Although this faculty has been mentioned last, it is not less important than the other two. After all, it is volition that invests every action, whether in body, speech or mind, with the potentiality of producing results. And devotion as an act leading to deliverance must necessarily have a powerful volition. In fact, all these three faculties are mutually complimentary in the realisation of the common goal, Nibbāna.

It may not be inappropriate if the simile of the construction of a building is used to illustrate the functions of these faculties; for devotion is also a constructive activity after all. Understanding is like the plan and estimates; will is the actual execution of the work of construction according to the plan; and faith, *saddhā*, is like the building materials needed for the construction.

Without a proper plan, a construction may prove positively dangerous, and the exclusion of the other two would mean no construction whatsoever. Thus the task of building a spiritual structure is accomplished in Buddhist devotion with the mutual cooperation and assistance of all the various faculties of the mind.

Salutation to the Triple Gem

By Ven. Dhammapāla

Lord of great compassion, voyager, Thou,
Across the knowledge-sea, to Thee I bow.
Thou by method fine, vivid and profound,
The path dost well proclaim.

What leads from the world the men who bring,
Life-mode and love to fullness, that Best Thing,
To which the Perfect One both homage pay,
That Thing do I revere.

Who in path and fruition steadfast stand,
With virtue and such goods, the noble band,
Unrivalled field for reaping merit rich,
That band do I revere.

From the Udāna Commentary
Translated by Soma Thera

Flower Offering

by Kassapa Thera

Nirodha-samāpattito vuṭṭhahitvā viya nisinnassa Bhagavato Arahato Sammā-sambuddhassa, iminā, pupphena pūjemi, pūjemi, pūjemi. Idam puppha-pūjaṃ Buddha-Paccekabuddha-Aggasāvaka-Mahāsāvaka-Arahantānam sabhāvasīlaṃ, aham'pi tesam anuvattako homi.

Idam pupphaṃ idāni vaṇṇenapi suvaṇṇaṃ, gandhenapi su-gandhaṃ saṇṭhānenapi susaṇṭhānaṃ, khippameva dubbaṇṇaṃ duggandhaṃ dussaṇṭthānaṃ pappoti.

Evameva sabbe saṅkhārā, aniccā, sabbe saṅkhārā dukkhā, sabbe dhammā anattā'ti. Iminā vandanamānana-pūja-paṭipattyānubhāvena āsavakkhayāvahaṃ hotu cittaṃ sabba-dukkhā pamuccatu.

An English rendering of the above Pali formula repeated while offering flowers, is as follows:

"As if to the Blessed One, the Holy One, the Perfectly Awakened One—newly arisen from uttermost ecstasy, with these flowers, reverentially I make offering.

"This reverential flower-offering was a virtuous practice of the Buddhas, Pacceka Buddhas, the Chief Disciples, the Great Disciples and the Arahats. I also am following on their path hereby.

"These flowers are now in colour lovely, in scent sweet, in shape beautiful; soon they will be discoloured, ill-smelling and ugly. So too all things compounded: they pass away, are pain-laden and soulless.

"May this worship, adoration, and reverential offering, through the lofty dignity and psychic power of the practice, help to root out the corruptions. May I gain release from all suffering".

Flower gifts to those loved, trusted and respected have been an ancient and honoured custom of the East. Flower-offering was made by the Buddha Dīpaṅkara to the ascetic Sumedha, who too having resolved to be a Buddha then obtained from the Perfect One the first *niyata vivaraṇa*—or assurance of success in the aspiration for Buddhahood.

It is recorded that the gods offered flowers to the future Buddha at his birth, and again on his enlightenment and death (*parinibbāna*).

The Buddhists offer flowers to the Buddha, the Dhamma and the Sangha. The Buddha is the embodiment of wisdom, he is the supremely Enlightened One; he who, out of compassion for the countless throng of sentient beings, crossed this Sea of Saṃsāra, of Birth, Decay and Death, after a ceaseless effort extending over aeons. The Dhamma is the *Navalokuttara Dhamma* (the ninefold supramundane or hypercosmic), i.e., the four Paths (*magga*) and Fruits of Sanctitude (*Phala*) thereof and Nibbāna, which does not exist outside Buddhism and which alone offers a solution to the Riddle of Life.

The Sangha are those who have attained these Paths and Fruits: Sotāpatti, Sakadāgāmī, Anāgāmī and Arahat. The monks of the present day too are making an earnest endeavour to attain to these sublime states. Hence it is a mistake to suppose that Buddhist monks are a lazy lot, for they are engaged in wholly meritorious work; the difference in the several individuals is only in the degree of earnestness and zeal displayed. Theirs is a life of renunciation. Only the good Buddhist layman knows and can appreciate this.

There being no Buddha living, the Buddhists worship the three *cetiyas* (stupas; literally meaning, pegs on which to hang one's thoughts). They are: (1) *pāribhogika,* the things used by the Buddha, e. g. the Bo-tree at his Enlightenment, which now serves as a symbol of Bodhi or enlightenment; (2) *sarīrika*, the body relics of the Buddha which are now mostly enshrined in the several *cetiyas*; and (3) *uddesika*, the image beautiful of the Buddha. He sees in his mind the golden figure of the Buddha, and a six-rayed aura around his head, a radiantly perfect body and the brilliant glory of his mind. It is the mind's eye and not the physical eye that is active. The offering is to the One who worked through many aeons out of compassion for the ones who take refuge in him. It is only an acknowledgement of one worthy of honour.

But in no wise does the Buddhist ask of him pardon or blessings. He only reflects on his perfections, learns to be self-reliant like him, to be humble and to honour those worthy of honour and so dispel pride. This last, be it noted, is what an envious man is unable to do.

Dāna, sīla, bhāvanā (charity, a virtuous life and meditation) help to root out greed, hatred and ignorance which make this life of ours what it is, a state of painful flux. Let us, as Buddhists would naturally do, submit this act of flower-offering to the cold light of reason and watch its results.

The flower is the acme of nature's perfection. It is beauty itself. Its lovely colour pleases the sight. Its softness pleases the sense of touch. The thought of it also is gratifying. The gift or *dāna* of it must indeed kill greed or *lobha* in the giver.

Of the two kinds of *sīla* (virtue), the negative and the positive, the flower-offering is of the positive kind, a good action. It is productive of a *kusala cetanā*, a meritorious thought, for at the time of offering one reflects that this has been the virtuous practice of the good and saintly of old, and that one is thus striving to follow those noble footsteps; and this is the *sīla*, or right observance, where hatred finds no room.

The *bhāvanā* here is meditation on *anicca, dukkha, anattā* (the transiency, sorrow and soullessness of life). It is this aspect of the flower-offering that raises this act to the highest psychic levels, to one of real usefulness in helping one to make headway along the grand highway—the noble Eightfold Path.

The flower blooms and is beautiful, in that it has lovely colours, emanates sweet scent, and is soft to the touch. But all this is not for long; for soon the flower will fade. This beauty which we adore and covet is a passing show. It is this same beauty that makes us cling to life. It is not real. It is only a mental concept, which varies even geographically.

Each nation has its own ideal of perfection of the human form. The Negro has his own and thinks his ideal the best. The Mongolian has one type of beauty, and the Caucasian another. What then is "beauty"? It is only an idea. To the Buddhist, beauty is *anicca*. This beautiful body is food for worms. All things we value eventually turn to ashes in our grasp. Saṃsāra's "beauty" is a stumbling block on the Noble Path to Nibbāna, which is the only beautiful.

That all things are transitory and therefore painful is not appreciated by the average Westerner, wrapt as he is in the world of sense. *Paññā* or wisdom, according to a Buddhist, is the due realisation of these all-pervading facts, the *anicca, dukkha* and *anattā* (transiency, sorrow and soullessness) of ourselves and all that is about us. The ultimate Truth is understood only thus. Therefore a Buddhist *bhāvanā* is on a higher level than that of the yogi who is merely bent on gaining trances, by the cultivation of a "soul-force" delusion, which the Buddhist knows is a hindrance to ultimate salvation, and therefore to be suppressed.

The nature of a flower-offering is not to be despised; say not that it is "exoteric" Buddhism. Truly, it is exoteric, in its simple grandeur, to most Westerners and some Westernised Easterners. For the direct result of flower-offering is a *ti-hetuka* merit, one that is free from greed, hatred and ignorance, and the death of a person in that state of mind results in a *tihetuka* birth.

The last words of the Buddha, to the Thera Ānanda, on this subject should be borne in mind, and the flower-offering must not be merely a "gift" of love and reverence. The surest way to worship the Lord is to follow his precepts, to live the life as detailed by him. Therefore *dāna, sīla* and *bhāvanā*, especially the last, must be included in this act of flower-offering. The flowers themselves serve as the peg on which to hang one's aspiring thoughts, the mind does the rest; it makes the simple act sublime.

The Foundations of Mindfulness

Satipaṭṭhāna Sutta

Translated by

Nyanasatta Thera

WHEEL PUBLICATION NO. 19

Introduction

The Philosophy of Buddhism is contained in the Four Noble Truths[1]

The *truth of suffering* reveals that all forms of becoming, all the various elements of existence comprised in the "five aggregates" or groups of existence—also called the "five categories which are the objects of clinging" (*pañcupadānakkhandhā*)—are inseparable from suffering as long as they remain objects of grasping or clinging. All corporeality, all feelings and sensations, all perceptions, all mental formations and consciousness, being impermanent, are a source of suffering, are conditioned phenomena and hence not-self (*anicca, dukkha, anattā*). Ceaseless origination and dissolution best characterize the process of existence called life, for all elements of this flux of becoming continually arise from conditions created by us and then pass away, giving rise to new elements of being according to one's actions or kamma.

All suffering originates from craving, and our very existence is conditioned by craving, which is threefold: the craving for sense pleasures (*kāma-taṇhā*), craving for continued and renewed existence (*bhava-taṇhā*), and craving for annihilation after death (*vibhava-taṇhā*). This is the *truth of the origin of suffering.*

The attainment of perfect happiness, the breaking of the chain of rebirths and suffering through the realization of Nibbāna, is possible only through the utter extirpation of that threefold craving. This is the *truth of suffering's cessation.*

The methods of training for the liberation from all suffering are applied by following the Noble Eightfold Path of Right Understanding, Right Thought, Right Speech, Right Action, Right Living, Right Exertion, Right Mindfulness and Right Concentration of Mind. The Noble Eightfold Path consists of

1. An exhaustive exposition of the Four Noble Truths is found in *The Word of the Buddha* by Nyanatiloka Mahāthera. See also *Three Cardinal Discourses of the Buddha,* translated by Ñāṇamoli Thera (BPS Wheel No. 17) and *The Four Noble Truths* by Francis Story (BPS Wheel No. 34/35).

three types of training summed up in: virtuous conduct (*sīla*), concentration (*samādhi*) and wisdom (*pañña*). This is the *truth of the way that leads to the cessation of suffering.*

The prevalence of suffering and absence of freedom and happiness is due to man's subjection to the three roots of all unskill and evil, and all unwholesome actions (*akusalakamma*), viz. lust, hatred and delusion (*lobha, dosa, moha*).

Virtuous conduct casts out lust. The calm of true concentration and mental culture conquers hatred. Wisdom or right understanding, also called direct knowledge resulting from meditation, dispels all delusion. All these three types of training are possible only through the cultivation of constant *mindfulness* (*sati*), which forms the seventh link of the Noble Eightfold Path. Mindfulness is called a controlling faculty (*indriya*) and a spiritual power (*bala*), and is also the first of the seven factors of enlightenment (*satta bojjhaṅga*).[2] Right Mindfulness (*samma-sati*) has to be present in every skillful or karmically wholesome thought moment (*kusalacitta*). It is the basis of all earnest endeavour (*appamāda*) for liberation, and maintains in us the sense of urgency to strive for enlightenment or Nibbāna.

The Discourse on the Foundations of Mindfulness, the *Satipaṭṭhāna Sutta,* is the tenth discourse of the Middle Length Collection (Majjhima Nikāya) of the Discourses of the Enlightened One. It is this version which is translated in the present publication. There is another version of it, in the Collection of Long Discourses (Dīgha Nikāya No. 22), which differs only by a detailed explanation of the Four Noble Truths.

The great importance of the Discourse on Mindfulness has never been lost to the Buddhists of the Theravada tradition. In Sri Lanka, even when the knowledge and practice of the Dhamma was at its lowest ebb through centuries of foreign domination, the Sinhala Buddhists never forgot the Satipaṭṭhāna Sutta. Memorizing the Sutta has been an unfailing practice among the Buddhists, and even today in Sri Lanka there are large numbers who can recite the Sutta from memory. It is a common sight to see on full-moon days devotees who are observing the Eight Precepts, engaged in

---

2. See Piyadassi Thera, *The Seven Factors of Enlightenment* (BPS Wheel No. 1).

community recital of the Sutta. Buddhists are intent on hearing this Discourse even in the last moments of their lives; and at the bedside of a dying Buddhist either monks or laymen recite this venerated text.

In the private shrine room of a Buddhist home, the book of the Satipaṭṭhāna Sutta is displayed prominently as an object of reverence. Monastery libraries of palm-leaf manuscripts have the Sutta bound in highly ornamented covers.

One such book with this Discourse written in Sinhala script on palm-leaf, has found its way from Sri Lanka as far as the State University Library of Bucharest in Rumania. This was disclosed while collecting material for the Encyclopaedia of Buddhism, when an Esperantist correspondent gave us a list of a hundred books on Buddhism found in the Rumanian University Libraries.

Mindfulness of Breathing (Ānāpānasati)

The subjects dealt with in the Satipaṭṭhāna Sutta are corporeality, feeling, mind and mind objects, being the universe of right Buddhist contemplation for deliverance. A very prominent place in the Discourse is occupied by the discussion on mindfulness of breathing (*ānāpānasati*). To make the present publication of greater practical value to the reader, an introductory exposition of the methods of practicing that particular meditation will now be given.

Mindfulness of breathing takes the highest place among the various subjects of Buddhist meditation. It has been recommended and praised by the Enlightened One thus: "This concentration through mindfulness of breathing, when developed and practiced much, is both peaceful and sublime, it is an unadulterated blissful abiding, and it banishes at once and stills evil unprofitable thoughts as soon as they arise." Though of such a high order, the initial stages of this meditation are well within the reach of a beginner though he be only a lay student of the Buddha-Dhamma. Both in the Discourse here translated, and in the 118th Discourse of the same Collection (the Majjhima Nikāya), which specifically deals with that meditation, the initial instructions for the practice are clearly laid down:

Herein, monks, a monk, having gone to the forest or the root of a tree or to an empty place, sits down with his legs crossed, keeps his body erect and his mindfulness alert. Ever mindful he breathes in, mindful he breathes out. Breathing in a long breath, he knows, "I am breathing in a long breath"; breathing out a long breath, he knows, "I am breathing out a long breath." Breathing in a short breath, he knows, "I am breathing in a short breath"; breathing out a short breath, he knows, "I am breathing out a short breath." "Experiencing the whole (breath-) body, I shall breathe in," thus he trains himself. "Experiencing the whole (breath-) body, I shall breathe out," thus he trains himself. "Calming the activity of the (breath-) body, I shall breathe in," thus he trains himself. "Calming the activity of the (breath-) body, I shall breathe out," thus he trains himself.

These are instructions given by the Enlightened One to the monks who, after their alms round, had the whole remaining day free for meditation. But what about the lay Buddhist who has a limited time to devote to this practice? Among the places described as fit for the practice of meditation, one is available to all: *suññagara,* lit. "empty house," may mean any room in the house that has no occupant at that moment, and one may in the course of the twenty-four hours of the day find a room in one's house that is empty and undisturbed. Those who work all day and feel too tired in the evening for meditation may devote the early hours of the morning to the practice of mindfulness of breathing.

The other problem is the right posture for meditation. The full "lotus posture" of the yogi, the *padmasana,* as we see it in the Buddha statues, proves nowadays rather difficult to many, even to easterners. A youthful meditator, however, or even a middle-aged one, can well train himself in that posture in stages. He may, for instance, start with sitting on a low, broad chair or bed, bending only one leg and resting the other on the floor; and so, in gradual approximation, he may finally master that posture. There are also other easier postures of sitting with legs bent, for instance the half-lotus posture. It will be worth one's effort to train oneself in such postures; but if one finds them difficult and uncomfortable at the outset it will not be advisable to delay or disturb one's start with meditation proper on that account. One may allow a special time for sitting-practice, using it as best as one can for contemplation and reflection; but for the time being, the practice of meditation aiming at higher degrees of concentration may better be done in a posture that is comfortable. One may sit on a straight backed chair of a height that allows the legs to rest comfortably on the floor without strain. As soon however, as a cross-legged posture has become more comfortable, one should assume it for the practice of mindfulness of breathing, since it will allow one to sit in meditation for a longer time than is possible on a chair.

The meditator's body and mind should be alert but not tense. A place with a dimmed light will be profitable since it will help to exclude diverting attention to visible objects.

The right place, time and posture are very important and often essential for a successful meditative effort.

Though we have been breathing throughout our life, we have done so devoid of mindfulness, and hence, when we try to follow each breath attentively, we find that the Buddhist teachers of old were right when they compared the natural state of an uncontrolled mind to an untamed calf. Our minds have long been dissipated among visible data and other objects of the senses and of thought, and hence do not yield easily to attempts at mind-control.

Suppose a cowherd wanted to tame a wild calf: he would take it away from the cow and tie it up apart with a rope to a stout post. Then the calf might dash to and fro, but being unable to get away and tired after its effort, it would eventually lie down by the post. So too, when the meditator wants to tame his own mind that has long been reared on the enjoyment of sense objects, he should take it away from places where these sense objects abound, and tie the mind to the post of in-breaths and out-breaths with the rope of mindfulness. And though his mind may then dash to and fro when deprived of its liberty to roam among the sense objects, it will ultimately settle down when mindfulness is persistent and strong.

When practicing mindfulness of breathing, attention should be focused at the tip of the nose or at the point of the upper lip immediately below where the current of air can be felt. The meditator's attention should not leave this "focusing point" from where the in-coming and out-going breaths can be easily felt and observed. The meditator may become aware of the breath's route through the body but he should not pay attention to it. At the beginning of the practice, the meditator should concentrate only on the in-breaths and out-breaths, and should not fall into any reflections about them. It is only at a later stage that he should apply himself to the arousing of knowledge and other states connected with the concentration.

In this brief introduction, only the first steps of the beginner can be discussed. For more information the student may refer to the English translation of the *Visuddhimagga* (*The Path of Purification,* chap. VIII) by Bhikkhu Ñāṇamoli, or to *Mindfulness of Breathing* by Bhikkhu Ñāṇamoli, and to *The Heart of Buddhist Meditation* by Nyanaponika Thera.[3]

The lay Buddhist who undertakes this practice will first take the Three Refuges and the Five Precepts; he will review the reflections on the Buddha, Dhamma, and Sangha, transmit thoughts of loving-kindness (*mettā*) in all directions, recollect that this meditation will help him to reach the goal of deliverance through direct knowledge and mental calm; and only then should he start with the mindfulness of breathing proper, first by way of counting.[4]

Counting

The Buddhist teachers of old recommend that a beginner should start the practice by counting the breaths mentally. In doing so he should not stop short of five or go beyond ten or make any break in the series. By stopping short of five breaths his mind has not enough room for contemplation, and by going beyond ten his mind takes the number rather than the breaths for its objects, and any break in the series would upset the meditation.

When counting, the meditator should first count when the in-breath or the out-breath is completed, not when it begins. So taking the in-breath first, he counts mentally 'one' when that in-breath is complete, then he counts 'two' when the out-breath is complete, 'three' after the next in-breath, and so on up to ten, and then again from one to ten, and so he should continue.

After some practice in counting at the completion of a breath, breathing may become faster. The breaths, however, should not

3. All published by the Buddhist Publication Society.
4. On the Refuges and Precepts, see *The Mirror of the Dhamma* (BPS Wheel No. 54).

be made longer or shorter intentionally. The meditator has to be just mindful of their occurrence as they come and go. Now he may try counting 'one' when he *begins* to breathe in or breathe out, counting up to five or ten, and then again from one to five or ten. If one takes both the in-breath and out-breath as 'one,' it is better to count only up to five.

Counting should be employed until one can dispense with it in following the sequence of breaths successively. Counting is merely a device to assist in excluding stray thoughts. It is, as it were, a guideline or railing for supporting mindfulness until it can do without such help. There may be those who will feel the counting more as a complication than a help, and they may well omit it, attending directly to the flow of the respiration by way of "connecting the successive breaths."

Connecting

After the counting has been discarded, the meditator should now continue his practice by way of connecting (*anubandhana*); that is, by following mindfully the in and out breaths without recourse to counting, and yet without a break in attentiveness. Here too, the breaths should not be followed beyond the nostrils where the respiratory air enters and leaves. The meditator must strive to be aware of the whole breath, in its entire duration and without missing one single phase, but his attention must not leave the place of contact, the nostrils, or that point of the upper lip where the current of air touches.

While following the in-breaths and out-breaths thus, they become fainter and fainter, and at times it is not easy to remain aware of that subtle sensation of touch caused by the respiration. Keener mindfulness is required to keep track of the breaths then. But if the meditator perseveres, one day he will feel a different sensation, a feeling of ease and happiness, and occasionally there appears before his mental eye something like a luminous star or a similar sign, which indicates that one approaches the stage of access concentration. Steadying the newly acquired sign, one may cultivate full mental absorption (*jhāna*) or at least the preliminary concentration as a basis for practicing insight.

The practice of mindfulness of breathing is meant for both mental calm and insight (*samatha* and *vipassanā*). Direct knowledge being the object of Buddhist meditation, the concentration gained by the meditative practice should be used for the clear understanding of reality as manifest in oneself and in the entire range of one's experience.

Though penetrative insight leading to Nibbāna is the ultimate object, progress in mindfulness and concentration will also bring many benefits in our daily lives. If we have become habituated to follow our breaths for a longer period of time and can exclude all (or almost all) intruding irrelevant thoughts, mindfulness, self-control and efficiency are sure to increase in all our activities. Just as our breathing, so also other processes of body and mind, will become clearer to us, and we shall come to know more of ourselves.

It has been said by the Buddha: "Mindfulness of breathing, developed and repeatedly practiced, is of great fruit, of great advantage, for it fulfils the four foundations of mindfulness; the four foundations of mindfulness, developed and repeatedly practiced, fulfil the seven enlightenment factors; the seven enlightenment factors, developed and repeatedly practiced, fulfil clear-vision and deliverance." Clear vision and deliverance, or direct knowledge and the bliss of liberation, are the highest fruit of the application of mindfulness.

The Foundations of Mindfulness

Satipaṭṭhāna Sutta

Thus have I heard. At one time the Blessed One was living among the Kurus, at Kammāsadamma, a market town of the Kuru people. There the Blessed One addressed the bhikkhu thus: "Monks," and they replied to him, "Venerable Sir." The Blessed One spoke as follows:

This is the only way, monks, for the purification of beings, for the overcoming of sorrow and lamentation, for the destruction of suffering and grief, for reaching the right path, for the attainment of Nibbāna, namely, the four foundations of mindfulness. What are the four?

Herein (in this teaching) a monk lives contemplating the body in the body,[5] ardent, clearly comprehending and mindful, having overcome, in this world, covetousness and grief; he lives contemplating feelings in feelings, ardent, clearly comprehending and mindful, having overcome, in this world, covetousness and grief; he lives contemplating consciousness in consciousness,[6] ardent, clearly comprehending and mindful, having overcome, in this world, covetousness and grief; he lives contemplating mental objects in mental objects, ardent, clearly comprehending and mindful, having overcome, in this world, covetousness and grief.

I. The Contemplation of the Body

1. Mindfulness of Breathing

And how does a monk live contemplating the body in the body?

Herein, monks, a monk, having gone to the forest, to the foot of a tree or to an empty place, sits down with his legs crossed, keeps his body erect and his mindfulness alert.[7]

Ever mindful he breathes in, mindful he breathes out. Breathing in a long breath, he knows, "I am breathing in a long breath"; breathing out a long breath, he knows, "I am breathing out a long breath"; breathing in a short breath, he knows, "I am breathing in a short breath"; breathing out a short breath, he knows, "I am breathing out a short breath."

---

5. The repetition of the phrases 'contemplating the body in the body,' 'feelings in feelings,' etc. is meant to impress upon the meditator the importance of remaining aware whether, in the sustained attention directed upon a single chosen object, one is still keeping to it, and has not strayed into the field of another contemplation. For instance, when contemplating any bodily process, a meditator may unwittingly be side-tracked into a consideration of his *feelings* connected with that bodily process. He should then be clearly aware that he has left his original subject, and is engaged in the contemplation of feeling.

6. Mind (Pali *citta,* also consciousness or *viññāṇa*) in this connection means the states of mind or units in the stream of mind of momentary duration. Mental objects, *dhamma,* are the mental contents or factors of consciousness making up the single states of mind.

7. Literally, "setting up mindfulness in front."

"Experiencing the whole (breath-) body, I shall breathe in," thus he trains himself. "Experiencing the whole (breath-) body, I shall breathe out," thus he trains himself. "Calming the activity of the (breath-) body, I shall breathe in," thus he trains himself. "Calming the activity of the (breath-) body, I shall breathe out," thus he trains himself.

Just as a skillful turner or turner's apprentice, making a long turn, knows, "I am making a long turn," or making a short turn, knows, "I am making a short turn," just so the monk, breathing in a long breath, knows, "I am breathing in a long breath"; breathing out a long breath, he knows, "I am breathing out a long breath"; breathing in a short breath, he knows, "I am breathing in a short breath"; breathing out a short breath, he knows, "I am breathing out a short breath." "Experiencing the whole (breath-) body, I shall breathe in," thus he trains himself. "Experiencing the whole (breath-) body, I shall breathe out," thus he trains himself. "Calming the activity of the (breath-) body, I shall breathe in," thus he trains himself. "Calming the activity of the (breath-) body, I shall breathe out," thus he trains himself.

Thus he lives contemplating the body in the body internally, or he lives contemplating the body in the body externally, or he lives contemplating the body in the body internally and externally.[8] He lives contemplating origination factors[9] in the body, or he lives contemplating dissolution factors[10] in the body, or he lives contemplating origination-and-dissolution factors[11] in the body. Or his mindfulness is established with the thought:

---

8. 'Internally': contemplating his own breathing; 'externally': contemplating another's breathing; 'internally and externally': contemplating one's own and another's breathing, alternately, with uninterrupted attention. In the beginning one pays attention to one's own breathing only, and it is only in advanced stages that for the sake of practicing insight, one by inference at times pays attention also to another person's process of breathing.

9. The origination factors (*samudaya-dhamma*), that is, the conditions of the origination of the breath-body; these are: the body in its entirety, nasal aperture and mind.

10. The conditions of the dissolution of the breath-body are: the destruction of the body and of the nasal aperture, and the ceasing of mental activity.

11. The contemplation of both, alternately.

"The body exists,"[12] to the extent necessary just for knowledge and mindfulness, and he lives detached,[13] and clings to nothing in the world. Thus also, monks, a monk lives contemplating the body in the body.

2. The Postures of the Body

And further, monks, a monk knows, when he is going, "I am going"; he knows, when he is standing, "I am standing"; he knows, when he is sitting, "I am sitting"; he knows, when he is lying down, "I am lying down"; or just as his body is disposed so he knows it.

Thus he lives contemplating the body in the body internally, or he lives contemplating the body in the body externally, or he lives contemplating the body in the body internally and externally. He lives contemplating origination factors in the body, or he lives contemplating dissolution factors in the body, or he lives contemplating origination-and-dissolution factors in the body.[14] Or his mindfulness is established with the thought: "The body exists," to the extent necessary just for knowledge and mindfulness, and he lives detached, and clings to nothing in the world. Thus also, monks, a monk lives contemplating the body in the body.

3. Mindfulness with Clear Comprehension

And further, monks, a monk, in going forward and back, applies clear comprehension; in looking straight on and looking away, he applies clear comprehension; in bending and in stretching, he applies clear comprehension; in wearing robes and carrying the bowl, he applies clear comprehension; in eating, drinking, chewing and savouring, he applies clear comprehension; in walking, in standing, in sitting, in falling

12. That is, only impersonal bodily processes exist, without a self, soul, spirit or abiding essence or substance. The corresponding phrase in the following contemplations should be understood accordingly.

13. Detached from craving and wrong view.

14. All contemplations of the body, excepting the preceding one, have as factors of origination: ignorance, craving, kamma, food, and the general characteristic of originating; the factors of dissolution are: disappearance of ignorance, craving, kamma, food, and the general characteristic of dissolving.

asleep, in waking, in speaking and in keeping silence, he applies clear comprehension.

Thus he lives contemplating the body in the body...

4. The Reflection on the Repulsiveness of the Body

And further, monks, a monk reflects on this very body enveloped by the skin and full of manifold impurity, from the soles up, and from the top of the head-hairs down, thinking thus: "There are in this body hair of the head, hair of the body, nails, teeth, skin, flesh, sinews, bones, marrow, kidney, heart, liver, midriff, spleen, lungs, intestines, mesentery, gorge, faeces, bile, phlegm, pus, blood, sweat, fat, tears, grease, saliva, nasal mucus, synovial fluid, urine."

Just as if there were a double-mouthed provision bag full of various kinds of grain such as hill paddy, paddy, green gram, cow-peas, sesamum, and husked rice, and a man with sound eyes, having opened that bag, were to take stock of the contents thus: "This is hill paddy, this is paddy, this is green gram, this is cow-pea, this is sesamum, this is husked rice." Just so, monks, a monk reflects on this very body enveloped by the skin and full of manifold impurity, from the soles up, and from the top of the head-hairs down, thinking thus: "There are in this body hair of the head, hair of the body, nails, teeth, skin, flesh, sinews, bones, marrow, kidney, heart, liver, midriff, spleen, lungs, intestines, mesentery, gorge, faeces, bile, phlegm, pus, blood, sweat, fat, tears, grease, saliva, nasal mucus, synovial fluid, urine."

Thus he lives contemplating the body in the body...

5. The Reflection on the Material Elements

And further, monks, a monk reflects on this very body, however it be placed or disposed, by way of the material elements: "There are in this body the element of earth, the element of water, the element of fire, the element of wind."[15]

Just as if, monks, a clever cow-butcher or his apprentice, having slaughtered a cow and divided it into portions, should be

15. The so-called 'elements' are the primary qualities of matter, explained by Buddhist tradition as solidity (earth), adhesion (water), caloricity (fire) and motion (wind or air).

sitting at the junction of four high roads, in the same way, a monk reflects on this very body, as it is placed or disposed, by way of the material elements: "There are in this body the elements of earth, water, fire, and wind."

Thus he lives contemplating the body in the body...

6. The Nine Cemetery Contemplations

(1) And further, monks, as if a monk sees a body dead one, two, or three days; swollen, blue and festering, thrown in the charnel ground, he then applies this perception to his own body thus: "Verily, also my own body is of the same nature; such it will become and will not escape it."

Thus he lives contemplating the body in the body internally, or he lives contemplating the body in the body externally, or he lives contemplating the body in the body internally and externally. He lives contemplating origination-factors in the body, or he lives contemplating dissolution factors in the body, or he lives contemplating origination-and-dissolution-factors in the body. Or his mindfulness is established with the thought: "The body exists," to the extent necessary just for knowledge and mindfulness, and he lives detached, and clings to nothing in the world. Thus also, monks, a monk lives contemplating the body in the body.

(2) And further, monks, as if a monk sees a body thrown in the charnel ground, being eaten by crows, hawks, vultures, dogs, jackals or by different kinds of worms, he then applies this perception to his own body thus: "Verily, also my own body is of the same nature; such it will become and will not escape it."

Thus he lives contemplating the body in the body...

(3) And further, monks, as if a monk sees a body thrown in the charnel ground and reduced to a skeleton with some flesh and blood attached to it, held together by the tendons...

(4) And further, monks, as if a monk sees a body thrown in the charnel ground and reduced to a skeleton blood-besmeared and without flesh, held together by the tendons...

(5) And further, monks, as if a monk sees a body thrown in the charnel ground and reduced to a skeleton without flesh and blood, held together by the tendons...

(6) And further, monks, as if a monk sees a body thrown in the charnel ground and reduced to disconnected bones, scattered in all directions—here a bone of the hand, there a bone of the foot, a shin bone, a thigh bone, the pelvis, spine and skull...

(7) And further, monks, as if a monk sees a body thrown in the charnel ground, reduced to bleached bones of conchlike colour...

(8) And further, monks, as if a monk sees a body thrown in the charnel ground reduced to bones, more than a year-old, lying in a heap...

(9) And further, monks, as if a monk sees a body thrown in the charnel ground, reduced to bones gone rotten and become dust, he then applies this perception to his own body thus: "Verily, also my own body is of the same nature; such it will become and will not escape it."

Thus he lives contemplating the body in the body internally, or he lives contemplating the body in the body externally, or he lives contemplating the body in the body internally and externally. He lives contemplating origination factors in the body, or he lives contemplating dissolution factors in the body, or he lives contemplating origination-and-dissolution factors in the body. Or his mindfulness is established with the thought: "The body exists," to the extent necessary just for knowledge and mindfulness, and he lives detached, and clings to nothing in the world. Thus also, monks, a monk lives contemplating the body in the body.

II. The Contemplation of Feeling

And how, monks, does a monk live contemplating feelings in feelings?

Herein, monks, a monk when experiencing a pleasant feeling knows, "I experience a pleasant feeling"; when experiencing a painful feeling, he knows, "I experience a painful feeling"; when experiencing a neither-pleasant-nor-painful feeling," he knows, "I experience a neither-pleasant-nor-painful feeling." When experiencing a pleasant worldly feeling, he knows, "I experience a pleasant worldly feeling"; when experiencing a pleasant spiritual feeling, he knows, "I experience a pleasant spiritual feeling"; when experiencing a painful worldly feeling, he knows, "I experience a painful worldly feeling"; when experiencing a painful spiritual feeling, he knows, "I experience a painful spiritual feeling"; when experiencing a neither-pleasant-nor-painful worldly feeling, he knows, "I experience a neither-pleasant-nor-painful worldly feeling"; when experiencing a neither-pleasant-nor-painful spiritual feeling, he knows, "I experience a neither-pleasant-nor-painful spiritual feeling."

Thus he lives contemplating feelings in feelings internally, or he lives contemplating feelings in feelings externally, or he lives contemplating feelings in feelings internally and externally. He lives contemplating origination factors in feelings, or he lives contemplating dissolution factors in feelings, or he lives contemplating origination-and-dissolution factors in feelings.[16] Or his mindfulness is established with the thought, "Feeling exists," to the extent necessary just for knowledge and mindfulness, and he lives detached, and clings to nothing in the world. Thus, monks, a monk lives contemplating feelings in feelings.

III. The Contemplation of Consciousness

And how, monks, does a monk live contemplating consciousness in consciousness?

Herein, monks, a monk knows the consciousness with lust, as with lust; the consciousness without lust, as without lust; the consciousness with hate, as with hate; the consciousness without hate, as without hate; the consciousness with ignorance, as with ignorance; the consciousness without ignorance, as without ignorance; the shrunken state of consciousness, as the shrunken state;[17] the distracted state of consciousness, as the distracted state;[18] the developed state of consciousness as the developed state;[19] the

16. The factors of origination are here: ignorance, craving, kamma, and sense-impression, and the general characteristic of originating; the factors of dissolution are: the disappearance of the four, and the general characteristic of dissolving.

17. This refers to a rigid and indolent state of mind.

18. This refers to a restless mind.

19. The consciousness of the meditative absorptions of the fine-corporeal and uncorporeal sphere (*rūpa-arūpa-jhāna*).

undeveloped state of consciousness as the undeveloped state;[20] the state of consciousness with some other mental state superior to it, as the state with something mentally higher;[21] the state of consciousness with no other mental state superior to it, as the state with nothing mentally higher;[22] the concentrated state of consciousness, as the concentrated state; the unconcentrated state of consciousness, as the unconcentrated state; the freed state of consciousness, as the freed state;[23] and the unfreed state of consciousness as the unfreed state.

Thus he lives contemplating consciousness in consciousness internally, or he lives contemplating consciousness in consciousness externally, or he lives contemplating consciousness in consciousness internally and externally. He lives contemplating origination factors in consciousness, or he lives contemplating dissolution-factors in consciousness, or he lives contemplating origination-and-dissolution factors in consciousness.[24] Or his mindfulness is established with the thought, "Consciousness exists," to the extent necessary just for knowledge and mindfulness, and he lives detached, and clings to nothing in the world. Thus, monks, a monk lives contemplating consciousness in consciousness.

---

20. The ordinary consciousness of the sensuous state of existence (*kāmāvacara*).
21. The consciousness of the sensuous state of existence, having other mental states superior to it.
22. The consciousness of the fine-corporeal and the uncorporeal spheres, having no mundane mental state superior to it.
23. Temporarily freed from the defilements either through the methodical practice of insight (*vipassanā*) freeing from single evil states by force of their opposites, or through the meditative absorptions (*jhāna*).
24. The factors of origination consist here of ignorance, craving, kamma, body-and-mind (*nāma-rūpa*), and the general characteristic of originating; the factors of dissolution are: the disappearance of ignorance, etc., and the general characteristic of dissolving.

IV. The Contemplation of Mental Objects

1. *The Five Hindrances*

And how, monks, does a monk live contemplating mental objects in mental objects?

Herein, monks, a monk lives contemplating mental objects in the mental objects of the five hindrances.

How, monks, does a monk live contemplating mental objects in the mental objects of the five hindrances?

Herein, monks, when *sense-desire* is present, a monk knows, "There is sense-desire in me," or when sense-desire is not present, he knows, "There is no sense-desire in me." He knows how the arising of the non-arisen sense-desire comes to be; he knows how the abandoning of the arisen sense-desire comes to be; and he knows how the non-arising in the future of the abandoned sense-desire comes to be.

When *anger* is present, he knows, "There is anger in me," or when anger is not present, he knows, "There is no anger in me." He knows how the arising of the non-arisen anger comes to be; he knows how the abandoning of the arisen anger comes to be; and he knows how the non-arising in the future of the abandoned anger comes to be.

When *sloth and torpor* are present, he knows, "There are sloth and torpor in me," or when sloth and torpor are not present, he knows, "There are no sloth and torpor in me." He knows how the arising of the non-arisen sloth and torpor comes to be; he knows how the abandoning of the arisen sloth and torpor comes to be; and he knows how the non-arising in the future of the abandoned sloth and torpor comes to be.

When *agitation and remorse* are present, he knows, "There are agitation and remorse in me," or when agitation and remorse are not present, he knows, "There are no agitation and remorse in me." He knows how the arising of the non-arisen agitation and remorse comes to be; he knows how the abandoning of the arisen agitation and remorse comes to be; and he knows how the non-arising in the future of the abandoned agitation and remorse comes to be.

When *doubt* is present, he knows, "There is doubt in me," or when doubt is not present, he knows, "There is no doubt in me." He knows how the arising of the non-arisen doubt comes to be; he knows how the abandoning of the arisen doubt comes to be; and he knows how the non-arising in the future of the abandoned doubt comes to be.

Thus he lives contemplating mental objects in mental objects internally, or he lives contemplating mental objects in mental objects externally, or he lives contemplating mental objects in mental objects internally and externally. He lives contemplating origination factors in mental objects, or he lives contemplating dissolution factors in mental objects, or he lives contemplating origination-and-dissolution factors in mental objects.[25] Or his mindfulness is established with the thought, "Mental objects exist," to the extent necessary just for knowledge and mindfulness, and he lives detached, and clings to nothing in the world. Thus also, monks, a monk lives contemplating mental objects in the mental objects of the five hindrances.

2. *The Five Aggregates of Clinging*

And further, monks, a monk lives contemplating mental objects in the mental objects of the five aggregates of clinging.[26]

How, monks, does a monk live contemplating mental objects in the mental objects of the five aggregates of clinging?

Herein, monks, a monk thinks, "Thus is *material form;* thus is the arising of material form; and thus is the disappearance of material form. Thus is *feeling;* thus is the arising of feeling; and thus is the disappearance of feeling. Thus is *perception;* thus is the arising of perception; and thus is the disappearance of perception. Thus are *formations;* thus is the arising of formations; and thus is the disappearance of formations. Thus

25. The factors of origination are here the conditions which produce the hindrances, such as wrong reflection, etc., the factors of dissolution are the conditions which remove the hindrances, e.g., right reflection.

26. These five groups or aggregates constitute the so-called personality. By making them objects of clinging, existence, in the form of repeated births and deaths, is perpetuated.

is *consciousness;* thus is the arising of consciousness; and thus is the disappearance of consciousness."

Thus he lives contemplating mental objects in mental objects internally, or he lives contemplating mental objects in mental objects externally, or he lives contemplating mental objects in mental objects internally and externally. He lives contemplating origination factors in mental objects, or he lives contemplating dissolution factors in mental objects, or he lives contemplating origination-and-dissolution factors in mental objects.[27] Or his mindfulness is established with the thought, "Mental objects exist," to the extent necessary just for knowledge and mindfulness, and he lives detached, and clings to nothing in the world. Thus also, monks, a monk lives contemplating mental objects in the mental objects of the five aggregates of clinging.

3. *The Six Internal and External Sense Bases*

And further, monks, a monk lives contemplating mental objects in the mental objects of the six internal and the six external sense-bases.

How, monks, does a monk live contemplating mental objects in the mental objects of the six internal and the six external sense-bases?

Herein, monks, a monk knows the eye and visual forms and the fetter that arises dependent on both (the eye and forms);[28] he knows how the arising of the non-arisen fetter comes to be; he knows how the abandoning of the arisen fetter comes to be; and he knows how the non-arising in the future of the abandoned fetter comes to be.

---

27. The origination-and-dissolution factors of the five aggregates: for material form, the same as for the postures (Note 10); for feeling, the same as for the contemplation of feeling (Note 12); for perception and formations, the same as for feeling (Note 12); for consciousness, the same as for the contemplation of consciousness (Note 20).

28. The usual enumeration of the ten principal fetters (*saṃyojana*), as given in the Discourse Collection (Sutta Piṭaka), is as follows: (1) self-illusion, (2) scepticism, (3) attachment to rules and rituals, (4) sensual lust, (5) ill-will, (6) craving for fine-corporeal existence, (7) craving for incorporeal existence, (8) conceit, (9) restlessness, (10) ignorance.

He knows the *ear* and *sounds* ... the *nose* and *smells* ... the *tongue* and *flavours* ... the *body* and *tactual objects* ... the *mind* and *mental objects,* and the fetter that arises dependent on both; he knows how the arising of the non-arisen fetter comes to be; he knows how the abandoning of the arisen fetter comes to be; and he knows how the non-arising in the future of the abandoned fetter comes to be.

Thus he lives contemplating mental objects in mental objects internally, or he lives contemplating mental objects in mental objects externally, or he lives contemplating mental objects in mental objects internally and externally. He lives contemplating origination factors in mental objects, or he lives contemplating dissolution factors in mental objects, or he lives contemplating origination-and-dissolution factors in mental objects.[29] Or his mindfulness is established with the thought, "Mental objects exist," to the extent necessary just for knowledge and mindfulness, and he lives detached, and clings to nothing in the world. Thus, monks, a monk lives contemplating mental objects in the mental objects of the six internal and the six external sense-bases.

4. *The Seven Factors of Enlightenment*

And further, monks, a monk lives contemplating mental objects in the mental objects of the seven factors of enlightenment.

How, monks, does a monk live contemplating mental objects in the mental objects of the seven factors of enlightenment?

Herein, monks, when the enlightenment-factor of *mindfulness* is present, the monk knows, "The enlightenment-factor of mindfulness is in me," or when the enlightenment-factor of mindfulness is absent, he knows, "The enlightenment-factor of mindfulness is not in me"; and he knows how the arising of the non-arisen enlightenment-factor of mindfulness comes to be; and

29. Origination factors of the ten physical sense-bases are ignorance, craving, kamma, food, and the general characteristic of originating; dissolution factors: the general characteristic of dissolving and the disappearance of ignorance, etc. The origination-and-dissolution factors of the mind-base are the same as those of feeling (Note 12).

how perfection in the development of the arisen enlightenment-factor of mindfulness comes to be.

When the enlightenment-factor of *the investigation of mental objects* is present, the monk knows, "The enlightenment-factor of the investigation of mental objects is in me"; when the enlightenment-factor of the investigation of mental objects is absent, he knows, "The enlightenment-factor of the investigation of mental objects is not in me"; and he knows how the arising of the non-arisen enlightenment-factor of the investigation of mental objects comes to be, and how perfection in the development of the arisen enlightenment-factor of the investigation of mental objects comes to be.

When the enlightenment-factor of *energy* is present, he knows, "The enlightenment-factor of energy is in me"; when the enlightenment-factor of energy is absent, he knows, "The enlightenment-factor of energy is not in me"; and he knows how the arising of the non-arisen enlightenment-factor of energy comes to be, and how perfection in the development of the arisen enlightenment-factor of energy comes to be.

When the enlightenment-factor of *joy* is present, he knows, "The enlightenment-factor of joy is in me"; when the enlightenment-factor of joy is absent, he knows, "The enlightenment-factor of joy is not in me"; and he knows how the arising of the non-arisen enlightenment-factor of joy comes to be, and how perfection in the development of the arisen enlightenment-factor of joy comes to be.

When the enlightenment-factor of *tranquillity* is present, he knows, "The enlightenment-factor of tranquillity is in me"; when the enlightenment-factor of tranquillity is absent, he knows, "The enlightenment-factor of tranquillity is not in me"; and he knows how the arising of the non-arisen enlightenment-factor of tranquillity comes to be, and how perfection in the development of the arisen enlightenment-factor of tranquillity comes to be.

When the enlightenment-factor of *concentration* is present, he knows, "The enlightenment-factor of concentration is in me"; when the enlightenment-factor of concentration is absent, he knows, "The enlightenment-factor of concentration is not in me"; and he knows how the arising of the non-arisen enlightenment-factor of concentration comes to be, and how perfection in the development of the arisen enlightenment-factor of concentration comes to be.

When the enlightenment-factor of *equanimity* is present, he knows, "The enlightenment-factor of equanimity is in me"; when the enlightenment-factor of equanimity is absent, he knows, "The enlightenment-factor of equanimity is not in me"; and he knows how the arising of the non-arisen enlightenment-factor of equanimity comes to be, and how perfection in the development of the arisen enlightenment-factor of equanimity comes to be.

Thus he lives contemplating mental objects in mental objects internally, or he lives contemplating mental objects in mental objects externally, or he lives contemplating mental objects in mental objects internally and externally. He lives contemplating origination-factors in mental objects, or he lives contemplating dissolution-factors in mental objects, or he lives contemplating origination-and-dissolution-factors in mental objects.[30] Or his mindfulness is established with the thought, "Mental objects exist," to the extent necessary just for knowledge and mindfulness, and he lives detached, and clings to nothing in the world. Thus, monks, a monk lives contemplating mental objects in the mental objects of the seven factors of enlightenment.

5. *The Four Noble Truths*

And further, monks, a monk lives contemplating mental objects in the mental objects of the four noble truths.

How, monks, does a monk live contemplating mental objects in the mental objects of the four noble truths?

Herein, monks, a monk knows, "This is suffering," according to reality; he knows, "This is the origin of suffering," according to reality; he knows, "This is the cessation of suffering," according to reality; he knows "This is the road leading to the cessation of suffering," according to reality.

Thus he lives contemplating mental objects in mental objects internally, or he lives contemplating mental objects in mental objects externally, or he lives contemplating mental objects in

30. Just the conditions conducive to the origination and dissolution of the factors of enlightenment comprise the origination-and-dissolution factors here.

mental objects internally and externally. He lives contemplating origination-factors in mental objects, or he lives contemplating dissolution-factors in mental objects, or he lives contemplating origination-and-dissolution-factors in mental objects.[31] Or his mindfulness is established with the thought, "Mental objects exist," to the extent necessary just for knowledge and mindfulness, and he lives detached, and clings to nothing in the world. Thus, monks, a monk lives contemplating mental objects in the mental objects of the four noble truths.

* * *

Verily, monks, whosoever practices these four foundations of mindfulness in this manner for seven years, then one of these two fruits may be expected by him: highest knowledge (arahantship) here and now, or if some remainder of clinging is yet present, the state of nonreturning.[32]

O monks, let alone seven years. Should any person practice these four foundations of mindfulness in this manner for six years... five years... four years... three years... two years... one year, then one of these two fruits may be expected by him: highest knowledge here and now, or if some remainder of clinging is yet present, the state of nonreturning.

O monks, let alone a year. Should any person practice these four foundations of mindfulness in this manner for seven months... six months... five months... four months... three months... two months... a month... half a month, then one of these two fruits may be expected by him: highest knowledge here and now, or if some remainder of clinging is yet present, the state of nonreturning.

O monks, let alone half a month. Should any person practice these four foundations of mindfulness in this manner for a week,

---

31. The origination-and-dissolution factors of the truths should be understood as the arising and passing of suffering, craving, and the path; the truth of cessation is not to be included in this contemplation since it has neither origination nor dissolution.

32. That is, the non-returning to the world of sensuality. This is the last stage before the attainment of the final goal of arahantship

then one of these two fruits may be expected by him: highest knowledge here and now, or if some remainder of clinging is yet present, the state of nonreturning.

Because of this it was said: "This is the only way, monks, for the purification of beings, for the overcoming of sorrow and lamentation, for the destruction of suffering and grief, for reaching the right path, for the attainment of Nibbāna, namely the four foundations of mindfulness."

Thus spoke the Blessed One. Satisfied, the monks approved of his words.

The Three Signata: Anicca, Dukkha, Anattā

(With extracts from the Buddha's discourses)

by

Dr. O. H. de A. Wijesekera
Professor of Sanskrit
University of Ceylon

WHEEL PUBLICATION NO. 20

The Three Signata

1. Anicca

The concept of the three signata (*tilakkhaṇa*) forms the essential basis for understanding the Buddha's scheme of emancipation (*vimokkha*). The three signata, the three universal properties of all existing things of the phenomenal world, are *anicca* (impermanence, transience or transitoriness), *dukkha* (unsatisfactoriness, ill, suffering or painfulness), and *anattā* (non-self, absence of a permanent ego, or insubstantiality). It is the contemplation of these three universal characteristics of all compounded things and processes (*saṅkhāra*), or of all phenomena (*dhamma*), that leads to true insight (*vipassanā*) and enlightenment (*bodhi-ñāṇa*). The realisation of these three fundamental truths can thus be regarded as the key to the highest spiritual perfection afforded by the Buddha Dhamma.

The first of the three signata, *anicca* (impermanence, transitoriness of all things in the universe), is a doctrine constantly and emphatically insisted upon in the Buddhist texts. According to the Buddha's Teaching, the Buddha Dhamma, there is nothing divine or human, animate or inanimate, organic or inorganic, which is permanent or stable, unchanging or everlasting.

This Buddhist concept of the transitoriness of all things, the Buddhist law of impermanence, finds classic expression in the famous formula "*sabbe saṅkhārā aniccā*" occurring in the Cūlasaccaka Sutta (MN 35), and in the more popular statement "*aniccā vata saṅkhārā.*" Both these formulas amount to saying that all conditioned things or processes are transient or impermanent. This is not given as the result of metaphysical inquiry, or of any mystical intuition, but as a straightforward judgement to be arrived at by investigation and analysis. It is founded on unbiased thought and has a purely empirical basis. In the Mahāvagga of the Aṅguttara Nikāya (AN 7:62/A IV 100ff.) the Master admonishes his disciples thus: "Impermanent, monks, are [all] *saṅkhāras*, unstable [not constant], monks, are [all] *saṅkhāras*, [hence] not a cause for comfort and satisfaction are [all] *saṅkhāras*, so much so that one must get tired of all these *saṅkhāras*, be disgusted with them, and be completely free of them."

There is no doubt here as to what is meant by the term *saṅkhāra*, for the Master himself continues by way of illustration:

> There will come a time, monks, maybe hundreds of thousands of years hence, when no more rains will fall and consequently all plants and trees, all vegetation, will dry up and be destroyed with the scorching due to the appearance of a second sun; streams and rivulets will go dry; and with the appearance of a third sun, such large rivers as the Ganges and Yamunā will dry up; similarly, the lakes and even the great ocean itself will dry up in the course of time, and even such great mountains as Sineru, nay even this wide earth, will begin to smoke and be burnt up in a great and universal holocaust ... Thus impermanent, monks, are all *saṅkhārā*, unstable, and hardly a cause for comfort, so much so that one [contemplating their impermanent nature] must necessarily get tired of them.

It is easy to understand from this discourse in what an all-embracing sense the term *saṅkhāra* is used: it includes all things, all phenomena that come into existence by natural development or evolution, being conditioned by prior causes and therefore containing within themselves the liability to come to an end, to be dissolved from the state in which they are found.

According to the Buddha, there is no "being," but only a ceaseless "becoming" (*bhava*). Every thing is the product of antecedent causes, and, therefore, of dependent origination (*paṭiccasamuppanna*).[1] These causes themselves are not ever-lasting and static, but simply antecedent aspects of the same ceaseless becoming. Thus we may conceive everything as the result of a concatenation of dynamic processes (*saṅkhāra*) and, therefore, everything created or formed is only created or formed through these processes and not by any agency outside its own nature. In Buddhism everything is regarded as compounded (*saṅkhata*). Thus *saṅkhata* in these contexts implies everything arisen or become (*bhūta*), which depends on antecedent conditions (*sahetu-*

1. See The Wheel, No. 15, *Dependent Origination*, by Piyadassi Thera.

sappaccaya). It is for this very reason (namely, that everything conceivable in this world has come to be or become depending on antecedent conditions or processes) that everything is to be regarded as liable to pass away. As it is declared in the Saṃyutta Nikāya (SN 12:31/S II 49): "Whatever has become is of the nature of passing away (*yaṃ bhūtaṃ taṃ nirodhadhammaṃ*)." This law, if one may call it so, holds in the case of the mightiest of gods, such as Mahā-Brahmā, as much as of the tiniest creature. In the 11th discourse of the Dīgha Nikāya it is regarded as ludicrous that even God or Brahma should imagine himself to be eternal. As Professor Rhys Davids remarked:

> The state of an individual, of a thing or person, distinct from its surroundings, bounded off from them, is unstable, temporary, sure to pass away. It may last as, for instance, in the case of the gods for hundreds of thousands of years; or, as in the case of some insects, for some hours only; or as in the case of some material things (as we should say some chemical compounds), for a few seconds only. But in every case as soon as there is a beginning, there begins also at that moment to be an ending.[2]

The ethical significance of this law of impermanence is well brought out in the Mahā-Sudassana Suttanta (DN 17). There the Buddha tells Ānanda, his favourite disciple, about the glories of the famous king of the past, Mahā Sudassana; about his cities, treasures, palaces, elephants, horses, carriages, women, and so on, in the possession of which he led a wonderful life; about his great regal achievements; and finally his death; only to draw the moral conclusion: "Behold, Ānanda, how all these things (*saṅkhāra*) are now dead and gone, have passed and vanished away. Thus, impermanent, Ānanda, are the *saṅkhāras*; thus untrustworthy, Ānanda, are the *saṅkhāras*. And this, Ānanda, is enough to be weary of, to be disgusted with and be completely free of such *saṅkhāras*."

When the Buddha characterized all compounded things and conditioned processes as impermanent and unstable, it must be understood that, before all else, stood out that particular heap

2. *American Lectures.*

of processes (*saṅkhārapuñja*) that is called man; for at bottom it was with man chiefly that Buddha had to do, in so far as it was to man primarily that he showed the way to emancipation. Thus the chief problem was to find out the real nature of man, and it is precisely in this great discovery that the uniqueness of the Dhamma is visible. The Buddha's conclusion regarding man's nature is in perfect agreement with his general concept of impermanence: Man himself is a compound of several factors and his supposedly persistent personality is in truth nothing more than a collection of ceaselessly changing processes; in fact, a continuous becoming or *bhava*. The Buddha analysed man into five aggregates: *rūpa, vedanā, saññā, saṅkhāra*, and *viññāṇa*, that is to say, material form, sensations, perceptions, dynamic processes and consciousness. In discourse after discourse, the Master has emphatically asserted that each of these aggregates is impermanent and unstable. In the famous discourse of the Dīgha Nikāya (DN 22/D II 301) entitled "The Discourse on the Establishment of Mindfulness" (Mahā Satipaṭṭhāna Sutta) the Master teaches the disciple to view all these categories as being of the nature of arising (*samudayadhamma*) and of passing away (*vaya-dhamma*): "Such is material form, such is its genesis, such its passing away; and so on with the other three groups: perceptions, dynamic processes and consciousness." In fact, the highest consummation of spiritual life is said to result from the true perception of the evanescent nature of the six spheres of sense contact. The 102nd discourse of the Majjhima Nikāya ends with the words: "This, indeed, monks, is the perfect way of utter peace into which the Tathāgata has won full Enlightenment, that is to say, the understanding, as they really are, of the six spheres of sense-contact, of their arising and passing away, their comfort and misery, and the way of escape from them free of grasping" (M II 237). It is these six spheres of sense-contact that cause the continuity of *saṃsāra*, in other words, *bhava* or becoming, and thus they are to be understood as involving the most important *saṅkhāras*. Hence the oft repeated stanza in the Pali Canon: "All compounded things indeed are subject to arising and passing away; what is born comes to an end; blessed is the end of becoming; it is peace."

II. Dukkha

The fact of impermanence as the leading characteristic of all compounded things and processes of the phenomenal world has been dealt with above. The next, according to the concept of the three signata (*tilakkhaṇa*), is the fact of *dukkha* which signifies the universal characteristic of all saṃsāric existence, viz. its general unsatisfactoriness. It must be admitted that this Pali word "*dukkha*" is one of the most difficult terms to translate. Writers in English very often use as its equivalent the English word "sorrow" or "ill" and some even translate it as "pain," "suffering" and so on. But none of these English words covers the same ground as the Pali *dukkha*, they are too specialized, too limited and usually too strong. The difficulty is increased by the fact that the Pali word itself is used in the Canon in several senses.

There is what one may call the general philosophical sense, then a narrower psychological sense, and a still narrower physical sense. It is as indicating the general philosophical sense of *dukkha* that the word unsatisfactoriness has been selected. This is perhaps the best English term, at least in this particular context of the "three signata."

Whatever some writers of Buddhism may have said, the recognition of the fact of *dukkha* stands out as the most essential concept of Buddhism. In the very first discourse after attaining Enlightenment the Master formulated this concept in the following terms:

> This, indeed, monks, is the Noble Truth of *dukkha,* namely the fact that birth itself is *dukkha,* disease is *dukkha*, death is *dukkha;* to be joined with what is unpleasant is *dukkha*, to be separated from what is pleasant is *dukkha*, failure in getting what one wants is *dukkha*, in short the five groups of physical and mental qualities making up the individual due to grasping are themselves *dukkha*. (Vin I 10; cp. S V 421)

This observation of the universal fact of unsatisfactoriness is, as any unbiased student of Buddhism will soon realize, the central pivot of the whole system of spiritual and moral progress discovered and proclaimed by the Buddha.

According to the Buddha, the beginning, continuity and ending of all experience (i.e. the whole world [*loka*]) for a sentient being, are centred in its own individuality (*nāma-rūpa*), that is to say, the five groups of grasping that constitute the individual (the *pañcupadānakkhandhā* viz. material form, sensations and feelings, perceptions [physical and mental], dynamic processes, and consciousness [*rūpa, vedanā saññā, saṅkhāra* and *viññāṇa*]). Now, the physical form or the body of the individual is the visible basis of this individuality, and this body, as every one knows, is a product of material components derived from the four great elements, viz. the watery, the fiery, the airy and the earthy (*āpo tejo, vayo, paṭhavī*). It is said to be built up of these four chief elements (*cātummahābhūtika*) and therefore, it is conditioned by these. As was explained in the previous article, the universal characteristic of the four great elements is their impermanence (*anicca*), and not much science is needed to understand this fact which is self-evident to the thoughtful person. The Buddha says:

> "A time will come when the watery element will rise in fury, and when that happens, the earthy element will disappear, unmistakably revealing itself as transient and subject to ruin, destruction and vicissitude... There may also come a time when the watery element will dry up and no more water is left in the great ocean than will cover one joint of a finger. On that day this great watery element will unmistakably reveal itself as transient and subject to ruin, destruction and vicissitude. A time will come when the fiery element will rage furiously and devour the whole surface of the earth, ceasing only when there is nothing more to devour. On that day this great fiery element will unmistakably reveal itself as transient and subject to destruction. A time will come when the airy element will rage in fury and carry away village and town and everything upon the earth ... till it exhausts itself completely. On that day this great airy element will unmistakably reveal itself as transient and itself subject to ruin, destruction and all vicissitude." (MN 28/M I 187)

Thus everything that is comprised within the four great elements shows itself subject to the universal law of transitoriness, and it is not a difficult inference to conclude that this fathom-long body which is a derivative of these four elements will itself go the way of its elemental source.

Now the Buddha goes on to show the impermanence or transitoriness of the remaining components of our individuality which are based upon the body and its organs:

> The corporeal form, monks, is transient, and what underlies the arising of corporeal form, that too is transient. As it is arisen from what is transient, how could corporeal form be permanent? Sensations and feelings are transient; what underlies the arising of these [viz. the sense organs, depending on the body] is also transient. Arisen from what is transient, how could sensations and feelings be permanent? Similarly, perceptions, dynamic processes of the mind, and consciousness: all these, arising from the transient, cannot but be transient. (SN 22:15/S III 23)

In all these are observed arising, vicissitude and passing away. This real, impermanent nature of everything constituting the individual can only lead to one conclusion: that as they are transitory and by nature unabiding, they cannot be the basis for a satisfactory experience dependent on them. In short, whatever is transient, is (by that very fact) unsatisfactory (*yadaniccaṃ taṃ dukkhaṃ*, SN 22:15). Hence is established the great Truth of Buddhism that the whole personality or individuality (wherever that may take shape, whether in this world or in another, as is possible in *saṃsāra*) and therefore the whole world of experience which simply depends on this individuality, all this is unsatisfactory or *dukkha*.

> What do you think, monks; is the body permanent or is it transient?
>
> It is transient, Sir.
>
> Now, that which is transient: is it satisfactory or unsatisfactory?
>
> It is unsatisfactory, Sir.
>
> What do you think, monks, sensation, perception, mental processes and consciousness: are all these permanent or transient?
>
> They are transient, Sir.

Now, what is transient: is it satisfactory or unsatisfactory?
It is unsatisfactory, Sir. (SN 22:57).

Thus this general unsatisfactoriness is to be regarded as the universal characteristic of all saṃsāric experience, and this fact constitutes the Noble Truth of *dukkha.* To the intelligent person all this must sound axiomatic. But, then, why are the large majority of people unconvinced of, or unconcerned with, this great Truth which forms the bedrock of the Buddha Dhamma? To answer this we have to probe into the working of man's own mind which alone can realize this conception of the universality of *dukkha.*

The Master has said that the sentient being is psychologically so constituted that he seeks what is pleasurable and shuns what is non-pleasurable (*sukhakāmo dukkhapaṭikkūla*); to use the above employed terminology, he hankers after what is satisfactory for himself and recoils from what is unsatisfactory. Critics of Buddhism may wonder whether it is justifiable to regard the whole psychology of the sentient being as being so strongly ruled by this principle of hankering for the pleasurable and shunning what is unpleasant. That a similar conclusion was arrived at by Freud, the founder of the modem school of psychoanalysis, should cause such critics or sceptics to pause and reflect upon the scientific validity of such an observation. Freud begins his famous dissertation on "Beyond the Pleasure Principle" with the following significant words: "In the theory of psychoanalysis we have no hesitation in assuming that the course taken by mental events is automatically regulated by the pleasure principle. We believe, that is to say, that the course of those events is invariably set in motion by an unpleasurable tension, and that it takes a direction such that its final outcome coincides with a lowering of that tension, that is, with an avoidance of unpleasure or a production of pleasure." Freud thus introduces what he calls an "economic" principle into his study of mental processes, and is it not a noteworthy fact in the history of human ideas that the Buddha had nearly twenty five centuries earlier formulated the same principle in practically the same terms? Now, if man by nature is driven by his own unconscious processes to seek for the pleasant and avoid what is unpleasant, it stands to reason that he would be unwilling to accept a philosophy whose basic idea is the characterization of all his experiences as impermanent and therefore liable to bring unhappiness or *dukkha*. That is why the Buddha soon after his Enlightenment considered that only a very few in the world had their vision sufficiently clear to grasp this great Truth of the universality of *dukkha*.

Before concluding this brief exposition of *dukkha* a doubt should be cleared which is often seen to cloud this conception and erroneously leads certain people to conclude that if the fact of *dukkha* is such a universal characteristic of experience, Buddhism must be regarded as a profession of pessimism. That such a view is totally wrong is seen clearly from certain passages of the Canon itself. According to Buddhism there is a point of view from which experiences, that is to say, sensations and feelings (*vedanā*) can be considered to be threefold: they can be pleasant or happy (*sukha*), or they can be unpleasant or unhappy (*dukkha*), or they can be neutral, i.e., neither pleasant nor unpleasant (*adukkhamasukha*). From this lower or relative point of view which holds good for all individual experience, there is what may be called happiness in the world just as much as unhappiness, the degree of predominance of the one over the other varying according to personal and environmental conditions prevailing at a given moment. But further contemplation of such happiness and unhappiness and neutral feelings shows unmistakably that there is a common denominator between all these three types of experiences, namely, the fact that all three are subject to the universal property of impermanence or transience. Thus the Venerable Sāriputta assures the Master that if questioned on the real nature of sensations and feelings, he would reply: "Threefold, indeed, friend, are those feelings and sensations: pleasant, unpleasant and neither-pleasant-nor-unpleasant; but, friend, [all] these three [experiences] are transient, and when one realizes that whatever is transient [and fleeting] must give rise to *dukkha* [in other words, is unsatisfactory], no hankering after them arises."

It can easily be seen that in the last sentence, *dukkha* is used in the wider philosophical sense, as referred to at the beginning of this article. Hence is the Master's joyful approval of Sāriputta's words: "Well said, well said, Sāriputta, this exactly is the manner in which one should summarily dispose of such a question: Whatever experience there is, such [being transitory] must fall within the category of *dukkha*" (*yaṃ kiñci vedayitaṃ tam dukkhasmiṃ*; SN 12:32/S II 53). All saṃsāric experience is in this sense *vedayita* and thus arises the incontrovertible proposition that all becoming (*bhava*) in *saṃsāra* is *dukkha* or unsatisfactory from the highest point of view (*paramattha*). Herein is also based that absolutely certain optimism of Buddhism, viz. that there is a way out of this saṃsāric *dukkha*, a haven of utter peace and tranquillity, which is the absolute happiness of Nibbāna. *Nibbānaṃ paramaṃ sukhaṃ*.

III. Anattā

The above discussion of the two signata of impermanence and unsatisfactoriness naturally leads to the basic Buddhist concept of *anattā*, non-self or insubstantiality.[3]

Every student of Buddhism knows that this concept is the most controversial of all the basic ideas of the system, and that a hundred and one interpretations have been suggested by commentators, scholars and critics. To the Western student of Buddhism the so-called "*anattā*-doctrine" has been the hunting ground, not always a happy one, for the display of personal ingenuity and dialectical jumbling, and it is significant that this idea has been the cause of the most glaring contradictions among themselves, and even within the writings of the same authority. Even our own historical schools of Buddhist interpretation have found this concept the most difficult. The main difficulty confronting the interpreters has, in my opinion, been the lack of a clear definition of the term *attā*. It is curious how writers, particularly those of the West, have plunged into discussions of this doctrine equipped with no other definition of it than the ideas of Soul or Ego borrowed from theistic and pantheistic systems of philosophy or religion, as they were accustomed to before taking up the study of Buddhism. It is not intended to pursue the criticism of such interpretation in this article, but to emphasize the important fact that by the word *attā* or *atta* books of the Pali Canon refer to a number of historical concepts that prevailed in India about the sixth century before Christ, and, therefore, the term must be defined accordingly in

3. See Anattalakkhaṇa Sutta in *Three Cardinal Discourses of the Buddha*, translated by Ñāṇamoli Thera (The Wheel, No. 17).

relation to the particular context under review. Here then we shall confine ourselves to those contexts where the adjective *anattā* is used as the universal characteristic of all *dhammas* (*sabbe dhamma anattā*) which is the third of the three signata or *tilakkhaṇa*.[4]

The two previous articles dealt with the facts of the impermanence of all compounded things and processes, and of the general unsatisfactoriness of all states derived from these, namely, the five groups of physical and mental properties dependent on grasping (*pañcupadānakkhandhā*); in particular those feelings and sensations that go to make up individual experience (*vedanā*) which could be classified as pleasant, unpleasant, and neither-pleasant-nor-unpleasant. The relevant texts were cited to show that the latter characteristic of general unsatisfactoriness is derived directly from the first characteristic of impermanence. It is now opportune to show how as a necessary corollary of this general unsatisfactoriness of all experience arises the realization of the third and last verity included in the three signata, *viz.* the universal characteristic of all physical and mental states and phenomena as *anattā.*

In the words of the Master himself: "Physical form, monks, is transient [*anicca*] and whatever is transient is unsatisfactory [*dukkha*]; whatever is unsatisfactory, that is *anattā* [non-self]; and whatever is non-self, that is not of me, that I am not, that is not my self." This same rigorous logic is in turn applied to the four other groups constituting individuality, viz. the feelings and sensations (*vedanā*), perception and cognitions (*saññā*), mental processes and reflexes (*saṅkhāra*) and finally, the individual's consciousness itself (*viññāṇa*). This last application of the universal characteristic of non-self to consciousness is in several ways the most significant act in this statement, and when we remind ourselves that the Pali word *viññāṇa* includes even the innermost mental experiences of the sentient being, we can see clearly the exact force of the *anattā* characteristic as conceived by the Buddha. The most rarified concept of Self or Ego that any philosopher, before or after the Buddha, ever conceived was somehow or somewhere concerned with a state of self-consciousness, the consciousness that "I am I."

4. See *Vedanta and Buddhism* by H. von Glasenapp (The Wheel, No. 2) p. 6 ff and *Anattā and Nibbāna* by Nyanāponika Thera (The Wheel, No. 11).

To the Buddha, even this self-consciousness or "I-ness" is subject to the inexorable characteristics of impermanence and unsatisfactoriness, and since whatever is subject to these characteristics is non-self, this I-consciousness must be regarded as an illusion or an error. This is, in short, the significance of the adjective *anattā* as used in the above mentioned doctrine. In the Chachakka Sutta (MN 148) a detailed analysis of this concept occurs:

> "If any one regards the eye [i.e. seeing] as the self, that does not hold, for the arising and the passing away of the eye is [clear from experience]. With regard to that which arises and passes away, if anyone were to think, 'myself is arising and passing away' [such a thought] would be controverted by the person himself. Therefore, it does not hold to regard the eye as the self. Thus the eye [or seeing] is [proved to be] non-self. Similarly if anyone says that the forms [*rūpā* or visual objects] are the self, that too does not hold."

So both the eye and the visual objects [cognized by it] are non-self. The same argument applies to visual perception or the eye-consciousness [*cakkhuviññāṇa*] if one were to consider this as self. Similarly, it applies to visual sense-contact [*cakkhu-samphassa*], so that the eye, its sense objects, visual consciousness and visual sense-contact are all four non-self [*anattā*]. It applies also to feelings [that arise due to the above four], so that the eye, its sense-objects, visual consciousness, visual sense-contact, and the resultant feelings, are all five non-self. It applies lastly to the [instinctual] craving [*taṇhā*] that is associated with above five, so that the eye, its sense objects, visual consciousness, visual contact, the resultant feelings, and the craving behind them all, these six are non-self. And, what thus applies to the eye or the sense of sight, applies equally to the other five senses [the last being the mind (*mano*) as an organ of sense]. Thus, if it be said that the mind is self [*mano attā' ti*], that too does not hold. Similarly, it is inadmissible to assert that the mind, or its sense-objects [*dhamma*] or mental-consciousness [*manoviññāṇa*], or mental contact [*manosamphassa*], or the feelings [*vedanā*] that result from all the craving [*taṇhā*], that is associated with all these, are the self. They are non-self, all of them. The way that leads to the origination of the [concept of] permanent individuality or personality [*sakkāya-samudaya*] is to regard as mine, or as "I am this," or as "This is my self" either the sense of seeing, or the visual data, or visual consciousness, or visual contact, its feelings or its craving or similarly, to regard hearing and the four other senses [including mind] with their adjuncts. The way that leads to the cessation of the [view of] permanent personality [*sakkāya-nirodha-gāmaṇi-paṭipadā*] is to cease regarding as mine and so forth, either [the functions of] seeing, or hearing, or smelling, or tasting, or touching, or thinking, or their adjuncts.

Now, the Buddha goes on to discuss the ethical implications of this view of self (*attā*) or permanent personality (*sakkāya*):

> "From sight and visual objects arises visual consciousness and the meeting of all three is contact, from which contact come feelings which may be pleasant, or unpleasant, or neither. When experiencing a pleasant feeling, a man rejoices in it, hails it and clings tight to it, and a trend to passion [attachment] ensues. When experiencing an unpleasant feeling a man sorrows, feels miserable, wails, beats his breast and goes distraught, and a trend of repugnance ensues. When experiencing a feeling that is neither pleasant nor unpleasant he has no true and causal comprehension of that feeling's origin, disappearance, agreeableness, perils and outcome, and a trend of ignorance ensues. It can never possibly result that, without first discarding the pleasant feeling's trend to passion, without first discarding the unpleasant feeling's trend to repugnance, and without getting rid of the neutral feeling's trend to ignorance, without discarding ignorance, and stopping it from arising, he will put an end, here and now, to *dukkha*. And what is true of sight, is equally true of the other five senses."

Thus the Buddha admonishes his disciples to analyse the whole conception of self or abiding personality and thereby the whole of experience (*loka*) along with every single component of the process, whereby the fallacy of Self or abiding personality arises, viewing this whole process of the arising of individuality (*nāmarūpa*) in a perfectly objective manner.

From all this it becomes clear that the three concepts of *anicca, dukkha* and *anattā,* the three signata or *tilakkhaṇa,* are the three cornerstones of the whole edifice of Buddhism. To be convinced of their validity is to accept the Dhamma in its entirety and therefore there can be no halfway house in this process of conviction. It behoves each one of us, who call ourselves Buddhists, to contemplate these three permanent characteristics of the world as we experience it, both objectively and subjectively, and apply in our individual and social lives the ethical principles that, as the Master pointed out, derive from such conviction and lead us to that state free from these three signata, viz. the eternal bliss of Nibbāna.

The Three Signata

Gleanings from the Pali Scriptures

These texts have been selected by the editors of this series and partly adapted from various translations.

Anicca—Impermanence

Whatever has origination, all that is subject to cessation.

(MN 56)

"There is no materiality whatever, O monks, no feelings no perception, no formations,[5] no consciousness whatever that is permanent, everlasting, eternal, changeless, identically abiding for ever." Then the Blessed One took a bit of cow dung in his hand and he spoke to the monks. "Monks if even that much of permanent, everlasting, eternal, changeless individual Selfhood [*attabhāva*], identically abiding forever, could be found, then this living of a life of purity [*brahmacariya*] for the complete eradication of ill [*dukkhakkhaya*] would not be feasible." (SN 22:96)

5. *Saṅkhāra* is rendered elsewhere in this essay as "dynamic processes." It means "kamma formations."

Here a monk abides contemplating rise and fall in the five categories affected by clinging thus: "Such is materiality, such its origin, such its disappearance, [and so with the other four]." Cultivating this kind of concentration conduces to the eradication of taints [*āsavakkhaya*]. (DN 33)

Monks, formations are impermanent; they are not lasting; they provide no real comfort; so that that is enough for a man to become dispassionate, for his lust to fade out, and for him to be liberated. (AN 7:62)

Here, monks, feelings, perceptions and thoughts are known to him as they arise, known as they appear present, known as they disappear. Cultivating this kind of concentration conduces to mindfulness and full awareness. (DN 33)

When a man abides thus mindful and fully aware, diligent, ardent and self-controlled, then, if pleasant feeling arises in him, he understands, "This pleasant feeling has arisen in me; but that is dependent, not independent. Dependent on what? Dependent on this body. But this body is impermanent, formed and dependently originated. Now how could pleasant feeling, arisen dependent on an impermanent, formed, dependently arisen body, be permanent?" In the body and in feeling he abides contemplating impermanence and fall and fading and cessation and relinquishment. As he does so, his underlying tendency to lust for the body and for pleasant feeling is abandoned. Similarly when he contemplates unpleasant feeling his underlying tendency to resistance [*paṭigha*] to the body and unpleasant feelings is abandoned; and when he contemplates neither-unpleasant-nor-pleasant feeling his underlying tendency to ignorance of the body and of that feeling is abandoned. (SN 36:7)

Monks, when a man sees as impermanent the eye [and the rest], which is impermanent, then he has right view. (SN 35:155)

Consciousness comes into being [*sambhoti*] by dependence on a duality. What is that duality? It is the eye, which is impermanent, changing, becoming-other, and visible objects, which are impermanent, changing and becoming-other; such is the transient, fugitive duality [of eye-cum-visible objects], which is impermanent, changing and becoming-other. Eye-consciousness is impermanent, changing and becoming-other; for this cause and condition [namely eye cum-visible objects] for the arising of eye-consciousness being impermanent, changing and becoming-other, how could eye-consciousness, arisen by depending on an impermanent condition, be permanent? Then the coincidence, concurrence and confluence of these three impermanent dhammas is called contact [*phassa*]; but eye-contact too is impermanent, changing becoming-other; for how could eye-contact arisen by depending on an impermanent condition, be permanent? It is one touched by contact who feels [*vedeti*], likewise who perceives [*sañjānāti*]; so these transient, fugitive dhammas too [namely, feeling, choice and perception] are impermanent, changing and becoming, other. (And so with ear-cum-sounds, nose-cum-odours, tongue-cum-flavours, body-cum-tangibles, mind-cum-ideas.) (SN 35:93)

When a monk abides much with his mind fortified by perception of impermanence, his mind retreats, retracts and recoils from gain, honour and renown, and does not reach out to it just as a cock's feather or a strip of sinew thrown on a fire retreats, retracts and recoils and does not reach out to it. (AN 7:46)

Perception of impermanence should be cultivated for the elimination of the conceit "I am," since perception of not-self becomes established in one who perceives impermanence; and it is perception of not-self that arrives at the elimination of the conceit "I am," which is extinction [*nibbāna*] here and now. (Ud 4.1)

Fruitful as an act of [lavish] giving is, yet it is still more fruitful to go with confident heart for refuge to the Buddha, the Dhamma and the Sangha and undertake the five precepts of virtue ... Fruitful as this is, yet it is still more fruitful to cultivate even as little as a whiff of fragrance of loving-kindness. Fruitful as that is, still more fruitful it is to cultivate the perception of impermanence even for only as long as the snapping of a finger. (AN 9:20)

Better a single day of life perceiving how things rise and fall than to live out a century yet not perceive their rise and fall. (Dhp 14)

When a monk sees six rewards it should be enough for him to establish unlimitedly perception of impermanence in all formations. What six? "All formations will seem to me insubstantial. My mind will find no relish in all the world. My mind will emerge from all the world. My mind will incline towards Nibbāna. My fetters will come to be abandoned. And I shall be endowed with the highest in monkhood." (AN 6:102)

All life and all existence here
With all its joys and all its woe,
Rests on a single state of mind,
And quick passes that moment by.

Nay, even gods whose life does last
For four and eighty thousand *kalpas*,
Do not remain one and the same,
Not even for two single thoughts.

Those groups that passed away just now,
Those groups that will pass later on,
Those groups just passing in between,
They're not in nature different.

Not in the future moment does one live,
One now lives in the present moment.
"When consciousness dissolves, the world is dead";
This utterance is true in the highest sense.

No hoarding up of things passed by,
No heaping up in future time!
And things arisen are all like
The mustard seed on pointed awl.

The groups of life that disappeared
At death, as well as during life,
Have all alike become extinct,
And never will they rise again.

Out of the unseen did they rise,
Into the unseen do they pass.
Just as the lightning flashes forth,
So do they flash and pass away.

(Vism Ch. 20)

The monk in deepest solitude,
Grown still and tranquil in his heart,
Feels superhuman happiness
Whilst clearly he perceives the truth.

Whenever he reflects upon
The rise and passing of the groups,

He's filled with rapture and with bliss
Whilst he beholds the Deathless Realm.

(Dhp 373f.)

Transient are formations all.
Their law it is to rise and fall.
Arisen—soon they disappear.
To make them cease is happiness.

(SN 6:15, DN 16)

Dukkha—Suffering or Unsatisfactoriness

This only do I teach: suffering, and its end. (MN 22)

Suffering only arises when anything arises; suffering only ceases when anything ceases. (SN 12:15)

Suffering is threefold: intrinsic suffering [*dukkha-dukkha*], suffering in change [*viparināma-dukkha*] and suffering due to formations [*saṅkhāra-dukkha*]. Bodily and mental painful feeling are called intrinsic suffering because suffering is their very nature, their common designation and because they are in themselves suffering... . Bodily and mental pleasant feeling are called suffering in change because they are a cause for the arising of pain when they change. Neutral feeling and the remaining formations of the three planes of existence are called suffering due to formations because they are oppressed by rise and fall. (Vism XVI)

Pleasant feeling is agreeable while it lasts and is disagreeable when it changes; painful feeling is disagreeable while it lasts and is agreeable when it changes; the neither-pleasant-nor-unpleasant feeling is agreeable when there is knowledge and disagreeable when there is no knowledge. (MN 44)

A heedless man is vanquished by the disagreeable in the guise of the agreeable, by the unloved in the guise of the loved, by suffering in the guise of happiness. (Ud 2.8)

In the past, sense-pleasures were a painful experience, intensely burning and searing; in the future too, sense-pleasures will be a painful experience, intensely burning and searing; and also now in the present, sense-pleasures are a painful experience, intensely burning and searing. But these beings have not yet lost their greed for sense-pleasures, are consumed by craving for sense-pleasures, burning in feverish passion for sense-pleasures; and with their faculties clouded, they have, in spite of that painful experience, the illusion of happiness. (MN 75)

Whoso delights in materiality, in feeling, in perception, in formations, and in consciousness, he delights in suffering; and whoso delights in suffering, will not be freed from suffering. Thus I say. (SN 22:29)

The arising, presence and manifestation of materiality, feeling, perception, formations, and consciousness is but the arising of suffering, the presence of maladies, the manifestation of decay and death. The cessation, the stilling, the ending of materiality, feeling, perception, formations and consciousness is but the cessation of suffering, the stilling of maladies, the ending of decay and death. (SN 22:30)

Inconceivable is the beginning of this *saṃsāra*; not to be discovered is a first beginning of beings who, obstructed by ignorance and ensnared by craving, are hurrying and hastening through this round of rebirths. Which do you think, O monks, is more: the flood of tears which, weeping and wailing, you have shed upon this long way, hurrying and hastening through this round of rebirths, united with the undesired, separated from the desired; this or the waters of the four great oceans? Long have you suffered the death of father and mother, of sons, daughters, brothers and sisters. And whilst you were thus suffering you have, indeed, shed more tears upon this long way than there is water in the four great oceans. And thus, O monks, have you long undergone torment, undergone misfortune, filled the graveyards full; verily, long enough to be dissatisfied with all forms of existence, long enough to turn away and free yourselves from them all. (SN 15:3)

How can you find delight and mirth
Where there is burning without end?
In deepest darkness you are wrapped!
Why do you not aspire for light?

Look at this puppet here, well rigged,
A heap of many sores, piled up,
Diseased and full of greediness,
Unstable and impermanent!

Devoured by old age is this frame,
A prey to sickness, weak and frail;
To pieces breaks this putrid body,
All life must truly end in death!

(Dhp 146–48)

For those who know not Ill and how Ill grows,
who neither know how Ill is stilled and quenched
nor know the Way to lay Ill to rest,
—those miss Release, alike of heart and mind;
they cannot end it all and reach the goal;
they tramp the round of birth, decay and death.

But they who know both Ill and how Ill grows,
and also know how Ill is stilled and quenched
and know the Way that lays all Ill to rest;
—these win Release of heart, Release of mind;
these surely end it all and reach the goal;
these nevermore shall know decay and birth.

(Sn 724–727)

When a monk sees six rewards, it should be enough for him to establish unlimited perception of suffering in all formations. What six? "The thought of turning away from all formations will be established in me, like unto a murderer with drawn sword. My mind will emerge from all the world. I shall see peace in Nibbāna. The underlying [evil] tendencies will be eliminated in me. I shall be dutifull and I shall attend well upon the Master, with a loving heart." (AN 6:103)

Anattā: Not-self or Egolessness

Give up what does not belong to you! Such giving-up will long conduce to your weal and happiness. And what is it that does not belong to you? Materiality, feelings, perception, formations and consciousness; these do not belong to you and these you should give up. Such giving-up will long conduce to your weal and happiness. (SN 22:33)

All ascetics and brahmins who conceive a self in various ways, all those conceive the five groups [as the self] or one or another of them. Which are the five? Herein an ignorant worldling conceives materiality, feeling, perception, formations or consciousness as the self; or the self as the owner of any of these groups; or that group as included in the self; or the self as included in that group. (SN 22:47)

It is impossible that anyone with right view should see anything [or idea, *dhamma*] as self. (MN 115)

The learned and noble disciple does not consider materiality, feeling, perception, formations, or consciousness as self; nor the self as the owner of these groups; nor these groups as included within the self; nor the self as included within the groups. Of such a learned and noble disciple it is said that he is no longer fettered by any group of existence, [his] own or external. Thus I say. (SN 22:117)

It is possible that a virtuous man while contemplating the five groups as impermanent, woeful, ... empty, not-self may realize the Fruit of Stream-entrance. (SN 22:122)

One should not imagine oneself as being identical with the eye, should not imagine oneself as being included within the eye, should not imagine oneself as being outside the eye, should not imagine: "The eye belongs to me." And so with ear, nose, tongue, body and mind. One should not imagine oneself as being identical with visual objects, sounds, odours, tactile and mental objects. One should not imagine oneself as being included in them or outside of them; one should not imagine: "They belong to me." One should not imagine oneself as being identical with eye-consciousness... ear-consciousness... nose-consciousness... body-consciousness... mind-consciousness; should not imagine oneself as being included within mind-consciousness; should not imagine oneself as being outside of mind-consciousness, should not imagine: "Mind-consciousness belongs to me." One should not imagine oneself as being identical with the totality of things [the All, *sabbaṃ*] should not imagine oneself as being included in the totality of things; should not imagine oneself as being outside the totality of things; should not imagine: "The totality of things belongs to me." Thus not imagining any more, the wise disciple clings no longer to anything in the world. Clinging no longer to anything, he trembles not. Trembling no longer, he reaches in his own person the extinction of all vanity: "Exhausted is rebirth, lived the holy life, the task is done, and nothing further remains after this." Thus he knows. (SN 35:90)

It would be better for an untaught ordinary man to treat as self [*attā*] this body, which is constructed upon the four great primaries of matter [*maha-bhūta*], than mind. Why? Because the body can last one year, two years ... even a hundred years: but what is called "mind" and "thinking" and "consciousness" arises and ceases differently through night and day. (SN 12:61)

Consciousness is not-self. Also the causes and conditions of the arising of consciousness, they likewise are not-self. Hence, how could it be possible that consciousness, having arisen through something which is not-self, could ever be a self? (SN 35:141)

When a monk sees six rewards it should be enough for him to establish unlimited perception of not-self concerning all things [dhamma]. What six? "I shall be aloof from all the world. No impulses of 'I' [egotism] will assail me. No impulses of 'mine' will assail me. With extraordinary insight shall I be endowed. I shall clearly see causes and the causally-arisen phenomena."

(AN 6:104)

The Removal of Distracting Thoughts

Vitakka-saṇṭhāna Sutta

A Discourse of the Buddha
(Majjhima Nikāya No. 20)

With the Commentary and Marginal Notes

Translated by

Soma Thera

WHEEL PUBLICATION NO. 21

The Discourse on the Removal of Distracting Thoughts

Thus have I heard. At one time the Blessed One was staying at Sāvatthī, in Jeta's Grove, Anāthapiṇḍika's Pleasance. The Blessed One addressed the bhikkhus, saying, "Bhikkhus," and they replied to him saying, "Reverend Sir." The Blessed One spoke as follows :

"Five things should be reflected on from time to time, by the bhikkhu who is intent on the higher consciousness. What five?

When evil unskilful thoughts connected with desire, hate and delusion arise in a bhikkhu through reflection on an adventitious object, he should (in order to get rid of that) reflect on a different object which is connected with skill. Then the evil unskilful thoughts are eliminated; they disappear. By their elimination, the mind stands firm, settles down, becomes unified and concentrated, just within (his subject of meditation).

Like an experienced carpenter or carpenter's apprentice, striking hard at, pushing out, and getting rid of a coarse peg with a fine one, should the bhikkhu in order to get rid of the adventitious object, reflect on a different object which is connected with skill. Then the evil unskilful thoughts connected with desire, hate and delusion are eliminated; they disappear. By their elimination the mind stands firm, settles down, becomes unified and concentrated, just within (his subject of meditation)

If the evil unskilful thoughts continue to arise in a bhikkhu, who in order to get rid of an adventitious object reflects on a different object which is connected with skill, he should ponder on the disadvantages of unskilful thoughts thus: Truly these thoughts of mine are unskilful blameworthy and productive of misery. Then the evil unskilful thoughts are eliminated; they disappear. By their elimination, the mind stands firm, settles down, becomes unified and concentrated, just within (his subject of meditation).

Like a well-dressed young man or woman who feels horrified, humiliated and disgusted because of the carcase of a snake, dog or human that is hung round his or her neck, should the bhikkhu in whom unskilful thoughts continue to arise in spite of his reflection on the object which is connected with skill, ponder on the disadvantages of unskilful thoughts thus: Truly, these thoughts of mine are unskilful, blameworthy and productive of misery. Then the evil, unskilful thoughts are eliminated; they disappear. By their elimination, the mind stands firm, settles down, becomes unified and concentrated, just within (his subject of meditation).

If evil, unskilful thoughts continue to arise in a bhikkhu who ponders on their disadvantageousness, he should in regard to them, endeavour to be without attention and reflection. Then the evil, unskilful thoughts are eliminated; they disappear. By their elimination, the mind stands firm, settles down, becomes unified and concentrated, just within (his subject of meditation).

Like a keen-eyed man shutting his eyes and looking away from some direction in order to avoid seeing visible objects come within sight, should the bhikkhu in whom evil, unskilful thoughts continue to arise in spite of his pondering on their disadvantageousness, endeavour to be without attention and reflection as regards them. Then the evil, unskilful thoughts are eliminated; they disappear. By their elimination, the mind stands firm, settles down, becomes unified and concentrated, just within (his subject of meditation).

If evil, unskilful thoughts continue to arise in a bhikkhu in spite of his endeavour to be without attention and reflection as regards evil, unskilful thoughts, he should reflect on the removal of the (thought) source of those unskilful thoughts. Then the evil, unskilful thoughts are eliminated; they disappear. By their elimination, the mind stands firm, settles down, becomes unified and concentrated, just within (his subject of meditation).

Just as a man finding no reason for walking fast, walks slowly; finding no reason for walking slowly, stands; finding no reason for standing, sits down; and finding no reason for sitting down, lies down; and thus getting rid of a posture rather coarse resorts to a easier posture, just so should the bhikkhu in whom evil, unskilful thoughts arise, in spite of his endeavour to be without attention and reflection regarding them, reflect on the removal of the (thought) source of those unskilful thoughts. Then the evil, unskilful thoughts are eliminated; they disappear. By their elimination, the mind stands firm, settles down, becomes unified and concentrated, just within (his subject of meditation).

If evil, unskilful thoughts continue to arise in a bhikkhu in spite of his reflection on the removal of the source of unskilful thoughts, he should with clenched teeth and the tongue pressing on the palate, restrain, subdue and beat down the (evil) mind by the (good) mind. Then the evil, unskilful thoughts connected with desire, hate and delusion are eliminated; they disappear. By their elimination, the mind stands firm, settles down, becomes unified and concentrated, just within (his subject of meditation).

Like a strong man holding a weaker man by the head or shoulders and restraining, subduing and beating him down, should the bhikkhu in whom evil, unskilful thoughts continue to arise in spite of his reflection on the source of unskilful thoughts, restrain, subdue and beat down the (evil) mind by the (good) mind, with clenched teeth and the tongue pressing on the palate. Then the evil, unskilful thoughts connected with desire, hate and delusion are eliminated; they disappear. By their elimination, the mind stands firm, settles down, becomes unified and concentrated, just within (his subject of meditation).

When, indeed, bhikkhus, evil unskilful thoughts due to reflection on an adventitious object are eliminated, when they disappear, and the mind stands firm, settles down, becomes unified and concentrated just within (his subject of meditation), through his reflection on an object connected with skill, through his pondering on the disadvantages of unskilful thoughts, his endeavouring to be without attentiveness and reflection as regards those thoughts, his reflection on the removal of the source of those thoughts or through his restraining, subduing and beating down of the evil mind by the good mind with clenched teeth and tongue pressing on the palate, that bhikkhu is called a master of the paths taken by the courses of thought. The thought he wants to think, that, he thinks; the thought he does not want to think, that, he does not think. He has cut off craving, removed the fetter, rightly mastered pride, and made an end of suffering.

The Blessed One said this, and the bhikkhus glad at heart, approved of his words.

The Commentary to the Discourse on the Removal of Distracting Thoughts

With Marginal Notes from the Subcommentary

Thus have I heard:[1] *evaṃ me sutaṃ*. This Discourse on the Removal of Distracting Thoughts (Vitakkasaṇṭhāna Sutta) was heard by me in this way.

"I" refers to the Elder Ānanda who recited the Discourse-collection (*Sutta Piṭaka*) of the Pali Canon at the first Council of purified ones (*arahants*) held at Rājagaha after the passing away of the Buddha.

By the bhikkhu who is intent on the higher consciousness: *adhicittaṃ anuyuttena bhikkhunā*. Consciousness connected with the practice of the ten courses of skilful action (*dasa kusala-kamma-pathā*) is referred to here as just (wholesome) consciousness (*cittameva*). Superior to that (merely wholesome consciousness) is the consciousness of the eight absorptions become a basis for the development of insight (*vipassanā pādakaṃ aṭṭha-samāpatti-cittaṃ*). This (superior) consciousness is the higher consciousness.

> *Consciousness connected with the practice of the ten courses of skilful action* is just an example of what is not meant here by the term higher consciousness. Consciousness of the ten courses of skilful action is just consciousness not forming a part of things supernormal (*uttarimanussadhamma*).[2]
>
> *Consciousness of the eight absorptions* that has become a basis for the development of insight, is meant here by *higher consciousness*. Some (i.e., dwellers of the Abhayagiri Vihāra at Anurādhapura) say that the consciousness associated with

1. The commentarial passages (in bold) are translated from the Venerable Buddhaghosa's *Papañcasūdani*, the commentary to the Majjhima Nikāya.
2. Indented passages are 'marginal' notes taken from the Subcommentary (*ṭīkā*) to the Majjhima Nikāya.

insight is the higher consciousness (*vipassanāya sampayuttaṃ adhicittan'ti keci*).

By one who is intent on (*anuyuttena*) means: by one who is diligently occupied with (*yutta-payuttena*).

This bhikkhu is not intent on the higher consciousness the while he is going forth, sitting-mat in hand, to a place near a tree in a jungle—thicket, at the bottom of a hill, or on a slope, with the thought, "I shall do the recluse's duty." He is also not intent on that, when removing grass and leaves for the sitting place, with hands or feet. When, however, having sat down, after washing his hands and feet, he remains with legs crossed, having taken up his preliminary subject of meditation, he is indeed intent on the higher consciousness.

> *Intent on* means: intent on producing the yet unarisen higher things and zealously developing to completion the higher things that have already arisen.
>
> *The preliminary subject of meditation* (*mūla-kammaṭṭhāna*) is the subject of meditation the bhikkhu is fostering (*pārihāriya-kammaṭṭhāna*).
>
> *When ... he remains ... having taken up* means: when having taken up the preliminary subject of meditation, he remains applying himself to it (or when having taken up the preliminary subject he applies himself to the development of it). Though full absorption is not reached through the meditation he is still one intent on the higher consciousness.

Things: *nimittāni* are practical methods—reasonable ways (*kāraṇāni*).

From time to time: *kālena kālaṃ* means: on different occasions (*samaye samaye*).

Is not the subject of meditation to be reflected on always, without putting it aside even for a moment? Why did the Blessed One say "from time to time"?

There are thirty-eight subjects classified in the text (*pāḷiyaṃ*). By the bhikkhu who having selected one of these, one which appeals to him, and is seated there is no reflection on these five things (*nimittāni*) so long as imperfections (*upakkilesa*) do not appear.

When an imperfection appears, the danger should be driven away by means of these things.

Pointing out this, the Blessed One said: "From time to time..."

> The opinion of the objector is as follows: Because it is said "by him who is intent on the higher consciousness (*adhicittaṃ anuyuttena*)" and as the term "intent on the higher consciousness" means "diligently applying oneself to the meditation without a break," is it not the fact that the Blessed One began this exposition with the words, "these five things should be reflected on from time to time," in order to point out the method of driving out danger to the meditation that progresses?
>
> The other stated that *there are thirty-eight subjects of meditation in the text*, and so forth, in order to point out that the Master said, "From time to time" because these five things have to be reflected on at the proper time for the purpose of purifying the mind of the beginner devoted to inner culture when sometimes imperfections of meditation (*bhāvanā upakkilesā*) arise in him.

Connected with desire (*chandūpasaṃhita*): means associated with desire, associated with lust (*rāgasampayutta*). The field (*khetta*) and the object (*ārammaṇa*) of these three obsessive thoughts should be known.

The eight kinds of consciousness associated with greed are the field of obsessive thoughts connected with desire. The two kinds of consciousness associated with hatred are the field of obsessive thoughts connected with hate.

Even the twelve kinds of unwholesome consciousness are the field of obsessive thoughts connected with delusion. The two kinds of consciousness combining with scepsis and restlessness, indeed are equally the field of these obsessive thoughts connected with delusion. To even all three kinds of obsessive thought, just living beings and inanimate things are the object, since these obsessive thoughts come into being in regard to living beings and inanimate things viewed unimpartially by way of liking and disliking them.

> *Living beings and inanimate things* are unimpartially viewed by way of liking and disliking when the dear and the not dear are unequally seen, are wrongly seen.

Viewing unimpartially (*asamapekkhanaṃ*) is the laying hold of an object with unsystematic attention through looking on ignorantly in a worldly way (*gehasita-aññāṇupekkha-vasena ārammaṇassa ayoniso gahaṇaṃ*).

He should... reflect on a different object which is connected with skill: *aññam nimittaṃ manasikātabbaṃ kusalūpasaṃhitaṃ* means: an object different from the adventitious object, and one which is connected with skill, should be reflected on.

Here the explanation of the term "different object" is as follows: When a thought connected with desire for living beings arises, the development of the idea of the unlovely (*asubha-bhāvanā*) is a different object, and when a thought connected on with desire for inanimate things arises, the reflection on impermanence (*anicca-manasikāra*) is a different object.

When a thought connected with hate towards living beings arises, the development of the idea of friendliness (*metta-bhāvanā*) is a different object, and when a thought connected with hate for inanimate things arises, the reflection on the modes of materiality (*dhātumanasikāra*) is a different object.

Wheresoever a thought connected with delusion concerning living beings or things arises, the fivefold reliance associated with the doctrine (*pañca dhammūpanissayo*) is the different object.

An object different from the adventitious object: *tato nimittato aññam nimittaṃ*. A different, new object separate from the cause for the arising of unskilful thought connected with desire, hate and delusion (*tato chandūpasaṃhitādi-akusala-vitakkuppatti-kāraṇato*).

One which is connected with skill: *kusala-nimitto taṃ*. The cause for the proceeding of states of consciousness that is with skill.

Should be reflected on: *manasikātabbaṃ*. Should be placed in the mind, should be thought upon as a meditation, or should go on in the mind-flux (*citte ṭhapetabbaṃ*).

The unlovely (*asubhaṃ*) is indeed the unlovely object (*asubha-nimittaṃ*).

When greed arises in regard to living beings with thoughts like the following: "This one's hands are beautiful," "This one's feet are beautiful," one should think by way of the unlovely thus: To what are you attached? Are you attached to the hair of the head, the hair of the body, nails, teeth, skin ... or urine?[3]

This body (*attabhāva*) held up by three hundred bones, bound with nine hundred nerve strings, plastered over with nine hundred lumps of flesh, wrapped completely in a wet skin, covered with the colour of the cuticle (*chavi-rāgena*), drips filth from the nine open sores and the ninety-nine thousand pores of the hairs of the body. It is filled with a collection of bones, is bad-smelling, contemptible, repellent, and is the sum of the thirty-two parts. There is neither essence not excellence in it. To one who thinks thus of the unlovely (nature of the body), the greed connected with living beings is cast out. Therefore the different object is the thinking on the object (*nimitta*) which produces greed, by way of the meditation on the unlovely (nature of the body).

When there is greed for inanimate things like bowls and robes, it is cast out through reflection of two kinds of bringing about detachment for inanimate things, namely those on ownerlessness and temporariness, taught in the section of the enlightenment factors (*bojjhaṅga*) in the commentary to the Satipaṭṭhāna Sutta. Therefore the thinking on the object (which produces greed), by way of the reflection of impermanence is the different object.

> *Reflection ... on ownerlessness and temporariness*; this bowl gradually ends up as broken pieces, having changed color, became old, developed cracks and holes or having smashed up; this robe, having faded, worn out will have to be thrown away with the end of a stick, after it is used as a rag to wipe the feet with. If these had an owner, he would prevent them from being destroyed. In this manner should the reflection on ownerlessness be done. And the reflection on temporariness should be done with the thought that these cannot last long, that these are of brief duration.

When there is hatred towards living beings, friendliness should be developed as taught in the Discourse on the Overcoming

3. This refers to the thirty-two parts of the body.

of Ill-will (*āghāta-vinaya-sutta*), the instruction with the Parable of the Saw[4] (*kakacūpamovāda*), and the like. In one developing friendliness, hatred vanishes. Therefore the development of friendliness for the object (which produces anger) is the different object.

> *The Discourse on the Overcoming of Ill-will* in the Aṅguttara Nikāya[5] is as follows:
>
> "Bhikkhus, these are the five ways of overcoming ill-will. Whenever ill-will is arisen in a bhikkhu it should altogether be overcome. What are the five?
>
> "Should ill-will arise at any time in a person, friendliness should be developed in him ... compassion should be developed in him ... equanimity should be developed in him ... the state of being without mindfulness and reflection (in regard to the object producing hate) should be developed in him ... consciousness of the fact of one's own karma as one's own property should be developed in him ... Thus should ill-will be overcome in that person. Indeed, these are five ways of overcoming ill-will. Wherever it is arisen in a bhikkhu, it should be overcome entirely."
>
> *And the like*: similes like that of the firebrand from funeral pyre[6] (unclean, untouchable).
>
> *Friendliness should be developed* having overcome hate in the manner taught in the above mentioned teachings.

Further, when one gets angry with the stump (of a tree), a thorn, grass or leaves one should ask oneself:

With whom are you angry? Is it with the earth-element or the water-element? Or who is it that is angry? Is it the earth-element or the water-element? To one who reflects on the elements (*dhātu-manasikāra*) anger in regard to inanimate things vanishes. Therefore the reflection on the elements of the object (internal or external—the thinker or the thought which produces anger) is the different object.

4. Majjhima Nikāya Sutta 21.
5. AN 5:156/A III 185.
6. Itivuttaka Sutta 91.

When, however, delusion appears, in any circumstances, there should be dependence on, reliance on, or the resorting to five things (five expedient things). They are as follows:

1. The practice of living under the guidance of a teacher.
2. The work of learning the doctrine.
3. The work of inquiring into the meaning of doctrines learnt.
4. The act of listening to the doctrine at suitable times.
5. The work of inquiring into what are and what are not causes.

Through dependence on these five things or through resorting to these five expedients the element of delusion (*moha-dhātu*)[7] is eliminated.

In this way also a bhikkhu's delusion is eliminated: When he, while learning too, becomes energetic through the thought: The teacher punishes him who does not learn at the proper time, him who does not recite well and him who does not recite at all.

In this way also a bhikkhu's delusion is eliminated: When he, while inquiring from esteemed and respected bhikkhus, after going into their presence: "Reverend Sir, how is this? What does this mean?" dispels doubts. In this way also, a bhikkhu's delusion is eliminated: When to him the meaning of various passages becomes clear while listening carefully to the doctrine, after going to a place where the doctrine is expounded to the public.

In this way also a bhikkhu's delusion is eliminated: While he becomes expert in discerning the cause of a thing from what is not its cause saying thus: "This is the reason for this; this not the reason."

Further, unskilful thoughts are surely eliminated in one practising by any one of the thirty-eight subjects of meditation; but the lust, hatred and delusion which are eliminated by their direct opposites, by what is contrary to them, namely these five objects (or practical methods) are thoroughly eliminated.

It is like this: a fire may surely be put out after its being struck with firebrands, earth and branches, but when it is extinguished with water which is directly opposed to it, it is extinguished well. In the same way the lust, hatred and delusion which is eliminated with these five objects (*pañca nimittāni*, mentioned at

7. *Moha-dhātu* is just *moha* (*ṭīkā*).

the beginning of the discourse) are eliminated well. Therefore, it should be understood, were these stated.

> *Becomes energetic* (*yatta-paṭiyatto*). The bhikkhu who is possessed of the desire for things like the asking of permission to go to the village becomes energetic (*yatto*) and active (*sajjito*).
>
> *The meaning of various passages becomes clear* (*tesu tesu ṭhānesu attho pākaṭo hoti*) = to one listening to the doctrine the meaning of different passages explained becomes clear with the comprehension thus: "Here, virtue is expounded, here concentration; here wisdom."
>
> *Expert in discerning the cause of a thing from what is not its cause* (*ṭhānāṭhānā vinicchaye cheko*) by knowing for instance that the eye, visible object, light and so forth are the reasons for eye-consciousness and not for ear-consciousness.

Connected with skill (*kusalūpasaṃhitaṃ*). Dependent on skill, become a condition of skill.

Just within (*ajjhattikaṃ eva*). Just inside the pasture (*gocarajjhattikam eva*), that is, just within the resort, the subject-of-meditation of the bhikkhu devoted to the higher consciousness.

Carpenter (*palagaṇḍho*) = joiner (*vaḍḍhaki*).

With a fine peg (*sukhumāya āṇiyam*). A peg of heartwood, finer than some peg one wishes to take out (or draw out) of a board (*yaṃ āṇiṃ niharitukāmo hoti, tato sukhumatarāya sāradaru āṇiyā*).

Coarse peg (*olārikāṃ āṇiṃ*). An incongruous peg in a board or plank of sandalwood or of a heartwood (of sandal) (*candanaphalake vā sāraphalake va ākotitaṃ visamāniṃ*).

> *In a board* (*or plank*) *of ... heartwood* (*sāraphalake*) = in a plank of sandal heartwood (*candanamaye sāraphalake*).
>
> *An incongruous peg* (*visamāṇim*) = a peg standing incompatibly there, in a board or plank of sandalwood (*visamākārena tattha thitaṃ āṇim*).

The mind of the bhikkhu intent on the higher consciousness is like the plank of sandal heartwood; the unskilful thoughts are like the incongruous peg: the skilful object of meditation on things such as the unlovely which is different from the object producing unskilfulness is like the fine peg. The removal of unskiflul objects such as the meditation on the unlovely is like the removal of the coarse with the fine peg.

If the yogin who, like a person shocked by the carcase slung round his neck by an enemy who has brought it (*paccatthikena ānetvā kaṇṭhe baddhena*), thinks wisely, by himself, of these unskilful thoughts as blamable and productive of suffering, in many ways, the unskilful thoughts are eliminated in him.

> *In many ways* (*imināpi imināpi kāraṇena*). These thoughts are blamable and productive of suffering in many ways because of their being produced through unskilfulness (*akosallasambhūtatāya*); because of their being opposed to skill (*kusalapaṭipakkhatāya*); becasue of their unhealthiness through being afflicted with the disease of sense-desire called worldliness (*gehasita-rogena sarogatāya*); becasue of their being subject to the censure of the wise (*viññugarahitabbatāya*); because of their loathsomeness (*jigucchatāya*); because of the unpleasantness of their results (*anitthaphalatāya*); and because of their nature of bringing about no satisfaction (*nirassādasaṃvattaniyatāya*).

But he who is unable to think wisely by himself should see his teacher and tell the teacher about the troubles (in meditation). Or he should see his preceptor, a respected fellow-bhikkhu or the chief of the order for the same purpose. Or he should ring the bell (or strike the gong), assemble even the order of bhikkhus and inform the order of the troubles (in meditation). For, at a meeting of many persons, there surely will be one learned man who will explain to him who is troubled: "Thus should the disadvantages of these thoughts be understood," or he will check these thoughts of the person troubled in meditation with the talk that is intended for the removal of desire for the body (*kāyavicchandanīya kathā*) and so forth.

Should endeavour to be without attention and reflection (*asati-amanasikāro āpajjitabbo*). Those unskilful thoughts should just not be remembered, not be dwelt upon. One should be occupied with something else.

Just as a man who does not want to see a certain object, shuts his eyes, just so should the bhikkhu in whom an unskilful thought arises, while he is meditating on the subject of meditation to which he resorts repeatedly (*mūla-kammaṭṭhāna*) occupy himself with something else. By doing that his unskilful thought is eliminated. When that unskilful thought is eliminated he should again sit down to meditate on the subject of meditation he is keeping to, the preliminary object of meditation to which he repeatedly resorts (*mūla-kammaṭṭhāna*).

If the unskilful thought is not eliminated, he should recite aloud some composition of doctrinal explanation he knows by heart. If when being occupied with something else in this way, too, it is not eliminated, he should take out from his bag a manual, if he has one, in which the virtues of the Buddha and the Doctrine are written and by reading it occupy himself with something else.

If by that, too, it is not eliminated, he should take out of the bag such things like the pair of fire-sticks and by turning his attention to them, saying, "This is the upper fire-stick, this is the lower," and so forth occupy himself with something else.

If by that, too, it is not eliminated, he should, having taken out the receptacle (*sipāṭika*), by contemplating the requisites thus: "This is the awl; this is the pair of scissors; this is the nail-cutter; this is the needle." occupy himself with something else.

If by that, too, it is not eliminated, he should occupy himself with something else by darning the worn-out parts of the robe. So long as the unskilful thought is not eliminated, he should by doing various skilful actions occupy himself with something else. When it is eliminated he should again sit down to meditate on the subject he is keeping to (the preliminary object to which he resorts repeatedly).

> *Composition of doctrinal explanation* (*dhammakathā pabandha*) = a composition helpful to the subject-of-meditation (*kammaṭṭhānassa upakāro dhammakathā pabandho*).
>
> *Manual* (*muṭṭhipotthako*, lit: fist-book, a hand-book). A book carried about and which is about the size of the fist (hand).
>
> *By contemplating* (*samannāmentena*) = by concentrating (*samannāharantena*).

But building work (erecting new buildings and repairing of old ones etc). should not be begun. Why? Because when the unskilful thought is destroyed there will be no time for reflection on the subject-of-meditation. But wise ones of old (*porāṇakā paṇḍitā*) destroyed unskilful thought having done building work too (*nava kammāni pana na paṭṭhāpetabbaṃ; kasmā? vitakke pacchinne kammaṭṭhāna-manasikārassa okāso na hoti*).

> (*There will be*) *no time* (*okāso na hoti*) because of the making complete (or bringing to completion) of what is begun (*āraddhassa pariyosāpetabbato*). The bringing to an end of what is begun or not beginning (not starting some new work) is the counsel of the elder (*āraddhassa antagamanaṃ anārabbho vā'ti theravādo*).

This is a story connected with building activity. The preceptor (*upajjhāya*) of Tissa and a novice, it is said was staying at the great monastery of the city of Tissa (Tissamahāvihāra; in Southeast Sri Lanka).

"Reverend Sir," said the novice to the preceptor, "I am dissatisfied." Then the elder said to the novice: "Water for bathing is scarce in this monastery. Take me to Cittalapabbata (Cittala Hill)." The novice did that. There (at Cittalapabbata) the Thera told him: "This monastery is very largely property made over to the use of the Order as a whole (*saṅghika*). Make me a personal dwelling place."

"Good, Reverend Sir," said the novice. He began to do three things at once: the learning of the Saṃyutta Nikāya from the beginning; the clearing of a cave on a hill; and work on the preliminary stage of practice on the meditation on fire (*tejokasiṇa-parikamma*). He reached absorption in the subject-of-meditation, learned the Saṃyutta Nikāya to the end, and finished clearing the cave. Having done all, he informed the preceptor about the completion of the tasks, The preceptor said: "Novice, it was done by you with difficulty. Today you yourself first stay there."

The novice, while staying that night in the cave (he had cleared), having obtained suitable weather conditions, developed insight, reached arahatship and passed away, just there (*tattheva parinibbāyi*).

Having taken his bones (*dhātuyo*), they (the people) built a shrine. To this day that shrine is known as the shrine of the elder Tissa (*Tissattheracetiyanti paññāyati*).

While exerting himself in clearing the cave just to check unskilful thoughts, in reciting the Saṃyutta Nikāya, and in the practice of the preparatory part of the meditation on the fire-device for doing the work that precedes the function of seeing the truth through Stream-winning, he accumulated the merit of the three kinds of skilful action of body, speech and mind.

The elder said: "Water for bathing is scarce in this monastery. Take me to Cittalapabbata" having known the novice's latent tendency (to good) and his particular meditation-device. Therefore, everything was effected according to his intention (*Thero tassa āsayaṃ kasiṇañca savisesam jānitvā imasmiṃ vihārehi ādiṃ avoca. Tenasā yathādhippāyaṃ sabbaṃ sampāditaṃ*).

This is called the section dealing with "non-attention" on account of the explanation in it of the manner of checking the flow of unskilful thoughts by not attending to them (*asatipabbaṃ nāma asatiyā vitakka-niggahaṇa-vibhāvanato*).

He again said: "If evil unskilful thoughts continue to arise in a bhikkhu" and so forth in order to set forth the section of "inquiry into the source of the unskilful thoughts" (*vitakka-mūla-bheda-pabbaṃ*).

The section of inquiry into the source of the unskilful thoughts is the making clear of the source of the source of unskilful thoughts (*vitakka-mūlassa tammūlassa ca bheda-vibhāvanaṃ*).

He should reflect on the removal of the thought source of those unskilful thoughts (*vitakka-saṅkhāra saṇṭhānaṃ manasikātabbaṃ*).

What is forming is formation (*saṅkhāro'ti saṅkhāro*), condition (*paccayo*), cause (*kāraṇaṃ*), source (*mūlaṃ*), is the meaning (*attho*). That state in which there is stopping or ending is stopping or ending (*santiṭṭhati etthā ti saṇṭhānaṃ*). (Removal is the stopping or ending of a thing in the sense of getting rid of it.)

This is stated: What is the cause of this unskilful thought? What is its condition? By what reason has it arisen? Thinking thus, the source of the unskilful thoughts and the source of the source should be reflected on by the yogin.

Just as if, bhikkhus, a man should walk fast, and then to him it should occur thus: "But why do I walk fast? Now, let me walk slowly." And as if, then, he should walk slowly and it should occur to him thus: "Why do I walk slowly? Now let me stand." (*Seyyathāpi bhikkhave puriso sīghaṃ gaccheyya tassa evamassa kinnukho ahaṃ sīghaṃ gacchāmi yannunāhaṃ saṇikaṃ gaccheyyanti so saṇikaṃ gaccheyya, tassa evamassa kinnu kho ahaṃ saṇikaṃ gaccheyya, tassa evamassa kinnu kho ahaṃ saṇikaṃ gacchāmi yannunāhaṃ tiṭṭheyyan'ti.*) (The above is paraphrased in the translation of the discourse as follows: "Just as a man finding no reason for walking fast walks slowly: finding no reason for walking slowly, stands.")

"But why do I walk fast": owing to what reason (or cause) do I walk fast?

"Now let me walk slowly": He thinks thus: "What profit is there to me by this fast walking? I shall walk slowly."

"And as if, then, he should walk slowly"; as if he, having thought in the foregoing way, should walk slowly. This is the method of explanation throughout (this simile).

The man's walking fast is comparable to the bhikkhu's entry into the state of unskilful thinking; the walking slowly, to the cutting off of unskilful thought-conduct (*vitakka-cāra*);[8] the standing, to the descent of the subject-of-meditation into the bhikkhu's mind, with the cutting off of unskilful thought-conduct; the sitting down to the attainment of arahatship through the development of insight; the lying down, to passing the day in the attainment of the fruit that has Nibbāna for its object.

In him, who goes to (find) the source and the source of that source of unskilful thoughts questioning himself thus: "Possessed of what cause, due to what condition, are the unskilful thoughts?" there is a slackening of unskilful thoughts. (Owing to an access of energy) when the slackening of unskilful thought conduct reaches its highest point, unskilful thoughts are entirely dissolved (*vitakkā sabbaso nirujjhanti*).

---

8. Might also be translated as "unskilful thought-movement or unskilful mental behaviour or conduct".

What produces unskilful thoughts is the source of unskilful thought (*vitakkaṃ saṅkhāroti vitakka-saṅkhāro*). It is the condition for unskilful thoughts (*vitakka-paccayo*), (and that condition is) unwise reflection (even) on the sensuously favourable etc. taking them as lovely etc. (*subhanimitādisu pi subhādinā ayoniso manasikāro*).

The state, indeed, by which the production of unskilful thoughts ends is called (the ending or) the removal of the source of unskilful thought (*so pana vitakka-saṅkhāro santiṭṭhati ettha'ti vitakka-saṅkhāra-saṇṭhānaṃ*). The source of unskilful thought is the delusion of perceiving unlovely things and so forth as lovely and so forth (*asubhe subhanti ādi saññāvipallāso*). Therefore it is said: the source, and the source of that source, of thoughts should be reflected on (*tenāha vitakkānaṃ mūlañca mūlamūlañca manasikātabbaṃ*).

In him who goes to (find) the source of unskilful thoughts (*vitakkānaṃ mūlaṃ gacchantassa*) = in him who goes along the domain of knowledge, by way of investigation, to the root of wrong thoughts, to the cause of their arising (*upaparikkhana-vasena micchā vitakkānaṃ mūlaṃ, uppati-kāraṇaṃ ñāṇa-gatiyā gacchantassa*).

There is a slackening of unskilful thought-conduct (*vitakkacāro sithilo hoti*). In him who knows according to reality, unskilful thoughts do not continuously proceed, as in the time before be knew truly (*yathāvato jānantassa pubbe viya abhiṇhaṃ nappavattanti*).

When the slackening of unskilful thought-conduct reaches its highest point (*tasmiṃ sithilibhūte matthakaṃ gacchante*), through arriving at a stable state, gradually (*anukkamena thirabhāvappattiyā*).

Unskilful thoughts are entirely dissolved (*vitakkā sabbaso nirujjhanti*). Even all wrong thoughts go, do not assail one or owing to the completion of the meditation are eliminated without remainder (*micchā vitakkā sabbe pi gacchanti, na samudācaranti bhāvanā pāripuriyā va anavasesā pahīyanti.*

The meaning should be brought out through the "Daddabha birth-story."

It is said that a ripe bael fruit having been cut off from its stalk, fell close to the ear of a hare which was asleep at the foot of the bael tree. Getting up on hearing that noise, it thought: "The earth is being destroyed," and fled. The other beasts which were in front of him, fled, too, seeing the hare's flight.

At that time the Bodhisatta was a lion and he thought: "The earth is destroyed at the end of an aeon (*kappavināse*). In the interval (between the beginning and the end of an aeon) there is no destruction of the earth. Now, let me after going from source to source (*mūlā mūlaṃ gantvā*) find out (*anuvijjeyyaṃ*)."

The lion questioned each animal separately beginning with the elephant. When he came to the hare, he asked: "Dear, did you see the earth being destroyed?" The hare: "Yes, lord." The lion: "Come, friend, show." The hare, "I am not able, sire." Saying, "Hey, come; don't fear," the lion using gentle speech alternately with firm speech (*taddha-mudukena*) took the hare along with him.

The hare standing not far from the bael tree said: "May there be blessing to thee! In that place in which I stayed, it echoed. I do not know why it echoed."

The Bodhisatta told the hare: "You stay here," and went up to the tree. He saw where the hare had lain, saw the ripe (fallen) bael fruit and looking upwards saw the fruit-stalk from which the fruit had fallen and concluded as follows: "This hare whilst lying asleep here got the idea that the earth was being destroyed when he heard the sound of the fruit that fell near his ear." Then he questioned the hare to see if the facts he had found out were true. The hare said: "Yes, lord," confirming the lion's conclusions. The lion, thereupon, uttered this stanza:

> "The hare ran, after hearing the echoing sound of the bael fruit that fell;
>
> Having listened to the hare's words, the army of frightened beasts ran."

After that the Bodhisatta comforted the beasts saying: "Don't fear." Thus unskilful thoughts are eliminated in him who goes (investigating things) from source to source.

> It is said that beneath the place where the hare was sleeping there was a huge rat hole—a big excavation made by rats—and

that the fruit falling on the ground above it caused a loud sound (*tassa kira sasakassa heṭṭhā mahāmūsikāhi khatamahāvātaṃ umaṅgasadisaṃ ahosi; tenassa pātena mahāsaddo ahosi*).

With the repetition of the words, "If evil unskilful thoughts continue to arise," the Master points out to the bhikkhu who fails to check the unskilful thoughts according to the instruction in the section of inquiring into the source of unskilful thoughts, another method.

With clenched teeth (*dantehi dantaṃ ādhāya*). The upper teeth placed on the lower.

The mind by the mind (*cetasā cittaṃ*). The unskilful state of mind should be checked by the skilful state of mind.

Strong man (*balavā puriso*). Just as if a brawny man—a person with great physical strength—should, having caught hold of a weaker one by head or body, restrain, subdue and beat down that weaker person—make him wearied, exhausted and to faint—just so, should the unskilful thoughts be checked by the bhikkhu who wrestles with the unskilful thoughts, having overcome them saying, "Who are you and who am I," and after whipping up great, energy saying, "Let the flesh and blood of this body dry up; let skin sinews and bones, remain." To point out the foregoing meaning, the Master gave the simile of the strong man.

> *By the skilful state of mind* (*kusala-cittena*) = by means of the mind associated with right thinking (*balavā sammā-saṅkappa-sampayuttena*).
>
> *The unskilful state of mind* (*akusala-cittaṃ*) = the unskilful state of mind with such things like sensual thought (*kāmavitakka-ādisahitaṃ*).
>
> *Should be checked* (*abhiniggahitabbaṃ*). Should after overcoming be checked. Thus: in such a way that in the future no unskilful thoughts assail the bhikkhu. The state of the non-arising of things should be produced is the meaning (*yathā taṃ āyatiṃ samudācāro na hoti evaṃ, abhibhāvitvā niggahetabbaṃ anuppatti-dhammatā āpadetabbā ti attho*).

When, indeed, Bhikkhus (*yato kho bhikkhave*). This is called the division of summing up (*pariyādānabhājaniyaṃ nāma*). The meaning of the phrase is even clear (*uṭṭhāna-mattameva*).[9]

> The division of that which was pointed out from the beginning thus: "Five things should be reflected on from time to time, by the bhikkhu who is intent on the higher consciousness," by way of the (taking up completely) summing up of the time of reflection of his object mentioned in the passage.

As a teacher of archery[10] having taught the art of the five weapons to a prince come from a foreign country spurs him on thus: "Go and take up the rulership of your country," after showing him what ought to be done with the five weapons thus: "If robbers meet you on the way, use the bow; if that is destroyed or broken, use the spear, the sword ... and go (free)." And having done this, having gone to his own country and taken up the rulership, the prince enjoys the fortune of sovereignty.

In just the same way the Blessed One taught what is in these five sections while spurring on the bhikkhu intent on the higher consciousness towards the realization of saintship.

If to the bhikkhu who is intent on the higher consciousness objects productive of unskilfulness (*akusalanimitta*) arise during his meditation he, having established himself in the instruction of the section of "the "different object" (*añña-nimitta-pabba*) and checked those unskilful thoughts, he will reach saintship after developing insight; unable to do it in that way, he will do it by the instruction of the section on disadvantages (*adīnava-pabba*); unable to do it in that way he will do it by the instruction of the section on non-attention and non-reflection (*asati-amanasikāra-pabba*); unable to do it in that way too, by the instruction of the section of searching the cause (*mūla-bheda-pabba*): unable to do it in that way too, by the instruction of the section of restraining (*abhiniggaṇhaṇa-pabba*) he will develop insight and reach saintship.

9. The commentary to the Sabbāsava Sutta, Majjima Nikāya No. 2, has the following comment on "*yato kho bhikkhavo.*" The "*to*" of "*yato*" is gen. in sense. "*Yato kho*"—"*yassa kho*" (of whom). That is said (by the commentator). But the ancient teachers (*porāṇā*) explain it by "in which time," when or what time (*yamhi kāle*).

10. *Satthācariyo'ti dhanubhedācariyo* (*ṭīkā*)—a master of weapon is a teacher of the knowledge of archery.

He is called a master of the paths taken by the courses of thought (*vasī vitakkapariyāya-pathesu*). He is called one who is an expert of control in the paths taken by the course of thoughts, one who is conversant with the art of control in the paths taken by the courses of thought (*vitakka-cārapathesu ciṇṇavasī paguṇavasī ti vuccati*).

The thought he wants (to think) (*yaṃ vitakkaṃ ākaṅkhissati*). This was said to show his expertness of control. Formerly he was not able to think as he wanted and thought what he did not want to think about. Now, owing to his expertness in the control of thought, he is able to think as he wishes. Therefore it was said: The thoughts he will want to think, those thoughts he will think. The thoughts he will not want to think, those thoughts he will not think.

He has cut off craving (*acchejji taṇhan'ti*). This and the rest should be understood as taught in the Sabbāsava Suttanta Commentary.

Buddha the Healer

The Mind and its Place in Buddhism

Edited by

Dr. Ānanda Nimalasuria

WHEEL PUBLICATION NO. 22

Preface

The Buddha means the Enlightened One, and is the title that was given to Siddhattha Gotama on his attaining enlightenment The religion preached by the Buddha is known as Buddhism.

Siddhattha Gotama was born on the full moon day of the month of May in the year 623 BCE in Lumbini near the Indian border of Nepal. His parents were King Suddhodana and Queen Mahāmāyā. As a prince he was brought up in the lap of luxury. At his birth a sage predicted that this prince, out of compassion for humanity, would one day leave his home in search of true happiness. He married Yasodharā, a beautiful princess, in his sixteenth year, and thirteen years later, at the time of the birth of his son, Rāhula, he renounced all his worldly possessions and left the palace to wander as an ascetic in search of happiness. He went from teacher to teacher, but was dissatisfied with them all. In the sixth year of the life of an ascetic, at the age of thirty-five years, while meditating under a Bodhi-tree at Gayā in Northern India, he realised the Supreme Truth and became the Enlightened One. He proclaimed his readiness to teach the Path of Deliverance in the words,

> "Open are the doors of the deathless,
> Let them that have ears repose trust."

His first sermon was preached at Sarnath, near Benares. It was on the four Noble Truths: the existence of unhappiness or suffering; the cause of it; that there can be an end to it; and the path that leads to the end of unhappiness or suffering. For forty-five years he preached the Path of Deliverance to all that came to hear him, from the lowliest to the highest. He established the Order of Monks (Sangha) which exists even to this day. At the age of eighty years he finally passed away at Kusināra. His last words to his followers were,

"Behold now, O monks, I exhort you: Transient are all compounded things. With heedfulness work out your deliverance."

His teachings gradually spread throughout India, and from India to Sri lanka, Burma, Thailand, Tibet, China, Japan, Indo-China and other countries. Wherever it spread Buddhism exercised a very powerful influence on the life of the people. It elevated their moral stature, stimulated art, spread education, encouraged the care of the sick and infirm, abolished slavery, established morality as the yardstick of nobility, and introduced a humanising influence over their lives. It was propagated with missionary zeal, but without compulsion or bloodshed.

Gradually, the initial fervour was lost. Nevertheless, something of the moral code remained and high ideals such as loving-kindness were woven into the fabric of the lives of the people; Buddhist philosophy and literature continued its fructifying impact. In this state the religion lay dormant for a few more centuries. It is true to say that in practically all countries of Asia, philosophy and art among the cultured and the way of life among the poor are to a great extent influenced by the teachings of the Buddha.

This present century has been marked by a revival of Buddhism. The teachings of the Buddha, which are in the Pali language and are enshrined in the collection of works known as the Tipiṭaka, are being translated into European as well as Asian languages, and many philosophers and men of religion in the world are giving thought to the teachings contained in them.

Wherein lies the appeal of Buddhism to modern man, and especially to great thinkers, philosophers and scientists? In what way does Buddhism differ from other religious?

The way of life enjoined by the Buddha is methodical and based on the three cardinal features of individual existence—impermanence, unhappiness or suffering, and soullessness or egolessness. Life consists of body and mind (*nāma-rūpa*), and there is nothing that is permanent or unchanging in either of these components. On the other hand both are themselves compounded, the former consisting of units of matter, the latter of units of mind. The units of matter are being continually replaced, and so are the units of mind, which are even more rapidly replaced; although there is continuity of the individual, there is neither permanence of mind nor matter. The second cardinal feature is unhappiness or suffering. The third is soullessness or egolessness. We all like to feel and even assert there is in us something stable, something unchanging which is our inner self, but the more we analyse it, the more we realise that there is no such entity we can call a permanent ego or a soul. The quest of man is in search of happiness, and the path of deliverance of the Buddha is based on these cardinal features of individual existence.

Buddhism's greatest appeal to modern man is its freedom from dogma. Among all leaders of religion, the Buddha alone asked his followers to accept the doctrine if it appealed to their reason and its practice brought them solace.

> "Do not go upon what has been acquired by repeated hearing; nor upon tradition; nor upon rumour; nor upon what is in a scripture; nor upon surmise; nor upon an axiom; nor upon specious reasoning; nor upon a bias towards a notion that has been pondered over; nor upon another's seeming ability; nor upon the consideration, 'The monk is our teacher.' Kālāmas, when you yourselves know: 'These things are good; these things are not blamable; these things are praised by the wise; undertaken and observed, these things lead to benefit and happiness,' enter on and abide in them."
>
> (Kālāma Sutta)

This little book entitled *Buddha the Healer* should be regarded as one of the whole series of publications undertaken by the Buddhist Publication Society with its headquarters in Kandy, Ceylon. It emphasises an aspect of Buddhism—the healing of the mind as the cure of all worldly ills. When something goes wrong and we are unhappy we are inclined to attribute it to our environment or to others. But quite often it is a wrong view that we have taken that produces unhappiness, and the correction lies more frequently in our own ways of thought than in our environment.

The Buddha has shown this on many occasions. In the articles that follow are numerous examples. They are brought together in the hope they might be of special interest to doctors and psychologists—for it is they that have a wide knowledge and understanding of human ills. It is claimed that Buddhist psychology is rational, in that it has a yardstick of morality and that it works towards the gradual uplift of the individual from the mire of emotional conflict with its centre on "Self" to a position where emphasis on sense impressions are reduced and the emphasis on self is replaced by compassion towards others as well.

Ānanda Nimalasuria

Homage to the Buddha

who rooted out and removed all diseases like lust, and so on, which cause delusion and indolence, and are spread over all living beings, sticking to them always. To that unique physician I Pay homage.

Introductory stanza to Vāgbhaṭa's manual of medicine.[1]

The Story of Kisā-Gotamī

In this Buddha era she was reborn at Sāvatthī, in a poor family. Gotamī was her name, and because of the leanness of her body, she was called "Lean Gotamī." She was disdainfully treated when married, and was called a nobody's daughter. But when she bore a son, they paid her honour. Then, when her son was old enough to run about and play, he died. She was distraught with grief. Mindful of the change in folk's treatment of her since his birth, she thought, "They will even try to take my child and throw it out." So, taking the corpse upon her hip, she went, crazy with sorrow, from door to door, saying: "Give me medicine for my child!" And people said with contempt: "Medicine! What's the use?"

She did not understand them. But one sagacious person thought: "Her mind is upset with grief for her child. He of the Tenfold Power (the Buddha) will know of some medicine for her." And he said: "Dear woman, go to the very Buddha, and ask him for medicine to give your child." She went to the monastery at the time when the Master taught the Doctrine, and said:

"Exalted One, give me medicine for my child!" The Master, seeing the potential in her, said: "Go, enter the town, and bring a little mustard seed from any house where no one has yet died."

"It is well, lord!" she said, with mind relieved; and going to the first house in the town said: "Let me take a little mustard seed that I may give as medicine to my child. If in this house no one has died yet, give me a little mustard seed."

1. Vāgbhaṭa, a Buddhist physician of medieval India, was the author of a manual of medicine called *Aṣṭāṅgahṛdayasaṃhitā*, which is still used by the students and practitioners of the Ayurvedic system of medicine.

"Who may say how many have not died here?" "With such mustard, then, I have nought to do," so she went on to a second and a third house until, by the might of the Buddha, her frenzy left her, her natural mind was restored and she thought: "Even this will be the order of things in the whole town."

"The Exalted One foresaw this out of his pity for my good." And, thrilled at the thought, she left the town and laid her child at the charnelfield, saying:

"No village law is this, no city law,
No law for this clan, or for that alone;
For the whole world—ay, and the gods in heaven—
This is the law: All is impermanent!"

So saying, she went to the Master. And he said: "Gotamī, have you gotten the little mustard seed?" And she said: "The work, Lord, of the little mustard seed has been done. Give me your confirmation." Then the Master spoke thus:

"To him whose heart on children and on goods
Is centred, cleaving to them in his thoughts,
Death comes like a great flood in the night,
Bearing away the village in its sleep."

When he had spoken, she was confirmed in the fruition of the First (the Stream-entry) Path, and asked for ordination. He consented, and she, thrice saluting him by the right, went to the Bhikkhunīs (nuns), and was ordained. And not long afterwards, studying the causes of things, she caused her insight to grow. Then the Master said an inspired verse:

"The man who, living for an hundred years,
Beholds never the Ambrosial Path
Had better live no longer than one day,
So he beholds within that day the Path."

When he had finished, she attained Arahantship (Sainthood).

(From the Commentary to the Therigāthā [*Songs of the Sisters*].)

The Peerless Physician

by
Dr. C. B. Dharmasena, M.B., B.S. (Lond.)

"Subject to birth, old age, disease,
Extinction will I seek to find
Where no decay is ever known,
Nor death, but all security."[2]

The Buddha was the peerless physician. He it was who recognised the fatal malady affecting all sentient beings, to which he gave the name dukkha or suffering. It constitutes the first of the Four Noble Truths described by him.[3] The diagnosis is not difficult for the expert psychiatrist, who however has an extremely difficult task before him to convince his "patient" that he is really ill.

Avijjā or ignorance, and *taṇhā* or craving, are the root causes of the disease; this is the second of the Four Noble Truths.

Dukkha nirodha or cessation of ignorance and craving constitutes the prognosis; and this is the third of the Four Noble Truths. The prognosis is excellent provided the necessary effort to acquire the details of the prolonged and difficult course of treatment is forthcoming, and the treatment itself is carried out with enthusiasm, with diligence, with constant mindfulness, and with wisdom. The cure once achieved is complete and permanent, without complications, and without the possibility of a relapse.

Dukkhanirodhagāmini paṭipadā or the Noble Eightfold Path is the detailed course of treatment which leads to the cessation of all suffering. It forms the last of the Four Noble Truths.

Symptoms and Diagnosis

The key to the diagnosis of this universal malady is offered to us by the Buddha when he says,[4]

---

2. W. "The Story of Sumedha." Ch. 1. (18).
3. SN 56:11/S V 420, vide footnote 2 page 4; DN 22 & MN 141.
4. *Path to Deliverance*, Ven. Ñāṇatiloka, Introduction, para 16: A IV 182.

> "Four things, O monks, nobody can bring about, no ascetic, priest, or heavenly being, no god nor devil, nor anybody in this world. And what are these four things? That that which is subject to decay may not decay, that that which is subject to sickness may not fall sick, that that which is subject to death may not die, that those evil, impure, frightful, and pain-bestowing actions, which ever again and again lead to rebirth, old age and death may not bring results."

The Buddha in his very first sermon after his Enlightenment[5] and on many other occasions[6] said,

> "Now, this, O Bhikkhus, is the Noble Truth of Suffering: Birth is suffering, decay (ageing) is suffering, disease is suffering, death is suffering, to be united to the unloved is suffering, to be separated from the loved is suffering, not to receive what one craves for is suffering, in brief the five Aggregates of attachment are suffering."

All conditioned things are impermanent, because of their continued rise and fall and change; what is impermanent is painful because of continued oppression, for the pain commencing to be felt in any body posture adopted at the moment is concealed by repeated change into a fresh position.[7] The knowledge that all conditioned things are transient and are therefore subject to suffering is the pivot on which Buddhism rests. Buddhism has no meaning except for those who feel that all life is transient and therefore painful, which observation stands in natural contrast to freedom from pain, to blessedness regarded as something changeless, i.e. Nibbāna.

---

5. Dhammacakkappavattana Sutta; translation in *Bodhi Leaves* No. 12 and *The Wheel* No. 17: *Three Cardinal Discourses of the Buddha*—both issued by the Buddhist Publication Society.

6. DN 22, p. 305–315, Mahā Satipaṭṭhāna Sutta & MN 141, Sacca Vibhaṅga Sutta.

7. Vism XXI.6.7.

Cause

The root causes of this malady besetting all sentient beings are ignorance (*avijjā*) and craving (*taṇhā*); ignorance being an outstanding cause of kamma (action) that leads to unhappy destinies[8]

> "The man who lives for sensuous joys,
> And finds his delight therein
> When joys of sense have taken flight,
> Doth smart as if with arrows pierced."[9]

On the other hand craving for becoming is an outstanding cause of kamma that leads to "happy" destinies in various heaven worlds.[10]

Prognosis or Cure

The above view of life may make the unthinking reader conclude that Buddhism is a pessimistic and melancholic religion which hinders effort. But this view is a very superficial one, the very antithesis of the truth, for the Buddha has not only given the diagnosis of disease, but an infallible remedy as well. The patient is told he has an operable cancer, or is suffering from early pulmonary tuberculosis. He is further told that a definite cure is available. In these circumstances after the patient gets over the initial shock of his discovery, is he not likely to consider himself lucky that his illness has been discovered in time, and will he not thereafter cooperate with enthusiasm, and with optimism in the carrying out of his treatment? It is this optimistic expectation and calm assurance that keeps the Buddhist happy and serene in his surroundings, and makes it possible to include joy (*pīti*), as one of the seven factors of enlightenment found in Buddhism.

In dealing with the causal law formula in terms of happiness the Buddha states,[11]

> "Suffering (understood as change and transience) leads to confidence (*saddhā*); confidence to joy (*pāmojja*); joy to rapture (*pīti*); rapture to tranquillity (*passaddhi*); tranquillity

8. Vism XVII.39.
9. W. Ch. 26. c.
10. Vism XVII.40.
11. SN 12 *Introduction* page ix & SN 12:23, Upanisā sutta.

to happiness (*sukha*); happiness to concentration (*samādhi*); concentration to knowledge and vision of things as they truly are (*yathābhūtañāṇadassana*); the knowledge and vision of things as they truly are to disgust or repulsion (*nibbidā*); disgust to detachment or passionlessness (*virāga*); detachment to deliverance (*vimutti*); deliverance to knowledge of the extinction of passions (*khaye-ñāṇa*)."

The above text clearly points out "how every tear can become a tutor," how suffering and sorrow may ultimately lead to sainthood, deliverance, and happiness, even as Kisā Gotamī[12] in her distress went about asking for medicine for her dead child, until she came to the Buddha, who told her that she did well to have come to him for medicine, and requested her to go to the city and bring a mustard seed from a house where no one had died. She was cheered at this simple request, and readily went round from house to house asking for the mustard seed which, however, she could not procure under the conditions specified. She thereupon realised the truth that death was common to all, and that the Buddha in his compassion had sent her round to learn the truth, which she did to such good effect that she reached then and there the first stage of sainthood, and reached Arahatship not long after. How very different to this is Tennyson's attitude to the death of his friend, as expressed in the following lines:[13]

> "One writes, that "Other friends remain,"
> That loss is common to the race...
> That loss is common would not make
> My own less bitter, rather more."

We have in these two different attitudes towards sorrow a beautiful illustration of the truth that the results of sorrow depend solely on the attitude that one takes towards suffering and pain; sorrow merely experienced is pain and suffering, whilst on the other hand sorrow understood, through meditative contemplation, is change and transience leading to disgust, to passionlessness, to detachment and finally to deliverance. This is the fundamental difference between the hasty critic of Buddhism

12. See above.
13. *In Memoriam*, VI, Alfred Tennyson.

as a pessimistic religion, and the one who makes a genuine effort to understand sorrow. The Buddha does not deny that there is pleasure derived through the senses, but he warns us,[14] that such pleasures are temporary, and quite insignificant by comparison with the numerous dangers and perils involved in the indulgence in sense-pleasures.

Further, in the Bahuvedanīya Sutta,[15] whilst admitting that there is happiness in sense-pleasures, the Buddha adds there is other happiness more excellent and more exquisite. This happiness may be enjoyed by the one who relinquishes the coarse pleasures of the senses, and by meditative development of concentration (*samādhi*) attains the first *jhāna* (absorption or musing). Thereafter are seven further grades of happiness, each one more excellent and more exquisite than its predecessor; e.g. the second, third, and the fourth *rūpa-jhānas* (absorptions of the fine material sphere), and the first, second, third and fourth *arūpa-jhānas* (absorptions of the immaterial sphere).

Still further in the Aṭṭhakanāgara Sutta,[16] in reply to a question repeated over and over again by the householder Dasama of Aṭṭhaka, as to whether there is any one thing pointed out by the Buddha, whereby if a bhikkhu dwells diligent, ardent and self-resolute, his mind is freed, and he attains the destruction of the cankers, and the matchless security from the bonds, the Venerable Ānanda answers in the affirmative and adds,

> "A bhikkhu detached from the pleasures of the senses, detached from unskilled states of the mind, enters and enjoys the happiness, excellent and exquisite, of the first *rūpa-jhāna*, of the second, of the third, or of the fourth *rūpa-jhāna*, or likewise he enters and enjoys the more and more exquisite happiness of the *arūpa-jhānas*, or likewise he dwells having suffused the whole world, everywhere, in every way with friendliness (*mettā*) or with compassion (*karuṇā*), with sympathetic joy (*muditā*), or with equanimity (*upekkhā*); and attains the freedom of the mind that is friendliness, that is compassion, that is sympathetic joy, or that is equanimity.

14. MN 13 and 14 Mahā and Cūla Dukkhakkhandha Suttas.
15. MN 59.
16. MN 52.

> Having reached any one of these high states, the bhikkhu by reflection comprehends that the happiness of each one of these states, however excellent, however exquisite it may be, is effected, is thought out, is impermanent, and is liable to stopping. Firm in this conviction the bhikkhu attains the matchless security, not yet attained, from the bonds."

In other words the thoughtful disciple, although he enjoys the bliss of *jhānas* in this life, assesses such happiness at its true worth, and does not hanker after rebirth in the celestial worlds which would make him wander from the straight path, away from his final goal of Nibbāna. Buddhism is unique in that the happiness provided for those who reach their goal may be experienced by the one who so wishes it, here and now in the state known as *samāpatti-phala*, without the necessity to wait until his death.

> "This too is an attainment which
> A Noble One may cultivate;
> The peace it gives is recorded as
> Nibbāna here and now."[17]

Treatment

Whatever definition critics may give to the words religion and philosophy it is certain that Buddhism is a way of life to be lived energetically and actively from day to day, not a subject for mere academic study, discussion or debate; for the Buddha is the all-compassionate healer, and we are his patients. His only concern is to cure his patients and not to satisfy their curiosity, or solve for them the riddle of the universe. Accordingly his main concern is first to convince his patient that he is really ill and that his illness is of a serious nature. This is no easy task.

> "For in the fatness of these pursy times
> Virtue itself of vice must pardon beg,
> Yea, curb and woo for leave to do him good."[18]

---

17. Vism XXIII.8.30, 31, and 52. *Buddhist Dictionary*, Ven. Ñāṇatiloka, entry on *nirodha samāpatti*.

18. *Hamlet* III iv (153-155)

The task becomes still more difficult if his patient is a young adult, enjoying good physical health and is well provided with the comforts of life; for in such an event the symptoms of his illness are hardly noticeable; moreover there are long periods of apparent remissions in between such symptoms as may occasionally strike him as abnormal.

> "Sorrow disguised as joy, the hateful as the loved,
> Pain in the form of bliss the heedless overwhelms."[19]

In these circumstances the chances are he will not even see a physician until the disease is far advanced. Second, the Buddha inspires in his patient hope, confidence, and enthusiasm born of personal knowledge and conviction that a complete cure is definitely possible, although prolonged, difficult, irksome, and perhaps painful. He explains the necessity quite early in the course of his treatment, requiring a clear conception of his illness and the outlines of its treatment as is compatible with the current level of each patient's understanding, and for periodically improving upon that knowledge, so that the patient may follow this difficult course of treatment uninterruptedly, intelligently and with enthusiasm throughout the various stages into which it is divided. Over and over again, and in various ways suited to the intelligence of his particular audience the Buddha emphasised the basis of his doctrine as consisting of these four Noble Truths:[20] the Noble Truth of Suffering, of the Origin of Suffering, of the Extinction of Suffering, and of the Path leading to the Extinction of Suffering.

Numerous are the occasions on which the Buddha uttered the following words:[21]

> "It is through not understanding, not penetrating these four Noble Truths, O Bhikkhus, that we have had to wander so long in this weary round of rebirths, both you and I" And, "By not seeing the Noble Truths as they really are, long is the path that is traversed through many a birth; when these are grasped, the cause of rebirth is removed, the root of sorrow uprooted, and then there is no more birth."

19. Udāna 2.8.
20. Vide footnote 2, page 1.
21. DN 16, Ch. II 2.3: Ch. 4.2.

The necessity for this emphasis even during the lifetime of the Buddha was amply demonstrated; for he had, on various occasions to send for a disciple who had misunderstood his doctrine and was spreading heretical dogmas, and subsequently to point out his error. Even today we find well-meaning Buddhists stating that the Four Noble Truths are a great stumbling block in the way of non-Buddhists, even suggesting that they do not form a part of the original teaching, but are a later accretion by the monks. Says the Buddha,[22] "One thing only do I teach, that is sorrow, and escape from sorrow." And again,[23] "Just as the mighty ocean is of one flavour, the flavour of salt; even so, O bhikkhus, the doctrine is of one flavour, the flavour of deliverance." There is certainly no room for ambiguity or cause for misunderstanding in the above language.

Further the Buddha has always emphasised that a man can only reap what he himself has sown, whilst on the other hand he was not bound to reap all he has sown; for says the Buddha in the Aṅguttara Nikāya,[24] "If anyone says that a man must reap according to his deeds, in that case there is no religious life, nor is an opportunity afforded for the entire extinction of sorrow."

The Buddha has therefore made it clear that vicarious sacrifice by another can never secure one's salvation, and that on the other hand any kind of fatalism or predestination has no place in his doctrine. Medical and scientific men who have been trained to observe will not find the teaching of the Buddha likely to do violence to their training, or their habit of drawing scientific deductions from their observations. In Buddhism there is no Divine Power, or Divine Revelation, nor is there a belief in dogmas, or in supernatural occurrences necessary for the "patient" to commence his treatment, nor is the result of the treatment dependent on the caprice and approval of a Divine Being. The following lines:[25]

> "Strong Son of God, immortal Love,
> Whom we, that have not seen thy face,
> By faith, and faith alone, embrace,
> Believing where we cannot prove"

---

22. MN 22; N. Ch. IX, last page.
23. Udāna 5.5.
24. AN 3:99/A I 249; N. Ch. XV, first page.
25. *In Memoriam*, Alfred Tennyson, the opening lines.

have no place in Buddhism, nor do the following words cause any misgiving, or hold any terror for the Buddhist:[26]

> "Though justice be thy plea, consider this,
> That in the course of justice none of us
> Should see salvation"

The Buddha guarantees a lasting cure for every one of his patients, who persists in his course of treatment; not as a result of his intervention, except as a guide who merely shows the way; nor as the result of any Divine Grace; but only as the logical consequence of the treatment followed by the patient himself. The beginner in Buddhism is attracted to the Buddha even as a sick man who hears of others being cured goes to the physician, and makes up his mind to follow the course of treatment prescribed by the latter, though at first his faith in the physician may not amount to much.

Faith in Buddhism really begins with knowledge based on probable evidence. It develops with progress in morality (*sīla*), and increases rapidly with progress in concentration (*samādhi*), until complete confidence is gained through progress in the meditative development of understanding (*paññā*). The Buddha does not expect from his followers a blind respect, or admiration for himself, or for his doctrine. Says the Buddha,[27]

> "Do not accept anything on the mere fact that it has been handed down by tradition, or just because it is in one's scriptures, or merely because it agrees with one's preconceived notions, or because the speaker seems to be a good and respected person and his words should be accepted; when, Kālāmas, you know for yourselves these things are moral, these things are blameless, these things are praised by the wise; these things when performed and undertaken conduce to well-being and happiness, then do you live acting accordingly."

And again when Upāli a celebrated follower of another religious teacher was once so pleased with the exposition of the

26. *Merchant of Venice*. IV. 1 (197-200).
27. AN 3:65/A I 188ff. See *The Wheel* No. 8: *Kālāma Sutta* (Buddhist Publication Society).

Buddha's doctrine that he wished to become a follower, the Buddha cautioned him with these words,[28]

> "Of a verity, householder, make a thorough investigation. It is well for a distinguished man like you to first make a thorough investigation." Upāli's admiration at this unexpected request expressed itself in the following words, "Lord, if I had become the follower of another teacher, his followers would have taken me round the streets in procession proclaiming that such and such a millionaire had renounced his former religion and embraced theirs. The more pleased am I with this remark of yours."

Or again the Buddha questions,[29]

> "A man comes by a great stretch of water, and sees no way of crossing to the opposite shore, which is safe and secure, and so he makes an improvised raft out of sticks, branches, leaves and grass, and utilises it to cross over to the opposite shore. Suppose now, O bhikkhus, he were to say 'this raft has been useful to me, I will therefore put it on my head and proceed on my journey,' will he be doing what should be done with the raft?" "No, Lord," say the bhikkhus in reply; and the Buddha himself gives the obvious answer, and adds, "Even so, O bhikkhus, the doctrine taught by me, is for crossing over, and not for retaining."

The doctrine of the Buddha is clearly meant for daily practice, and not for mere academic discussion, nor for staring in a museum for relics as a mark of veneration and respect for its founder. Two final illustrations of the fact that the Buddha did not expect a blind admiration:[30]

> "Bhikkhus, if outsiders should speak against me, or against the Doctrine, or the Order you should not on that account either bear malice or suffer hatred, or feel ill-will, for if you feel angry and displeased you will not be able to judge how far that speech of theirs is well said or ill."

28. MN 56. Translated in The Wheel No. 98/99.
29. MN 22, Alagaddūpama sutta; translated in *The Wheel* No 48/49.
30. DN 1.1.5. The Brahmajāla sutta,

And his unique declaration, made by no other founder of a religion, to the effect that any one of his disciples may if he so desires become a Buddha himself.

The essence of the treatment consists of the Noble Eightfold Path (*aṭṭhaṅgika-magga*), which forms the last of the Four Noble Truths. No attempt is made in this essay to give anything more than the briefest reference to each of the eight links of the path, which consist of:

Wisdom (*paññā*)

1. Right Understanding (*sammā-diṭṭhi*)
2. Right Thoughts (*sammā-saṅkappa.*)

Morality (*sīla*)

3. Right Speech (*sammā-vācā*)
4. Right Action (*sammā-kammanta*)
5. Right Livelihood (*sammā-ājīva*)

Concentration (*samādhi*)

6. Right Endeavour (*sammā-vāyāma*)
7. Right Mindfulness (*sammā-sati*)
8. Right Concentration (*sammā-samādhi*)

Right Understanding is the penetration of the truth of the universality of suffering, its origin, its cure, and its treatment. Right Thoughts are threefold: thoughts free from sensuous desire, from ill-will, and from cruelty, replacing them with thoughts of renunciation of sensuous desires (*nekkhamma*), of loving-kindness (*mettā*), and of compassion (*karuṇā*). Right Speech is abstention from lying, tale bearing, harsh talk, and foolish babble. Right Action is abstention from killing, stealing, and unchastity. Right Livelihood is abstention from livelihood that brings harm to other beings. Right Endeavour is the effort of avoiding or overcoming evil and unwholesome things, and of cultivating and developing wholesome things. Right Mindfulness is mindfulness and awareness contemplating the body, feelings, mind, and mental objects. Right Concentration is one-pointedness of the mind, which eventually may reach the *jhānas* (absorptions or musings).

The Buddha, the all-compassionate physician, has explained ways suited to the mental capacities of each one of us the serious illness that we are suffering from, and how its dangerous symptoms are often masked. He has explained the cause of this illness, and he has told us that an infallible remedy exists. Further he has explained the details of his treatment and has given us the prescription. It is up to us to study the nature of the treatment offered, to reason it out, and then take the remedy ourselves.

The Buddha has spoken of three grades of wisdom, i.e., by learning (*sutamāyapaññā*), by reasoning (*cintāmāyapaññā*), and thirdly by meditative development (*bhāvanāmāyapaññā*). The first two grades come under the term knowledge, whilst it is only the third grade that may be correctly classified as understanding. The "taking of the remedy" consists of the gradual development of knowledge, side by side with faith and devotion (*saddhā*), so that neither of these faculties is in excess of the other (*indriya-samatta*). Excessive faith with deficient wisdom leads to blind and perhaps foolish belief, whilst excessive wisdom with deficient faith leads to cunning.

One cannot conceive of any other system of treatment, which has been so thoroughly analysed, so clearly explained, and apparently so reasonable as to fit in with our own observations. Let those of us who are not satisfied with things as they are accept tentatively the remedy offered by the Buddha as a working hypothesis, until we gradually prove to ourselves that the hypothesis fits in with each one of our limited observations. Let us thereafter increase the number of our observations by utilising the appropriate instruments for the purpose, e.g., by meditative development of understanding, so that each fresh observation that is found to agree with the tentative hypothesis may add to our confidence, and ultimately convert what was at the beginning merely a working hypothesis into a well established fact, i.e., convert knowledge into understanding; for this is the only means by which the remedy offered by the peerless physician for this universal malady of dukkha may be utilised successfully.

Two Kinds of Disease

Monks, there are these two kinds of disease. What are they? Bodily disease and mental disease. People are seen who say they have been physically healthy for a year, or two years, three years, four years, five years, ten years, twenty years, thirty years, forty years, fifty years, or one hundred years, or for more than one hundred years. But, apart from those whose cankers are destroyed (i.e., the saints or Arahants), beings who say that they have been mentally healthy for even a moment are rare in the world.

From AN 4:157

Buddhist Mental Therapy

by Francis Story
(Anāgārika Sugatānanda)

It has been estimated that one out of every four persons in the world's great cities today is in need of psychiatric treatment, which is equivalent to saying that the percentage of neurotics in present-day civilisation runs well into two figures.

This high incidence of personality disorders is believed to be a new phenomenon, and various factors have been adduced to account for it, all of them typical features of modern urban life. The sense of insecurity arising from material economic discord; the feeling of instability engendered by excessive competition in commerce and industry, with booms, slumps, redundancy and unemployment; the fear of nuclear war; the striving to "keep up" socially and financially with others; the disparity between different income levels combined with a general desire to adopt the manner of life of more privileged groups; sexual repression which is at the same time accompanied by continual erotic titillation from films, books and the exploitation of sex in commercial advertising — all these and a host of subsidiary phenomena are characteristic of our age. As a disturbing influence not least among them is the need to feel personally important in a civilisation which denies importance to all but few.

Each of these factors is doubtless a potential cause of psychological unbalance. Taken all together they may well be expected to produce personality maladjustments of a more or less disabling nature, particularly in the great capitals where the pressures of modern life are felt most acutely. The widespread emotional unbalance among the younger generation which has developed into an international cult with its own mythology and folklore and its own archetypal figures symbolic of the "beat generation" seems to substantiate the belief that we are living in an era of psychoneurosis.

Yet it is necessary to review this startling picture with caution. We have no statistical means of judging whether people of former days were less subject to neuroses than those of the present. The evidence of history does not entirely bear out the assumption. Patterns of living change radically, but human nature and its themes remain fairly constant in the mass. When Shakespeare, in the robust and full-blooded Elizabethan era, drew his picture of neurosis in Hamlet he was drawing from models that had been familiar from classical times and could doubtless be matched among his contemporaries. Greek and Roman history records many outstanding cases of behaviour which we now recognise as psychotic, while the Middle Ages abounded in symptoms of mass neurosis amounting to hysteria. The fear of witchcraft that held all Europe in its grip for three centuries was a neurosis so prevalent that it constituted a norm, while almost the same may be said of the more extravagant forms of religious behaviourism characteristic of that and later periods. The extraordinary Children's Crusade of 1212, when thousands of children from France and Germany set out on foot to conquer the Holy Land for Christendom, and never returned, is one example. Here the influence of a prevailing idea on young and emotionally unstable minds is comparable to the international climate of thought which in our own day has produced the "beat generation."

There is no strict line of demarcation between a religious ecstasy and a nihilistic expression of revolt, as we may learn from Dostoyevsky, himself a neurotic of no mean stature. The private mystique of the neurotic may be caught up in the larger world of mass neurotic fantasy, where it adds its contribution to a world that is apart from that of its particular age but which reflects it as in the distortions of a dream. Because of this, the neurotic is often found to be the spokesman and prophet of his generation. Modern communication has made this more than ever possible, creating a mental climate of tremendous power that knows no barriers and can only with difficulty be kept within the bounds of the prevailing norm. Adolph Hitler turned a large section of German youth into psychopaths, first because his personal neurosis found a response in theirs, and then because he was able to communicate it to them directly by means of radio, newspapers and other modern media of propaganda. At the same time, the unstable personality of the neuropath drew support and an intensification of its subliminal urges from the response it evoked in countless people who had never come into personal contact with the source. The real danger of neurosis today is its increased communicability; people are in contact with one another more than they have ever been before. The tendency to standardize, undesirable in itself, has the further disadvantage that it too often results in the wrong standards being accepted. Epidemic diseases of the mind are more to be feared than those of the body.

But those who are inclined to believe that personality disorders are a phenomenon of recent growth may draw comfort from Burton's *Anatomy of Melancholy*. There we have a compendium of cases of individual and collective neuroses gathered from all ages, showing every variety of hallucinatory and compulsive behaviour ranging from mild eccentricity to complete alienation from reality classed as insanity. Psychopathic degeneration, criminality, alcoholism, suicidal and homicidal tendencies are as old as the history of mankind.

Nor is there any real evidence that people living in simpler and more primitive societies are less prone to psychological disturbances than those of modern urban communities. The rural areas of any European country can show their proportion of neurotics in real life no less than in fiction, while in those parts of the world least touched by Western civilisation the symptoms of mental sickness among indigenous peoples are very common, and are prone to take extreme forms. Where an inherent tendency to confuse the world of reality with that of dreams and imagination is worked upon by superstitious fears, morbid neurotic reactions are a frequent result. The psychosomatic sickness produced by the witch doctor's curse, which so often culminates in death, is even more common than are the mentally induced diseases of the West that are its counterpart.

In one respect primitive societies are superior to those of today, and that is in the preservation of initiation ceremonies. These give the adolescent the necessary sense of importance and of "belonging"; they serve as tests which justify the place in tribal life that the initiate is to take up. By their severity they satisfy the initiate that he is worthy. Initiation rites have survived to some extent in the boisterous "ragging" given to new arrivals in most institutions for the young, but they have no official sanction and do not confer any acknowledged status. To be psychologically effective an initiation ceremony must be either religious or in some way demonstrative of the new manhood or womanhood of the initiate. It then dispels feelings of inferiority and the self-doubtings which are a frequent cause of neurosis, and sometimes of delinquent behaviour in young people. Primitive societies, however, have their own peculiar cause of mental disturbance and it is a mistake to suppose that they are superior in this context to more sophisticated social structures.

More attention is given to minor psychological maladjustments today than in former times. Departures from the normal standards of behaviour are more noticeable in civilised than in primitive societies. The instinct to run to the psychiatrist's couch has become a part of contemporary mores. It is true that modern life produces unnatural nervous stresses; but strain and conflict are a part of the experience of living, in any conditions. There has been merely a shifting of points of tension. The more man is artificially protected from the dangers surrounding primitive peoples, the more sensitive he becomes to minor irritants; yet man in a completely safe environment and free from all causes for anxiety—if that were more than theoretically possible—would be supremely bored, and boredom itself is a cause of neurosis.

Human beings can be psychologically as well as physically overprotected. As the civilised man falls a prey to psychological conflicts brought about by situations which are much less truly anxiety-producing than those that menace the lives of primitive peoples every day. Habituated by education and example to expect more of life than the human situation gives him any reason to expect, the modern man feels the impact of forces hostile to these expectations more keenly than he need do. Modern commercial civilisation is continually fostering and propagating desires which all men cannot satisfy equally, and desire, artificially stimulated only to meet with frustration, is a prime cause of psychological disorders. Herein lies the chief difference between our own and former eras. There is a need for periods of true relaxation which many people deny themselves in their desire to be continually entertained.

The systematic study of abnormal psychology began with the work of J.M. Charcot in 1862. The advent of psychoanalysis closely followed, bringing the subject of personality disorders into prominence. Then came a breaking down of distinctions formerly made between normal and abnormal psychology. The two became merged in what is now called dynamic psychology. It was found that the obsessions and compulsions of neurosis are not something distinct from the ordinary modes of behaviour but are only extreme and sharply defined forms of the prejudices and habit patterns of the "normal" person. In defining abnormality it has become the custom to place the line of demarcation simply at the point where the extreme symptoms make some form of treatment necessary for the person who deviates persistently from the average standards of his group. Thus "normal" and "abnormal" are purely relative terms whose only point of comparison is that provided by the generally accepted habit patterns of a particular group. If the group itself is collectively abnormal its units must be considered "normal," with the result that we are compelled to make a reinterpretation of what is meant by these terms of reference.

All behaviour is a form of adjustment, and this is true equally of behaviour that is socially acceptable (the "norm") or socially unacceptable. It is really the active response of a living organism to some stimulus or some situation which acts upon it. The ways in which certain persons deviate from normal standards in behaviour are nothing but individual ways of meeting and adjusting to situations. This new way of regarding the problem is of the utmost importance, particularly when we come to examine the Buddhist system of psychology. In Buddhism, all modes of consciousness are seen as responses to sensory stimuli, and these responses are conditioned by the predetermining factors from past volition. For example, where one person sees an object and is attracted to it, whilst another is repelled by the same object, the cause is to be found in mental biases set up in the past: All reactions, furthermore, are conditioned by a universal misapprehension of the real nature of the object as it is cognised through the senses.

There is therefore a common denominator of misunderstanding which takes the form of collective delusion; it constructs the world of sensory apperceptions and values out of the abstract world of forces which is the actuality of physics. Where there is in reality nothing but processes and events, an ever-changing flux of energies, the mind construes a world of things and personalities. In this world the human consciousness moves selectively, clinging to this, rejecting that, according to personal preferences of habit and prior self-conditioning. The dominating factors known to Buddhism as *avijjā* (nescience), *moha* (delusion) or *vipallāsa* (misapprehension) are a condition of mental disorder, a hallucinatory state. The Pali axiom *sabbe puthujjanā ummattakā*,[31] "all worldlings are deranged," indicates the whole purpose of Buddhism is to apply mental therapy to a condition which, accepted as the norm, is in truth nothing but a state of universal delusion.

The *puthujjana* or "worldling" who is thus described is the average man; that is, all human beings except those who have entered on the four stages of purification, the *sotāpanna* (stream-enterer), *sakadāgāmi* (once-returner), *anāgāmi* (non-returner) and *arahant* (saint). The *puthujjana* is characterised by mental reactions of craving for states which are impermanent, subject to suffering, devoid of reality and inherently impure. These he wrongly imagines to be permanent, productive of happiness, invested with self-existence and pleasurable. His hankering for them is accompanied by mental biases (*āsavas*), mind-defiling passions (*kilesa*) and psychological fetters (*saṃyojana*), which in Buddhism are seen as the root causes of wrong action and consequent unhappiness. What

31. *Vibhaṅga Aṭṭhakathā*.

we call the "norm" is an average balance of these mental factors and their opposites, in exactly the same way that a state of normal physical health is merely the "balance of power" between the various classes of bacteria in the body. If one class of bacteria gains ascendancy over the others it begins to have a destructive effect on the living tissues, and a state of disease supervenes. Psychologically, an increase in any one of the mental defilements constitutes the change over from a normal to an abnormal psychology. Since all "worldlings" are deranged, what we are concerned with in dynamic psychology is the degree of derangement and its underlying causes. This is the case also in Buddhist psychology.

Freudian psychoanalysis works on the assumption that when the origin of a personality disorder is known its influence on unconscious motivation will automatically disappear. Freud endeavoured to trace all psychic traumas to experiences in infancy or early childhood, and made the libido the basis of his system. His work opened up many hitherto unsuspected areas of personality and made a great contribution to our knowledge of the subject. But the defects of Freud's theories can be understood in terms of his system, for he tended to exaggerate certain motives unduly, and in deliberately searching for these he worked on a method of personal selectivity that was bound to become apparent to Jung and others among his successors. His therapeutic methods may also be questioned, for the conflicts engendered by unconscious motivation do not always cease when the original cause of the trauma is brought to the surface. For this and other reasons psychotherapy has not so far produced the benefits which were once expected of it. In many cases the most it can do is to enable the subject to come to terms with himself and "live with" his condition. The limited nature of its success is indicated by the need to resort to physical treatment for cases that have passed from neurosis to psychosis, such as electroconvulsive therapy for acute depressive moods, insulin injections for the early stages of schizophrenia, frontal lobotomy for prolonged anxiety states and the use of the class of drugs known as tranquillizers which act upon the vegetative interneurotic circuits of the brain.

In contrast to the expedients of Western psychiatry, Buddhist mental therapy aims at total integration of the personality on a higher level. Since craving is the root cause of suffering it is necessary to diminish, and finally extinguish, craving. But desire is also the mainspring of volition, so the first stage of the process must be the substitution of higher objectives for the motivations of the libido and their offshoots. The libido-actuated urges must give place to the consciously-directed motives of the *adhicitta* or higher mind. It is here that Buddhism introduces a point of reference which Western psychotherapy has been unable to fit comfortably into its theories—the field of ethical values.

The discarding of many conventional and religious moral attitudes, on grounds they are for the most part contingent and arbitrary, has left the psychologist without ethical determinants in certain important areas of his work. Whilst accepting as the norm the standards of contemporary life he has not been able to work out any universal basis on which what is "right" and what is "wrong" in some aspects of human conduct can be established. The defect has been a serious handicap in the treatment of anti-social and delinquent behaviour. The psychiatrist confronted with examples of deviationist and unacceptable behaviour finds himself unable to decide on what authority he is setting up as the "norm" a standard which he knows to be mostly a product of environment and social convenience. Clinical diagnoses and moral judgements do not always point in the same direction.

Buddhist ethical-psychology cuts through the problem by asserting boldly the measure of immoral behaviour is simply the degree to which it is dominated by craving and the delusion of selfhood. This at once gives an absolute standard and an unchanging point of reference. It is when the ego-assertive instinct overrides conventional inhibitions that behaviour becomes immoral and therefore unacceptable; it is when the over-sensitive ego fears contact with reality that it retreats into a fantasy of its own devising. The neurotic creates his own private world of myth with its core in his own ego, and around this revolve delusions of grandeur, of persecution or of anxiety. Neurosis then passes imperceptibly into psychosis. The ordinary man also, impelled by ego-assertiveness and the desire for self-gratification, is continually in danger of slipping across the undefined border between normal and abnormal behaviour. He is held in check only by the inhibitions imposed by training. The attainment of complete mental health requires the gradual shedding of the delusions centred in the ego;

and it begins with the analytical understanding that the ego itself is a delusion. Therefore the first of the fetters to be cast away is *sakkāyadiṭṭhi*, the illusion of an enduring ego-principle.

The doctrine of non-self (*anattā*) is a cardinal tenet of Buddhism and the one that distinguishes it from all other religious systems, including Hindu Yoga. Ever since the time of Aristotle the "soul," the *pneuma* or *animus* which is supposed to enter the body at birth and permeate its substance, has been taken as the entelechy of being in Western thought. Buddhism denies the existence of any such entity, and modern psychology and scientific philosophy confirm this view. Everything we know concerning states of consciousness can be postulated without reference to any persisting ego-principle. Like the body, the mind is a succession of states, a causally-conditioned continuum whose factors are sensation, perception, volition and consciousness. Introspective examination of the states of the mind in order to realise this truth is one of the exercises recommended in Buddhism.[32]

Understanding Buddhist principles of impermanence, of suffering (as being the product of craving) and of non-ego brings about a reorientation of mind characterised by greater detachment, psychological stability and moral awareness. But Buddhism points out this is not an effect which can be obtained by external means; it is the result of effort, beginning with and sustained by the exercise of will. First of all there must be the desire to put an end to suffering, and that desire must be properly canalised into *sammappadhāna*, the Four Great Exertions; that is, the effort to eliminate existing unwholesome states of mind; to prevent the arising of new unwholesome states; to develop new wholesome states and to maintain them when they have arisen. The unwholesome states of mind are nothing but products of mental sickness that derive from the ego and its repressed desires.

Here it should be pointed out Buddhist teaching is non-violent, and nonviolence is to be exercised towards one's own mind as well as towards the external world. To repress natural desires is merely to force them below the surface of consciousness where they are liable to grow into morbid obsessions, breaking out in hysteria or

32. This is part of Satipaṭṭhāna on which see *The Heart of Buddhist Meditation* by Nyanaponika Thera (BPS) and The Wheel No. 18; 60; 121/122.

manic depressive symptoms. Buddhism does not favour this rough treatment of the psyche, which has produced so many undesirable results in Western monasticism. Instead of repression Buddhism works by attenuation and sublimation. Visualising the passions as fire, Buddhism seeks to extinguish them by withholding the fuel. For example, sensuality is reduced in stages by contemplation of the displeasing aspects of the body so there comes a turning away from the sources of physical passion. Attraction is replaced by repulsion, and this finally gives way to a state of calm indifference. Each impure state of mind is counteracted by its opposite.

Techniques of meditation (*bhāvanā*) in Buddhism are designed for specific ends according to the personality of the meditator and the traits necessary to eliminate. They are prescribed by the teacher just as treatment is given by a psychiatrist; the mode of treatment is selected with the requirements of the individual patient in view. The forty subjects of meditation, known as *kammaṭṭhāna* (bases of action), cover every type of psychological need and every possible combination of types. Their salutary action is cumulative and progressive from the first stages to the ultimate achievement. From the beginning, the Buddhist system of self-training makes a radical readjustment within the mental processes, a readjustment which is founded on the acceptance of certain essential concepts that differ from those ordinarily held. The old scale of values, with its emphasis on the cultivation of desires, is seen to be false and a source of unhappiness; but this realisation does not result in a psychic vacuum. As the old, unwholesome ideas are discarded, new and invigorating ones take their place, while the lower motivations give place to consciously-directed impulses on the higher levels of being. So the personality is moulded anew by introspective self-knowledge.

One defect of psychoanalysis as practised in the West is that it often reveals ugly aspects of the personality before the patient is ready to accept them. This sometimes has highly undesirable side effects and may even cause disintegration of the personality. The Buddhist system of mental analysis teaches us to confront every revealed motivation in a spirit of detached and objective contemplation in the knowledge there is nothing "unnatural" in nature, but that an impulse which is "natural" is not necessarily also desirable. The Buddhist who has brought himself to think in terms of the kinship of all living organisms, a concept inherent in the doctrine of rebirth, is not appalled by the coming to light of subconscious desires that are contrary to those permitted in his particular social environment.

The distinction between human and animal conduct, which science has done much to prove illusory, is not sharply defined in Buddhist thought, where all life is seen as the product of craving-impulses manifesting now on the human, now on the animal level. Where sadistic or masochistic impulses exist they are viewed realistically and with detachment as residual factors of past motivation, and they can be dealt with accordingly. Terms such as "perversion," already obsolete in modern psychology although they survive in popular writing and speech, have never existed in Buddhist thought. All Buddhism recognises is craving and its various objects and degrees. Because of this, the moral climate of Buddhist thought as it concerns libidinal impulses and inclinations is different from that of the West with its Judeo-Christian discriminations.

The distinction that this craving is "good" while that is "bad" is foreign to Buddhism, for Buddhism is not concerned with the morality of fluctuating social conventions but with a concept of mental hygiene in which all craving is seen as a source of misery, to be first controlled and then eradicated. Thus, although its ultimate ideals are higher, the rational morality of Buddhism as it still operates in many Buddhist communities is not so destructive in its effects as the discriminative theological morality prevailing in the West. No Buddhist feels himself to be a "lost soul" or an outcast from society because his desire-objects are different from those of the majority, unless his ideas have been tainted with Judeo-Christian influences. The Western psychiatrist who seeks to reassure a patient whom he cannot "cure" suffers from the disadvantage that he has the whole body of theological popular morality against him and nothing can remove this devastating knowledge from his patient's mind. Hence we find that guilt and inferiority complexes, a dangerous source of psychological maladjustment, are certainly more prevalent, coming from this particular cause, than they are where standards common to the antique world still survive.

The three unwholesome roots of conduct, greed, hatred and delusion, are nourished by unhealthy thoughts that arise spontaneously in association with memories of past experiences. The mind also absorbs a great deal of poison from its environment. Through the channels of sense perception there is continual exposure to suggestions from the outside world. This, together with the natural desire to conform to the behaviour patterns and ways of thinking characteristic of one's particular generation or society, brings an almost compulsive pressure to bear upon the individual. The norms of primitive societies are directed towards conformity with the laws of the tribe, enforcing respect for taboo and inter-tribal relations; but in the complex civilisations of today, disruptive influences that deny or at least weaken the traditional patterns of behaviour, often bringing them into contempt, are gathering force end momentum. An increasing part is being played in this process by the media of mass entertainment.

It would be well if more attention were to be paid by present-day moralists to the cult of violence that has arisen as the outcome of commercially exploited sadism in films, popular literature and "comics" which give children and adolescents a morbid taste for the torture and extermination of their fellow beings. Aggression is another instinct natural to man, but to encourage it for profit is certainly one of the true sins against humanity. Here again, of course, we have nothing entirely new; cruelty is a prominent feature of many traditional and classic stories for children. What is new is the enormous quantity of such entertainment and the facility with which it is distributed on a global scale to create an international climate of thought and a subconscious reversal of all the standards that civilisation nominally upholds. We should not feel surprised at the psychological dichotomy it produces. Sooner or later we shall again have to pay heavily for the cult of outrage we have encouraged.

This however is a question of social psychology; we are now dealing with individual psychology as it is affected by modern conditions and in the light of the Buddhist axiom, *Sabbe puthujjanā ummattakā.* We have already noted the four stages of mental purification beyond the *puthujjana* state begin with the attainment of *sotāpatti-magga*, the "path" of one who has "entered the stream" of emancipation. This is followed immediately by *sotāpatti-phala*, the "fruit of stream winning." It is at this point the erstwhile *puthujjana* becomes one of the four (or eight) classes of Noble Persons. In the scheme of the ten *saṃyojanas* (fetters) he has eliminated the first three fetters: ego-delusion, doubt as to the truth, and addiction to vain rituals which have no place in the higher endeavour. He then goes on to the next stage, that of the *sakadāgāmi*. This is marked by the weakening of the next two fetters in the series: sensuous passion and ill-will.

In the next phase of development he completely frees himself from these first five, which are called the "lower fetters." The remaining five fetters are attachment to existence on the higher levels of being (intellectualised existence), craving for existence on the purely mental plane (the spiritual life freed from the body), pride (the "pride of the saint in his sainthood"), restlessness (the perturbed condition of the mind distracted by desires) and nescience. The last of these is the root-condition referred to previously; it is only eliminated in full at the last stage. The aspirant has then gained the full mental liberation of an Arahant. While the mental and bodily formations continue to function he experiences *sa-upādisesa-nibbāna*, or Nibbāna with the elements of existence still present: At death this becomes *an-upādisesa-nibbāna* or *parinibbāna*, the complete extinction of the life-asserting, life-sustaining factors. No form of Nibbāna can be attained before this last stage; the three classes of Noble Personalities that precede it gain assurance of the reality of Nibbāna but they do not experience the actual *sa-upādisesa-nibbāna* until all the defilements are removed.

It is not the purpose of this article to deal with the state of Nibbāna, but merely to indicate the difference between the condition of the "worldling" with his illusions and cravings, and that of the fully emancipated and mentally healthy being. Buddhism itself is concerned more with the path than with the end, since it is the path which has to be followed, and the end must automatically reveal itself if the path is followed rightly. It is true the goal Nibbāna is never very far from Buddhist thought; it is the motivating principle and raison d'être of the entire Buddhist system.

But the stages on the way are our immediate concern. They involve an approach which is fundamentally therapeutic and progressive. Buddhist meditation is of two types, complementary to each other: *samatha-bhāvanā*, the cultivation of tranquillity, and *vipassanā-bhāvanā*, the cultivation of direct transcendental insight. For the latter it is necessary to have a teacher, one who has himself taken the full course of treatment, but much benefit can be obtained by an intelligent application of Buddhist ideas in the preliminary stages without a guide other than the original teachings of the Buddha. Everyone can, and should, avoid what he knows to be unwholesome states of mind, should cultivate universal benevolence in the systematic Buddhist manner, should endeavour to impress on his deepest consciousness the truths of impermanence, life-suffering and its cause, and the unreality of the ego. A period of quiet meditation, in which the mind is withdrawn from externals, ought to be set aside every day for the purpose. By this method Buddhism enables every man to be his own psychiatrist, and avoids those dependences on others which so often produce further emotional entanglements in the relationship between the psychotherapist and patient.

Any philosophy of life which does not include rebirth must be incomplete and morally unsatisfactory, and the same is true of psychological systems. Some psychological disorders have their origin in past lives: they are then often congenital and sometimes involve the physical structure of the brain or neural system. These are the psychosomatic conditions which call for the use of surgery, drugs and the other physical treatments already mentioned. As resultants of past kamma they may respond to treatment or they may not; all depends upon the balance of good and bad kamma and the interaction of causes, not excluding external and material ones. But in any case, the knowledge that no condition is permanent, and the certainty that the disorder will come to and end with the exhaustion of the bad kamma-result, be it in this life or another, gives courage and fortitude to the sufferer.

By understanding our condition we are able to master it, or at least to endure it until it passes away. This salutary understanding can also be applied beneficially in the case of those who have developed personality disorders through bad environmental influences, childhood traumas or any other cause traceable in this present life. Feelings of inadequacy, grievances against the family or social framework, emotional maladjustments can all be understood in terms of kamma and rebirth. The question "Why has this thing happened to me?" with the sense of injustice that comes from experiencing undeserved pain, is answered fully and logically by Buddhism. With that comes the beginning of an adjustment to circumstances which is in itself therapeutic. Together with this, the knowledge one can be the sole and undisputed master of one's own future fate comes as the most effective psychological tonic and corrective that can be administered.

On Egolessness

From the Discourses of the Buddha

Better it would be to consider the body as the "Ego" rather than the mind. And why? Because this body may last for ten, twenty, thirty, forty or fifty years, even for a hundred years and more. But that which is called "mind, consciousness, thinking," arises continuously, during day and night, as one thing, and as something different again it vanishes.

Saṃyutta Nikāya 12:61

There is no corporeality, no feeling, no perception, no mental formations, no consciousness that is permanent, enduring and lasting, and that, not subject to any change, will eternally remain the same. If there existed such an ego that is permanent, enduring and lasting and not subject to any change, then holy life leading to the complete extinction of suffering will not be possible.

Saṃyutta Nikāya 22:96

One should not imagine oneself as being identical with the six sense organs (including mind) with the six sense objects (including mind objects) and with the (corresponding) six kinds of consciousness; one should not imagine, oneself as being outside them; one should not imagine "they belong to me." Nor should one imagine oneself as being identical with the totality of things.

Thus not imagining any more, the wise disciple clings no longer to anything in the world. Clinging no longer to anything, he trembles not. Trembling no longer, he reaches in his own person the extinction of all vanity: "Exhausted is rebirth, lived the holy life, and no further existence have I to expect," thus he knows.

Saṃyutta Nikāya 35:90

The Teaching of Egolessness (*Anattā*)

A Solace in Illness by
Dr. Anton Kropatsch, Vienna

Quite frequently the Discourses of the Buddha make reference to the problem of disease, and of man as a being unavoidably afflicted with disease. We find such reference, for instance, in a Discourse of the Buddha, called "Nakulapitā."[33]

Nakulapitā, an old and sick man, comes to see the Buddha for obtaining solace in the afflictions of old age: "I am decrepit and old, O Lord, aged, advanced in years, have come to the end of my life. My body is ailing and I am frequently unwell. Rarely now, O Lord, can I enjoy the sight of the Enlightened One and of his venerable monks. May the Exalted One instruct me, may the Exalted One teach me so that it may be for my benefit and happiness for a long time!"

And the Buddha replied: "Yes, householder. Truly this body of ours is feeble, fragile and delicate. If one who carries this kind of body along and deems it free of illness even for a moment, what else could that be called but ignorance! Therefore, householder, you should train yourself in the thought: "May not my mind be ill, though my body be ill!" Thus, householder, should you train yourself." The Buddha and his monks are thoroughly realistic in their way of thinking. They accept things as they are, they

33. Saṃyutta Nikāya Vol. 3 Discourse No 1. (SN 22:1)

do not hide facts nor do they embellish them; they see in them neither more nor less than what is actually involved. Therefore the Buddha listens calmly to Nakulapitā's complaint about his illness, without contradicting him and without trying to persuade him that his condition was not serious as far as his aged body was concerned. The Buddha admits that Nakulapitā's complaints are justified, but he tries to turn his attention from his ailing body to his unimpaired mind which may well stay healthy even in bodily illness, and is sure to be healthy if the patient does not cherish wrong ideas, but preserves his clarity of thinking,

The Buddha's words first dispose of a theoretical misunderstanding that is very often attached to that well-known Latin saying *Mens sana in corpore sano*, "sound mind in sound body". There is certainly truth in that tag if it is taken as pointing to the close interrelations existing between body and mind. But then it should consistently be supplemented by the statement *Corpus sanum in mente sana*, "A healthy body, with a healthy mind." For there is no doubt about it: as frequently as a sound mental life will develop based on a sound body likewise wrong ideas and misconceptions about life will harm the body and cause illness.

Furthermore, those words of the Buddha to old Nakulapitā, if they are fully understood and practically applied, will help mitigate the actual suffering of the patient, and in some cases make his ailment cease.

After Nakulapitā had listened to the Buddha's advice and had left him, he meets one of the Master's chief disciples, the venerable Sāriputta, and requests him to elucidate further that brief utterance so that he may better grasp its implications. What Sāriputta now explains, offering it as a solace in old-age and illness, may well surprise us at first. Sāriputta tells the ailing man true health of mind manifests itself in the rejection of wrong ideas about one's personality, for instance the belief that the five aggregates (*khandha*) which, according to Buddhist doctrine constitute the so-called individual or personality, have anything to do with an abiding core, an eternal soul, ego or self. These five aggregates are corporeality, feeling, perception, volition and other mental formations, and consciousness. They implicitly comprise the entire world of our perception. They are also called "the groups of clinging" (*upādānakkhandhā*) because, through ignorance, they are made the objects of clinging and craving, the targets of possessive greed by which a deluded mind identifies itself with these groups, calling them "I" or "mine." But reality, so teaches the Buddha, has no equivalent for these erroneous conceptions.

To hold out this denial of an abiding Ego against the harsh experience of old-age and illness may first appear as a rather poor consolation. But let us listen to how Sāriputta continues his exposition. "Suppose," says Sāriputta, "man's so-called self were identical with any of these five aggregates, or it were their rightful owner; or they were inherent within the Self, or the Self were enveloped in them. If that were the case, then an ailing man would have good reason for being mortally afraid of the illness that constantly attacks the one or the other of the five aggregates," and afflicts also the other aggregates with resulting repercussions. His fear, in that case, will be so deep-rooted because he believes it is his imagined Self that undergoes all these painful changes, and that hence the possibility of complete destruction of that Self cannot be excluded. But if, in the light of the Buddha's teaching of *anattā* (not-self), the ailing man sees all constituents and functions of the body as but transient life-processes in which no self is hidden and hence cannot perish; if he understands that no abiding ego exists and that the belief in it is a myth; that the conception of an ego is produced, mirage-like, by the interplay of the five aggregates; if in this way the ailing man comes to understand that in truth there is no self or soul, then he will regard his organism as something alien, even as the objects of the external world. He will feel no regrets about the changes in the five aggregates, their arising and then passing away. He will recognise and accept it as a fundamental fact of reality and will not cherish any grief or sorrow about it. With a serene mind, he will face the impending disintegration of the body and of the physical and mental processes bound up with it. Calm and collected will be his death. An event dreadful in itself may lose half of its impact if it is clearly understood and thoroughly examined in the light of Buddhist methods of thinking. To gain such insight or helping others to gain it, does not of course signify a cure of illness but it does take the sting out of it.

In addition, the cultivation of such a way of thinking may be of decisive importance for one's future if, following the Buddha, one accepts the view that the energy set free in death cannot vanish but will continue to be active, searching a new womb, a new physical basis for its activity, in conformity with the volitional tendencies developed during previous lives. Now a mind that accepts the teaching of egolessness, that thereby has shed many disquietening illusions and has found serene equanimity, will in consequence have much better chances for a favourable rebirth than a mind agitated by fear of death and confused by the passionate clinging to an imagined self—thus torn between fear and hope. Moreover, a mind that has seen through the illusion of self, may, under favourable circumstances, become capable of freeing itself entirely from the ever-revolving Wheel of Life, and reach Nibbāna, the final cessation of life-affirming passions and life-creating energies. This, however, will come to pass only if the teaching of *anattā* (egolessness) has been grasped not merely intellectually, but if it has been realised fully through a completely transformed and truly selfless way of life.

Thus it was not an empty and false consolation but a practical help, and a beneficial clarity of insight, which the Buddha and his disciple bestowed upon ailing Nakulapitā. The same realistic outlook will become evident when considering another aspect of Sāriputta's words. In his explanations he deals with wrong ideas about a self only to the extent of actual experience. Beyond that we cannot know more about ourselves than what Buddhist psychology teaches us: what we call "man" or "person" is the interplay of the five aggregates: corporeality, feeling, perception, mental formations and consciousness. These five groupings are classifications of all physical and mental phenomena that constitute the human being. The Discourses of the Buddha and later Buddhist psychology give many interesting details about them.

Modern psychology of the West has developed quite kindred ideas which have been summarized by Bertrand Russell in his *History of Western Philosophy*: "What can we know about Mr. Smith? When we look at him, we see a pattern of colours; when we listen to him talking, we hear a series of sounds. We believe that, like us, he has thoughts and feelings. But what is Mr. Smith apart from all these occurrences? A more imaginary hook from which the occurrences are supposed to hang. They have in fact no need of a hook, no more than the earth needs an elephant to rest upon... Mr. Smith is a collective name for a number of occurrences. If we take it as anything more, it denotes something completely unknowable."

If a thinker wishes to remain on the firm ground of experience and yet postulates an abiding ego, he will have to assume that this ego is identical with one of the five aggregates or with the totality of the physical and mental processes of life which these groups represent. But this belief will collapse as soon as the arising and vanishing of these aggregates has been perceived; because what arises and thus constantly changes can never constitute an eternal and abiding self.

However, those who believe in a soul only too often override the limits set by experience and concern themselves with "something completely unknowable," as Russell says. Moving along these wrong tracks of thought, they readily admit that all cognizable and experiential constituents of the "personality" are subject to constant change, to an unceasing rise and fall; and for that reason they of course cannot be considered as an abiding ego. But it is, so they believe, just from behind or beyond the cognizable and experiential components of the personality that the true eternal self or soul appears which, naturally, must be beyond cognition and experience. What is wrong in such a position and in these conclusions, has chiefly to be attributed to the fact that an empty concept has been raised to the dignity of man's true essence or core—a concept obtained by mere abstract ratiocination, having no longer anything in common with observation and experience. The futility of such a play with words has been shown by Kant. For him a way of thinking that transgresses the limits drawn by experience is a playing with ideas, and the alleged vision of something imperceptible is "a poetic fiction transcending everything imaginable, a mere whim."

The Buddha and his monks, however, are no dreamers chasing after metaphysical phantoms. They are sober realists who will not admit such groundless speculations even to the range of their considerations or refutations. This may be the reason why the Buddha and his followers appear so realistic and quite modern in their outlook.

From the Questions of King Milinda

Certain drugs, O king, have been made known by the Blessed One: drugs by which the Blessed One delivers the whole world of gods and men from the poison of evil dispositions. And what are these drugs? The four Noble Truths made known by the Blessed One, that is to say, the truth as to sorrow, and the truth as to the origin of sorrow, and the truth as to the cessation of sorrow, and the truth as to that path which leads to the cessation of sorrow. And whosoever, longing for the highest insight (the insight of Arahatship), hear this doctrine of the four truths, they are set quite free from rebirth, they are set quite free from old age, they are set quite free from death, they are set quite free from grief, lamentation, pain, sorrow, and despair.

> "Of all the drugs in all the world,
> The antidotes of poison dire,
> Not one equals that Doctrine sweet.
> Drink that, O Bhikkhus. Drink and live!"

Certain medicines, O king, have been made known by the Blessed One, medicines by which he cures the whole world of gods and men. And they are these: "These four Foundations of Mindfulness, the four Right Endeavours, the four Roads to Power, the five Faculties, the five Powers, the seven Factors of Enlightenment, and the Noble Eightfold Path." By these medicines the Blessed One purges men of wrong views, purges them of low aspirations, purges them of evil speaking, purges them of evil deeds, purges them of evil modes of livelihood, purges them of wrong endeavours, purges them of attention to the wrong, purges them of erroneous meditation; and he gives emetics to the vomiting up of lusts, and of malice, and of dullness, and of doubt, and of pride, and of sloth of body and inertness of mind, and of shamelessness and hardness of heart, and of all evil.

"Of all the medicines found in all the world,
Many in number, various in their powers,
Not one equals this medicine of the Truth.
Drink that, O Bhikkhus. Drink and live!

For having drank that medicine of the Truth,
You shall have passed beyond old age and death,
And—evil, lusts, and kamma rooted out,
Thoughtful and seeing, you shall be at rest!"

Buddhism in the Modern Age

by Nimalasuria

Scientific achievement has revolutionised the way of human life. The most characteristic feature of the modern age is its material progress. Modern men and women, whatever their social condition, expect a higher degree of physical comfort and a greater satisfaction of their material needs than their ancestors. The machine with its high productivity is responsible for this.

Another feature of the modern age is the very large number of people every country has to support.

Increased material needs and the vast populations which states have to support have made organisation the only means of "delivering the goods to the people." In all the far-reaching changes that have taken, those religious beliefs and moral attitudes without the sanction of science or reason have been or are in danger of being swept away. Buddhism alone stands firm and the belief in it becomes stronger every day. The reason is Buddhism is based on fundamentals—the acceptance that impermanence, unsatisfactoriness and soullessness are characteristics of individual existence, of which craving (*taṇhā*) is the root cause, and that the change that occurs in the individual from moment to moment follows the law of "dependent origination".

How may the basic truths of Buddhism and the way of life it enjoins be used for the benefit of modern society? The answer, perhaps oversimplified, is by the encouragement of those states of consciousness that are productive of good, and the discouraging of those states that are productive of evil.

"*Pañcasīla*" may be accepted as the universal code of moral conduct—the first four precepts regarding the taking of life, stealing, wrongful sexual relations and the deceiving of others—are an endeavour to live one's life without interfering with the legitimate rights of others. The fifth is to refrain from taking intoxicants which have the effect of lowering man from a poise of high endeavour and calm judgment to a coarse expression of emotional behaviour.

The ordinary layman spends much of his time in the pursuit of his livelihood. His first requirement therefore is that the nature of his work should be such as not to bring him into conflict with the practice of the five precepts, or to make him an intermediate link in encouraging others to break them. In modern society, the acceptance by science of a diet which satisfies the physiological requirements of man, but which does not involve the slaughter of animals, is a pressing need.

The work of many people today tends to be dull and monotonous. It may involve, for example, the repetition of a certain movement several hundred times a day. Few have the satisfaction of creative work, of seeing a job to its finish. The lack of creative work dulls the mind, but little has been done to correct this during the hours of leisure. If leisure time is spent in the pursuit of pleasure alone, there can be little or no improvement of the individual or of society as a whole. The reason for the failure to use leisure time to the best advantage of the individual and society is the lack of a rational view of morality—a defect in modern society which Buddhism alone can correct.

In the pursuit of a moral life a positive attitude towards good is as important as a negative attitude towards evil. In the ordinary world of sense desires the opportunity for good lies in selfless service and in giving. Whatever one's livelihood, it should be possible to render this service, and however poor one is one should still be able to share what one has with another.

An opportunity to practise the "higher *sīla*" (morality) is a necessary part of the Buddhist way of life. Without a recognition of this need, neither the individual nor society as a whole can make any progress. Observing of the eight precepts on full moon days by lay people gives an opportunity at least once a month for the practice of the higher *sīla* as well as for *bhāvanā*" (meditation) which should accompany it.

In the Buddhist way of life, monks are those who have abandoned worldly pleasures, and with it worldly cares. They should live in temples or places of meditation and be strictly guided by the rules of the order. With the clarity of thought born of detachment, their capacity for higher understanding is great. They are a help not only to themselves but to all those who wish to tread the path of Buddhism, and to society itself. In the organisation of modern life, the place of the monk as one who devotes his whole life to his calling must be accepted. His endeavour must be supported not only for his own sake, but also for the benefit of society as a whole. A society which does not accept this responsibility will suffer sooner or later from moral degradation.

Abbreviations

All translations published by the Pali Text Society, except:

N.: Nārada Thera, *The Buddha and His Teachings*, BPS 1980.
Vism: *Visuddhimagga* or *The Path of Purification*, translated by Ñāṇamoli and published by the B.P.S.
W.: Warren, *Buddhism in Translation*, Harvard 1896, New York 1972, Delhi 1987.

The Nature and Purpose of the Ascetic Ideal

Ronald Fussell

WHEEL PUBLICATION NO. 23

Arthur Schopenhauer

In commemoration of the centenary of his death
21st September 1860

Arthur Schopenhauer, one of the greatest German philosophers, lived from 1788 to 1860. His first major philosophical work, *The Fourfold Root of the Principle of Sufficient Reason*, was published when he was only twenty-five. His whole life was devoted to working out his great philosophical system, the main statement of which is in *The World as Will and Representation.* He followed on from Kant in Western philosophy, but acclaimed the first works of Hinduism and Buddhism that were beginning to reach Europe. He said that the 19th Century in Europe would be remembered as noteworthy because of this new influence. Because of his great understanding and reaffirmation of Buddhist teaching, some people think he must have been a reincarnated Buddhist.

He said, "If I were to take the results of my philosophy as a yardstick of the Truth, I would concede to Buddhism the pre-eminence of all religions in the world."

Ronald Fussell

The Ascetic Ideal

One of the most remarkable developments connected with the inner side of the religious life in the nations of Asia and Europe has been that of asceticism and the monastic life. Its understanding can be of great value in the understanding of Buddhism, indeed of religion as a whole. Though appearing in the most diverse races and ages and clothing itself in the forms of different traditions, there is an impressive unanimity of spirit and purpose in the lives and experiences of the men and women concerned; so much so that no one can deny its importance as expressing the very essence and meaning of the spiritual life without putting himself out of court.

Schopenhauer, writing on this subject in 1810, commented, "Unless we are made eye-witnesses by an especially favourable fate, we shall have to content ourselves with the biographies of such persons. Indian literature, as we see from the little that is so far known to us through translations, is very rich in descriptions of the lives of saints, penitents, *Samanas*, *Sannyāsis*, and so on."

The position in Europe is more favourable than this now. Not only is the literature much more extensive, but many of us have had contact with Buddhist *Bhikkhus*, either from Eastern countries or from Europe itself and thereafter know something of their lives. In addition to this, Buddhism, by its great frankness and fearless facing of the fact of suffering leads the thoroughgoing Buddhist, if not to become a monk, at least to understand the aspect of the Noble Eightfold Path that appears as renunciation.

The questions that the lives of such men pose, illustrate the deepest problems of philosophy, i.e. of life. An insight into these questions is the same as an insight into philosophy itself. An attempt is made to deal with them here under the following headings:

(1) Why do men take up the ascetic path?
(2) What is its purpose?
(3) What are its results?

Men take up the ascetic path because there develops in them 'a strong spirit of renunciation,' as Shri Rāmakrishna so often called it when it manifested in his disciples. This renunciation is based on the development of an insight whereby 'self' and the 'world' come to be seen in quite a different way from their superficial picture in the minds of the ignorant. Buddhism teaches that such insight arises dependent on an ethical life, on the practice of the ethical section of the Noble Eightfold Path along with the practice of meditation and the development of insight. Buddha gained enlightenment because his efforts were based on moral excellence, not the other way round. Therefore, it is to be assumed that such men have trodden the path in previous lives and so, as Buddhism would say, they have but "little dust of ignorance in their eyes."

Insight sees the element of illusion (*māyā*), of ignorance (*avijjā*), of misapprehension (*vipallāsa)* in the world accepted by the ignorant. Moreover, the very nature of this world-illusion is seen to produce suffering, nay to *be* suffering, whether regarded as the unquenchable thirst of a separative self or the impermanence of a phenomenal universe. Realizing they are caught in an illusion, there arises a great longing to find out the truth of things; feeling that they are in prison there is a great urge for freedom. Buddhists would say that insight has arisen into the First Noble Truth of Sorrow.

The Buddha was supremely frank, as Schopenhauer witnesses, in putting this fact right in the forefront of his teaching. Whether we accept it, decides whether we are thoroughgoing Buddhists or whether we are still clinging to some form of self-affirming and world-affirming optimism. Optimism, in the philosophical sense, means that we hope to get the fulfilment of desire. Pessimism means that we see the only final freedom from desire in the extirpation of desire. This is *Nirvāna.* The basic clash between the views of optimism and pessimism is the most important in all philosophy. Only if we accept the latter can we enter on the path.

Incidentally, it would be worth while for anyone, Buddhist or Christian, to read (or re-read) the New Testament, if only to see how near to Buddhism it is in spirit (though, needless to say, there are many an important differences).

It is the same with the great Christian mystics. "If we turn from the forms, produced by external circumstances, and go to the root of things, we shall find generally that *Sākya Muni* and Meister Eckhart teach the same thing; only that the former dared to express his ideas plainly and positively whereas the latter is obliged to clothe them in the garment of the Christian myth, and to adapt his expressions thereto. In the same respect, it is noteworthy that the turning of St. Francis from prosperity to a beggar's life is entirely similar to the even greater step of the Buddha *Sākya Muni* from prince to beggar, and that accordingly the life of St. Francis, as well as the order founded by him, was only a kind of *Sannyāsi* existence. In fact, it is worth mentioning that his relationship with the Indian spirit also appears in his great love for animals, and his frequent association with them, when he calls them his sisters and his beautiful 'Cantico' is evidence of his inborn Indian spirit through the praise of the sun, moon, stars, wind, water, fire, and earth."[1]

It has, in fact, been forgotten by most Christians that in the New Testament 'world' is used as a synonym for 'evil,' that the 'prince of this world' is the 'devil', and that Christ said clearly enough "my kingdom is not of this world." It is because some men begin to see for themselves what this means that they seek the ascetic path.

Schopenhauer's philosophy gives two remarkable keys for the clearer understanding of Buddhist teaching. Having penetrated deeply into Buddhism by his own genius, he makes what may appear as abstruse to us, because of its unfamiliar forms, into the most clear of commonsense. He follows Plato in placing the beginnings of philosophy in man's awakening wonder at himself. This is a thing no being but man can do. No cat, or dog, or elephant can do just this. Whether we are evolutionists or not we can see that the great difference between man and the animals is the preponderance of intellect. It is his intellect that makes birth as a man such a great opportunity.

The other key, unique in Western philosophy, was Schopenhauer's observation and explanation of the "will-to-live." Its nature is identical with the *taṇhā* of Buddhism—an unquenchable thirst. Philosophically, it is a direct intuition into the one being we can know in this way—our 'self.' It answers the problem posed by Kant as to the possibility of knowledge of the 'thing-in-itself' (Ding-an-sich).

---

1. *The World as Will and Representation*, by Arthur Schopenhauer, Vol. II. p. 614

Man's intellect, then, comes to know his inner nature as will-to-live (*tanhā*). The form of this will-to-live, appearing in time and space, is mere phenomenon—body. Conversely, the body is the visible aspect of the 'will-to-live' or desire. Desire seeks satisfaction in time, for time is a form of our very consciousness. But, by definition, this satisfaction must be temporal and so pass away. Fresh desire arises continually. So *Saṃsāra* comes to be, and we are *Saṃsārins*, i.e. wanderers in the phenomenal universe, in space and time.

This comes to be dimly perceived by the man in whom insight is awakening. The knowledge comes to him through his intellect, but when he decides to seek the 'final emancipation' from this state of affairs he must deal with the will or desire. This is where the ascetic path starts; and it ends where its goal is reached: in the ending of desire, *Nirvāna*.

Irving Babbitt, who was Professor of French Literature at Harvard University, made a translation of the *Dhammapada*, and appended to it an essay on "Buddha and the Occident." He has this profound comment on *Nirvāna:*

"No religious teacher was ever more opposed than Buddha, in his scheme of salvation, to every form of postponement and procrastination. He would have his followers take the cash and let the credit go—though the cash in this case is not the immediate pleasure but the immediate peace.

"The peace in which the doctrine culminates is not, the Buddhist would insist, inert but active, a rest that comes through striving. In general the state that supervenes upon the turning away from the desires of the natural man is not, if one is to believe the Buddhist, a state of cool disillusion. One may apply to it, indeed, the term enthusiasm, though the enthusiasm is not of the emotional type with which we are so familiar, but rather of the type that has been defined as 'exalted peace.' Buddha himself seems to speak from an immeasurable depth of calm, a calm that is without the slightest trace of languor." [2]

Nevertheless, the same writer had realized for himself the danger of trying to define *Nirvāna* positively:

2. "Buddha and the Occident" p. 98

"Negatively, *Nirvāna* is defined as 'escape from the flux,' positively as the 'immortal element.' Strictly speaking, what is above the flux cannot be defined in terms of the flux, and 'mind' is for Buddha an organ of the flux. Anyone, therefore, who demands at the outset a firm intellectual formulation of *Nirvāna* has, from the Buddhist point of view, missed the point."[3] Buddha was, therefore, very wise when he stated over and over again, "One thing alone I teach: sorrow and the ending of sorrow." For this is the way of experience. At the outset of this article it was stated that men enter this path because of the arising of a new view of life. If this view is the true one, then what was held before must have had a basic error or inconsistency in it. This basic error is put very clearly by Schopenhauer as the belief that we exist *in order* to be happy. This is the optimistic view. It means that we expect our desires to be satisfied in this world, and that we are disappointed if they are not, envious of others who appear to be happy and ready to act selfishly and even cruelly to get our desires. This is all part of the egoistic illusion.

Conversely, both the Buddha and Schopenhauer have been charged with 'pessimism.' Understood as the emotional reaction of shallow people this is one thing, but understood in its deep metaphysical meaning it is quite another. It is true of their teaching just as it is of *Vedanta* and of New Testament Christianity. It should be accepted as a term of praise and not of abuse, as may be seen by its result. It means that a man who professes such a view sees through the illusions of optimism, does not expect a selfish happiness for himself, feels compassion for the suffering of others, and is ready to enter on the spiritual path. Many people are in fact naive realists or disguised Christians while professing to be Buddhists, but this question is the touchstone of their sincerity.

If however, the terms optimism and pessimism are understood in their conventional sense, it must be said that Buddhism is neither optimistic nor pessimistic but realistic. In the *Majjhima Nikāya* (Further Dialogues of the Buddha Vol. I. *Dīghanakha Sutta*), the Buddha, in answer to a questioner, rejects both emotional generalizations: the optimistic view ('all is satisfactory') and the pessimistic view ('all is dissatisfactory'). But the Buddha says that

3. Ibid. p. 96

the latter, the pessimistic view, "is allied to passionlessness and freedom, aloof from pleasure, attachment and clinging," while the optimists, those who find everything satisfactory, hold a view that "is allied to passion, to bondage, to pleasure to attachment and clinging." Nevertheless, both these one-sided views of optimism and pessimism are said by the Buddha to lead to dogmatism and to conflict. This remarkable Discourse ends with teaching that the abandonment of those one-sided views is effected by a growing detachment from body and feelings which is a salient feature of the Ascetic Path. Such statements are, of course, likely to bring up the charge that the Buddha was an annihilationist. It was expressly denied by him that he was either an annihilationist or an eternalist; nevertheless *Nirvāna* remains a puzzle and an intellectual mystery. It can, however, be shown why *Nirvāna* must be, from the intellectual point of view, a negation or a mystery, though not what *Nirvāna* is.

Again to quote Irving Babbitt, "*Nirvāna* is, in its literal meaning, the 'going out' or extinction of (these) desires—especially of the three fires of lust, ill-will, and delusion. The notion that what ensues upon this extinction is mere emptiness is not genuinely Buddhist. The craving for extinction in the sense of annihilation or non-existence (*vibhava-taṇhā*) is indeed expressly reprobated in the Buddhist writings."[4]

Schopenhauer had such a profound intellectual grasp of the nature of *Nirvāna* and was at the same time so much in sympathy with Buddhism that some people have considered him to be a re-incarnated Buddhist. It should be remembered that when he wrote *The World as Will and Representation* in 1818, the first translations of Buddhist books had only just reached Europe and he read the *Dhammapada* in Latin.

"The moral virtues are not really the ultimate end, but only a step towards it. In the Christian myth, this step is expressed by the eating of the tree of knowledge of good and evil, and with this moral responsibility appears simultaneously with original sin. This original sin itself is in fact the affirmation of the will-to-live; on the other hand, the denial of this will, in consequence of the dawning of better knowledge, is salvation. There, what is

4. "Buddha and the Occident" p. 96

moral is to be found between these two; it accompanies man as a light on his path from the affirmation to the denial of the will or, mythically, from the entrance of original sin to salvation, through faith in the mediation of the incarnate God (*Avatār*): or, according to the teaching of the *Veda*, through all the rebirths that are the consequence of the works in each case, until right knowledge appears, and with it salvation (final emancipation), *Moksha*, i.e. reunion with *Brahmā*. But the Buddhists, with complete frankness, describe the matter only negatively as *Nirvāna*, which is the negation of this world or of *Saṃsāra*. If *Nirvāna* is defined as nothing, this means only that *Saṃsāra* contains no single element that could serve to define or construct *Nirvāna*."[5]

"To free it from this (*Saṃsāra*) is reserved for the *denial* of the will-to-live; through this denial, the individual tears itself away from the stem of the species, and gives up that existence in it. We lack concepts for what the will now is; indeed, we lack all data for such concepts. We can only describe it as that which is free to be or not to be the will-to-live. For the latter case, Buddhism describes it by the word *Nirvāna* ... It is the point that remains for ever inaccessible to all human knowledge precisely as such."[6]

"Philosophy has its value and virtue in its rejection of all assumptions that cannot be substantiated, and in its acceptance as its data only of that which can be proved with certainty in the external world given by perception, in the forms constituting our intellect for the apprehension of the world, and in the consciousness of one's own self common to all. For this reason it must remain cosmology and cannot become theology. Its theme must restrict itself to the world; to express from every aspect what this world *is*, what it may *be* in its innermost nature, is all that it can honestly achieve. Now it is in keeping with this that, when my teaching reaches its highest point, it assumes a *negative* character, and so ends with a negation. Thus it can speak here only of what is denied or given up; but what is gained in place of this, what is laid hold of, it is forced ... to describe as nothing; and it can add only the consolation that it may be merely a relative, not an absolute nothing. For, if something is no one of all the things that we know, then certainly

5. *The World as Will and Representation*, Vol. II. p. 608
6. *The World as Will and Representation*, p. 560

it is for us in general nothing. Yet it still does not follow from this, that it is nothing absolutely, namely that it is nothing from every possible point of view and in every possible sense, but only that we are restricted to a wholly negative knowledge of it; and this may very well lie in the limitation of our point of view. Now it is precisely here that the mystic proceeds positively, and therefore, from this point, nothing is left but mysticism."[7]

If these quotations are lengthy and if I have repeated myself somewhat I offer no apology; it is done deliberately for the subject is so important that we cannot deal with it too thoroughly or too exhaustively.

The nature of *Saṃsāra*, the path that leads from it and the inner change which that path means in our psychology have all been clearly expounded by Schopenhauer also. *Saṃsāra* is the will-to-live expressed as the phenomenal world in the forms of time and space. The path to freedom from *Saṃsāra* appears in his teaching as the "Doctrine of the Denial of the Will-to-live." This is expounded in the *World as Will and Representation,* Vol. I. Bk. 4, and Vol. II. in the chapter with the above title.

As a commentary on these two important subjects I would like here to quote from a volume of unpublished letters by K. J. Tarachand, an Indian Buddhist and a deep student of Schopenhauer:

"The relation of the will-to-live to the will-not-to-live may be studied from different standpoints—intellectual, moral, spiritual, emotional, aesthetic, or medical. If intellectually the will is error and ignorance, morally it is sin, spiritually it is exile, and emotionally it is suffering; then aesthetically it is ugly and from the medical standpoint it is diseased ...

"We must never lose sight of the fact that the will-to-live is exile from *Nirvāna*, and all its strivings have only one object—a return to its true home, to *Nirvāna.* Thirst for knowledge, search for truth, the sense of right and wrong, the insatiable desire to be happy and free from stress, strain, and suffering, the love of beauty, and the quest for health—all these represent temporary homes. We attain them with great effort only to lose them after a time; for we live in time and nothing therein can be permanent and abiding ..."

7. The World as Will and Representation, Vol. II. p. 612

It may be seen from this, how, desiring ceaselessly, finding abiding satisfaction nowhere, we are brought at last to the Buddha's teaching and see in his Noble Eightfold Path the Fourth Noble Truth, the Way that Leads to the Ceasing of Sorrow. One subsidiary, but valuable element of the experience of some men was pointed out by Schopenhauer as a foretaste of the nature of *Nirvāna*. It is the experience of 'pure aesthetic contemplation.' This arises in the perception of the artist at the moment of creation or in the mind of the man who appreciates the work of art. At such moments the will (desire) is still; and part, perhaps the most important part, of the experience, is the deep sense of peace that accompanies it. Thus beautiful natural phenomena may induce this state of mind. When I gaze at the landscape or the moon in the mood of the artist I may know it, but if I am planning to build a housing estate on the landscape or land a rocket on the moon I will not.

"To desire *Nirvāna*" is a statement that, of course, involves a contradiction. It is often posed as a catch-question to Buddhists. "If you desire *Nirvāna* how can you be said to end desire?" The answer is that the question is wrongly put. *Nirvāna* is desirelessness. By putting an end to all desires, to the very will-to-live that manifests as desire, *Nirvāna* comes to be. This brings us to the psychological aspect of the path, to the methods used, to why they are used, and to a consideration of what takes place between *Saṃsāra* and *Nirvāna*, between the state of the 'worldling' and that of the *Arahat* or *Jnāni*.

All moral systems imply that some improvement is necessary in the characters of the people following them. Many such systems are, however, merely conventional; under some form of orthodoxy many gross forms of egotism may flourish unchecked. Ultimate problems are neither faced nor solved. The paths of the great religions, on the other hand, put before us the necessity of a change so fundamental that both the self and the world will be radically altered. This great change is the true 'conversion,' the 'salvation' of Christianity, the 'inconceivable transformation-death' (*acintya-parināma-cyuti*) of the *Laṅkāvatāra Sūtra*.[8]

The *Bhikkhu*, Ascetic or *Sannyāsi*, then, sets out to conquer the will-to-live, in himself. He takes upon himself voluntary rules

8. *Laṅkāvatāra Sūtra* (LKS) p. 129

of chastity, poverty, humility and obedience. Though they may be taken as vows and embodied in monastic rules, it is in the first place a voluntary act by which he accepts them. The rules are so well known that almost any educated adult could repeat them. They refer to the strongest forms of affirmation of the will-to-live, which they seek to deny. By denying each aspect of the will, that will is in the end entirely extirpated and *Nirvāna* is reached.

In sex is seen the most vehement expression of the will-to-live, for it has as its objects the preservation of the species. Many people, speaking as advocates of the will, object that the ascetic path would mean the end of the human race *if everybody went in for it.* This is purely hypothetical. Though for thousands of years ascetic orders have existed, the human race is now increasing so rapidly that there is danger of food scarcity. Seeing what the race has achieved in that time it might not be a great loss if it were to end. But it can only end if everyone becomes an *Arahat* (a Saint, in the Buddhist sense), surely 'a consummation devoutly to be wished.'

Possessions are bound up with *ahaṃkāra* and *mamaṅkāra* (I-ness and My-ness), two deceptive forms of the will appearing as 'self.' The ascetic is even advised not to sleep too often under the same tree in case he develops too much attachment to it.

Humility and obedience strike at the deep root of *māna* (pride) in the will, which, according to Buddhism, is the last fetter to be cast off.

'Love' that was looked on as such a spiritual quality in the West was in fact compassion *(agape)*, and compassion is taught in Buddhism, as the great complementary virtue to wisdom, for, as I have explained above, compassion arises through the realization of the inevitable suffering which the will-to-live imposes on all beings. On this Irving Babbitt comments, "How many persons, for example, exalt the 'love' of St. Francis who, in their total outlook on life, are almost inconceivably remote from the humility, chastity, and poverty from which, in the eyes of St. Francis himself—the love was inseparable."[9] Even in the confines of a monastic or ascetic life it is, indeed, not easy to live consistently a life based upon the principles of love, compassion and unselfishness.

9. "Buddha and the Occident" p. 100–101

The entry upon the Ascetic Path is obviously a very serious undertaking and needs unusual qualities, if there is to be any hope of success.

If we cannot, however, accept the ascetic life we may find some comfort in the words of Schopenhauer, who advocates the acceptance of the inevitable suffering of our own life as 'the next best course.'

"Life then presents itself as a process of purification, the purifying lye of which is pain. If the process is carried out, it leaves the previous immorality and wickedness behind as dross, and there appears what the *Veda* says: 'Whoever beholds the highest and profoundest has his heart's knot cut, all his doubts are resolved, and his works come to nought.'[10]

It should not be forgotten that Gotama, even on the threshold of Buddhahood, spent a great part of his six years' search in great austerities. The famous *Buddha-rūpa* of him in his emaciated state gives a vivid impression of what this entailed. When he founded his order he advocated a less stringent set of rules, but, as we shall see, what he did lay down were extreme by our standards. He was still charged by the Hindus with a dangerous relaxation of standards, for many of them had carried asceticism to the point of self-torture. If the principle be understood as denial and reversal of self-will, a criterion is at once established for what does and what does not conduce to this. The ascetic, or even the householder, may guide his conduct by the light of reason.

The Christian term 'self-naughting,' Schopenhauer's 'denial of the will-to-live,' and the Buddhist 'Path to the Ceasing of Sorrow,' are all negative definitions and may impress people with the negative aspect of the path only. Why negative definitions are used has been partly explained above, but the path may be seen in another aspect that is both more positive as a definition and that may illustrate some of its positive results.

The path is a healing process, leading from the 'dis-ease' of *Saṃsāra* to the health, wholeness of *Nirvāna*. The Buddha refers to himself in the *Itivuttaka* and many other *Suttas* as the 'Incomparable Physician and Surgeon.'

10. *The World as Will and Representation*, Vol. II. p. 639

"Buddha aims at wholeness, a type of wholeness that is hard for us to grasp because breadth is for us something to be achieved expansively and even by an encyclopedic aggregation of parts; whereas the wholeness at which Buddha aims is related in fact, as it is etymologically, to holiness and is the result of concentration. To define the quality of concentration that Buddha would have us put forth psychologically—that is, by his own method—is to go very far indeed in the understanding of his doctrine."[11]

"This (effort of concentration) is in all its aspects a will to refrain and in its more radical aspects a will to renounce. What the Buddhist renounces are the expansive desires. *Nirvāna* is, in its literal meaning, the going out or extinction of these desires—especially of the three fires of lust, ill-will, and delusion. The notion that what ensues upon this extinction is mere emptiness is not genuinely Buddhist."[12]

This example of one Buddhist practice is valuable as illustrating the path as a whole. Just as the 'three fires' and the 'five hindrances' are temporarily renounced, left behind and escaped from in meditation, so this happens permanently in *Nirvāna*, but this, of course, necessitates that reversal of our whole nature to which I have already referred. Just as joy at this freedom arises together with peace of mind, so these are the eternal nature of *Nirvāna*—the 'peace that passes all understanding,' because it is beyond mental activity. Those who think that anything of permanent value has been renounced should consider the nature of the 'five hindrances' mentioned above, for they are the creators of the external world, as may immediately be seen by observation.

Psychologically, the effect of the reversal of our inner nature may be explained thus: The egoist is deeply involved in the phenomenal illusion of his own body and his own 'self.' This being so, he feels the separation between himself and others acutely and is intensely concerned with his own well-being and happiness, even to the point of inflicting injury on others. He, therefore, feels himself surrounded by hostile phenomena. This feeling reflects the truth of the impermanence and insecurity of his life, but because of *avijjā*, is not related to its true cause, but to

11. "Buddha and the Orient" p. 83
12. Ibid. p. 96

other people, towards whom aversion and vindictiveness is felt. Desire and aversion almost completely dominate him and greater and greater suffering may be his lot.

The man who begins to tread the path begins to see through the illusion of 'self.' He does not cherish the error of *sakkāya-diṭṭhi* (personality belief). In one scripture the Buddha is credited with the statement on the night of his enlightenment, "Blissful is he who has rid his mind of the conceit of self." Such a man makes less distinction between 'self' and others than is usually made. Consideration for their weal and woe affects him as much as his own. Compassion for their sufferings leads him to unselfish actions. His interest, spread over a number of people, increases his *mettā* (loving-kindness) and lessens his fear or pain at his own misfortune. He feels himself surrounded by friendly phenomena. The very height of this achievement is embodied in Buddha's 'Parable of the Saw,' and, indeed, in Buddha's search for truth on behalf of all mankind,

"Who cast away my world to find my world."

It is also seen to perfection in the example of Christ on the cross who prayed for his executioners, "Father, forgive them, for they know not what they do."

In such examples may be seen the phenomenal appearance of that process known only negatively as 'denial of the will-to-live.' The *Laṅkāvatāra Sūtra* describes it positively in the language of mysticism thus: "Before they had attained realization of Noble Wisdom they had been influenced by the self-interests of egoism, but after they attain realization they will find themselves reacting spontaneously to the impulses of a great and compassionate heart endowed with skilful and boundless means and sincerely and wholly devoted to the emancipation of all beings."[13]

This is the nature of the Enlightened One, the *Jīvanmukta* (he who is liberated in this life)—the *Arahat*. It may be seen that the path to that state appears as a process in time, though this is a part of the illusion, for how can a process in time lead to a timeless, eternal state. The experience of this process is one of progressive awakening (intellectual element), progressive compassion (feeling

13. LKS p. 105–106

element), and progressive goodness (ethical element). The culmination of these is in the life of the *Bhikkhu* whose example may be truly said to be the most sublime this world has to offer.

It has often occurred to me that the lines of Shelley on the death of Keats ("Adonais") might be applied to such a one:

"No, No! He is not dead, he does not sleep,
He has awakened from the dream of life,
'Tis we, oppressed by stormy visions, keep
With phantoms an unprofitable strife,
And in blind trance strike with our spirit's knife
Invulnerable nothings; we decay
Like corpses in a charnel, fear and grief
Convulse us and consume us day by day
And cold hopes swarm like worms within the living clay."
But He, "He has outsoared the shadow of our night!"

Asceticism

Selected Passages from Arthur Schopenhauer's

The World as Will and Representation
Translated by E. F. J. Payne14

If we consider the will-to-live as a whole and objectively, we have to think of it ... as involved in a *delusion*. To return from this, and hence to deny its whole present endeavour, is what religions describe as self-denial or self-renunciation *abnegatio sui isuis* (denial of ones own self); for the real self is the will-to-live. The moral virtues, hence justice and philanthropy, if pure, spring, as I have shown, from the fact that the will-to-live, seeing through the *principium individuationis* recognizes itself again, in all its phenomena; accordingly they are primarily a sign, a symptom, that the appearing will is no longer firmly held in that delusion,

14. 1958. With kind permission of the translator and The Falcon's Wing Press, Indian Hill, Colorado, USA.

but that disillusionment already occurs. Thus it might be said figuratively that the will already flaps its wings, in order to fly away from it. Conversely, injustice, wickedness, cruelty are signs of the opposite, that is, of deep entanglement in the delusion. But in the second place, these moral virtues are a means of advancing self renunciation, and accordingly of denying the will-to-live.

For true righteousness, inviolable justice, that first and most important cardinal virtue, is so heavy a task, that whoever professes it unconditionally and from the bottom of his heart has to make sacrifices which soon deprive life of the sweetness required to make it enjoyable, and thereby turn the will from it, and thus lead to resignation. Yet the very thing that makes righteousness venerable is the sacrifices it costs; in trifles it is not admired. Its true nature really consists in the righteous man's not throwing on others, by craft or force, the burdens and sorrows incidental to life, as is done by the unrighteous, but in his bearing what has fallen to his lot. In this way he has to endure undiminished the full burden of the evil imposed on human life.

Justice thereby becomes a means for advancing the denial of the 'will-to-live,' since want and suffering, those actual conditions of human life, are its consequence; but those lead to resignation. *Caritas*, the virtue of philanthropy which goes farther, certainly leads even more quickly to the same result. For on the strength of it, a person takes over also the sufferings that originally fall to the lot of others; he therefore appropriates to himself a greater share of these than would come to him as an individual in the ordinary course of things.

He who is inspired by this virtue has again recognized in everyone else his own inner nature. In this way he now identifies his own lot with that of mankind in general; but this is a hard lot, namely, that of striving, suffering, and dying. Therefore, whoever, by renouncing every accidental advantage, desires for oneself no other lot than that of mankind in general, can no longer desire even this for any length of time. Clinging to life and its pleasures must now soon yield, and make way for a universal renunciation; consequently, there will come about the denial of the will.

Now, since, according to this, poverty, privations, and special sufferings of many kinds are produced by the most complete exercise of moral virtues, *asceticism* in the narrowest sense, the giving up of all property, the deliberate search for the unpleasant and repulsive, self-torture, fasting, the hairy garment, mortification of the flesh; all these are rejected by many as superfluous and perhaps rightly so. Justice itself is the hairy garment that causes its owner constant hardship and philanthropy that gives away that which is necessary provides us with constant fasting. For this reason *Buddhism* is free from that strict and excessive asceticism that plays a large part in Brahmanism, and thus from deliberate self-mortification. It rests content with the celibacy, voluntary poverty, humility, and obedience of the monks, with abstinence from animal food, as well as from worldliness[15].

Quietism, i.e. the giving up of all willing, asceticism, i.e. intentional mortification of one's own will, and mysticism, i.e. consciousness of the identity of one's own inner being with that of all beings, or with the kernel of the world, stand in the closest connection, so that whoever professes one of them is gradually led to the acceptance of the others, even against his intention. Nothing can be more surprising than the agreement among the writers who express those teachings, in spite of the greatest difference of their age, country, and religion, accompanied as it is by the absolute certainty and fervent assurance with which they state the permanence and consistency of their inner experience. They do not form some *sect* that adheres to, defends, and propagates a dogma theoretically popular once adopted; on the contrary, they generally do not know of one another; in fact, the Indian, Christian, and Mohammedan mystics, quietists, and ascetics, are different in every respect except in the inner spirit and meaning of their teachings.

A most striking example of this is afforded by the comparison of Madame de Guyon's *Torrens* with the teaching of the *Vedas*, especially with the passage in the *Oupnekhat,* Vol. I. p. 63. This contains the substance of that French work in the briefest form, but accurately and even with the same figures of speech, and yet it could not possibly have been known to Madame de Guyon in 1680. In the *German Theology* (the only, unmutilated edition, Stuttgart, 1851), it is said in Chapters 2 and 3 that the fall of the devil as well as that of Adam consisted in the fact that the one, like

15. *The World as Will and Representation*, Vol. II. p. 606/7

the other, had ascribed to oneself I and me, mine and to me. On page 89 it says, "In true love there remains neither I nor me, mine, to me, thou, thine, and the like." In keeping with this, it says, in the *Kural*, translated from the Tamil by *Grauh*, p. 8, "The passion of the mine directed outwards and that of the I directed inwards cease" (cf. verse 346).

And in the *Manual of Buddhism* by Spence Hardy, p. 258, the Buddha says, "My disciples, reject the idea that I am this or this is mine." If we turn from the forms, produced by external circumstances, and go to the root of things, we shall find generally that *Sākya Muni* and Meister Eckhart teach the same things; only that the former dared to express his ideas plainly and positively, whereas the latter is obliged to clothe them in the garment of the Christian myth, and to adapt his expressions thereto. This goes to such lengths, that with him, the Christian myth is little more than a metaphorical language, in much the same way as the Hellenic myth is to the Neo-Platonists; he takes it throughout allegorically. In the same respect, it is noteworthy that the turning of St. Francis from prosperity to a beggar's life is entirely similar to the even greater step of the Buddha *Sākya Muni* from prince to beggar, and that accordingly the life of St. Francis, as well as the order founded by him, was only a kind of *Sannyāsi* existence[16].

If we go to the bottom of things, we shall recognize that even the most famous passages of the Sermon on the Mount contain an indirect injunction to voluntary poverty, and thus to the denial of the will-to-live. For the precept to comply unconditionally with all demands made on us (Matth. V. 40 Seq.), to give also our cloak to him who will take away our coat, and so on; likewise (Matth. vi, 25-34) the precept to banish all cares for the future, even for the morrow, and so to live for the day, are rules of life whose observance inevitably leads to complete poverty. Accordingly, they state in an indirect manner just what the Buddha directly commands his followers to do, and confirmed by his own example, namely, to cast away everything and become *Bhikkhus*, that is to say, mendicants. This appears even more decidedly in the passage Matthew X, 9–15, where the Apostles are not allowed to have any possessions, not even shoes and staff, and

16. *The World as Will and Representation*, p. 613/4

are directed to go and beg. These precepts afterwards became the foundation of the mendicant order of St. Francis (Bonaventura, *Vita S. Francisci c. 3*). I say therefore that the spirit of Christian morality is identical with that of Brahmanism and Buddhism. In accordance with the whole view discussed here, Meister Eckhart also says (*Works*, Vol. I. p. 492): "Suffering is the fleetest animal that bears you to perfection."[17]

"All these considerations furnish a fuller explanation of the purification, the turning of the will, and salvation, which were denoted in the previous chapter by the expression 'the next best course,' and which are brought about by the sufferings of life, and are undoubtedly the most frequent; for they are the way of sinners as we all are. The other way, leading to just the same goal by means of mere knowledge and accordingly the appropriation of the sufferings of a whole world, is the narrow path of the elect, of the saints, and consequently is to be regarded as a rare exception. Therefore, without that first path, it would be impossible for the majority to hope for any salvation. But we struggle against entering on this path and strive rather with all our might to prepare for ourselves a secure and pleasant existence, whereby we chain our will ever more firmly to life.

"The conduct of ascetics is the opposite of this, for they deliberately make their life as poor, hard, and cheerless as possible, because they have their true and ultimate welfare in view. Fate and the course of things, however, take care of ourselves better than we ourselves do, since they frustrate on all sides our arrangements for a Utopian existence, whose folly is apparent enough from its shortness, uncertainty, emptiness, and termination in bitter death. Thorns upon thorns are strewn on our path and everywhere we are met by salutary suffering, the panacea of our misery. What gives our life its strange and ambiguous character is that in it two fundamental purposes, diametrically opposed, are constantly crossing each other. One purpose is that of the individual will, directed to chimerical happiness in an ephemeral, dreamlike, and deceptive existence, where, as regards the past, happiness and unhappiness are a matter of indifference, but at every moment the present is becoming the past. The other purpose is that of fate,

17. *The World as Will and Representation*, Vol. II. p. 633

directed obviously enough to the destruction of our happiness, and thus to the mortification of our will, and to the elimination of the delusion that holds us chained to the bonds of this world.

"... If we put this purpose in the complete reversal of this nature of ours ... a reversal brought about by suffering, the matter assumes a different aspect, and is brought into agreement with what actually lies before us. Life then presents itself as a process of purification the purifying lye of which is pain. If the process is carried out, it leaves the previous immorality and wickedness behind as dross, and there appears what the *Veda* says: 'Whoever beholds the highest and profoundest, has his heart's knot cut, all his doubts are resolved, and his works come to nought.'"[18]

* * *

The inner spirit and meaning of genuine monastic life, as of asceticism generally, are that a man has recognized himself as worthy and capable of an existence better than ours and wants to strengthen and maintain this conviction by despising what this world offers, casting aside all its pleasures as worthless, and now awaiting calmly and confidently the end of this life that is stripped of its empty allurements, in order one day to welcome the hour of death as that of salvation. The *Sannyāsis* have exactly the same tendency and significance, and so too have the Buddhist monks. Certainly in no case does practice so rarely correspond to theory as in that of monasticism just because its fundamental idea is so sublime; and *abusus optimi pessimus* (The worst is the abuse of the best). A genuine monk is exceedingly venerable, but in the great majority of cases the mere mask behind which there is just as little of the real cowl is monk as there is behind one at a masquerade.

From *Parerga and Paralipomena* § 168. Translated by E. F. J. Payne.

18. *The World as Will and Representation*, Vol. II. pp. 638–39.

Epilogue

The happiness of renunciation

Sayings of the Buddha

There are two kinds of happiness, O monks: the happiness of the householder and the happiness of the ascetic. But the greater of the two is the happiness of the ascetic.

There are two kinds of happiness, O monks: the happiness of the senses and the happiness of renunciation. But the greater of the two is the happiness of renunciation.

Aṅguttara-Nikāya, Duka-Nipāta

The wise man will give up a lesser happiness to obtain a greater happiness.

Dhammapada, v. 290

Ah, happily we live, hateless among haters;
midst men of hate, hateless we dwell!
Ah, happily do we live healthy among those ailing;
Amidst ailing men, healthy we dwell!
Ah, happily do we live, greedless among the greedy;
Amidst greedy men, greed-free we dwell!
Ah, happily do we live, free of impediments!
Feeders on joy shall we be even as the Radiant Gods.

Dhammapada, vv. 197-200.

Happy is he contented in solitude,
Seeing the Truth he has learned,
Happy is he, who abstains from harming,
Living restrained towards all that lives.
Happiness true is freedom from passion,
If senses' cravings are left behind.
But highest happiness is his
Who has removed the self-conceit.

Udāna, 2.1

Live Now

Buddhist Essays

By

Ānanda Pereira

WHEEL PUBLICATION NO. 24/25

Foreword to the Third Edition

The essays collected here appeared first in the years 1951–1952, as editorials in the fortnightly paper, *The Buddhist World* (Colombo), edited by the late U Tun Hla Oung, whose service to the cause of Buddhism we remember with appreciation.

The author of these essays passed away on 19th September 1967, having been Deputy Solicitor General at the time of his death. He was the son of the late Venerable Kassapa Thera (formerly Dr. Cassius A. Pereira), whose poems precede some of the essays in this volume.

A second selection of his essays appears under the title *Escape to Reality* as No. 45/46 of *The Wheel* series.

Buddhist Publication Society

Live Now

There's no tomorrow,
No yesterday.
No reason for sorrow
Or need to say,
'This thing I remember;
For that I pray.'
There's only today.

Ānanda Pereira

Look to this day.
In its brief course
Lie all the verities of existence—
Action, love, transience.
Yesterday is but a dream,
and tomorrow veiled.
Live now!

(Adapted from a poem by Kālidāsa)
Kassapa Thera

The secret of happy, successful living lies in doing what needs to be done now, and not worrying about the past and the future. We cannot go back into the past and reshape it; nor can we anticipate everything that may happen in the future. There is but one moment of time over which we have some conscious control—the present.

This truth has been recognized not only by the Buddha but by all the great thinkers of the world. They saw that it is futile to live in memories of the past and in dreams of the future, neglecting the present moment and its opportunities. Time moves on. Let us not stand idly by and see our hopes for success turn into memories of failure. It lies in our power to build today something that will endure through many tomorrows, something more solid than castles in the air. The Buddha has shown us the way. The time is now and the choice is ours.

Indomitability

We are battalions of Him who said,
"Confidence have I, and understanding,
Power to wrest freedom for myself, and all
This can I do, and will. Let blood dry up
And let my flesh shrink up and waste to naught,
Till bones and skin remain: yet will I not
From this seat rise till victory be won.
A Muñja-crest I wear in this last fight!
What boots this living on in endless ill?
Rather will I die in battle, ardent
Than miss high aim and like a craven live."
Such was our leader: and beneath His flag,
Shall we, who know the road we have to tread,
The road by Him revealed, who mapless went,
And dauntless won the Goal for us: shall we
Who bear His name not fight on, happily,
For all, our leader stood?—For justice, truth,
And peace for all, and love, and final bliss?
We shall—or die; that truth may thereby live.

Kassapa Thera

The Buddha did not preach fatalism, nor is the doctrine of kamma a doctrine of predetermination. The past influences the present but does not dominate it, for kamma is action, both past and present.

The past *and present* influence the future. The past is a background against which life goes on from moment to moment. The future is yet to be. Only the present moment exists and the responsibility of using the present moment for good or for ill lies with each individual. No living being can avoid this responsibility and no intelligent being will seek to do so.

Right through the Buddha's teaching repeated stress is laid on such attributes as self-reliance, mindfulness, resolution and energy. If there was one thing that he did *not* teach, it was fatalism. He taught that all conditioned things (*saṅkhāra*) are impermanent (*anicca*). Character also is a conditioned thing, and in this very quality of impermanence, of changeableness, lies the secret of ultimate deliverance. That which is impure can be purified. That which is weak can be strengthened. That which is immature can be developed into maturity.

The heights are not reached by a sudden leap but by quiet, persistent endeavour. "A journey of a thousand miles starts with one step." There is a quality of mind, which literally makes any attainment possible. It pushes on, steadily, and doggedly, refusing to be discouraged by handicaps and disappointments, refusing to be discouraged by obstacles, refusing to admit defeat, whatever happens. It fights on in spite of all.

This is the sort of mind the Buddha wanted his followers to cultivate—the indomitable mind.

It is more glorious than the sun, more dependable than the stars, more potent than any other force in the world.

It is invincible.

Action

For good or ill, three doors of action open
To lead the actor up, or down to woe.
Speech-door is lowest, body-door comes next,
Mind is most potent of the fateful three.
Low is all action that the wise will scorn,
Vain are fine words that lag unbacked by deeds,
Ill are the deeds unguided by wise mind,
Baneful are thoughts of foolish hate and lust.
Noble is action that the wise will prize.
Grand are fine words that leap to life in deeds.
High are the deeds directed by wise mind,
Lofty are thoughts of selfless sympathy.

Kassapa Thera

"Having slain mother (craving), father (conceit), two warrior kings (views of eternalism and nihilism), and having destroyed a country (senses and sense objects) together with its treasure (clinging), ungrieving goes the Arahat."

Dhammapada 294

The Buddha Dhamma is a virile teaching. It has no use for sickly sentimentality. It appeals to the practical minded, those who face facts and are prepared to exert themselves. The facts are greed, hatred and ignorance. Everywhere we see them, in the palaces of the rich and the hovels of the poor, in hospitals, at holiday resorts and in the courts of law. Wherever we see them, we must recognize them, because one cannot fight an enemy that one does not recognize.

Greed, hatred and ignorance—the ugly trio—these are our true enemies, and have always been so from the beginning of time. Against each of these enemies there is a weapon, sure and deadly, in the hand of him who is strong enough to wield it.

The weapon that destroys greed is liberality (*dāna*). That is simple enough to think about, and beautiful enough to admire. But it is a heavy weapon and only the strong can wield it. Let us be strong in giving, as the Bodhisatta was strong, giving wealth, giving limbs, eyes, blood, life itself. There was no limit to His giving, as there is no limit to the courage of a hero.

The weapon that destroys hatred is love (*mettā*). This is not the selfish, clinging love that novelists and film producers exploit to such advantage. Such love is a puny thing compared with the Buddha's *mettā*, because *mettā* has nothing of self in it and nothing of clinging. It is limitless, extending to all beings as friends, making no distinction between this person and that. It is not easy to love in this way, but it is worth trying, and the time is *now*. It may yet save humanity from self-destruction.

The weapon that destroys ignorance is meditation (*bhāvanā*). Buddhist meditation is not day dreaming, musing, or the building of castles in the air. It is the systematic training of the mind in concentrated thought and the focussing of that trained mind on the nature of life itself. Seen clearly, it is seen as impermanent, unsatisfactory and devoid of any core of reality. This weapon, meditation, is the most difficult of all to wield and master. It calls for training in self-discipline, a training that we all need. The beginning of this training lies in the strict observance of the five precepts. These precepts strictly observed, build a character strong enough to wield the weapon *of bhāvanā.* Let us strengthen ourselves, arm ourselves, arm ourselves with these three mighty weapons and attack the three enemies, like happy warriors.

Ideals and Ideologies

I seek the Highest, for myself
And those who trusted me.
I shall not bend down to my will
The folk who seek poor clods
Of earthy compromise.
What boots it if one dies
Or if the way be dark and grim!
I'll light it with a smile of love
And keep on searching still—
I seek the highest.

Kassapa Thera

History, with an abundance of instances, proves that whenever a group of people formulates an ideology and sets out to create a Utopia in accordance with its principles, there is trouble ahead for other people. The original reformers may be idealists, well-meaning and intelligent. Indeed, they usually are. But the misery they bring about appears to be in almost direct proportion to the goodness of their intentions.

Sooner or later, consciously or unconsciously, these men of destiny come to accept the principle that the end justifies the means; and once that is conceded unpleasant things begin to happen very quickly. Emotion deliberately excited, usurps reason; slogans take the place of argument, and people find themselves at each other's throats without knowing exactly why.

No Buddhist, however simple he may be, should ever let himself be duped into such stupid and unseemly behaviour. The Truth he seeks admits of no half-truths and lesser loyalties. It is to be sought and found by each individual for himself and within himself. Nobody, not even a Buddha, can confer Enlightenment upon another. With the example of the Buddha and the Arahants to inspire him, every Buddhist must strive for himself.

It is for this reason that Buddhists have no need for ideologies and no need to pretend that the end justifies the means. We do not seek to impose our way of life upon others. Our history is not written in the blood of prospective converts; nor do we believe that people can be dragged to Nibbāna in chains. In proclaiming the Buddha Dhamma, we speak as free men to free men.

The Buddha Dhamma points to ultimate and final truth as the end. It teaches self-control, mental culture and clear thinking as the means to that end. The end merely directs the means and does not need to justify them. Self-control, mental culture and clear thinking justify themselves and are a blessing at every stage of a being's progress to Enlightenment.

Skilful Giving

To give, compassion-moved,
To give to one who needs,
With a heart of love:
These are the precious seeds

That stand above
All barren show of splendour.
To give with selfless love,
To give from deep respect

To teacher, parent, holy man,
Wisdom's elect,
Is even grander.
To give to help good cause,

To spread the Truth
And knowledge of the Way
To Virtue, Mindfulness,
To dawn of Wisdom's Day,
Skilful is such giving.

Kassapa Thera

Giving is an art; and like any other art, it can be cultivated by practice. The miser, the man who thinks only of himself, finds it very difficult indeed to give. For him, it is very difficult to give even to those who are near and dear to him, not because he does not love them but because he loves himself too much and is too dominated by clinging, to part with anything.

Higher on the scale come those who give, and can take pleasure in giving to those who are near and dear to them, but to no one else. They give to their parents and children and to a limited circle of relatives and friends; but beyond that their generosity does not extend. It is like a lamp that is shut up within a little box. The inside is illuminated, but not a single ray penetrates the box to brighten the outside world. Such people too are dominated by selfish clinging; but in their case "self" does not mean only "I" but extends a little further to whom they call "mine."

Most of us worldlings belong to this class of giver. The differences between us are only differences of degree. Those of us who have a large circle of friends, to whom we give freely and gladly, are known as generous. Those of us who have a small circle of friends to whom we give are known as stingy. But we keep our giving within this circle, whether it be large or small.

Highest on the scale are those few great ones whose giving knows no bounds. Their generosity extends without limit, to all beings, blazing forth like the light of the sun. Our Buddha was one such, not only in his final birth but in previous existences also, when he was perfecting *dāna pāramī*. In previous existences he gave his wealth, his eyes, his limbs, his life; and in his final existence he gave the greatest of all gifts—the peerless Buddha Dhamma. He gave it freely to those who had ears to hear and minds to understand.

With such a noble example to guide us, it is the business of each of us to practice the art of giving. We should constantly try to widen the circle of those to whom we give, and every now and then, ever more frequently, we should strive to break the circle and let our generosity shine out to someone beyond. So, in time, it will become limitless.

Confidence

The floods of Lust, of endless Birth,
Of tangled Views, of Ignorance—
One crosses these, not staying still,
Nor yet by fool precipitance.
Quenchless the courage on that quest
And absolute the confidence

Kassapa Thera

What is the essential difference between a swimmer and a non-swimmer? Both may be elderly, not particularly healthy, and in poor physical condition due to lack of exercise. Yet, if they happen to fall into deep water, the swimmer will survive while the non-swimmer, unless somebody else saves him, will drown. Why? Because the swimmer, through knowledge gained from previous experience, has confidence that the water will support him. He does not struggle and fight the water and try to climb right out of it. He trusts it and relaxes, knowing full well that he will not sink and all he needs do is to keep his nose and mouth above the surface. The non-swimmer has no such confidence. He does not trust the water and his ability to float in it. He does not relax. He fights for his life when no fight is necessary, and he loses the fight.

This is only one example of the importance of confidence—confidence born of knowledge. It is an essential quality for success in any activity and endeavour—from the threading of a needle to the practice of *bhāvanā*. It makes all the difference between efficiency and inefficiency, success and failure. Sometimes it means the difference between life and death.

Some people call it faith. That is as good a word as any other; but it has certain connotations that do not appeal to those of independent mind, to people who wish to see and know for themselves. Unfortunately there are some things we cannot experience for ourselves with any hope of survival—the taste of cyanide for instance. There is an old saying "Experience is a comb that a man gets when he has lost his hair." It is a wise man who profits by the experience of others.

Confidence born of knowledge need not necessarily be confidence born of one's own personal experience. That is why people pay big fees to instructors, to people who have specialized in the various sciences. They have made it their business to acquire the necessary experience and knowledge to be competent to advise others. People who are wise heed such advice and act on it with confidence. Is this mere blind faith, or is it confidence born of knowledge?

To the Buddhist, the Buddha is the greatest instructor of all time. Yet there are those who call themselves Buddhists but who do not act on his advice with confidence. They act with confidence, and with no sense of incongruity, on the advice of the family doctor and the golf coach. They adopt an attitude of scepticism towards a mental giant but humbly acknowledge the wisdom of a host of contemporary pygmies.

The Power of Mind

A lone seer from a tropic land
Sent forth rays of radiant love,
Intense and immeasurable,
Below, around, above.
And far away where snowflakes fell
Death knocked, and round a bed, folk sighed.
He past hope, starts, and whispers— "Look!
Look! Love's rose-light!"—and smiling died.

Kassapa Thera

Mind is power, just as electricity is power. Nobody will deny the power of electricity, but people tend to doubt the power of mind because as yet there is no instrument whereby it can be measured. But to those who have had some actual experience of its operation, the power of mind is a very real thing. Sometimes it can be a startling thing.

Since time immemorial the East has recognized the power of mind. While the West has progressed far in studying and exploiting the power of matter, the East has progressed far in studying and exploiting this subtler power. Phenomena such as telepathy, hypnotism, clairvoyance and clairaudience, have, for ages past, been regarded as almost commonplace in the East, whereas in the countries of the West they are still excitingly new.

Mind power, like all forces, is neither good nor evil in itself. It can kill as well as cure, destroy as well as create. And again like all forces, it operates in accordance with certain natural laws. Many have been those who studied these laws, in order that they might use this silent, unseen force. Some used it for evil and reaped the deadly harvest that it yielded. Others used it for good and their names are yet remembered with reverence.

Greatest of all teachers of mental culture was the Buddha. Understanding fully the rational laws in accordance with which mind power operates, He taught his followers how to develop and use it for the highest good, the attainment of final deliverance. The first step on the road to mental culture, according to the Buddha Dhamma, is *sīla* or virtue. The man who would control his mind must first learn to control his speech and deed.

The next step is *bhāvanā*, the practice of concentration and the cultivation thereby of a calm, steady, "one-pointed" mind. It is not easy. The Buddha has prescribed forty subjects of meditation for the cultivation of this "one-pointed" mind. In the absence of an experienced teacher, the aspirant to mental culture must analyse his own nature (always a difficult feat) and choose a subject that suits him.

One of the subjects of meditation that may with benefit be chosen by anybody is *mettā*, selfless love, sympathetic kindness towards all beings. It may be practiced with safety, and indeed with definite advantage, even by those whose *sīla* is yet imperfect. It is wholesome and good, bringing bodily health, mental calm and rapid attainment of concentration.

To the hurrying multitude, a person seated quietly in the practice of *mettā bhāvanā* may appear to be doing nothing. But those who are aware of the nature of mind power would know better, for such a person is a human dynamo, generating thoughts of love in a world that has forgotten how to love. Were there many such, their united power might yet save the world from self-destruction:

For not by hatred are hatreds ever quenched here in this world,
By love rather are they quenched. This is an eternal law.

Virtue

Who stainless lives
Both calmness gives
And power gains.
Their fear departs
Where virtue reigns
In righteous hearts.

Kassapa Thera

In the last essay we mentioned *sīla* or virtue as the first step on the road to mental culture as taught by the Buddha. By *bhāvanā* or the cultivation of a "one-pointed" mind, a person learns to concentrate mind power. But it is obvious that one can only concentrate the power that is available.

If you stand in the bright sunlight at noon on a clear day, and using a convex lens, concentrate the sun's rays on the back of your hand, you will almost immediately feel the sting of the concentrated radiant heat. If however you do the same thing at night, using the same lens, but substituting a 40-candle power electric bulb in place of the sun, you will not even notice the increased temperature caused by the concentrated, radiant heat unless your skin is exceptionally sensitive.

The same principle applies to the concentration of mind power. The power that can be developed by concentration is in direct proportion to the innate power of the mind, and this power varies in different individuals; what is more important, it varies in the same individual at different times. Even strong characters have their moments of weakness, and weak characters their moments of strength.

The first step then on the road to mind power is to develop a consistently firm and purposeful mind as the source of power to be concentrated. In other words, one must first develop a strong will, as that term is commonly understood. This can most readily and surely be achieved by the constant practice of self-control. Virtue, *sīla,* is the best form of self-control. It ranges from the five precepts of a lay Buddhist to the innumerable precepts of the Upasampadā Bhikkhu, the fully ordained monk. Of course self-control can be practised in other ways as well. One can balance for hours on one's head, or go without food for days on end or hold an arm up until it withers. But such practices will not tend to purify the mind while strengthening it, as the practice of *sīla* does.

Hasty and unthinking critics have said of Buddhist virtue that it is negative, in that it lies in abstention from evil and not in doing good. But this criticism is based on a misunderstanding of the purpose of *sīla* in Buddhism. It is a means to an end and not an end in itself. There is but one end towards which every Buddhist strives, the attainment of Nibbāna or final deliverance from the toils of saṃsāra, from the recurrent, painful and entirely disgusting round of birth, decay and death.

It behoves every lay Buddhist to observe the five precepts, *pañca sīla.* These are the abstentions from five kinds of wrong action—killing, stealing, sexual misconduct, lying or slanderous speech and the taking of intoxicants. He who observes these five precepts consistently and scrupulously develops strong will, a mind that can be concentrated to some effect. He becomes a very considerable source of power.

Concentration

Wouldst thou wield cosmic power?
Then, virtue-based
Seek thou to concentre mind
In one clean focus.
Success yields god-like ken;
Yea, more than gods';
For even they know not
The Hypercosmic.

Kassapa Thera

In *bhāvanā* or concentration, we come to the very heart of the system of mental culture taught by the Buddha. It is the key to the highest mental powers and the performance of feats of *iddhi* (supernormal power). Such feats and such powers are not the ultimate end to which the Buddhist aims. They are but by-products of mental culture and they too are transient. The true follower of the Fully Awakened One has just one aim—the attainment of final deliverance. All else is shoddy, subject to the law of impermanence, devoid of any core of reality.

But let us be frank. Although such powers as clairvoyance and clairaudience and the capacity to perform such feats as levitation do not constitute the ultimate aim of the Buddhist, they have their appeal. And like all things, they do have their uses. Imagine the influence of a reformer who could make his audience actually see the states of suffering and the states of bliss of which he speaks.

Those of us who are Buddhists in little more than name spend so much of time and energy in the unblushing pursuit of purely material ends that it would be hypocritical for us to pretend that we do not work for mental powers only because we realize that they are not the final goal. The true reasons lie much closer to hand. We feel that we cannot spare the necessary time and energy. Also we are somewhat skeptical about such things. They are so foreign to the normal course of our lives. In short, we are full-time worldlings.

But what is the normal course of our lives? A treadmill. We are so preoccupied with the business of earning a living that we have no time to live. We strive to keep up appearances. We work hard for this pathetic little prize and that, and try to feel important when we succeed. When we fail, as most of us must, we pretend that we do not care. And presently death comes to each of us and the sorry little tale is told only to begin again in the next existence. And so on interminably, life after life, like an endless serial story told in countless squalid installments.

Is it escapism to turn away from such futility? Is it escapism to outgrow one's swaddling clothes, and cast aside one's rattle? The practice of *bhāvanā* offers as mere by-products, prizes, which far surpass anything attainable by material means. These prizes can be won and have been won. They are not figments of the imagination. And ultimately the practice of *bhāvanā* leads to final deliverance.

The mind, grown calm and powerful, at last sees things as they actually are. With this clear sight there is a flinging away of existence and all that it implies, just as a man would fling away a rotting corpse that he has long carried on his shoulders, imagining it to be a load of sweet-smelling sandalwood. With this act of revulsion there comes the intuition of Nibbāna.

Insight

To see things as they are,
To shed all taints,
To win security,
The goal of saints!

Kassapa Thera

Having purified and strengthened his mind by the practice of *sīla*, virtue, and *bhāvanā*, concentration, the follower of the Buddha turns this pure, steady, clear-seeing mind to the contemplation of life itself. *Vipassanā bhāvanā*, concentration for insight, is usually undertaken in some quiet place, such as a forest hermitage or lonely mountain cave, because quietness of surroundings promotes quietness of mind.

Unthinking people with worldly minds are apt to regard such seclusion as a form of escapism, a running away from life. But it is just the opposite. It is the most direct approach to life humanly possible. The busy worldling it is who constantly runs away from life, dodging from this activity to that and never pausing long enough to see things as they actually are. It takes strength to be quiet.

Seven qualities, when combined, lead to the gaining of insight. They are known as the seven *bojjhaṅgā* or factors of enlightenment. They are: 1. *sati,* mindfulness, 2. *Dhamma-vicaya,* investigation of truth, 3. *viriya,* effort, 4. *pīti,* joy, 5. *passaddhi,* tranquility, 6. *samādhi,* concentration, and 7. *upekkhā,* equanimity. An examination of these seven qualities gives one some idea of the sort of individual who is mature enough in character and intellect for the practice of this contemplation, *vipassanā bhāvanā.* One gets an impression of the true ascetic, alert, keen-minded, dauntless, cheerful, calm, concentrated and poised. He is no weakling, running away from life. He is a hero, facing life as lesser beings dare not face it. His mind does not play about any longer with the surfaces of things, but seeks deeply.

In the steadfast practice of such contemplation a time comes when, in a flash of insight, the true nature of life is realized. It is seen as transitory, pain-laden, devoid of soul.

Insight is not achieved by a process of reasoning. It is a direct experience, profound and shattering in its effect. At the first flash of insight the seer becomes a *Sotāpanna,* a Stream-Winner. No longer can he be called a worldling, no longer is he common clay. The process of transmutation thus begun, proceeds as surely as day succeeds night. In succeeding flashes of insight the seer attains the stages of *Sakadagāmi* and *Anāgāmi*, until finally, full enlightenment is won and he is an *Arahat.* Of beings such as these the Blessed One has said:

> *"They whose minds are well perfected in the factors of enlightenment, they who, without craving, delight in the renunciation of attachment, they, the corruption-free shining ones, have attained Nibbāna even in this world."*
>
> Dhammapada 89

The Six Aspirations

1. Renunciation Part I

He who, in this world, giving up craving,
would renounce and become a homeless one,
he who has destroyed craving and becoming—
him, I call a Brāhmaṇa.

Dhammapada 415

Renunciation, *nekkhamma,* is the first of the six aspirations (*ajjhāsayas*) of a Bodhisatta. A Bodhisatta, in the strict sense, is one who has received assurance from a Buddha that one day, in the distant future, he too will become a Buddha. Gotama Buddha had received such an assurance from Dīpaṅkara Buddha. In that existence our Buddha was an ascetic, Sumedha by name, so highly evolved that he could have become an *Arahanta*, a Saint. But his was a heroic spirit. With a heart of love for all beings, he chose the immeasurably harder road of the aspirant to Supreme Buddhahood, so that countless others too might benefit.

This, in itself, was renunciation of the highest order. Thereafter, through incalculably long periods of time, he who was to be Gotama Buddha battled on, building his character to that towering stature, which Buddhas alone attain. His main aspiration when he could remember it was Buddhahood. To this end he performed the ten *pāramīs* (perfections) times without number, sacrificing life itself. But there were existences in the long gulf of time that pass between the appearances of Buddhas when this supreme aim was temporarily obscured.

A Bodhisatta is necessarily a powerful character, and power can lead to great evil as well as great good. The driving force that is a Bodhisatta, wrongly directed, can take a downward plunge, deeper and more appalling than anything lesser beings can even imagine. What is it then that keeps a Bodhisatta on a steady course, life after life, for millions and millions of lives, even when he has lost sight of his supreme aim? It can be only one thing—the inherent quality of his character.

For this reason alone, if for no other, the six aspirations of the Bodhisatta, *every* Bodhisatta, are of interest to us Buddhists. From a man's aspirations one can get a glimpse of his character. A Bodhisatta, life after life, has a deep, natural, inevitable leaning towards six things. They are: *nekkhamma, paviveka, alobha, adosa, amoha,* and *nissaraṇa* (renunciation, seclusion, non-craving, non-hating, non-ignorance and freedom).

There is good reason for the negative form in which the third, fourth, and fifth aspirations are couched. We will deal with that in due course. For the present, we confine ourselves to the first aspiration—renunciation. To the average worldling, the word "Enough!" signifies only one thing—satiety. He is by instinct a gobbler and cries "Enough!" only when, for the time being, he can gobble no more. It happens, recurrently, in the context of the grosser physical appetites. Hunger is a good example. But in certain other contexts it is so rare as to be virtually non-existent. Take the appetite for money for instance. The average worldling can never have enough of it, for the simple reason that his greed is insatiable. However much he may have, he goes on wanting more and doing all he can to grab it. To say "Enough!" would seem to him like madness.

The story is quite different in the case of one who, like a Bodhisatta, has an instinctive leaning towards renunciation. Whatever his immediate heredity or environment, however alluring the immediate prospect of wealth, power, worldly position or influence, he has a deep, natural, inevitable leaning towards renunciation. He says "Enough," not because he is temporarily gorged, but because *renunciation* itself appeals to him as something positively good.

It is not difficult to see the significance of such a trait in the case of a powerful character such as a Bodhisatta. Life after life, it guides him away from the pursuit of ignoble worldly ends. Life after life, he sheds his worldly shackles and goes free, as a homeless ascetic, even though it be for a period when the word "Buddha" is unknown. It is a rudder holding him steady on his way towards the Final Goal.

Renunciation Part II

Who outgrows all life's toys,
His childhood's o'er;
He no more cares to reap,
He's not a sower.

Kassapa Thera

Renunciation in Buddhism, *nekkhamma*, is not so much a giving up as a growing up. We may give up things that we possess, or think we possess, for various different reasons. We may do so in order to please somebody, whose goodwill we wish to secure. We may do so in order that other people may think highly of us. We may do so from a number of different motives, some good and some bad. But the motive which inspires the true act of renunciation is as simple as it is lofty—a wish to let go.

To take a simple illustration, let us consider the case of a child with a number of toys. He may give up some of them because he is generous, or because he wishes to make friends with another child, or because he is a self-conscious little prig who wishes to appear noble. But he still loves his toys and really wants to have them and play with them. Such acts of giving up are not true acts of renunciation. But this child grows older. His outlook widens, and a time comes when he feels that the toys are a burden to him. He has to look after them, clean them, keep them in working order, but they yield him no pleasure now. Then he thinks, "Why should I hang on to these things any longer? Let anybody take them who wishes to have them." With this thought he lets go of those toys, and does not care who takes them or what happens to them thereafter. He has outgrown them. That is true renunciation.

All through life we perform acts of true renunciation in the process of growing up. We leave things behind as we progress towards a greater and greater maturity. Possessions that we once valued and clung to begin to appear as burdens, and we let go of them, not caring who takes them. But, with all worldlings, there comes a stage of stagnation, of arrested development. And so it is that there are certain things to which all worldlings cling until death comes to them and says, "Leave everything and come with me." Then there is a wrench, a clinging to valued possessions, to loved ones, to life itself, and with this clinging the seed is sown for continued existence, fresh possessions, further suffering.

And so life goes on and, as a being develops in maturity, a time comes when even the valued possessions of the adult worldling appear to him as toys that have lost their appeal. He realizes that he does not even possess them in any real sense of the word, his hold on them being subject to certain happenings such as death, over which he has no control. He sees himself as nothing more than a part-time custodian of a heap of trash.

This is how worldly possessions appear to those who renounce the world. Is it surprising that they let go? Rid of all such burdens, they are progressing on the road to greater maturity. Some day they will attain the ultimate maturity, when every single burden is shed and deliverance is won.

2. Seclusion

He who sits alone, rests alone, walks alone, he
who is strenuous and who alone subdues self:
such a man finds delight in the forest depths.

Dhammapada 305

Seclusion, *paviveka,* is the second aspiration of every Bodhisatta. He seeks it naturally, not because he dislikes other people but because he finds something positively good and wholesome in seclusion. Life after life he leaves the crowd and walks alone, taking easily and instinctively to the ascetic life.

The herd instinct is strong in most of us. We like to be with others, all the time. We feel a sense of security in doing what they do, saying what they say, thinking what they think. When circumstances compel us to leave the herd even for a short time, we feel uneasy. We yearn to return as fast as possible.

Today, in many parts of the world, there seems to be an upsurge of childish behaviour among adults. People subscribe to all sorts of dogmas without knowing, or bothering to ask, the reason why. The violence with which Communism for instance as advocated by some is as unreasoning as the violence with which it is opposed by others. People are willing to do literally anything rather than think for themselves. They are willing to fight and die for ideologies that they do not understand. They hold "convictions" that they have acquired as involuntarily as they catch measles.

Seclusion is really a quality of aloofness, mental rather than mechanical. As Lord Horder has put it, seclusion is "a withdrawing of mind at times from the busyness of life." Most of us are too busy with trifles. We need to look at life at times, ourselves included, from a distance as it were. Only thus can we preserve a sense of proportion and a sense of humour. We need to ask "Why?" and we can do this only if we hold aloof.

A Bodhisatta is ever a truth-seeker. When a questing mind goes in search of truth it owes allegiance to truth alone. It is ruthless in its integrity. It cuts through the rough shell of dogma and examines the heart, and if that heart is rotten it rejects the dogma without hesitation or regret. If a Bodhisatta finds himself agreeing with the crowd, it is because he has thought things out for himself. He never agrees through cowardice or laziness or lack of integrity.

But, unfortunately, it is in the nature of crowds to be wrong about most things, most of the time. Even when they are right, it usually is for the wrong reasons. So it is inevitable that truth-seekers generally prefer to walk alone. With mind unfettered by prejudice, uncluttered with other people's opinions, the Bodhisatta goes his own road. Whenever it lies in his power to help others, he does so, gladly. But, being wise, he knows that interference in other people's affairs can lead to more harm than good. So, as a rule, he is content to be a witness.

In an environment of seclusion, he finds peace and strength. While others find a sense of security in being members of a herd, he feels safest when he is alone. The forest depths hold no terrors for him. The tremendous trifles of existence cease to worry him. His mind grows calm and concentrated. It bursts the fetters of sensual existence. It soars, clean, clear and serene—seeking, ever seeking. Where truth beckons the Bodhisatta goes.

3. Non-Craving

Whoso in the world controls
this stupid unruly craving,
from him sorrows fall away,
like water-drops from a lotus-leaf.

Dhammapada 336

Non-craving, *alobha,* is the third aspiration of every Bodhisatta, existence after existence on his long journey to final deliverance.

We said in a previous essay that there is good reason for the negative form in which this lofty aspiration is expressed. There are some who imagine that *alobha* means generosity or munificence, but they are wrong, and there is a real difference between the two ideas. The man who is generous wishes to accumulate, so that he may give to others. The man who cultivates the quality of non-craving does not wish to accumulate for *any* reason. The generous man crossing a desert and coming upon a bag of gold would pick it up and take it with him, thinking of the others to whom he might give the money. The man who has cultivated non-craving to a high degree would leave the gold where it lies and go his way, not wishing to burden himself with it for any reason whatsoever.

Most of us have excellent reasons for accumulating possessions of all sorts. We pride ourselves on our altruism, while grabbing as much as we can, as quickly as we can. Each of us feels oneself a wiser, more worthy custodian of wealth than most other people. We intend to be generous, of course, and give to those who deserve our charity. But in order to give, we must first have. And so we spend most of our time in the process of acquisition. When it comes to giving away, we are very, very cautious and discriminating.

An aspiration to non-craving goes directly to the root of the matter. To accumulate wealth in order that one might help others is something like eating a vast quantity of food in order that one might vomit. Certain animals do it to feed their young. It is mixed up with the idea of "me and mine." It is an essentially selfish operation. The generous father accumulates wealth in order that he might leave it to *his* children. But it is an eternal truth that *every* act of acquisition means a corresponding deprivation of others. To one who loves all beings equally, without distinction or reserve, this business of grabbing from the world in general in order to give to particular individuals seems utterly stupid.

It is more than stupid. It is dangerous. It can lead to every kind of wickedness and meanness. That is why the quality of non-craving is so important for a Bodhisatta. It keeps him on a clean straight road. He goes with safety past the traps, which ensnare lesser beings. His is a powerful character, and the pursuit of possessions, however altruistic the motive, can lead such a character into great evil. Even Hitler and Mussolini had good motives. So has a tigress, when she carries away your child in order to feed her children.

A Bodhisatta will not let himself be dominated by craving. He lives like a master, ruling his desires with wisdom. His road is long and steep. But his load is light, and he goes forward happily.

4. Non-Hating

"Whoever, by causing pain to others,
seeks to win happiness for himself,
becomes entangled in the bonds of hate.
Such a man is not freed from hatred."

Dhammapada 291

Non-hating, *adosa*, is the fourth characteristic aspiration of every Bodhisatta. Here too there is good reason for the negative form in which the aspiration is expressed. A Bodhisatta, in his successive existences, may not always be one who is set on good works. He may not be a social reformer or a member of the local anti-crime association. He may be a man who minds his own business and goes his own way. But he does not wish to be a slave, and no bondage is more foolish than that which we impose on ourselves by hating others.

No man can hate another without losing some measure of freedom. Time and energy are two of our most precious assets, whatever we are striving for. But, if we are stupid, we squander them on our enemies as recklessly as an infatuated lover squanders them on his beloved. And hatred is a destructive emotion. It is like a gun whose recoil is more dangerous than the bullet, which it discharges. The damage done in front is as nothing compared to the damage done behind.

We, as Buddhists, should realize that the road of hatred is the road of slavery and suffering. It is not a matter of forgiving our enemies. If we see things as they really are, which few of us do, we will know that we *cannot* harm our enemies. Whatever pain they may suffer at our hands is merely the result of their own bad kamma, the paying-off of their own debts. In the meantime, by making ourselves the agency through which they pay off their debts, we incur new debts, which we in our turn will have to pay. And so it will go on, life after life for countless lives, unless we see the folly of it all and put a stop to this meaningless self-torture. It is in the ultimate analysis, a matter of forgiving ourselves, of excusing ourselves from further participation in a painful and utterly stupid activity. Only a masochist would see things in this light and yet persist in hatred.

Just as the road of hatred is the road of suffering and bondage, so the road of non-hatred is the road of happiness and freedom. This is the road of all Bodhisattas, life after life, in their long striving for Supreme Buddhahood. They are not willing to be the tools of other peoples' bad kamma. They seek no worldly advance or seeming success that entails suffering to others. They are content to live and let live. They are not to be drawn into crusades and holy wars.

It is well for us Buddhists to remember this always. Hatred is an ugly word, but it can easily be disguised under the name of "righteous indignation" and held up as something worthwhile. We should be on our guard always.

5. Non-Ignorance

The fool who knows that he is a fool
is at least to that extent a wise man.
The fool who thinks he is wise is a fool indeed.

Dhammapada 63

Non-ignorance, *amoha*, is the fifth aspiration of every Bodhisatta. Once again, there is reason for the negative form in which the aspiration is put. A Bodhisatta may not, in every birth, be a student of the current arts or sciences. He may not even be an educated man in the worldly sense. But he is always one who strives to see things as they really are. He has a basic integrity of mind, which stubbornly refuses to be misled by appearances. He has no pretences, and he is not beguiled by the pretences of others.

Most of us go through life with certain mental reservations, which do not permit us to ask ourselves the questions that really matter. We are like children, obedient children, who take a lot of things on trust, accepting without question the voice of authority. Thus, authority tells us that patriotism is a good quality, that worldly success is praiseworthy, that the scout-movement helps to build character and that the "public school spirit" is the very essence of manly virtue. So we fight for our respective countries in time of war, try hard to make money in times of peace, send our children to scout camps and, if we can afford it, to public schools. If anybody presumes to question the wisdom of our actions, we "know" that he is either a fool or a knave.

A Bodhisatta must be one who does not mind being considered a fool or a knave. If it is foolish not to think that one's own country is always in the right, then he is a fool. If it is knavish not to make money when the opportunity offers, then he is a knave. If it is ignoble to think for oneself and try to see things as they really are, then he is content to be the meanest of men. He asks his own questions, finds his own answers, and is strong enough to abide by them.

One of the questions he asks, life after life, is whether any phenomenon whatsoever is eternal. Life after life he sees that all phenomena are transient. He sees, too, that in transient phenomena there can be no real happiness or contentment. And so he seeks something beyond everything that he knows, something that does not change, something real. His is necessarily a long quest, for the answer comes only with attainment of Buddhahood. But it is always a quest, never an assumption of having found the final answer until that answer has really been found.

How many of us are wise enough to admit that we are fools? We say, as Buddhists, that all things are transient. But to judge by our actions, our plans, our hope, that statement does not carry much conviction to our own minds. Why? Because *moha,* ignorance, dominates our minds.

6. Freedom

He who, discarding human bonds
and transcending celestial ties,
is completely delivered of all bonds—
him I call a Brāhmaṇa.

Dhammapada 417

Freedom, *nissaraṇa,* is the last of the six distinctive aspirations of every Bodhisatta. It is, perhaps, the strongest of them all. It is because he loves freedom that a Bodhisatta seeks to win it, and to teach others the way to win it. He seeks leadership in the true sense, not to dominate others but to liberate them.

It takes vision to see the bonds that bind us. Few have that kind of vision. We would heartily agree that income tax is a bond, but we find it hard to regard in this light the income on which the tax is levied. Debts, of course, are bonds, but what of the desires, which make us borrow money? We see that a man undergoing a jail sentence for some crime he has committed is in bondage, but most of us are inclined to regard the successful swindler as a free man.

Even before he attains final Enlightenment, a Bodhisatta has clarity of vision, and this vision helps him to see bonds where others see only blessings. Thus, wealth, children, sovereignty over others, and a host of other things which most worldlings regard as desirable, he sees as bonds. These so-called blessings, while they last, may bring a fleeting moment of pleasure. But a Bodhisatta gladly renounces such pleasure, just as any sane man would refrain from licking a drop of honey off the nose of a hungry python, whose coils would instantly flash around him.

It is precisely for this reason that the Bodhisatta, as Prince Themiya, underwent all manner of hardships in order to avoid becoming a king. He had been a king in a previous existence, which he remembered. And he remembered also the state of suffering into which his kamma took him, as a direct result of the exercise of kingly authority. The zest with which election campaigns are conducted, even in Buddhist lands, bears witness to the fact that the spirit of Themiya is absent in most politicians. Of course, every politician has noble reasons for wanting to be elected. He wishes to 'serve his country.' But thinking men might find it a little difficult to understand how the spirit of service and the spirit of Themiya could be so different in their manifestation.

We can always find excellent reasons for doing what our desires prompt us to do. In pandering to our desires we may be honest and admit the truth, or we may be cunning rogues and seek to conceal it, or we may even be so foolish as not to see it. But one thing we definitely cannot be, while dominated by desire: we cannot be free. Freedom means letting go.

A Bodhisatta, loving freedom, is not willing to trade it in exchange for the prize which the world has to offer. He, above all others, is imbued with the spirit of service, but a sure instinct tells him that no service can be worthwhile which is performed at the sacrifice of personal freedom. He avoids fresh bonds, and strives to break any that he already has. He seeks to help others neither as a master nor as a slave, but as a friend.

Escapism

Neither in the sky, nor in mid-ocean,
nor in entering a mountain cave is found
that place, where abiding, one may escape
the consequences of an evil deed.

Dhammapada 127

There are people who seek to find fault with the Buddha Dhamma on the ground that it teaches escapism. They do not know what they are talking about. Escapism may be broadly defined as the attempt to avoid facing disagreeable facts. It is a very different thing from the action of any sensible person who actually escapes, or tries to escape, from danger or suffering. For instance, if you find yourself in a burning house, it would be escapism to take a large dose of whisky and go to bed, assuring yourself that everything will be all right by the time you wake up. It would not be escapism to leave the house before it is too late.

Buddhism teaches people to face facts. It does not try to pretend that everything is for the best, either in this life or in the next. It does not seek to delude people into the belief that a benevolent, all powerful deity presides over their destinies, or that salvation can be attained by unquestioning faith in such a deity. It does not deal in dope, telling people, "Swallow this pill, and when death comes, it will bring you life, everlastingly beautiful and glorious."

Buddhism teaches us to use our own powers of observation and reasoning and *face the facts.* The truth of *anicca,* impermanence, is not an esoteric teaching, or something to be taken on trust. We can see it all about us, every day of our lives. Flowers bloom and fade. People grow up, then grow old, then die. Everything is in a process of change. Nothing is stable for two consecutive instants. If anything seems stable, it is only because the process of change is relatively slow. But it can be, and often is, speeded up, as when a healthy man gets infected with tuberculosis.

From this *truth of anicca,* the truth of *dukkha* follows necessarily. *Dukkha* means suffering, and suffering is inevitable when all life is associated with change. No sensitive adult can look upon the scenes of his childhood without a feeling of sadness. No sensitive person, even if he and all his present associates are healthy and prosperous, can think of the sick and the poor in this world without feeling sad. And health, even in the healthiest of us, is also subject to change. Sickness, old age and death are merely biding their time.

From these truths of *anicca* and *dukkha* emerges the truth of *anattā.* There is nothing in this process of which one can say, "This is mine. This am I. This is my soul." Seeking a soul in this process is like stripping away the sheaths of a plantain tree in order to find the heartwood. There is no heartwood. It is merely a compound of changing, unstable ingredients, giving an appearance of solidity and stability.

And Buddhism teaches us to face the fact of rebirth. It is easier to be a materialist, and to console oneself with the promise of deep, dreamless, eternal sleep at life's close. To many thinking people, the idea of total extinction at death is not in the least disagreeable. Indeed, it would be comforting, if it were true. But unfortunately, it is not true. The process goes on and on, life after life. We live again and again, interminably, reaping as we have sown, the present the result of the past, the future the result of the present and the past.

The Buddha teaches us to face these facts honestly. And yet he tells us not to despair, but to be of good courage, because there is a way of working out our deliverance—the way *of sīla, samādhi, paññā*, virtue, concentration of mind, and wisdom. Is this escapism?

The God Idea

The man who is not credulous,
who understands the Uncreated (Nibbāna),
who has cut off the link,
who has put an end to occasion (of good and evil),
who has vomited all desires—
he, indeed, is the noblest of men.

Dhammapada 79

Buddhists are sometimes asked by non-Buddhists whether they believe in God, and if not, why not? If they reply, as they should, that the Buddha has denied the existence of a God, in the sense of a Supreme Being or Creator of all that is, Buddhists are sometimes confronted with the time-worn, repeatedly resurrected, "watchmaker" argument.

It goes like this. Even so small and relatively simple a piece of machinery as a watch must have a maker. It cannot come into existence automatically. So it follows that the universe, with all its complex balance of forces, all its stars and planets and other celestial bodies working in perfect coordination, must have had a creator.

The objections to the argument are threefold, and fatal:

1. No watchmaker ever came into existence automatically. If one is to be logical, this should apply to the universe-maker as well. He too must have had a maker, who in his turn must have had a maker, and so on in a receding vista of makers. The argument thus ends in futility, for where is one to stop?

2. No watchmaker ever made a watch out of sheer nothingness. How, then, can we postulate a universe-maker who achieved this impossible feat? Granted that he too, like the watchmaker, had materials how did the materials come into existence? Did they always exist?

3. If the argument is an argument at all, it leads inevitably to the conclusion that there is no one universe-maker but a number

of them. Even so simple a mechanism as a watch or a motor car is the creation of several people, each a specialist. If the universe was created by a conscious and intelligent agency, that agency probably consisted of a syndicate, a team of makers, rather than one sole maker. We do not seek to maintain such a conclusion, but only point out that it is a logical conclusion, perfectly consistent with the data provided, and the reasoning sought to be applied thereto.

The Buddha spoke of gods: not one God, with a capital G, but many gods. He taught the hard truth that these gods too, like human beings, are subject to decay and death. The inexorable law of change applies to gods too, just as it applies to men. They may live long, much longer than humans, because of their own good kamma. They may be very powerful, again because of their good kamma. Such longevity and power may even lead them to the erroneous belief that they are eternal and all-powerful, but this is their greatest fallacy. In due time, when the good kamma which maintains them in their glory is expended, they too die as humans die, as cattle die, as butterflies die. And when they die, they too are reborn, for they have not won freedom from the round of birth and death.

All gods, however lofty, however powerful, are living beings in *saṃsāra*. As such they are mind-body (and in the case of the *arūpāvacaradevās*, pure mind) fluxes. Mind and body are ever changing. In this changing process, what is the creator? The Buddha said there is only one creator—desire. It is desire that keeps the process going, phoenix-like, life after life.

There is no exception to this rule. It is a basic truth. If there is a God, he too is constantly creating himself by reason of desire. That is all he creates. Is there then an Uncreated (*akata*)? According to the Buddha, yes. To us worldlings (*puthujjanas*) it is but a name—Nibbāna. It is a name that stands for happiness, final release from the round of rebirth. There is no God in this noble teaching, no supreme being to whom we must cringe. We stand on our own feet; we are our own creators, we are our own masters, and in the fullness of time we will be our own saviours.

The Soul Idea

"Soul-less is everything that is,"
When this with wisdom one discerns,
Disgusted then is one with ill,
This is the Path to Purity.

Dhammapada 279

There are some who, despite repeated and authoritative assurances to the contrary, still entertain the false view that the Buddha adopted an equivocal attitude with regard to belief in soul. This is only natural, as all worldlings, however learned and intelligent they may be, do cherish a belief in a soul. Reason plays a relatively small part in what people believe or do not believe. Whatever reasons may be urged against the soul idea, the idea itself persists until a being attains the first stage of sainthood. When that stage is reached, *sakkāyadiṭṭhi,* belief in a soul vanishes, never to return.

From this very phenomenon, as taught by the Buddha, the thinking person *must* deduce that the soul idea is false. One does not, surely, advance to the stage of *Sotāpanna* in order to rid oneself of a true belief! If the soul idea is correct, and a soul really does exist, then on the Buddha's own statement, the worldling is more enlightened in this respect than the *sotāpanna* or indeed, even the *arahat.* But this is absurd, for the Buddha taught a road of evolution to greater and greater understanding.

Such understanding is the fruit of growth, not of logic. We almost said spiritual growth, but did not, because the word "spiritual" has become somewhat debased through excessive use in other contexts. It now smacks of cheap emotionalism and spurious religiosity. The growth of the individual towards sainthood, in the Buddhist sense, is a very slow and gradual process, admitting of no short cuts and pretences. It takes, literally, aeons.

Of course, this does not mean that Buddhism denies the possibility of sudden "reformation" and achievement of sanctity. The notorious robber, Aṅgulimāla, who became an *arahat*, is a case in point. But, as in his case, the suddenness of such advance is only apparent, and due to the inability of the average observer to relate the present phenomenon to its true background in past existences. The potential saint, in such a being as Aṅgulimāla is already there in his character, needing but a shift in the balance of personality to be transmuted from potential to reality. Such a shift can only be effected by a Buddha, and that is why a Buddha is called "*Anuttaro purisa-damma-sārathi*" (guide incomparable for the training of individuals).

People sometimes tend to forget the reason why an aspirant to Buddhahood strives through incalculable periods of time to achieve his final goal. It is not in order that he might found yet another "ism," to titillate men's intellects and provide absorbing topics of debate in cultured circles. It is only in order that he might help others to win release from the round of rebirth and all its attendant miseries. The help a Buddha gives is his Teaching, for he teaches the eternal Dhamma, the way of release that other Buddhas have taught before him. The doctrine of *anattā*, soullessness, is an integral part of this eternal Dhamma. It is not a thing to be savoured intellectually and played with. It is reality, something that we worldlings can only barely glimpse intellectually, but which the saint realizes with a certitude that is final.

Me and Mine

"These sons are mine, this wealth I hold,"
The fool raves thus and comes to ruin;
When self itself owns not a "self,"
Who are thy sons, what is thy self!

Dhammapada 62

In the last essay we endeavored to state the doctrine of *anattā*, soullessness, taught by the Buddha. It was perforce a very bare statement and we therefore feel that some further thought should be devoted to the subject.

It should, first of all, be understood clearly that this doctrine is not a mere theory but a truth, propounded by one who saw things as they really are. The Buddha did not speak in the tentative and hypothetical terms adopted by lesser men for the simple reason that his Teaching was the result of *direct knowledge*, and not of logic.

It should be borne in mind that the *anattā* doctrine is of practical application in our everyday lives. It is not something of purely academic interest, to be stored away in some sealed compartment of our minds. The Buddha intended us to apply it to our own lives, to test it on the touchstone of personal experience and prove its truth for ourselves. It is true that ultimate realization can only come with the attainment of the four stages of sanctity; but short of that, we do have the ability to think things out and arrive at certain convictions based on personal experience.

Experience teaches us that a good deal of ill health, both physical and mental, is due to worry. Modern medical science is definitely of the view that such diseases as diabetes, high blood pressure and gastric ulcer are aggravated, if not actually brought about, by anxiety states. Doctors are inclining more and more to the opinion that, in the treatment of such diseases, and indeed most functional disorders, close attention should be paid to the mental condition of the patient.

Of all adverse mental states, the most obviously unhealthy and potentially dangerous is prolonged worry. Why, we naturally ask, do people worry? In the ultimate analysis there is only one answer. People worry because of thoughts of "me and mine." We yearn for security for ourselves and for those we love, in a changing world that offers no permanent security. He who builds sand castles on the beach is afraid of every wave. He who offers hostages to fortune becomes the plaything of fortune. He who identifies himself with any existing state of affairs and is anxious to preserve that state of affairs inviolate, knows no peace of mind. Thus we worry about our "selves," our health, our children, our friends, our possessions—yearning always to maintain stability in that which is inherently unstable.

The Buddha made no pretence of offering stability in the unstable. For this reason some foolish people call him a pessimist, just as a child who has built a sand castle will regard as pessimistic any prediction of its dissolution. But the Buddha did offer people something infinitely better than the stability they foolishly seek in unstable phenomena. He offered them a method to attain *ultimate stability, ultimate security, in that which is eternally stable and secure.* He said, in effect, "Do not imagine there is a soul, a core of permanence in body or mind. That is a road of anxiety and suffering. See these merely as changing phenomena and work for that which does not change." If we remember this message in our daily lives, we will have taken a big step in the right direction. We may not attain Nibbāna here and now, but we will at least realize that there is no substitute for Nibbāna, and we will worry less about the unstable environment in which we live.

Travel

Few indeed are they
Who go the Further Shore.
The rest of mankind only
Runs about on the hither bank.

Dhammapada 85

This body of flesh and blood and bones is a passing thing. So too is the flickering phenomenon called personality which is associated with it. There is nothing permanent here, nothing that can be called "a soul." And yet the Buddha tells us this compound of linked processes, which is called a living being, does not begin with birth or end with death. It goes on from life to life, ever-changing.

We have come a long way, all of us. Nobody can see a beginning. Each one of us, as a changing process, is very, very old. We are older than the solar system and the stars and the nebulae, in their present form.

The Buddha has said that in this long journey each of us has experienced everything there is to be experienced on the "hither bank," that is, in the world. We have loved and hated, 'joyed' and sorrowed, been everywhere, seen everything, done everything, many, many times. This business has been going on so long that if we could but remember the past, we would be heartily sick of the whole thing. But we do not remember. That is why, life after life, we keep on doing the same old things again and again. We are still running about on the "hither bank" playing with the things that are there.

From the highest heavens to the lowest hells we run. If somebody like a Buddha tells us quit fooling about and try to get across to the "Further Shore" we do not pay heed.

We can stay here as long as we wish. Indeed, we shall stay here for a long time even after it has dawned on us that we are making fools of ourselves. It is not easy to get to the "Further Shore" for the "Further Shore" is Nibbāna, which only Buddhas, Paccekabuddhas and Arahats attain. To cross over, we too must evolve as they evolved. That is the only journey we have not made, the only journey worth making.

People think that by going from one spot to another on the surface of the earth they are travelling. So they are like maggots crawling over a rotten orange. Other people, more ambitious and imaginative, dream of going from the earth to the moon, or to other planets. *That* they feel, will be *travelling! So* it will, like insects flying from one rotten orange to another. But the Buddha tells us that we have tried *all* the rotten oranges at one time or another. They are all on the "hither bank," and there is nothing new in them.

Out, far out in space, so far that the mind cannot imagine the distances, there are stars, many millions of them. It would be the height of egotism to deny that life must exist on some of the planets revolving about those other stars, just as the earth revolves about the sun. If there is life, why not human life? It may well be. And so what? It only means that out there, just as here, there is greed, there is hatred, there is ignorance. Need we travel out to such planets? Need we go so far to see the same foolish faces, hear the same ugly noises, smell the same stinks that are all around us here on earth? Speaking for ourselves, we have no desire to go to all that trouble merely to renew our acquaintance with the unpleasant.

The distance by which we separate ourselves from the unpleasant is not measured in miles. A good book can do it, for a while. So can meditation, if one has practised meditation and is good at it. Quietness is necessary. One will not sit to meditate on a railway line, which is in use, nor in the middle of a busy street, nor on a shooting-range while target practice is going on. One will not turn on the radio, especially if a race commentary is on the air. With quietness and stillness come concentration and clear thought. *This*, at last, is the preparation for a real adventure, a journey utterly new. Its end? The "Further Shore." Good luck!

Bewailing not the past,
Of the future incurious,
Living in the present—
By this health glows.

Anxious about the future
And bewailing the past,
Thus do fools wither away—
Like cut green reeds.

Atītaṃ nānusocanti, nappajappanti 'nāgataṃ
Paccuppannena yāpenti, tena vaṇṇo pasīdati.
Anāgatappajappāya atītassānusocanā
Etena bālā sussanti, naḷo'va harito luto.

Translated by Kassapa Thera
From the Samyutta Nikāya Vol. 1: Sāgāthā Vagga, No. 10

The Five Mental Hindrances and Their Conquest

Selected Texts from the Pali Canon and the Commentaries

Compiled and translated by

Nyanaponika Thera

WHEEL PUBLICATION NO. 26

Introduction

Unshakable deliverance of the mind is the highest goal in the Buddha's doctrine. Here, deliverance means: the freeing of the mind from all limitations, fetters, and bonds that tie it to the Wheel of Suffering, to the Circle of Rebirth. It means: the cleansing of the mind of all defilements that mar its purity; the removing of all obstacles that bar its progress from the mundane (*lokiya*) to the supramundane consciousness (*lokuttara-citta*), that is, to Arahatship.

Many are the obstacles which block the road to spiritual progress, but there are five in particular which, under the name of hindrances (*nivaraṇa*), are often mentioned in the Buddhist scriptures:

1. Sensual desire (*kāmacchanda*),
2. Ill-will (*byāpāda*),
3. Sloth and torpor (*thīna-middha*),
4. Restlessness and remorse (*uddhacca-kukkucca*),
5. Sceptical doubt (*vicikicchā*).

They are called "hindrances" because they hinder and envelop the mind in many ways, obstructing its development (*bhāvanā*). According to the Buddhist teachings, spiritual development is twofold: through tranquillity (*samatha-bhāvanā*) and through insight (*vipassanā-bhāvanā*). Tranquillity is gained by complete concentration of the mind during the meditative absorptions (*jhāna*). For achieving these absorptions, the overcoming of the five hindrances, at least temporarily, is a preliminary condition. It is especially in the context of achieving the absorptions that the Buddha often mentions the five hindrances in his discourses.

There are five mental constituents which are chiefly representative of the first meditative absorption, and are therefore called the factors of absorption (*jhānaṅga*). For each of these there is, according to Buddhist commentarial tradition, one of the five hindrances that is specifically harmful for it and excludes its higher development and refinement to the degree required for jhāna; and on the other hand, the cultivation of these five factors beyond their average level will be an antidote against the hindrances, preparing the road to jhāna. The relationship between these two groups of five is indicated in this anthology, under the heading of the respective hindrance.

Not only the meditative absorptions but also lesser degrees of mental concentration are impeded by these five hindrances. So is the "neighbourhood" (or "access") concentration (*upacārasamādhi*), being the preliminary stage for the fully absorbed concentration (*appanā*) reached in jhāna. Likewise excluded by the presence of the hindrances is the momentary concentration (*khaṇikasamādhi*) which has the strength of neighbourhood concentration and is required for mature insight (*vipassanā*). But apart from these higher stages of mental development, any earnest attempt at clear thinking and pure living will be seriously affected by the presence of these five hindrances.

This widespread harmful influence of the five hindrances shows the urgent necessity of breaking down their power by constant effort. One should not believe it sufficient to turn one's attention to the hindrances only at the moment when one sits down for meditation. Such last-minute effort in suppressing the hindrances will rarely be successful unless helped by previous endeavour during one's ordinary life.

One who earnestly aspires to the unshakable deliverance of the mind should, therefore, select a definite "working-ground" of a direct and practical import: a *kammaṭṭhāna*[1] in its widest sense, on which the structure of his entire life should be based. Holding fast to that "working-ground," never losing sight of it for long, even this alone will be a considerable and encouraging progress in the control and development of the mind, because in that way the directive and purposive energies of mind will be strengthened considerably. One who has chosen the conquest of the five hindrances for a "working-ground" should examine which of the five are strongest in one's personal case. Then one should carefully observe how, and on which occasions, they usually appear. One should further know the positive forces within one's own mind by which each of these hindrances can best be countered and, finally, conquered; and one should also examine one's life for any opportunity of developing these qualities which, in the following pages, have been indicated

1. I.e., subject of meditation: literally "working-ground."

under the headings of the spiritual faculties (*indriya*), the factors of absorption (*jhānaṅga*), and the factors of enlightenment (*bojjhaṅga*). In some cases, subjects of meditation have been added which will be helpful in overcoming the respective hindrances.

By the "worldling" (*puthujjana*),[2] however, only a temporary suspension and partial weakening of the hindrances can be attained. Their final and complete eradication takes place on the stages of sanctity (*ariyamagga*):

1) Doubt is eliminated on the first stage, the path of stream-entry (*sotāpatti-magga*).
2) Sensual desire, ill will and remorse are eliminated on the third stage, the path of non-returner (*anāgāmi-magga*).
3) Sloth and torpor and restlessness are eradicated on the path of Arahatship (*arahatta-magga*).

Hence the reward of the fight against the hindrances is not only the limited one of making possible a shorter or longer spell of meditation, but every step in weakening these hindrances takes us nearer to the stages of sanctity where deliverance from these hindrances is unshakable.

Though most of the following texts, translated from the Discourses of the Buddha and the commentaries, are addressed to monks, they are likewise valid for those living the worldly life. As the Old Masters say: "The monk (*bhikkhu*) is mentioned here as an example of those dedicated to the practice of the Teaching. Whosoever undertakes that practice is here included in the term 'monk.'

2. A "worldling," or *puthujjana*, who may be a monk or layman, is one who has not yet attained to the first stage of sanctity, the Path of stream-entry (*sotāpatti-magga*).

The Five Hindrances

I. General Texts

There are five impediments and hindrances, overgrowths of the mind that stultify insight. What five?

Sensual desire is an impediment and hindrance, an overgrowth of the mind that stultifies insight. Ill-will... Sloth and torpor... Restlessness and remorse... Sceptical doubt are impediments and hindrances, overgrowths of the mind that stultify insight.

Without having overcome these five, it is impossible for a monk whose insight thus lacks strength and power, to know his own true good, the good of others, and the good of both; nor will he be capable of realizing that superhuman state of distinctive achievement, the knowledge and vision enabling the attainment of sanctity.

But if a monk has overcome these five impediments and hindrances, these overgrowths of the mind that stultify insight, then it is possible that, with his strong insight, he can know his own true good, the good of others, and the good of both; and he will be capable of realizing that superhuman state of distinctive achievement, the knowledge and vision enabling the attainment of sanctity. (AN 5:51)

One whose heart is overwhelmed by unrestrained covetousness will do what he should not do and neglect what he ought to do. And through that, his good name and his happiness will come to ruin.

One whose heart is overwhelmed by ill-will... by sloth and torpor... by restlessness and remorse... by sceptical doubt will do what he should not do and neglect what he ought to do. And through that, his good name and his happiness will come to ruin.

But if a noble disciple has seen these five as defilements of the mind, he will give them up. And doing so, he is regarded as one of great wisdom, of abundant wisdom, clear-visioned, well endowed with wisdom. This is called "endowment with wisdom." (AN 4:61)

There are five impurities of gold impaired by which it is not pliant and wieldy, lacks radiance, is brittle and cannot be wrought well. What are these five impurities? Iron, copper, tin, lead and silver.

But if the gold has been freed from these five impurities, then it will be plaint and wieldy, radiant and firm, and can be wrought well. Whatever ornaments one wishes to make from it, be it a diadem, earrings, a necklace or a golden chain, it will serve that purpose.

Similarly, there are five impurities of the mind impaired by which the mind is not pliant and wieldy, lacks radiant lucidity and firmness, and cannot concentrate well upon the eradication of the taints (*āsava*). What are these five impurities? They are: sensual desire, ill-will, sloth and torpor, restlessness and remorse, and sceptical doubt.

But if the mind is freed of these five impurities, it will be pliant and wieldy, will have radiant lucidity and firmness, and will concentrate well upon the eradication of the taints. Whatever state realizable by the higher mental faculties one may direct the mind to, one will in each case acquire the capacity of realization, if the (other) conditions are fulfilled. (AN 5:23)

How does a monk practice mind-object contemplation on the mental objects of the five hindrances?

Herein, monks, when sensual desire is present in him the monk knows, "There is sensual desire in me," or when sensual desire is absent he knows, "There is no sensual desire in me." He knows how the arising of non-arisen sensual desire comes to be; he knows how the rejection of the arisen sensual desire comes to be; and he knows how the non-arising in the future of the rejected sensual desire comes to be.

When ill-will is present in him, the monk knows, "There is ill-will in me," or when ill-will is absent he knows, "There is no ill-will in me." He knows how the arising of non-arisen ill-will comes to be; he knows how the rejection of the arisen ill-will comes to be; and he knows how the non-arising in the future of the rejected ill-will comes to be.

When sloth and torpor are present in him, the monk knows, "There is sloth and torpor in me," or when sloth and torpor are absent he knows, "There is no sloth and torpor in me." He knows how the arising of non-arisen sloth and torpor comes to be; he knows how the rejection of the arisen sloth and torpor comes to be; and he knows how the non-arising in the future of the rejected sloth and torpor comes to be.

When restlessness and remorse are present in him, the monk knows, "There are restlessness and remorse in me," or when agitation and remorse are absent he knows, "There are no restlessness and remorse in me." He knows how the arising of non-arisen restlessness and remorse comes to be; he knows how the rejection of the arisen restlessness and remorse comes to be; and he knows how the non-arising in the future of the rejected restlessness and remorse comes to be.

When sceptical doubt is present in him, the monk knows, "There is sceptical doubt in me," or when sceptical doubt is absent he knows, "There is no sceptical doubt in me." He knows how the arising of non-arisen sceptical doubt comes to be; he knows how the rejection of the arisen sceptical doubt comes to be; and he knows how the non-arising in the future of the rejected sceptical doubt comes to be. (MN 10; Satipaṭṭhāna Sutta)

To note mindfully, and immediately, the arising of one of the hindrances, as recommended in the preceding text, is a simple but very effective method of countering these and any other defilements of the mind. By doing so, a brake is applied against the uninhibited continuance of unwholesome thoughts, and the watchfulness of mind against their recurrence is strengthened. This method is based on a simple psychological fact which is expressed by the commentators as follows: "A good and an evil thought cannot occur in combination. Therefore, at the time of knowing the sense desire (that arose in the preceding moment), that sense desire no longer exists (but only the act of knowing)."

II. The Hindrances Individually

Just as, monks, this body lives on nourishment, lives dependent on nourishment, does not live without nourishment—in the same way, monks, the five hindrances live on nourishment, depend on nourishment, do not live without nourishment.

SN 46:2

Sensual Desire

A. Nourishment of Sensual Desire

There are beautiful objects; frequently giving unwise attention to them—this is the nourishment for the arising of sensual desire that has not arisen, and the nourishment for the increase and strengthening of sensual desire that has already arisen.

SN 46:51

B. Denourishing of Sensual Desire

There are impure objects (used for meditation); frequently giving wise attention to them—this is the denourishing of the arising of sensual desire that has not yet arisen, and the denourishing of the increase and strengthening of sensual desire that has already arisen.

SN 46:51

Commentary to the Satipaṭṭhāna Sutta

Six things are conducive to the abandonment of sensual desire:

1) Learning how to meditate on impure objects;
2) Devoting oneself to the meditation on the impure;
3) Guarding the sense doors;
4) Moderation in eating;
5) Noble friendship;
6) Suitable conversation.

1. & 2. Meditation on the impure

(a) *Impure objects*
In him who is devoted to the meditation about impure objects, repulsion towards beautiful objects is firmly established. This is the result.

AN 5:36

"Impure object" refers, in particular, to the cemetery meditations as given in the Satipaṭṭhāna Sutta and explained in the *Visuddhimagga*; but it refers also to the repulsive aspects of sense objects in general.

(b) *The loathsomeness of the body*

Herein, monks, a monk reflects on just this body, confined within the skin and full of manifold impurities from the soles upward and from the top of the hair down: "There is in this body: hair of the head, hair of the body, nails, teeth, skin, flesh, sinews, bones, marrow, kidneys, heart, liver, pleura, spleen, lungs, intestines, bowels, stomach, excrement, bile, phlegm, pus, blood, sweat, fat, tears, lymph, saliva, mucus, fluid of the joints, urine (and the brain in the skull)."

MN 10

By bones and sinews knit,
With flesh and tissue smeared,
And hidden by the skin, the body
Does not appear as it really is...
The fool thinks it beautiful,
His ignorance misguiding him...

Sutta Nipāta v. 194, 199

(c) *Various contemplations*

Sense objects give little enjoyment, but much pain and much despair; the danger in them prevails.

MN 14

The unpleasant overwhelms a thoughtless man in the guise of the pleasant, the disagreeable overwhelms him in the guise of the agreeable, the painful in the guise of pleasure.

Udāna 2:8

3. Guarding the sense doors

How does one guard the sense doors? Herein, a monk, having seen a form, does not seize upon its (delusive) appearance as a whole, nor on its details. If his sense of sight were uncontrolled, covetousness, grief and other evil, unwholesome states would flow into him. Therefore he practices for the sake of its control, he watches over the sense of sight, he enters upon its control. Having heard a sound... smelt an odor... tasted a taste... felt a touch... cognized a mental object, he does not seize upon its (delusive) appearance as a whole... he enters upon its control.

SN 35:120

There are forms perceptible by the eye, which are desirable, lovely, pleasing, agreeable, associated with desire, arousing lust. If the monk does not delight in them, is not attached to them, does not welcome them, then in him thus not delighting in them, not being attached to them and not welcoming them, delight (in these forms) ceases; if delight is absent, there is no bondage. There are sounds perceptible by the ear... odors perceptible by the nose... if delight is absent, there is no bondage.

SN 35:63

4. Moderation in eating

How is he moderate in eating? Herein a monk takes his food after wise consideration: not for the purpose of enjoyment, of pride, of beautifying the body or adorning it (with muscles); but only for the sake of maintaining and sustaining this body, to avoid harm and to support the holy life, thinking: "Thus I shall destroy the old painful feeling and shall not let a new one rise. Long life will be mine, blamelessness and well-being."

MN 2; MN 39

5. Noble friendship

Reference is here, in particular, to such friends who have experience and can be a model and help in overcoming sensual desire, especially in meditating on impurity. But it applies also to noble friendship in general. The same twofold explanation holds true also for the other hindrances, with due alterations.

The entire holy life, Ānanda, is noble friendship, noble companionship, noble association. Of a monk, Ānanda, who has a noble friend, a noble companion, a noble associate, it is to be expected that he will cultivate and practice the Noble Eightfold Path.

SN 45:2

6. Suitable conversation

Reference is here in particular to conversation about the overcoming of sensual desire, especially about meditating on impurity. But it applies also to every conversation which is suitable to advance one's progress on the path. With due alterations this explanation holds true also for the other hindrances.

If the mind of a monk is bent on speaking, he (should remember this): "Talk which is low, coarse, worldly, not noble, not salutary, not leading to detachment, not to freedom from passion, not to cessation, not to tranquillity, not to higher knowledge, not to enlightenment, not to Nibbāna, namely, talk about kings, robbers and ministers, talk about armies, dangers and war, about food and drink, clothes, couches, garlands, perfumes, relatives, cars, villages, towns, cities, and provinces, about women and wine, gossip of the street and of the well, talk about the ancestors, about various trifles, tales about the origin of the world and the ocean, talk about what happened and what did not happen—such and similar talk I shall not entertain." Thus he is clearly conscious about it.

But talk about austere life, talk suitable for the unfolding of the mind, talk which is conducive to complete detachment, to freedom from passion, to cessation, tranquillity, higher knowledge, enlightenment and to Nibbāna, namely, talk about a life of frugality, about contentedness, solitude, aloofness from society, about rousing one's energy, talk about virtue, concentration, wisdom, deliverance, about the vision and knowledge of deliverance—such talk I shall entertain." Thus he is clearly conscious about it.

MN 122

These things, too, are helpful in conquering sensual desire:

1) One-pointedness of mind, of the factors of absorption (*jhānaṅga*);
2) Mindfulness, of the spiritual faculties (*indriya*);
3) Mindfulness, of the factors of enlightenment (*bojjhaṅga*).

C. Simile

If there is water in a pot mixed with red, yellow, blue or orange color, a man with a normal faculty of sight, looking into it, could not properly recognize and see the image of his own face. In the same way, when one's mind is possessed by sensual desire, overpowered by sensual desire, one cannot properly see the escape from sensual desire which has arisen; then one does not properly understand and see one's own welfare, nor that of another, nor that of both; and also texts memorized a long time ago do not come into one's mind, not to speak of those not memorized.

SN 46:55

Ill-Will

A. Nourishment of Ill-Will

There are objects causing aversion; frequently giving unwise attention to them—this is the nourishment for the arising of ill-will that has not yet arisen, and for the increase and strengthening of ill-will that has already arisen.

SN 46:51

B. Denourishing of Ill-Will

There is the liberation of the heart by loving-kindness; frequently giving wise attention to it—this is the denourishing of the arising of ill-will that has not yet arisen, and of the increase and strengthening of ill-will that has already arisen.

SN 46:51

Cultivate the meditation on loving-kindness! For by cultivating the meditation on loving-kindness, ill-will disappears.

Cultivate the meditation on compassion! For by cultivating the meditation on compassion, cruelty disappears.

Cultivate the meditation on sympathetic joy! For by cultivating the meditation on sympathetic joy, listlessness disappears.

Cultivate the meditation on equanimity! For by cultivating the meditation on equanimity, anger disappears.

MN 62

Six things are helpful in conquering ill-will:

1) Learning how to meditate on loving-kindness;
2) Devoting oneself to the meditation of loving-kindness;
3) Considering that one is the owner and heir of one's actions (*kamma*);
4) Frequent reflection on it (in the following way): Thus one should consider: "Being angry with another person, what can you do to him? Can you destroy his virtue and his other good qualities? Have you not come to your present state by your own actions, and will also go hence according to your own actions? Anger towards another

is just as if someone wishing to hit another person takes hold of glowing coals, or a heated iron-rod, or of excrement. And, in the same way, if the other person is angry with you, what can he do to you? Can he destroy your virtue and your other good qualities? He too has come to his present state by his own actions and will go hence according to his own actions. Like an unaccepted gift or like a handful of dirt thrown against the wind, his anger will fall back on his own head."

5) Noble friendship;
6) Suitable conversation.

Commentary to Satipaṭṭhāna Sutta

These things, too, are helpful in conquering ill-will:

1) Rapture, of the factors of absorption (*jhānaṅga*);
2) Faith, of the spiritual faculties (*indriya*);
3) Rapture and equanimity, of the factors of enlightenment (*bojjhaṅga*).

C. Simile

If there is a pot of water heated on the fire, the water seething and boiling, a man with a normal faculty of sight, looking into it, could not properly recognize and see the image of his own face. In the same way, when one's mind is possessed by ill-will, overpowered by ill-will, one cannot properly see the escape from the ill-will which has arisen; then one does not properly understand and see one's own welfare, nor that of another, nor that of both; and also texts memorized a long time ago do not come into one's mind, not to speak of those not memorized.

SN 46:55

Sloth and Torpor

A. Nourishment of Sloth and Torpor

There arises listlessness, lassitude, lazy stretching of the body, drowsiness after meals, mental sluggishness; frequently giving unwise attention to it—this is the nourishment for the arising of sloth and torpor that have not yet arisen and for the increase and strengthening of sloth and torpor that have already arisen.

SN 46:51

B. Denourishing of Sloth and Torpor

There is the element of rousing one's energy, the element of exertion, the element of continuous exertion; frequently giving wise attention to it—this is the denourishing of the arising of sloth and torpor that have not yet arisen and of the increase and strengthening of sloth and torpor that have already arisen.

SN 46:51

"May nothing remain but skin and sinews and bones; may flesh and blood dry up in the body! Not before having achieved what can be achieved by manly strength, manly energy, manly exertion shall my energy subside!"

MN 70

Six things are conducive to the abandonment of sloth and torpor:

1) Knowing that overeating is a cause of it;
2) Changing the bodily posture;
3) Thinking of the perception of light;
4) Staying in the open air;
5) Noble friendship;
6) Suitable conversation.

These things, too, are helpful in conquering sloth and torpor:

1. Recollection of Death

To-day the effort should be made,
Who knows if tomorrow Death will come?

MN 131

2. Perceiving the suffering in impermanence

In a monk who is accustomed to see the suffering in impermanence and who is frequently engaged in this contemplation, there will be established in him such a keen sense of the danger of laziness, idleness, lassitude, indolence and thoughtlessness, as if he were threatened by a murderer with drawn sword.

AN 7:46

3. Sympathetic joy

Cultivate the meditation on sympathetic joy! For by cultivating it, listlessness will disappear.

MN 62

Applied thought, of the factors of absorptions (*jhānaṅga*); Energy, of the spiritual facilities (*indriya*); Investigation of reality, energy and rapture, of the factors of enlightenment (*bojjhaṅga*).

When the mind is sluggish, it is not the proper time for cultivating the following factors of enlightenment: tranquillity, concentration and equanimity, because a sluggish mind can hardly be aroused by them.

SN 45:53

When the mind is sluggish, it is the proper time for cultivating the following factors of enlightenment: investigation of reality, energy and rapture, because a sluggish mind can easily be aroused by them.

4. Contemplation of the spiritual journey

"I have to tread that path which the Buddhas, the Paccekabuddhas and the Great Disciples have gone; but by an indolent person that path cannot be trodden."

Vism IV.55

5. Contemplation of the Master's greatness

"Full application of energy was praised by my Master, and he is unsurpassed in his injunctions and a great help to us. He is honoured by practicing his Dhamma, not otherwise."

Ibid.

6. Contemplation on the greatness of the Heritage

"I have to take possession of the Great Heritage, called the Good Dhamma. But one who is indolent cannot take possession of it."

Ibid.

7. How to stimulate the mind

How does one stimulate the mind at a time when it needs stimulation? If due to slowness in the application of wisdom or due to non-attainment of the happiness of tranquillity, one's mind is dull, then one should rouse it through reflecting on the eight stirring objects. These eight are: birth, decay, disease and death; the suffering in the worlds of misery; the suffering of the past rooted in the round of existence; the suffering of the future rooted in the round of existence; the suffering of the present rooted in the search for food.

Vism IV.63

8. How to overcome sleepiness

Once the Exalted One spoke to the Venerable Mahā-Moggallāna thus: "Are you drowsy, Moggallāna? Are you drowsy, Moggallāna?"—"Yes, venerable sir."

(1) "Well then, Moggallāna, at whatever thought torpor has befallen you, to that thought you should not give attention, you should not dwell on it frequently. Then it is possible that, by so doing, torpor will disappear.

(2) "But if, by so doing, that torpor does not disappear, you should think and reflect within your mind about the Dhamma as you have heard and learned it, and you should mentally review it. Then it is possible that, by so doing, torpor will disappear.

(3) "But if, by so doing, that torpor does not disappear, you should learn by heart the Dhamma in its fullness, as you have heard and learned it. Then it is possible...

(4) "But if, by so doing, that torpor does not disappear, you should shake your ears, and rub your limbs with the palm of your hand. Then it is possible...

(5) "But if, by so doing, that torpor does not disappear, you should get up from your seat, and after washing your eyes with

water, you should look around in all directions and look upwards to the stars in the sky. Then it is possible...

(6) "But if, by so doing, that torpor does not disappear, you should firmly establish the (inner) perception of light: as it is by day, so also by night; as it is by night, so also by day. Thus with a mind clear and unobstructed, you should develop a consciousness which is full of brightness. Then it is possible...

(7) "But if, by so doing, that torpor does not disappear, you should, conscious of that which is before and behind, walk up and down, with your senses turned inwards, with your mind not going outwards. Then it is possible...

(8) "But if, by so doing, that torpor does not disappear, you may lie down on your right side, taking up the lion's posture, covering foot with foot—mindful, clearly conscious, keeping in mind the thought of rising. Having awakened again, you should quickly rise, thinking: 'I won't indulge in the enjoyment of lying down and reclining, in the enjoyment of sleep!'

"Thus, Moggallāna, you should train yourself!"

AN 7:58

9. The five threatening dangers

If, monks, a monk perceives these five threatening dangers, it is enough for him to live heedful, zealous, with a heart resolute to achieve the unachieved, to attain the unattained, to realize the unrealized. Which are these five dangers?

(1) Here, monks, a monk reflects thus: "I am now young, a youth, young in age, black-haired, in the prime of youth, in the first phase of life. But a time will come when this body will be in the grip of old age. But one who is overpowered by old age cannot easily contemplate on the Teachings of the Buddha; it is not easy for him to live in the wilderness or a forest or jungle, or in secluded dwellings. Before this undesirable condition, so unpleasant and disagreeable, approaches me, prior to that, let me muster my energy for achieving the unachieved, for attaining the unattained, for realizing the unrealized, so that, in the possession of that state, I shall live happily even in old age."

(2) And further, monks, a monk reflects thus: "I am now free from sickness, free from disease, my digestive power functions smoothly, my constitution is not too cool and not too hot, it is

balanced and fit for making effort. But a time will come when this body will be in the grip of sickness. And one who is sick cannot easily contemplate upon the Teachings of the Buddha; it is not easy for him, to live in the wilderness or a forest or jungle, or in secluded dwellings. Before this undesirable condition, so unpleasant and disagreeable, approaches me, prior to that, let me muster my energy for achieving the unachieved, for attaining the unattained, for realizing the unrealized, so that, in the possession of that state, I shall live happily even in sickness."

(3) And further, monks, a monk reflects thus: "Now there is an abundance of food, good harvests, easily obtainable is a meal of alms, it is easy to live on collected food and offerings. But a time will come when there will be a famine, a bad harvest, difficult to obtain will be a meal of alms, it will be difficult to live on collected food and offerings. And in a famine people migrate to places where food is ample, and there habitations will be thronged and crowded. But in habitations thronged and crowded one cannot easily contemplate upon the Teachings of the Buddha. Before this undesirable condition, so unpleasant and disagreeable, approaches me, prior to that, let me muster my energy for achieving the unachieved, for attaining the unattained, for realizing the unrealized, so that, in the possession of that state, I shall live happily even in a famine."

(4) And further, monks, a monk reflects thus: "Now people live in concord and amity, in friendly fellowship as mingled milk and water and look at each other with friendly eyes. But there will come a time of danger, of unrest among the jungle tribes when the country people mount their carts and drive away and fear-stricken people move to a place of safety, and there habitations will be thronged and crowded. But in habitations thronged and crowded one cannot easily contemplate upon the Teachings of the Buddha. Before this undesirable condition, so unpleasant and disagreeable, approaches me, prior to that, let me muster my energy for achieving the unachieved, for attaining the unattained, for realizing the unrealized, so that, in the possession of that state, I shall live happily even in time of danger."

(5) And further, monks, a monk reflects thus: "Now the Congregation of Monks lives in concord and amity, without quarrel, lives happily under one teaching. But a time will come

when there will be a split in the Congregation. And when the Congregation is split, one cannot easily contemplate upon the Teachings of the Buddha; it is not easy to live in the wilderness or a forest or jungle, or in secluded dwellings. Before this undesirable condition, so unpleasant and disagreeable, approaches me, prior to that, let me muster my energy for achieving the unachieved, for attaining the unattained, for realizing the unrealized, so that, in the possession of that state, I shall live happily even when the Congregation is split."[3]

AN 5:78

These things, too, are helpful in conquering sloth and torpor:

1) Applied thought, of the factors of absorptions (*jhānaṅga*);
2) Energy, of the spiritual faculties (*indriya*);
3) Investigation of reality, energy and rapture, of the factors of enlightenment (*bojjhaṅga*).

When the mind is sluggish, it is not the proper time for cultivating the following factors of enlightenment: tranquillity, concentration and equanimity, because a sluggish mind can hardly be aroused by them.

When the mind is sluggish, it is the proper time for cultivating the following factors of enlightenment: investigation of reality, energy and rapture, because a sluggish mind can easily be aroused by them.

SN 46:53

C. Simile

If there is a pot of water, covered with moss and water plants, then a man with a normal faculty of sight looking into it could

3. This Discourse is one of the seven canonical texts recommended by the emperor Asoka in the Second Bhairat Rock Edict; "Reverend Sirs, these passages of the Law, to wit: ... 'Fears of what may happen (*anāgata-bhayāni*)..., spoken by the Venerable Buddha—these, Reverend Sirs, I desire that many monks and nuns should frequently hear and meditate: and that likewise the laity, male and female, should do the same. (Vincent A. Smith, *Asoka*. 3rd ed., p. 54).

not properly recognize and see the image of his own face. In the same way, when one's mind is possessed by sloth and torpor, overpowered by sloth and torpor, one cannot properly see the escape from sloth and torpor that have arisen; then one does not properly understand one's own welfare, nor that of another, nor that of both; and also texts memorized a long time ago do not come into one's mind, not to speak of those not memorized.

SN 46:55

Restlessness and Remorse

A. Nourishment of Restlessness and Remorse

There is unrest of mind; frequently giving unwise attention to it—that is the nourishment for the arising of restlessness and remorse that have not yet arisen, and for the increase and strengthening of restlessness and remorse that have already arisen.

SN 46:51

B. Denourishing of Restlessness and Remorse

There is quietude of mind; frequently giving wise attention to it—that is the denourishing of the arising of restlessness and remorse that have not yet arisen, and of the increase and strengthening of restlessness and remorse that have already arisen.

SN 46:51

Six things are conducive to the abandonment of restlessness and remorse:

1) Knowledge of the Buddhist scriptures (Doctrine and Discipline);
2) Asking questions about them;
3) Familiarity with the Vinaya (the Code of Monastic Discipline, and for lay followers, with the principles of moral conduct);
4) Association with those mature in age and experience, who possess dignity, restraint and calm;
5) Noble friendship;
6) Suitable conversation.

These things, too, are helpful in conquering restlessness and remorse:

1) Equanimity, of the factors of absorption (*jhānaṅga*);
2) Concentration, of the spiritual faculties (*indriya*);
3) Tranquillity, concentration and equanimity, of the factors of enlightenment (*bojjhaṅga*).

When the mind is restless it is not the proper time for cultivating the following factors of enlightenment: investigation of the doctrine, energy and rapture, because an agitated mind can hardly be quietened by them.

When the mind is restless, it is the proper time for cultivating the following factors of enlightenment: tranquillity, concentration and equanimity, because an agitated mind can easily be quietened by them.

SN 46:53

C. Simile

If there is water in a pot, stirred by the wind, agitated, swaying and producing waves, a man with a normal faculty of sight could not properly recognize and see the image of his own face. In the same way, when one's mind is possessed by restlessness and remorse, overpowered by restlessness and remorse, one cannot properly see the escape from restlessness and remorse that have arisen; then one does not properly understand one's own welfare, nor that of another, nor that of both; and also texts memorized a long time ago do not come into one's mind, not to speak of those not memorized.

SN 46:55

Doubt

A. Nourishment of Doubt

There are things causing doubt; frequently giving unwise attention to them—that is the nourishment for the arising of doubt that has not yet arisen, and for the increase and strengthening of doubt that has already arisen.

SN 46:51

B. Denourishing of Doubt

There are things which are wholesome or unwholesome, blameless or blameworthy, noble or low, and (other) contrasts of dark and bright; frequently giving wise attention to them—that is the denourishing of the arising of doubt that has not yet arisen, and of the increase and strengthening of doubt that has already arisen.

Of the six things conducive to the abandonment of doubt, the first three and the last two are identical with those given for restlessness and remorse. The fourth is as follows:

Firm conviction concerning the Buddha, Dhamma and Sangha. In addition, the following are helpful in conquering Doubt:

1) Reflection, of the factors of absorption (*jhānaṅga*);
2) Wisdom, of the spiritual faculties (*indriya*);
3) Investigation of reality, of the factors of enlightenment (*bojjhaṅga*).

C. Simile

If there is a pot of water which is turbid, stirred up and muddy, and this pot is put into a dark place, then a man with a normal faculty of sight could not properly recognize and see the image of his own face. In the same way, when one's mind is possessed by doubt, overpowered by doubt, then one cannot properly see the escape from doubt which has arisen; then one does not properly understand one's own welfare, nor that of another, nor that of both; and also texts memorized a long time ago do not come into one's mind, not to speak of those not memorized.

SN 46:55

From the Sāmaññaphala Sutta

I. The Sutta (Dīgha Nikāya No. 2)

Being endowed with noble mindfulness and clear comprehension, and endowed with noble contentedness, the monk resorts to a lonely place: to a forest, the foot of a tree, a mountain, a cleft, a rock cave, a cemetery, a jungle, an open space, a heap of straw.

After the meal, having returned from the alms-round, he sits down, crosslegged, keeping his body erect and his mindfulness alert. Having given up covetousness (= sensual desire) with regard to the world, he dwells with a heart free of covetousness, he cleanses his mind from covetousness. Having given up the blemish of ill-will, he dwells without ill-will; friendly and compassionate towards all living beings, he cleanses his mind from the blemish of ill-will. Having given up sloth and torpor, he dwells free from sloth and torpor, in the perception of light; mindful and clearly comprehending, he cleanses his mind from sloth and torpor. Having given up restlessness and remorse, he dwells without restlessness; his mind being calmed within, he cleanses it from restlessness and remorse. Having given up sceptical doubt, he dwells as one who has passed beyond doubt; being free from uncertainty about salutary things, he cleanses his mind from sceptical doubt.

Just as when a man taking a loan, engages in a trade, and his trade succeeds, he now not only disposes of his old debt but he has also, beyond that, a surplus for maintaining a wife. And at that he rejoices, is glad at heart...

Just as when a man is sick and in pain, suffering from a grave disease, his food does not agree with him, and he has no strength left in his body. But some time later he recovers from that sickness; he can again digest his food, and he regains his strength. And at that he rejoices, is glad at heart...

Just as when a man has been thrown into prison, but some time later he is released from prison; he is safe and without fears, and he did not suffer any loss of property. And at that he rejoices, is glad at heart...

Just as when a man is a slave, not independent, but dependent on others, unable to go where he likes, but some time later he is set free from slavery, is now independent, no longer dependent on others, a freeman who can go where he wants. And at that he rejoices, is glad at heart...

Just as when a man, rich and prosperous, travels through a wilderness where there is no food and much danger, but some time later he has crossed the desert, and gradually reaches safely the vicinity of a village, a place of safety, free from danger. And at that he rejoices, is glad at heart.

Similarly, so long as these five hindrances are not abandoned in him, a monk considers himself as indebted, as ailing, as imprisoned, as enslaved, as travelling in a wilderness.

But when these five hindrances are abandoned, he considers himself as free from debt, rid of illness, emancipated from the prison's bondage, as a free man, and as one arrived at a place of safety.

And when he sees himself free of these five hindrances, joy arises; in him who is joyful, rapture arises; in him whose mind is enraptured, the body is stilled; the body being stilled, he feels happiness; and a happy mind finds concentration.

Then detached from sensual desires, detached from unwholesome states, he enters into and dwells in the first absorption which is accompanied by applied thought and reflection, born of detachment, and filled with joy and rapture. He enters into and dwells in the second... third... fourth absorption.

II. The Commentary

A. The Similes for the Hindrances

The text of the discourse says: "Similarly, so long as these five hindrances are not abandoned in him, a monk considers himself as indebted, as ailing, as imprisoned, as enslaved, as travelling in a wilderness."

Hereby the Blessed One shows the unabandoned hindrance of sensual desire as similar to being in debt; and the other hindrances as similar to being ill, and so on. These similes should be understood as follows:

1. Sensual Desire

There is a man who has incurred a debt but has become ruined. Now, if his creditors, when telling him to pay back the debt, speak roughly to him or harass and beat him, he is unable to retaliate but has to bear it all. It is his debt that causes this forbearance.

In the same way, if a man is filled with sensual desire for a certain person, he will, full of craving for that object of his desire, be attached to it. Even if spoken to roughly by that person, or harassed or beaten, he will bear it all. It is his sensual desire that causes this forbearance. In that way, sensual desire is like being in debt.

2. Ill-Will

If a man suffers from a bilious disease, and receives even honey and sugar, he will not enjoy its flavour, owing to his bile sickness; he will just vomit it, complaining, "It is bitter, bitter!"

In the same way, if one of angry temperament is admonished even slightly by his teacher or preceptor who wishes his best, he does not accept their advice. Saying "You harass me too much!" he will leave the Order, or go away and roam about. Just as the bilious person does not enjoy the flavour of honey and sugar, so one who has the disease of anger will not enjoy the taste of the Buddha's Dispensation consisting in the happiness of the meditative absorptions, etc. In that way, ill-will resembles illness.

3. Sloth and Torpor

A person has been kept in jail during a festival day, and so could see neither the beginning nor the middle nor the end of the festivities. If he is released on the following day, and hears people saying: "Oh, how delightful was yesterday's festival! Oh, those dances and songs!" he will not give any reply. And why not? Because he did not enjoy the festival himself.

Similarly, even if a very eloquent sermon on the Dhamma is going on, a monk overcome by sloth and torpor will not know the beginning, middle or end. If after the sermon, he hears it praised: "How pleasant was it to listen to the Dhamma! How interesting was the topic and how good the similes!" he will not be able to say a word. And why not? Because, owing to his sloth and torpor, he did not enjoy the sermon. In that way, sloth and torpor are comparable to imprisonment.

4. Restlessness and Remorse

A slave who wants to enjoy himself at a festival is told by his master: "Go quickly to such and such a place! There is urgent work to do. If you don't go, I shall have your hands and feet cut off, or your ears and nose!" Hearing that, the slave will quickly go as ordered, and will not be able to enjoy any part of the festival. This is because of his dependence on others.

Similarly it is with a monk not well versed in the Vinaya (the Disciplinary Code), who has gone to the forest for the sake of solitude. If in any matter, down to the question of permissible meat (Sub-Cy: e.g., pork) he gets the idea that it was not permissible (taking it for bear's flesh), he has to interrupt his solitude and, to purify his conduct, has to go to one skilled in the Vinaya. Thus he will not be able to enjoy the happiness of solitude because of his being overcome by restlessness and remorse. In that way, restlessness and remorse are like slavery.

5. Sceptical Doubt

A man travelling through a desert, aware that travellers may be plundered or killed by robbers, will, at the mere sound of a twig or a bird, become anxious and fearful, thinking: "The robbers have come!" He will go a few steps, and then out of fear, he will stop, and continue in such a manner all the way; or he may even turn back. Stopping more frequently than walking, only with toil and difficulty will he reach a place of safety, or he may not even reach it.

It is similar with one in whom doubt has arisen in regard to one of the eight objects of doubt.[4] Doubting whether the Master is an Enlightened One or not, he cannot accept it in confidence, as a matter of trust. Unable to do so, he does not attain to the paths and fruits of sanctity. Thus, as the traveller in the desert is uncertain whether robbers are there or not, he produces in his mind, again and again, a state of wavering and vacillation, a lack of decision, a state of anxiety; and thus he creates in himself an obstacle for reaching the safe ground of sanctity (*ariya-bhūmi*). In that way, sceptical doubt is like travelling in a desert.

4. They are, according to the Vibhaṅga: doubt in regard to the Buddha, the Dhamma, the Sangha, the (threefold) training, the past, the future, both past and future, and the conditionality of phenomena dependently arisen.

B. The Abandonment of the Hindrances

The text of the Discourse says:

"But when these five hindrances are abandoned, the monk considers himself as free from debt, rid of illness, emancipated from the prison's bondage, as a free man, and as one arrived at a place of safety."

1. The Abandonment of Sensual Desire

A man, having taken a loan, uses it for his business and comes to prosperity. He thinks: "This debt is a cause of vexation." He returns the loan together with the interest, and has the promissory note torn up. After that he neither sends a messenger nor a letter to his creditors; and even if he meets them it depends on his wish whether he will get up from his seat to greet them, or not. And why? He is no longer in debt to them or dependent of them.

Similarly, a monk thinks: "Sensual desire is a cause of obstruction." He then cultivates the six things leading to its abandonment, and removes the hindrance of sensual desire. Just as one who has freed himself of debt no longer feels fear or anxiety when meeting his former creditors, so one who has given up sensual desire is no longer attached and bound to the object of his desire; even if he sees divine forms, passions will not assail him.

Therefore the Blessed One compared the abandonment of sensual desire to freedom from debt.

2. The Abandonment of Ill-Will

Just as a person suffering from a bilious disease, having been cured by taking medicine, will regain his taste for honey and sugar, similarly a monk, thinking, "This ill-will causes much harm," develops the six things leading to its abandonment and removes the hindrance of ill-will. Just as the cured patient partaking of honey and sugar appreciates the taste, so also this monk receives with reverence the rules of training, and observes them with appreciation (of their value). Therefore the Blessed One compared the abandonment of ill-will to the recovery of health.

3. The Abandonment of Sloth and Torpor

There is a person that once had been in jail on a festival day. But when freed and celebrating the festival on a later occasion, he will think: "Formerly, through the fault of my heedlessness, I was in prison on that day and could not enjoy this festival. Now I shall be heedful." And he remains heedful of his conduct so that nothing detrimental finds entry into his mind. Having enjoyed the festival, he exclaims: "Oh, what a beautiful festival it was!"

Similarly a monk, perceiving that sloth and torpor do great harm, develops the six things opposed to them, and so removes the hindrance of sloth and torpor. Just as the man freed from prison enjoys the whole length of the festival, even for seven days, so this monk who has given up sloth and torpor is capable of enjoying the beginning, the middle and the consummation of the Festival of the Dhamma (*dhamma-nakkhatta*), and finally attains to Arahatship together with the fourfold discriminating knowledge (*paṭisambhidā*)

Therefore the Blessed One spoke of the abandonment of sloth and torpor as being comparable to release from imprisonment.

4. The Abandonment of Restlessness and Remorse

There is a slave who, with the help of a friend, pays money to his master, becomes a free man, and is henceforth able to do what he likes. Similarly a monk, perceiving the great obstruction caused by restlessness and remorse, cultivates the six things opposed to them, and thus gives up restlessness and remorse. And having given them up, he is like a truly free man, able to do as he wishes. Just as no one can forcibly stop a free man from doing what he likes, so can restlessness and remorse no longer stop that monk from walking the happy path of renunciation (*sukha-nekkhamma-paṭipadā*).

Therefore the Blessed One declared the abandonment of restlessness and remorse as being similar to winning freedom from slavery.

5. The Abandonment of Sceptical Doubt

There is a strong man who, with his luggage in hand and well armed, travels through a wilderness in company. If robbers see him even from afar, they will take flight. Crossing safely the wilderness and reaching a place of safety, he will rejoice in his safe arrival. Similarly a monk, seeing that sceptical doubt is a cause of great harm, cultivates the six things that are its antidote, and gives up doubt. Just as that strong man, armed and in company, taking as little account of the robbers as of the grass on the ground, will safely come out of the wilderness to a safe place; similarly a monk, having crossed the wilderness of evil conduct, will finally reach the state of highest security, the deathless realm of Nibbāna. Therefore the Blessed One compared the abandonment of sceptical doubt to reaching a place of safety.

Going Forth
(Pabbajjā)

A Call to Buddhist Monkhood

An Essay, and Letters on Buddhism by

Sumana Sāmaṇera

Translated from the German

WHEEL PUBLICATION NO. 27/28

Preface

The essay that forms the first part of this booklet, bears in its German original the title *Pabbajjā* which, in Pali, the language of the Buddhist texts, means *Going forth,* namely from the household life to the homelessness of a Buddhist monk. The Pali word *Pabbajjā* is also the term for the first ordination bestowed for entry into the Buddhist monastic Order (Sangha) by which the candidate becomes a Novice or *Sāmanera* like the author of the writings presented here, whose illness and premature death deprived him of taking higher ordination.

Fritze Stange, the lay name of our author, was a German by birth, and received his novice ordination in 1906 at Mātara (Ceylon), under the nestor of the German Buddhist monk the Venerable Nyanatiloka Thera (d. 1957). Together with Sumano, a Dutchman called Bergendahl was ordained as the Sāmaṇera Suñño. They were the first two pupils of the Venerable Nyanatiloka who, on his part, had received novice ordination in 1903 and higher ordination in 1904, both in Burma. As related in the Appendix of this booklet, illness obliged Sumano to go back to Germany, but in the same year he returned again to Ceylon, together with the Venerable Nyanatiloka who had paid a short visit to Germany. He took ordination again and then lived in the undulating, grassy hillocks of Bandarawela, in Ceylon's up-country—a landscape of ascetical bareness, breathing seclusion and quietude. There he died and was cremated in January 1910. A spout just by the spot where he lived, still bears in the Sinhala language the name "German Phihilla" ("German spout").[1]

Sumano was held in great reverence by the people for his deep piety. He was of an unassuming nature; but his bearing emanated an atmosphere of saintliness and detachment, of maturity and

1. To those who have the opportunity of visiting Bandarawela some road directions may be welcome. The place where Sumano lived and died, is reached by going up the Grand Road to Uturu Kabillawela, a distance of about one and one-half miles from the Bandarawela Town Hall, and then walking down a little over one quarter mile on the foot path leading to Gediyarde village.

gentle firmness which obviously must have set him apart from the multitude.

The same atmosphere of the true ascetic's sincere and forceful simplicity radiates from the pages of his little book *Pabbajjā*. Its first publication in Germany, in the year 1910, deeply impressed and inspired the members of the small circles of German Buddhists. An English version by Bhikkhu Silācāra appeared in Ceylon the same year. This has been fully revised for the present edition, after comparison with the German original.

Sumano's letters first appeared in print in a German Buddhist magazine, *Die Buddhistische Warte*, and are published here for the first time in an English version prepared by the Venerable Nyanaponika Thera.

Both essays and letters served first to justify and explain Sumano's unusual step of entering Buddhist monkhood in the East. There is, however, nothing apologetic in his words, no diffident defence; they are rather a stirring call to kindred minds for proceeding on that hard but incomparably rewarding road towards the "unshakable deliverance of mind." In the same spirit they are offered here to the reader, as a companion to another booklet in this series of Buddhist publications, *The Ascetic Ideal* by Ronald Fussell (*The Wheel Publication* No 23).

Buddhist Publication Society
Forest Hermitage
Kandy, Ceylon
February, 1961

Pabbajjā

"He is beside himself"

"Marvellous is it, O Lord, extraordinary is it, O Lord, how the Exalted One has so clearly pointed out the Four Satipaṭṭhāna, which lead to the purification of beings, to the overcoming of sorrow and lamentation, to the cessation of pain and grief, to the attainment of the path, to the realization of Nibbāna! For we also, Lord, as householders, have from time to time fixed our minds upon the Four Satipaṭṭhāna."

"Whilst we thus dwell with earnest minds, eager, unweariedly, the memories of household things pass from us; and as they so pass, the heart grows ever more steady, becomes quieted and unified, finds peace."

The more frequently a man thus dwells all the more perceptibly does the alienation increase, does the world die away from him, for ever more clearly does the true nature of the world reveal itself to the mind through the persistent contemplation of this truth founded in experience:

"Thus is form, thus it arises, thus it passes away.
Thus is feeling, thus it arises, thus it passes away.
Thus is perception, thus it arises, thus it passes away.
Thus are the mental formations, thus they arise, thus they pass away.
Thus is consciousness, thus it arises, thus it passes away."

Always the same law, always the same song:

Aniccā vata saṅkhārā uppāda-vaya-dhammino;
Uppajjitvā nirujjhanti, tesaṃ vūpasamo sukho'ti:

"Transient are all compounded things;
To rise to fall, their nature is.
Having become, they pass away;
Their final rest is highest bliss."

"I know not, Ānanda, even of a single form whereby pleasure and satisfaction in form does not pass into sorrow and lamentation, pain, grief, despair, since it is transient and changeable"—and so with feeling, and so with perception, and so with the mental formations, and so with consciousness. "This world, however, seeks pleasure, loves pleasure, prizes pleasure. Only a few beings are stirred by things that are truly stirring, in comparison with the greater number who remain unstirred by truly stirring things. And again, there are only a few who, being stirred, earnestly strive, in comparison with the greater number who, being stirred, yet do not earnestly strive."

Unrestrained by the perception of the hollowness of things, the hot stream of foolish desire flows on: "O, that no birth lay before us, no old age, no death, no sorrow, no lamentation, no pain, no grief, no despair!—but this is not to be obtained by mere desiring; and not to get what one desires is suffering." Ah! if only our parents would remain alive; Ah! if only our loved one would not die... Ah! the misery of this law of nature! How many millions daily sob and weep over graves! The misery of this law of nature! "What is dear to one brings sorrow and lamentation, pain, grief, and despair: attachment is the root of suffering." Hence the uprooting of suffering is non-attachment, the way of escape from all this wretchedness is non-attachment, denial, renunciation. "Whoso cleaves to woe, follows after woe, is bound up with woe, and thus considers: 'That belongs to me, that I am, that is my self (attā, self, soul)—can such a one really comprehend woe, can such a one avoid the woe that encompasses him?' But he who withdraws himself from attachment and learns to renounce, to deny, and to turn away, deprives the heart's pain of its nourishment, and by degrees brings about its extinction. "The turning away of the will vanquishes all woe."

This turning away comes into operation where there is an understanding of *suffering*, of the arising of suffering, of the cessation of suffering, and of the path that leads to the cessation of suffering. Before understanding these truths, man hastens from birth to death in the sea of existence (*saṃsāra*), without deriving therefrom any true gain for his deliverance—worn out for naught, the body perishes. "It is through lack of understanding and insight into the Four Holy Truths, ye disciples, that we had to travel so long the weary round of Saṃsāra—both you and I. What think ye: which is greater—the floods of tears which, weeping and wailing, ye have shed on this long journey, ever and again hastening towards new birth and new death, united to the undesired, sundered from the desired—this or the waters of the four great seas? For long have ye experienced the death of a mother, for long the death of a father, for long the death of a son, for long the death of a daughter, for long the death of brothers and sisters; for long have ye suffered the loss of your property; for long ye were harassed by disease; and whilst experiencing the death of mother, of father, of son, of daughter, of brothers and sisters, the loss of property, the torment of disease, whilst being united with the undesired and sundered from the desired, thus hastening from birth to death and from death to birth ye have verily shed more tears on this long journey, than all the waters that are held in the four great seas! But how is that possible? Without beginning and without end is this Saṃsāra, unknowable is the beginning of beings sunk in ignorance (*avijjā*) who, seized by craving (*taṇhā*), ever and again are brought to renewed birth, and so hastened through the endless round of rebirths. Thus, for long have ye experienced suffering, experienced torment, experienced misery, and filled the graveyards—long enough truly to have become dissatisfied with all existence, long enough to turn away from all being, long enough to seek release from it all."

Who takes this exhortation to themselves? Those whose minds are stirred by these thoughts. And being stirred they will learn to understand, and will earnestly strive. "For them delight and pleasure in the world gradually pass away, they perceive the coarse as well as the subtle lures of Māra; wearied are they of intoxication, of self-deception; no longer do they shrink from the inevitable struggle for the overcoming of the world; yea, to this or that one, the widespread misery in the world reveals itself to his mind so nakedly, so powerfully, that the cry for the end of it drowns every other voice: "Forth, forth, forth to the other shore!" "Sunk am I in birth, in old age and death, in sorrow, lamentation and pain, in grief and despair, sunk in suffering, lost in suffering! O that it were possible to make an end of all this mass of suffering!" To such a comprehension, to such a longing, the meaning of asceticism becomes evident as that manner of living which really makes possible single-minded devotion to that most difficult of all tasks—the task of becoming perfectly good or pure or holy, and thereby, free from suffering and rebirth!

"If I truly understand the doctrine declared by the Exalted One, it is not easy for one who remains in household life to fulfil point by point the wholly stainless, wholly purified ascetic life." "Whoso lives in the house is busy over-much, is much occupied, anxious about many things, disturbed about many things; he is not always entirely devoted to truthfulness; not always and entirely zealous in self control, chaste, recollected, given to renunciation."

"Man falls as falls the fruit from off the tree,
Unripe or mayhap ripe, with sudden crash:
and so, O king, a beggar I become,
For, the sure pilgrim-life me seems the best."

"There has never been a householder, Vaccha, who without forsaking household-ties, has, at the dissolution of the body, made an end to suffering."

Therefore, whoso resolutely seeks the end, "after a time will leave behind a small property, or leave behind a large property; he forsakes a small circle of acquaintances, or he forsakes a large circle of acquaintances, and goes forth from home to homelessness"—*pabbajjā.*

But father and mother, wife and children, love and duty? The sense of duty depends on understanding. Once a duty has been understood as the higher one, it sets aside the lower conception of duty held formerly.

For years a man may have devoted himself to the care of wife and child, prizing nothing higher than his family's welfare. Then war comes to his country. The course of events stirs him profoundly; he is affected by new ideas, another view of things gains strength within him. "Sweet it is to die for the fatherland!" The feeling overpowers him: "What care I for wife, what care I for child!" Of his own free will he goes forth to meet the foes of the fatherland. The duty to his country now seems to him higher than the duty to his wife and children.

Another man has in former days, with full conviction, solemnly vowed faithfully to stand by his country even to death. Later on, in consequence of higher comprehension he gains a higher standpoint, a wider outlook; envisages politics as a citizen of the world, thinks in universal terms: "This Frenchman is a fellow human being, is a fellow sufferer. This Russian is a fellow human being, is a fellow sufferer. Life is a sacred thing; frightful, barbaric is this wholesale killing, called war—the visible aggravation of suffering." No longer can he slay his fellow-men. In case of a call to arms he willingly allows himself to be shot by his own countrymen. The duty "Thou shalt not kill!" stands higher in his eyes than any duty towards his fatherland.

Yet another, as pastor, for many a year enjoyed a secure living with his family. By degrees his views undergo a change. He finds himself unable any longer to give his assent to dogmas, to the doctrines of Revelation, of Grace, or of Forgiveness of Sins, or Vicarious Atonement; he can no longer believe in that deplorable and absurd doctrine of "eternal damnation for the deeds of a brief spell of thirty years." A higher knowledge has come to fruition within him. Clear and evident to him has become the universally ruling law, the unchangeable, equable relation of cause and effect, the unfailingly just recompensations of right or wrong action (*kamma*). He burdens his mind neither with thoughts about the unfathomable, nor with useless discussions: he understands suffering and the cessation of suffering—the saviour in man. As an honourable man how can he go on preaching as before? He will follow his altered convictions, give up his position as pastor—come what may!

Whoso acts according to his deepest understanding is always straight and candid, ever acts in accordance with truth—at least relatively so: for a man's truth is his degree of understanding.

> "This above all: to thine own self be true,
> And it must follow as the night the day;
> Thou canst not then be false to any man:
> Be true to the highest within you!"

To a man now, who has clearly perceived the pitiable condition of all beings that share a common existence, what higher, holier, or more urgent task can there be than to become perfectly kind, perfectly good or holy and thereby to get himself cured of this being born, growing old and dying, of this sorrow, lamentation, pain, grief, and despair? Hence if he has truly recognised the significance and value of asceticism for the fulfilment of this highest duty, and experienced the impossibility of its perfect realisation in household life, there follows the going forth into homelessness (*pabbajjā*) as necessarily as the fall of the drop that is full. "No man can serve two masters"—fully well. The man who devotedly strives for the fulfilment of the Doctrine experiences intensely the unsatisfactoriness of divided allegiance. Hence after a time, he gives it up, for the blessing of himself as well as of his family; an inward law of development that is beyond dispute. Only a mother knows the pangs of childbirth, and only a mother knows the succeeding joys of motherhood. Only he who has left home knows the relief of relinquishing accustomed bonds; only he who has left home, knows the happiness of being free: an inward experience—indisputable! "The joys of the family life and the joys of the homeless life—these are two different joys: and the nobler of the two is the joy the homeless life."

If millions of honest men in worldly life find *pabbajjā*, the Going Forth, obnoxious; if they condemn the incomprehensible act as wrong, as unnatural, or deplore it as a mental aberration, they are quite right from their own standpoint; no intelligent man will contradict them. They act in accordance with their conception of duty, and are "great, great in their place" if, before all things they care for beloved parents, for wife and children, and strive to fulfil the manifold important duties laid upon them by their life in the world. Also the few who have a bent for the ascetic life and honestly long for it, but feel themselves bound one way or another to their wanted way of life and therefore remain in its bondage—they also are right from their own standpoint. So also are those individuals right who go forth, being no longer bound inwardly. It is not the outward circumstances that bind a man; by himself is man really bound, by himself is he really free.

"Having left parents, son and wife,
Relations, wealth and land,
And all desires of sense,
Let him wander alone like the rhinoceros."

By logic, by reasoning or by eloquent words alone that act of going forth into homelessness can certainly not be argued or explained. But whoso sees this law, whoso sees this truth, no longer asks for proof. Quietly and with confidence he acts. What the world says about it, leaves him unconcerned.

"There are two goals, the holy goal and the unholy goal. But what is the unholy goal? One, himself subject to birth, seeks what also is subject to birth; himself subject to old age, to sickness, to death, to pain, to defilement seeks what also is subject to old age, to sickness, to death, to pain, to defilement. But what is subject to birth, old age, sickness, death, pain and defilement? Wife and child are subject to birth, old age, sickness, death, pain and defilement; servant and maid, lamb and goat... gold and silver are subject to birth, old age, sickness, death, pain and defilement. Subject to birth, old age, sickness, death, pain, to defilement are these things. And allured, blinded, enchanted, a man himself subject to birth, to old age, to sickness, to death, to pain, to defilement seeks what also is subject to birth, old age, sickness, death, to pain, to defilement! This is the unholy goal. But what is the holy goal?

"One himself subject to birth, perceiving the misery of this law of nature, seeks that which is free from birth: the incomparable surety of Nibbana; subject to old age, to sickness, to death, to pain, to defilement, perceiving the misery of this law of nature, seeks that which is free from old age, sickness, death, pain and defilement, the incomparable surety of Nibbana. This is the holy goal.

"Formerly, when but a Bodhisatta, myself subject to birth, I sought what also was subject to birth; myself subject to old age, sickness, death, pain, defilement, sought what also was subject to old age, sickness, death, pain, defilement. And it occurred to me as follows: 'Why, myself subject to birth, old age, sickness, death, pain, defilement, do I seek what also is subject to birth, old age, sickness, death, pain, defilement? What, if now, myself subject to birth, perceiving the misery of this law of nature, I were to seek the incomparable surety of Nibbāna free from birth: myself subject to old age, sickness, death, pain, defilement perceiving the misery of this law of nature, I were to seek the incomparable surety of Nibbāna free from old age, sickness, death, pain, defilement? And after a time while still young, with coal-black hair, possessed of radiant youth, in the prime of my life, against the wish of my weeping and wailing parents, I had my hair and beard shaved off, put on the yellow robe, and went forth from the household life to the houseless one..."

Whoso well in time sees the holy goal with penetrating clearness, he can no longer tie matrimonial bonds.

"Who dwells alone and seeks not any mate,
Though young in years yet bides not anywhere,
Averted, turned away from contact's transports:
Him the wise well and truly call a sage."

Whether, however, a man be old or young, whether he be married or not—at whatever period of his life that the urge in him for the ascetic life asserts itself, then along with the other bonds binding to the worldly life, the bonds of blood-relationship also lose their force. The mother has become an elder sister; the father has become a brother; the wife has become a sister; the son has become a brother... fellow beings, fellow sufferers. Attachment, longing have died away, alienation has set in. Such a one has no longer a place and use in the family. "Another law works in the members," a wider love. In love the ascetic goes forth from the family, out of love he leaves it. Truly difficult to understand is the love in genuine ascetic mind, yet relatives also learn to understand it. "And if the families out of which those noble men have gone forth from home into homelessness, think of these noble men with love, for long will it make for their weal and happiness."

Just as a man, who out of true feelings gives alms at the same time makes richer his family, though to outward appearance that family may suffer some loss in goods or money: so truly bestows a householder a rich treasure to an understanding family, if in a right frame of mind, moved by the highest of duties, he renounces the worldly life, even though that family may lose its external support. This loss which not seldom is brought about by premature death, can be made good and is unessential; but essential is: awakening from the slumber, thoughtfulness, insight, the perspective of *anattā* (not-self), turning away, detachment—that is what matters.

"Naught is the loss of relatives, riches and honour; but the loss of insight is the heaviest loss. Naught is the gain of relatives, riches and honour; but the gain of insight—that is the highest gain. Wherefore let your endeavour be: Insight will be gain! Let this be your endeavour!"

"And the former wife of the venerable Sangamaji had heard it said: 'The monk Sangamaji has arrived in Savatthi.' Then she took her child and went to the monastery at the Jeta Grove, near Savatthi. At that time, however, the venerable Sangamaji sat at the foot of a tree to spend the afternoon there, devoted to meditation. Then the former wife of the venerable Sangamaji betook herself thither and spoke to the venerable Sangamaji: Look at thy little son here, O ascetic! Give me food!' But to these words the venerable Sangamaji maintained silence. A second and a third time the former wife of the venerable Sangamaji so spoke: 'Look at thy little son here! Give me food!' And a second and a third time did the venerable Sangamaji preserve silence. Then the wife of the venerable Sangamaji laid the child down in front of the venerable Sangamaji and went away, saying: 'There is thy son, O ascetic; give him food!' The venerable Sangamaji however, neither looked at the child nor uttered a word. Now when the former wife of the venerable Sangamaji having gone some distance turned round, she saw that the venerable Sangamaji neither looked at the child nor said anything. Then she thought 'This ascetic cares not even for his child,' turned back, took up the child and went away."

> "If any man come to me, and hate not his father, and mother, and wife and children, and brethren and sisters, yea, and his own life also, he cannot be my disciple. Whosoever he be of you that forsaketh not all that he hath, he cannot be my disciple."
>
> (Luke XIV.26 and 33)

> "Think not that I am come to send peace on earth: I came not to send peace, but a sword. For I am come to set a man at variance against his father and the daughter against her mother, and the daughter-in-law against her mother-in-law. And a man's foes shall be they of his own household. He that loveth father and mother more than me is not worthy of me; and he that loveth son or daughter more than me is not worthy of me."
>
> (Matthew X.34-37)

"Let the dead bury their dead."

(Luke IX.60)

"My kingdom is not of this world."

(Luke IX.60)

Apart from the differences existing between the teachings of the Buddha and of the Christ, all these sayings have these ideas in common:

1. Void throughout is this world.
2. Whoso "hungers and thirsts" to overcome this world, will loosen all earthly bonds, count them but dirt. Commentators and scribes there are in abundance but "whoso has eyes will see."

Day after day, twenty-four hours older, a hundred thousand heart beats nearer to the grave inevitably! "O, put all wishes aside save the desire to know truth; recognize the truth and tell it, come what may!" Whoso does not act in that way, deceives himself and others. Whoso shrinks from the decision that truth demands, puts obstacles in the way of himself and others though it may not always be obvious.

"From life departing, man no refuge finds,
Nor friend, nor loved one, boon companions none.
The heirs, with strife, divide the heritage,
Himself fares forth according to his deeds."

"Put not thy trust in friends or relatives, and put not off thy salvation till the future, for man will forget thee sooner than thou thinkest. It is better to provide now in time and do the right than to trust to help of another. If thou art not solicitous for thyself now, who will be solicitous for thee in the future? Now is the time very precious, now is the day of salvation...!"

— Thomas a Kempis

None can do for another what is needed for deliverance. Here each has to rely on himself alone.

"Self alone is the lord of self.
What higher master can there be?

By self alone is evil done, by self one is defiled;
By self is evil left undone; by self alone one is purified,
Pure and impure on self alone depend;
No one can make another pure.
Hence give not up thine own best weal
For others' weal however great.
Once thou hast seen thine own best weal,
Pursue it keenly for thyself."

Concern for oneself, in that sense, is far from being reprehensible egotism. It has nothing to do with the oppression or exploitation of others, with harshness towards others.

"Once, Lord, in an hour of solitude and retirement the following thoughts came to me: 'To whom is one's self dear, to whom is it not dear?' And this, Lord, occurred to me: Those who do, and speak, and think evilly, to these their self is not dear. And even though they say: 'We love ourselves,' yet they do not love themselves. And why not? Whatsoever unlovely thing they do to one unbeloved, that they do to their own selves. Therefore is it that their self is not dear to them. Those, however, who act, and speak, and think rightly, to them their self is dear. And even though they may say: 'We love not ourselves,' yet they do love themselves. And why? Whatsoever lovely thing they do to one beloved, that they do to their own selves. Therefore is it that their self is dear to them."—"That is so, great king."

Not only is such true care for oneself irreprehensible, but it is the only way to become hale and holy oneself and to help others to become likewise. "A man may do ever so much good and take upon himself ever so many abnegations, and yet as long as he does not know himself he will not reach deliverance."—"The only limitations he imposes upon himself, are those arising from not knowing himself. In the degree, however, that he knows himself, he is able to do greatest service a man can render for another, namely: to help him to help himself; to bring him to a true knowledge of himself, of his own inner power." Hence, the more ardently a man devotes himself to the work of his own deliverance, all the sooner and more effectively can he become a blessing to others; for all the sooner can he learn and experience what will help himself and others to win true deliverance; the laws for it are the same for all. Any other helpful action, however meritorious it may be, is concerned with things external, not with the world within. "Can the blind lead the blind? Shall they not both fall into the ditch?" Whoso has ever offered to others "bread for stones," has first of all laboured within himself, "lonely, apart, untiringly, ardent and resolute."

The inward worker who has lived the truth, speaks from experience, with the assurance of an "expert": "So it is," he says, and not, "So it may be." Therefore his words produce in susceptible minds an inner crisis never experienced before, a crisis severe but wholesome: "The word of the wise heals." As is the speech of the inwards worker, so is his outward behaviour: true, straight and firm, serene, aloof, uncommon. Such venerable ones are the greatest benefactors of their fellow men, the best physicians; visible witnesses of the fact that detachment from the world is possible; by their very lives they point to the way by which that what continually produces and feeds new suffering can be eliminated. Therefore, whether householder or monk—above all, win to a true vision for thyself! "Know thyself!"—"Be ever mindful of thyself."

"The wise upon the path of truth
He first establishes himself:
Then only can he others teach.
Who thus, as he to others tells,
Can conquer and subdue himself,
May haply turn them to the true;
But hard it is to rule oneself."

"That, Cunda, one himself sunk into the mire should pull out of the mire another sunk therein—this cannot be. But that one, himself not sunk in the mire, can lift out of the mire another sunk therein—that may be. And that one, himself not subdued, not disciplined, not attained to the extinction of delusion, should lead others to become subdued and disciplined to attain to the extinction of delusion—this cannot be. But that one who himself is subdued and disciplined, and has attained to the extinction of delusion, should lead others also to become subdued and disciplined and to attain to the extinction of delusion—this may well be."

The most likely possibility of escape from the mire of ignorance (*avijjā*) is offered by the life of a true monk (*bhikkhu*). Though the Buddha's Teaching has been described as "running counter to the common current, profound, subtle and hard to realize," there are those in the world who, on hearing that Teaching, feel irresistibly attracted to the monk life. There are those who, once they become aware of the general misery of life and of the way of the speediest release from it, lay everything else aside and, without delay, go forth into the homeless life—"their insight needed only to be roused." Others again are able, only after a severe struggle, to break up all bridges behind them. Deep-rooted desires and ideas, coarse or subtle, so strongly ingrained in ordinary life, may obstruct for long an appreciation of the ascetic life; hence people are not in a hurry to turn to it, and the strength of character needed for renunciation, is lacking.

"Even that state of mind, Mahānāma, still exists in thee and causes thy heart to be overpowered at times by impulses of desire, by impulses of anger, by impulses of delusion. For, Mahānāma, if that state of mind no longer had any place in thee, thou wouldst not remain in the home life, in the enjoyment of desires."

It is quite true that noble characters can be found everywhere in society, also in family life; it is true that not a few householders die more ennobled in mind than many a monk; it is true that an earnest, devoted disciple, by virtue of an unusually developed character, due to his good *Kamma* of the past, may, without abandoning household ties, attain to almost all stages of holiness, that is up to the stage of the nonreturner (*anāgāmi*). But no one who knows will maintain that he who is determined to make an end of suffering, may to the same effect remain in the household life as lead the life of a monk. On the contrary, "the wisest of all times" teach that such a man will choose a mode of life detached from all worldly bonds: he will go the road that offers the least resistance to his aspirations.

"Even as the peacock, the blue-necked bird of the parks,
In its aerial flight never can rival the swan,
So the dweller in house can never equal the monk—
Him the thinker withdrawn, in forest abiding."

Separation, isolation, again and again, is necessary for bringing suffering to an end. Just as the steam which is asleep in the water and awakened by fire, does not develop its giant strength, does not become a concentrated power, unless it is shut in, likewise man's inner potentialities for lack of seclusion, for lack of isolation, cannot develop, cannot be converted into higher powers. "Many live far below their possibilities because they continually surrender their individualities to others." In the worldly life, full self-recollectedness, full devotion to the goal, do not come easily. The chaotic mass of uncontrolled impressions will divert and distract again and again, and will lead astray. Sadly great is the sum of energy daily expended to no profit. In home life, too much nutriment gross or subtle is supplied by the world of the five senses, and this will ever and again disturb those thoughts that in the noble-minded are naturally directed towards higher things; hence there is only very slow progress in discarding and uprooting obstructing qualities and evil propensities of the mind.

Quite different is it in the homeless state, in a life of solitude. There man is, as it were, forsaken by all the world, and thrown back entirely upon himself, without palliatives and self-deceptions. There he learns to be profoundly ashamed of all that is base, and feels himself impelled to strive for progress; mindfully he breathes in, mindfully he breathes out, and he wins to the insight that frees from suffering. In secluded places—in the depth of the forest, in a lonely cottage, a mountain cave, a cemetery—the five senses, in the absence of their usual objects of craving, are, as it were, put out of action; and the sixth sense, the mind, alone, detached, undisturbed, effectively collected, can do its work, can understand the workings of greed, hatred and delusion, can reject them.

"What are the characteristics of those venerable ones, what is so special to them that people should say of them, 'Truly, these venerable ones have lost greed and hatred and delusion, or are on the way to overcome them'? This question may be answered thus: 'Those venerable ones seek out lonely places in the depth of the forest: There are not to be found any forms entering the field of vision that can be looked at and craved for; no sounds entering the field of hearing to be listened to and craved for; no odours entering the field of smell to be smelled and craved for; no flavours entering the field of taste that can be tasted and craved for; no bodily contacts entering the field of touch that can be felt and craved for."

Bodily isolation (*kāya-viveka*) in secluded places facilitates isolation (*citta-viveka*) from craving and other hindrances. At the start, this purification and concentration of mind comes only temporarily, during specific meditative exercises; but later on, strengthened by these very exercises, that pure and concentrated state of mind can be maintained for an increasingly longer time, and will make possible a deep and penetrative insight (*pañña vipassanā*) into the true nature of things. And that vision, when completely cleansed of delusion, will finally bring about ultimate isolation, the freedom from every kind of attachment (*upadhi-viveka = nibbāna*). In other words: to a disciple tirelessly meditating in solitude, the transient, painful and unsubstantial nature of all constituents of existence will become apparent with an increasing clarity and certainty. To the degree, however, that ignorance and delusion (*avijjā, moha*) about this world disappear, also desire (*rāga*) for anything in it, and hate or anger (*dosa*) against anything in it, will die away: they will lose their objects, their foothold, their basis, their sanction. Thus, with the withdrawal of the fuel, this terrible conflagration of suffering is brought to extinction, sooner or later, according to previous action-force (*kamma*) and present effort.

True holiness is never born without solitude; never is it perfected without lonely struggle with the passions within. Yet, the untiring activity of Gotama, the Buddha, and of many of his disciples demonstrate that solitude and the happiness of seclusion are not, as many think, the aim and end of the ascetic life, but they are an essential means to the end, and are an incomparable mine of strength and inspiration to him who resolutely strives for the goal.

> "Ye should know that those people practise the most useful practices. Know ye that the kingdom is blessed where man is inwardly one. They produce more eternal gain in one moment than all works ever wrought outwardly."
>
> — Meister Eckehart

By a wrong view of life all ascetic endeavour will naturally be considered as egotism pure and simple; but right understanding will never regard it like that. The true ascetic who has wholeheartedly taken up the training knows that, in the absolute sense, there is no ego nor anything belonging to it, neither I nor mine. Neither corporeality nor feeling, perception, formations and consciousness contain any abiding substance, because they are transient, painful, subject to change. Therefore, no longer can one who has entered the path where deliverance is assured (the *sekha*) bestir himself for the sake of the ego; his striving aims at the final cessation of the conditioned personality (*kamma, khandha*), by the gradual elimination of all its roots. But during his more or less protracted struggle for final emancipation the *sekha* is not yet entirely cured of all self-affirmation, of all impulses connected with I and Mine; still the old *kamma* clings to him. Only in the Arahant, the Holy One, is the truth of *anattā* fully realised, and therewith all and every form of self-affirmation is done away; "through the cessation, rejection, removal, denial and relinquishment of all notions of I and mine, and all biases of self-conceit, he has won perfect deliverance." In other words:

> Much ignorance (and craving): Much self-affirmation (and suffering);
>
> Little ignorance (and craving): Little self-affirmation (and suffering);
>
> Free from ignorance (and craving): Free from self-affirmation (and suffering).
>
> "Ignorance is the root of all self-affirmation."

It is this very truth that none in this world period has as perfectly penetrated, as perfectly taught as the Buddha. The entire hard struggle for deliverance was called by the Enlightened One briefly "The liberation from the fetter of ignorance" that is, from self-illusion. "Hence, Sāriputta, thus should you train yourself: 'Concerning this body endowed with consciousness, there shall not arise any notions of I and Mine, nor any biases of self-conceit shall arise; and also concerning all external impressions, these notions and biases shall not arise! And we shall abide in the attainment of this deliverance of the heart, this deliverance by wisdom through which all these notions and biases cease.' Thus,

Sāriputta, should you train yourself. And insofar, Sāriputta, as a monk attains to this deliverance of the heart, this deliverance by wisdom, he is called one who has cut off craving, removed the fetters of existence, has made an end of suffering by the full elimination of self-conceit."

The more devotedly one strives towards this goal, the more selfless he becomes, and the earlier will he make an end of all egotism:

Saṅghaṃ saraṇaṃ gacchāmi

"I take refuge in the Order of Monks."

But, to be sure, mere outward asceticism is of no avail. "Whether one remains in the household life or whether one goes forth from it to the homeless state, if one lives wrongly I do not praise it. For, whosoever either remains at home or departs from home, if he lives wrongly, on account of that wrong way of life he can gain nothing on the good path of the Dhamma."—"I do not ascribe asceticism to a robe wearer just because he wears a monk's robe. I do not ascribe asceticism to a forest hermit just because he lives in the forest. I do not ascribe asceticism to a knower of text just because he knows many texts... Not because a man wears a robe, dwells in the forest, knows the texts, speaks much about the Doctrine, can he get rid of craving propensities, can he get rid of hating propensities, can he get rid of delusive propensities."

"There are people who, void of faith, go forth from home into homelessness, hypocrites, dissemblers, sham-ascetics, conceited men, busy talkers and chatterers, bad guardians of the doors of the senses, without moderation at meals, not devoted to wakefulness, indifferent to asceticism, without respect for the training, fond of luxury, importunate, preferring what is detrimental, shunning solitude as a heavy burden, lazy, without energy, heedless and uncomprehending; uncontrolled and distracted minds of small understanding, and stupid. Such a monk's asceticism appears to me, O monks, like a murderous weapon, meant for slaughter, double edged, well sharpened, covered and wrapped round with a robe. A knife taken up by the blade wounds the hand: misused asceticism drags one on the downward path."

"In error ye wander, O monks of Assaji, upon a false path ye wander, O monks of Assaji. How far apart have they strayed, the foolish, from this Doctrine and Discipline!" "Hard it is to serve the Exalted One, very hard it is to serve the Exalted One!"—meeting with this experience many a weak disciple, discouraged or displeased, has given up asceticism (see Majjhima Nikāya No. 67, 77).

Only to him who knows suffering, only to one who, true to the Doctrine, earnestly works within, fighting purposefully and persistently against Māra—to such a one only will the external circumstances of asceticism prove to be what actually they ought to be according to Buddha's declaration: the most suitable conditions which the world can offer for the complete overcoming of the world. Again and again did the Master place before his disciples the hollowness and futility of half-hearted asceticism, as well as the seriousness and difficulties of the true monk's life. Never did he attempt to persuade anyone to become his disciple or to lead the ascetic life under him. "He lays the Doctrine before the people, does not persuade them, does not dissuade them." "He shows the nature of this world after he himself has understood and penetrated it. The doctrine, excellent in the beginning, excellent in the middle, excellent in its consummation, does he proclaim, both in the spirit and in the letter; he sets forth the holy life in its fullness and purity." Now, if the nature and purpose of this ascetic life becomes overwhelmingly clear to a householder or a householder's son, he will become an ascetic of his own free will, following his inner urge. "Sunken I am in birth, in old age and death, in distress, lamentation and pain, in grief and despair; sunken in suffering, lost in suffering! Oh that it might be possible to make an end of this whole mass of misery!" In such a state of mind, filled with confidence, he renounces the worldly life, and such a renunciation is called in the texts "right-minded renunciation" (*nekkhammasaṅkappa*).[2]

With such a true renunciation, such a true *Pabbajjā* (Going Forth), "has he arrived in a clearing (of life's jungle)"—but no

2. *Nekkhamma-saṅkappa*, "the thought of renunciation," is one of the three kinds of Right Thought or Right Aspiration (*samma-saṅkappa*), the second factor of the Noble Eightfold Path.

further. "Whoso, as a noble son, has thus renounced, what has he to do? Whoso finds no detachment from desires, from evil states of mind, whoso finds no joy and happiness or other still better gain, his heart will be seized and bound by lust; will be seized and bound by ill-will; will be seized and bound by sloth and torpor; will be seized and bound by restlessness and worry; will be seized and bound by doubt; will be seized and bound by dissatisfaction; will be seized and bound by attachment. But whoso finds detachment from desires, from evil states of mind, and finds joy and happiness and other still better gain, his heart will not be seized and bound by lust, will not be seized and bound by ill-will, by sloth and torpor, restlessness and worry, by doubt, dissatisfaction and attachment." But this nobility of mind, how is it acquired? Only through meditation and again meditation (*satipaṭṭhāna*): "Here trees invite; there, lonely cottages. Go, meditate! Be not slothful, lest later ye repent!"

True asceticism is an obstinate, mute struggle. Mighty is Māra! Fearfully deep-embedded is delusion! "Dying and becoming! Dying and becoming!" No standing still should be permitted; no satisfaction with what has been attained! "Ever more strong must ye become to reach what is still unreached, to attain what is still unattained, to realise what is still unrealised!" "I declare unto you, O monks, I call upon you to give heed, ye that aspire to the goal of asceticism: see that the goal does not elude you while there is more to accomplish!"

Dying and becoming, again and again—until nothing can any more become, and hence there is nothing that can die! No rest, no stopping before Nibbāna is reached! "Also to the world beyond I shall not cleave, nor shall my consciousness be bound to that world. All nutriment is misery, heavenly food as well. To be conscious is to be suffering." An ascetic thus minded "has found and finds ever greater and loftier results; he is well satisfied with the ascetic life, does not give up the noble effort." "It is called 'death' in the Order of the Holy One, when a person gives up asceticism and turns back to the common life of the world"—this he now appreciates, depending upon none in that experience. "As the moth that has caught sight of the light does not turn back to the darkness, and as the ant dies on the sugar heap, so he turns not back to the worldly way of life but devotes himself fully to the noble training, so that he may reach the highest state, Nibbāna, the extinction of delusion."

"And so he becomes fit to eradicate the taints (*āsava*), and to attain, in this very lifetime, the taint-free deliverance of the heart, the deliverance by wisdom."

"Whoso, monks, practises the four Foundations of Mindfulness (*satipaṭṭhāna*) for seven years, may expect one of these two results: the Highest Knowledge (of Sainthood) in his present lifetime, or, if there is a remainder of clinging left, the state of Non-return (to this world; *anāgāmitā*). Setting aside seven years, whoso, monks, thus practises the four Foundations of Mindfulness for six years, five years, four years, three years, two years, one year—nay, setting aside one year: whoso practises the four Foundations of Mindfulness for seven months, may expect one of these two results: the Highest Knowledge in his present lifetime, or, if there is a remainder of clinging, the state of Non-return. Setting aside seven months, whoso, monks, practises these four Foundations of Mindfulness for six months, five months, four months, three months, two months, one month, or half a month —nay, setting aside half a month: whoso practises these four Foundations of Mindfulness for seven days, may expect one of these two results: the Highest Knowledge in his present lifetime, or if there is a remainder of clinging, the state of Non-return."

If weak men only knew themselves! The hero, verily, slumbers in many a one!

"Striving, have many won the deathless,
And still today by striving men can win
If they with wise endeavour persevere.
But none can do it who does shun the fight."

Five Letters About Buddhism

I

Letter of 9-8-1906
Dear —,
From your letter I hear the cry for deliverance. "Deliverance is born of knowledge." For attaining to that liberating knowledge, I can, from my own experience, only give the advice to you who are otherwise fairly well prepared; to imbibe for a period of years the spirit of the Discourses of the Buddha, and to set to work accordingly. There will then be no need for you to *believe* (as you write) that a system of thought can do justice to the world (i.e., to reality), but you will *know* it. Buddhism does justice to the world even to such a degree that it leads to the overcoming of it. It is an unspeakably vast task to struggle through and beyond all apparent contradictions, and to struggle free, from the most subtle fetters (*taṇhā*). Gotama, the Buddha says expressly: "Profound is this doctrine, hard to understand, hard to perceive, tranquil, sublime, beyond the realm of logic, intelligible only to the wise. You will hardly understand it without patience, devotion, guidance and effort." But, "there are beings whose eyes are only little covered by dust. Not hearing the truth, they will be lost. It is they who will understand the Dhamma." For it has been said that there are "two conditions of right understanding: the voice of others (be it orally or in writing) and wise reflection" (MN 43). Furthermore: "Also in this doctrine and discipline is it possible to show a gradual training, gradual practice, gradual progress" (MN 107). Gradually one will come to acquire a wise understanding of the teachings proclaimed by the Exalted One, and then "lofty results will gradually be experienced."

You write that the spirit of Buddhism is repugnant to you, owing to its rationalistic penetration of the world. I too had formerly that opinion; but it disappears with a more exact knowledge about man's composite nature and his way of development as taught by the Master. Meditation (*bhāvanā*, the four *Satipaṭṭhāna, Samādhi*) rests upon the fact that mind is the forerunner in evolution (thoughts, words and deeds: *kamma* or *sankhāra* within the Dependent Origination,[3] *paṭicca-samuppāda*). In brief, what man thinks, that he becomes. Meditation, in the Buddhist sense includes what we, in Christian lands, call feeling, heart, love, and so on. What commonly is called "feeling" or "emotion," is, in fact, only a "clinging," low or noble; it is but ties and fetters, gross or subtle. For me, for instance, music was formerly such an important factor that, when listening particularly to Beethoven's symphonies, I was clearly possessed by them, ravished, shaken. Even four or five years ago I busied myself with writing music and composition. My judgment of musical performances was generally appreciated. But art is just a means to lead us on to the *comprehending* of suffering, and not only to an emotional experience of it; it takes us from the "particular" to the "general" (aspect of suffering). But more subtle devices (than art) await us. All of them, however, are, as the entire Teaching, meant "for letting go, not for keeping a hold on them" (MN 22).

You say that you have suffered much, and yet you think that this world of suffering is a glorious place! But if you progress from the emotional experience of suffering to an understanding of life's general nature as ill, then there will come a turning point in your ideas. You will come to reflect deeply upon the fact that the entire existence, being something originated, is bound up with impermanence (*sabbe saṅkhārā aniccā*). *Everything* originated (body, feelings, perceptions, mental formations and consciousness) is *aniccā*. What ceases is woe, is suffering and not-self, unsubstantial *dukkham, anattā*. Among these three related characteristics of existence,[4] the most tangible one, *dukkha*, has been taken out, fully stated and defined in the First Truth of suffering; in the second, its cause: in the third its cessation; and in the fourth, the practical path of deliverance. He who has eyes, will perceive these things. The better one understands and practises the Eightfold Path, the less one will be assailed by suffering.

Taṇhā (craving), that 108-headed hydra, will gradually die away—beginning with the grossest, and ending with the most subtle craving which one notices only later. Then "done is, what

3. See The Wheel No. 15a/b: *Dependent Origination*, by Piyadassi Thera.
4. See The Wheel No. 20: *Three Signata*, by Prof. O.H. de A. Wijasekara.

ought to be done." Suffering is transcended, and thereby the world or life (= suffering) are transcended. "Ceased has rebirth, lived to its end is the holy life, the work is done, nothing more beyond this—thus he knows" (MN 94). To him who wishes to inquire further, the following texts are recommended for thorough reflection: the 63rd and 72nd Discourse of the Majjhima Nikāya, and further the Discourses 2, 22, 38, 140; and it is advisable to think slowly and carefully about causality (Dependent Origination).

Enough for today. Though Buddhism, as you say, is for you partly still unpalatable, yet in the first words of your letter, you admit the strict consistency and inner strength of my own way of action. I have understood Buddha's logic and love: "the shortest way between two points (i.e., the present stage of development, and deliverance) is the straight line."

The study of Pali will permit you a much quicker penetration of the teaching, since all translations are makeshifts (even the sound ones by Neumann); our words (concepts) are insufficient, and often they lead astray.

...If, in addition, you will learn by heart the most important Discourses, fully or partly, then you will have a solid foundation, inwardly and with regard to your linguistic studies.

II

Dear Sir,

One who has understood the universality of suffering and the importance of the ascetic life for the speediest elimination of that suffering, such a one will certainly sympathize with you. According to your valuable and frank confession you have "a strong sensuality." You may know that asceticism or the "holy life" is mostly called *brahmacariyaṃ* (the chaste life). It is significant that the same term is used in the third *sīla* (Precept) of the monk. "Having abandoned unchastity, he lives a life of chastity; he keeps aloof and abstains from that vulgar practice, sexual intercourse." "He keeps aloof," that is, he observes a prudent distance from women, lest he lend a hand to Māra, because he is still weak, and in the process of growth.

For the millions of those who live a worldly life, sexual intercourse within the limits indicated in MN 41 is not regarded as *akusala* (unwholesome);[5] but for the disciple proper who wishes "to bring suffering to an end," it is always *akusala*: unwholesome, wrong, and conducive to suffering. How could he gain a deeper, truly penetrating insight as long as that powerful affirmation of life vibrates through his organism and paralyzes his mind? Therefore, *kāmacchanda* or *kāmarāga* (sense-desire or sensual lust) is the first Hindrance, Fetter and Defilement; and its opposite *nekkhamma*, "renunciation," is the first help and aid in gaining *samma-samādhi*, "right concentration," which is required for the pure vision of truth (*vipassanā*). Although the entire realm of *kāma* (i.e., the five sense objects) are a hindrance to *samādhi* yet one has to recognize the sexual sphere as the most portentous in the realm of sensuality. One knows what an enormous amount of energy is expended here. He who is infatuated will be aware of it only faintly; but later when fighting and subduing his passion, it will become clear to him that he was formerly but a miserable specimen of humanity, a slave of Māra; he will then appreciate that a mind kept in a violent tremor by strong emotions, cannot possibly see reality as it is.

"The teaching that goes against the current,
that is deep, subtle and hidden —
invisible it remains to those infatuated by lust."

The Buddha-Dhamma is said to go against the current. The crowd goes along with the current: life-affirmation, lust, hatred, self-delusion. The true disciple goes against that stream; he negates it, because he wishes to transcend the world, get rid of it.

"The turning away of the will vanquishes all woe." Our blind fellowbeings, however, who float along with the current will say: "But sexual desire is something natural!" It is that very fact which a perspicuous Buddhist knows, and therefore turns away:

---

5. The author's use of the Buddhist technical term *akusala,* i.e., "karmically unwholesome," is here somewhat misleading; but the meaning intended by him is clear: For a layman, sexual intercourse in marriage is not immoral, being not a violation of the Five Precepts binding on him. Any form of lust (*lobha*), however, is karmically unwholesome, in the strict sense of the term *akusala,* though "unlawful lust" (*visama-lobha;* e.g., adultery) is so in a higher degree.—The Translator.

"This world, the other world as well
the Knowing One has clearly shown:
the realm of nature and its law,
and freedom ending all that woe." (MN 34)

He who understands *that,* has achieved much.

Also he who has strong sensual inclination, *can* live *brahmacariya,* the chaste life. "There is one who is by nature lustful, yet he preserves his chastity, even if passion often makes him feel pain and torment; but he is able, though with pain and torment, to live the noble, pure life of chastity (*brahmacariya*)" (Majjh. 45)

A disciple who has made himself familiar with the Buddha's instruction, is able to fight the passions with quite different weapons from other folk, but knowledge without application is dead. How, then, can a tendency be gradually expelled from one's nature, for instance that to sensuality? By displacing, eliminating and replacing. You may have observed how thoughts are placed in the sequence of time, how they follow each other, and how only *one* thought at one time can be present to consciousness, if ever so briefly.

Make a start now, and take matters into your own hands! Instead of allowing your thoughts to roam about aimlessly, in a confused way and impelled by emotions—you should first select a time of the day, a short half an hour, in which to give to your thought processes a definite direction by choosing a suitable subject of meditation such as *asubha-bhāvanā* (contemplation of the body's foulness). By doing so, gradually a counter tendency is developed, because during the 30 minutes of *asubha-bhāvanā,* lust has simply dropped out. If you now return to your routine life, the tendency developed during your practice will produce an after-effect which will grow more and more beneficial in proportion to the intensity and duration of the practice. Gradually, with strengthened mindfulness (*sati*), that noble tendency will permeate almost your whole thought process, always ready to step in with its beneficial effect whenever Māra wishes to intrude. Most of our fellowbeings "believe that they push while they are pushed themselves." But the true disciple actually pushes matters himself, because he has grasped "the law of elimination by disuse," and thus he displaces and eliminates, so that passions die away; until at the end there is nothing more to die away.

First a Buddhist should suffuse and saturate himself with the Master's words like those in (the "Revelation of the Body"), in the *Sutta Nipāta* (v. 193ff), the *Theragāthā,* suttas like Majjhima Nikāya No. 82; then, if he has noble aspirations, the powerful sexual urge will be reduced noticeably.

"Look how this puppet is decked out,
that skin-enveloped skeleton!
Fools are deluded by that sight;
Not those who seek the shore beyond."

According to the Master's injunction (MN 75), after listening (or reading), there should be thorough reflection about it (*yoniso manasikāra*), to be done best at a quiet place. You should contemplate and analyze this body as it is described (so simply but ever so true) in Majjhima Nikāya 10 (Satipaṭṭhāna Sutta): "He contemplates his body from the sole of the feet upwards, and from the crown of the head downward, covered by the skin, filled with many impurities." He understands it as a passing combination of elements; he visualizes it as a putrefying corpse, food for worms, as a skeleton and as decaying bones: "My body, too, is of that nature, will become like that, and cannot escape it."

After such thorough contemplation (*asubha-bhāvanā*), actual realization will unfailingly follow. If he now sees women, he is no longer dominated by the animal urge of carnal desire, but he sees *through* it; he sees them as skeletons. Looking ahead he, already now, perceives the flesh now, after death, it will be devoured by worms; and, then his prevailing feeling will be compassion: "Soon these bodies will perish and will add to the charnel field. May beings awake from their frenzy, so that it may no longer be said of them: 'Worn out in vain, the body dies away,' but may their *kamma* come gradually to rest!"

For him who is moved by such compassion, will it be possible to use a being for satisfying his lust? Only selfishness will be able to do so, even if it hides behind greatest learning. The Master has taught his disciples—of whom none was a eunuch—how to regulate that desire, and how to bring it to rest. If you make substantial progress in that respect, you will have achieved much. May you remain mindful of the fact that you do it for *your own* sake, for *other's* sake, and for the cause (of the truth).

"Him who as sage from mating keeps aloof,
Who, young in years, nowhere ensnares himself,
From heedless rapture free, detached,
Him as a sage the wise ones rightly hold."

(Sutta Nipāta v. 218)
Namo Buddhāya,
Sumano

III

Dear —,

Not many details can be told about your first question.[6] I became aware of the fact: "I am afflicted by birth, old-age and death, sunken into sorrow, lamentation, pain, grief and despair, submerged by suffering, lost in suffering! Oh, that it might be possible to make an end of that whole mass of suffering!" (With regard to your question) consider "evolution" in its widest sense. I mean to say: Beings understand and follow the teaching of the Blessed One according to the degree of their own development. "He who has eyes, will see."

Let us assume there is an "intelligent person," "a man of understanding." He perceives clearly (a) the impermanency of all that is originated, and he understands (b) the conclusion: what is impermanent is liable to suffering (*dukkha*) and it is not-self (*anattā*). Through both (a) and (b), he will understand the equation: life = suffering; and now, awakened from his slumber, he works with increasing intensity to make an end of suffering, and thereby, of life.

But how? "Deliverance results from knowledge." That liberating knowledge (=Right Understanding) is (and according to the above, cannot be anything else): 1. to know suffering; 2. to know the origin of suffering; 3. to know the cessation of

6. This question was, probably, about the Rev Sumano's reasons for entering the monkhood.

suffering; 4. to know the path leading to suffering's cessation. This is "the teaching particular to Enlightened Ones." "This only do I teach, now as before: suffering and the cessation of suffering." Any doubt as to whether that knowledge is actually the only one needful to us now, will disappear if one reflects carefully on the 63rd Discourse of Majjhima Nikāya.

From experience I may give the assurance that man will grow in his detachment, and that suffering will touch him less and less, the more mindfully and energetically he walks the path. *Taṇhā* (craving), the direct cause of suffering (2nd Truth) and of renewed existence (Paṭicca-samuppāda links 8, 9, 10;[7] Majjhima Discourses, 9, 38), is gradually brought to extinction. First its gross form dies away, and later the more subtle one that is imperceptible at the start (this Taṇhā-hydra has 108 heads).

Though, as a rule, only the genuine bhikkhu will be able to walk the path perfectly, yet the opinion which one sometimes finds expressed, that *only* the bhikkhu can do it at all, is erroneous. Everyone who leads the home life—more especially if living alone—can tread the Path and progress on it very far, "according to the nature of his actions." Everyone who has become a bhikkhu with the clear awareness of what he is doing, has once lived the worldly life before, but has prepared himself before he chose to lead the ascetic life that is so beneficial. Gotama Buddha, in the 43rd Discourse (Majjhima Nikāya) addressed to the citizens of Sala, has given very valuable instructions for right conduct in thoughts, words and deeds. Adherence to that conduct will, to the degree of one's success in doing so, contribute considerably to the overcoming of suffering. Without having fully understood the importance of a virtuous life (*sīla*) for purification and for mental concentration, it will be premature if the disciple desires to attain the meditative absorptions (*jhāna*). If you consider very carefully the following you will see clearly in that matter.

We find in the texts the following threefold division of the Path:

---

7. See "The Wheel" No. 15a/b.

I. *Sīla* (virtue):
3. sammā-vācā, Right Speech
4. sammā-kammanta, Right Action
5. sammā-ājiiva, Right Livelihood

II. *Samādhi* (concentration):
6. sammā-vāyāma, Right Effort
7. sammā-sati, Right Mindfulness
8. sammā-samādhi, Right Concentration

III. *Paññā* (wisdom):
1. sammā-diṭṭhi, Right Understanding
2. sammā-saṅkappa, Right Thought

Usually the factors numbered (1) and (2) are mentioned first, because the Path cannot be trodden without a degree of Right Understanding and Right Thought. In their *perfected* form, however, they constitute *paññā,* the highest wisdom.

Virtue comes first (being perfected later, by concentration and wisdom). Then follows Concentration, comprising the 6th, 7th and 8th factor of the Path. Among them, Right Effort consists of the Four Endeavours (Discourse 141); and these four are also called "implements of concentration." The four "Foundations of Mindfulness"[8] *(satipaṭṭhāna),* which according to Discourse 141 form the seventh Path factor, are "the objects of concentration"; and Concentration proper, the 8th factor, is explained by the four meditative absorptions *(jhāna).*

In other words, firstly strong energy (6th factor) has to be developed, and untiringly one should work, that is meditate, in accordance with the four Foundations of Mindfulness, for providing the inner training required for the entry into the First Absorption.

How then, can such mighty energy be developed? "If he sees with his eyes a visible object, he does not take up its general features nor its details. Because lust and grief, unwholesome and evil thoughts may overwhelm him who dwells with his sense of sight unrestrained, he practises that restraint, guards his sense of sight and watches over it." The same holds good for the other four physical senses and mind as the sixth.

---

8. See "The Wheel" No. 19: *The Four Foundations of Mindfulness.*

	I	II	III	IV	V	VI
1	eye	ear	nose	tongue	body	mind
2	forms	sounds	smells	tastes	tactile objects	mental objects

Through the six senses (the subjective side of reality; see the first line in the sketch) we communicate with the outer world (the objective side of reality; see the 2nd line). From this is seen the immense importance of controlling that [sense] apparatus (*saŷāyatana,* the 5th link of the Nidāna-chain, *Paṭiccasamuppāda*) for the specific purpose of gaining mental concentration, and for the general purpose of eliminating suffering. "He who does not know and understand according to reality, the eye (ear, etc.), visual (etc.) objects, visual (etc.) consciousness, visual (etc.) impression, the feelings produced by visual (etc.) impression—he will be delighted in the eye; being delighted in it and attached to it, he will allow himself to be allured by it, looking always for the enjoyment provided by it. To him the life process consisting of the five Groups (*khandha*) will continue to accumulate, and craving that leads to renewed existence, finding delight here and there, will continue to grow... But he who knows and understands according to reality, the eye..., will not be delighted in the eye..., seeing always the danger in it. To him the five Groups will decrease, and craving... will vanish."

"The concentration of one who has achieved that, is Right Concentration"...; "He who sees the Dependent Origination, sees the Dhamma; he who sees the Dhamma, sees the Dependent Origination."

This spiritual struggle will lead to victory chiefly through constant mindfulness and thought concerning the fact of origination (arising), in other words, impermanence. For instance: "Now this unpleasant feeling has arisen in me (e.g., by insult) produced by auditory impression (see Paticcasamuppada 5, 6), and it is conditioned, not unconditioned. Conditioned by what? By sense impression. And he knows: impression is impermanent; he knows: feeling is impermanent... Then his mind, thus discerning the elements, becomes gladdened, serene, strong and steady" (similarly with I, III-VI of the above sketch).

So far about Energy or Right Effort (the 6th path factor), being the implement by which to attain concentration (meditative absorption).

Information about the Four Foundations of Mindfulness will be found in MN 10 (*Satipaṭṭhāna-sutta*), 118 ("Mindfulness on Breathing"), 119 ("Mindfulness on the Body"), 62 ("Admonition to Rāhula"). Then, "while he thus dwells earnest, ardent and mindful, the memories bound up with home life will vanish in him."

I have experienced myself how important it is to meditate upon the four Foundations of Mindfulness (*Satipaṭṭhāna-sutta*). I have learned that Discourse by heart, in Pali, and daily I repeat one seventh part of it in my meditation; every week has brought new revelations (*sati*). But one must work for it. "He who does not work, cannot follow the truth." "It is not possible, thus I teach, to obtain assurance at once, at the start; but gradually fighting, progressing step by step, one will obtain assurance... And because he makes determined effort, he realizes for himself the highest truth and visualizes it by wise penetration." He who attends to the preparatory work, as indicated, will avoid the illusions of "wrong concentration" (*micchā-samādhi*), and will steer straight towards Right Concentration, because cultivation of *samādhi* means the cultivation of, and the training in just these things, i.e., Energy and Mindfulness.

The fact that also householders (lay followers) can practice mindfulness, is mentioned in Discourse 51: "We too, O lord, being householders, have from time to time established our mind in the four Foundations of Mindfulness; and we dwell, O Lord, contemplating the body in the body, ardent, clearly comprehending, mindful, having overcome covetousness and grief regarding the world."

If you now read a Discourse like the 27th, where the Master gives a connected summary, you will have confirmation of that sequence of practice mentioned above: first *sila* (virtue; but here more comprehensive, being intended for monks); then the control of the senses (i.e., energy) and mindfulness (the passage on Clear Comprehension from Discourse 10). Also the five Hindrances which have to be overcome before one can enter the first Absorption, are found in the 10th Discourse, at the beginning of the fourth Foundation of Mindfulness. How difficult it is, generally, to gain the Absorptions is shown by the Buddha's statements in the 128th Discourse; there, profoundly, and step by step, the hindrances and their overcoming are shown... But the difficulties mentioned there will not deter an earnest disciple. He knows that evolution does not proceed at a bound, but that, by an indefatigable application of the appropriate means, progress undreamt of may be achieved in a short time... However, the fact cannot be concealed: "Profound is this teaching, difficult to grasp... you will hardly understand it without patience, devotion, effort and guidance"; and "there are fools who study the teaching; but though they have studied it, they do not wisely examine the meaning of the teachings; without wisely examining the teachings their contemplation will not yield satisfaction;... they do not grasp the purpose for which they have studied the teaching. To them, their wrong grasp of the teaching will bring them harm and suffering for a long time."

Yet it has been said that the teaching is intelligible to every person of understanding, and that it grows in clarity for the earnest disciple. "There are no ascetics who know and understand everything at once. That is impossible." It is by *training*, by indefatigable training, that everything is nursed to maturity. "What a monk considers and reflects upon for a long time, to that his mind will incline."

If once the fundamental truths have been thoroughly grasped and experienced, and, through a faithful devotion to the inner work, "the gradual perception of a great result" has appeared, then from such a soil a beneficial and powerful *saddhā* (confidence) concerning the future work ("the achieving of the unachieved") will grow. This is the first of the five "qualities of spiritual striving" (*padhānaṅga*), by the help of which the disciple may achieve his aim quickly.

I am filled with an unshakable *saddhā* (confidence). A confidence rooted in understanding and experience surmounts difficulties met by one who is given to speculative thinking, a hair-splitter, or a petty critic. Though the way of expression (in the Discourses) may sometimes be difficult or strange (particularly in translations), and though, in some instances, the teachings given there, may remain unintelligible for some time, let us have

Saddhā! "Enlightened Ones do not speak imperfectly." "Work, Work!" as we have stressed above—that is the key word. Then the Dhamma will be realised, experienced and no longer requires proof or guidance, not even by a Buddha. "In the Liberated One is the knowledge of Liberation." Then there is no longer any difference as to liberation. "Equal to me will be those victorious ones who have destroyed craving."

Namo Tassa Bhagavato Arahato Sammā-sambuddhassa!

— Stg.

IV

Bandarawela (Monastery)
28th April 1909

Dear Mr. N.,

If you attach great significance to "Mindfulness of Breathing" (*ānāpāna-sati*) you have perceived an important fact. As the four Foundations of Mindfulness (*Satipaṭṭhāna*) may be called the heart of the doctrine, so is "Mindfulness of Breathing," if rightly understood, the heart of the heart. "Mindfulness of Breathing if developed well and regularly practised, brings to perfection the four Foundations of Mindfulness," thus it is said in the 118th Discourse. He who knows these means of deliverance, and applies them, will experience by himself that restlessness, desire, anger, misapprehensions and thereby all deep sorrows, will vanish, and will reappear only and always, when that mindfulness (*sati*) is absent. While our other fellowbeings—millions of them—go on living 'without any substantial gain' in liberation ("worn out in vain, this body dies away"), he who knows the laws of deliverance can purposefully take into his hands the work of their unfolding; he can loosen, and finally break, the chains of slavery.

First of all, three things are required here: 1. persistence; 2. persistence; 3. persistence. Without great devotion, without extraordinary patience even one who is otherwise gifted, will not be able to make progress. It is important that the beginner betakes himself to a quiet place, as secluded as possible, so that the habitual *taṇhā*—nourishment for the five senses (see end of Majjh.

150)—is reduced, and the numerous sounds, voices and noises which, particularly at the beginning, hinder so much any deeper concentration, do not constantly interfere. You will not have missed the fact that it is expressly stated in the Discourses 10, 62, 118 and 27, that the disciple should resort to the forest, an empty room, etc. Thus, whenever bonds of profession or family do not fetter you, you should make haste to go out of your town, like one who seeks hidden treasure, and should choose a suitable spot in forest environment. Then you should sit down there in a posture that allows you the longest time of sitting immovably. "Mindfully he breathes in, mindfully he breathes out"—that is the general practice of *ānāpāna-sati,* introducing the subsequent 16 specific exercises, and forming the transition from ordinary confused thinking to concentrated meditation focussed upon a definite mental object. The former kind of thinking, ordinary reflection, is called *vitakka,* i.e., "discursive thinking." By Mindfulness of Breathing that discursive thinking is suspended and silenced. *Ānāpāna-sati bhāvetabbā vitakk'upacchedāya:* "Mindfulness of Breathing ought to be practised for cutting off discursive thinking." How is it to be done?

"Breathing in long, he *knows* 'I breathe in long'; breathing out long, he knows 'I breathe out long'; breathing in short, he knows "I breathe in short"; breathing out short, he knows "I breathe out short." Now, at one and the same time only one single thought can be clearly present to consciousness; thoughts *follow* each other, they are placed in time. All exclusion of evil thoughts effected by meditation, rests upon that fact, is made possible by that fact. He who thinks for one minute a thought of kindness, has *at that time* no thought of hate in his mind; he who thinks of a corpse for one minute, has no lust while doing so; he who contemplates impermanence for one minute, will not have conceit. Whenever, and as long as, one knows "I breathe in, and out, long or short," for that time, even if it is only for a fraction of a second, other *vitakkā* (discursive thoughts) will be excluded.

You will, however, experience that, when you resolve to be strictly watchful, the first breaths that follow, will go in and out a clear awareness of them, but after that, habitual worldly thoughts (*vitakkā*) will appear again during a single breath. But if one considers that the complete tranquillization and exclusion of discursive thoughts is tantamount to the entry into the Second Absorption, one will, in spite of all relapses, persist in one's practice, week by week, month by month, year by year; and during a single session the meditator will apply mindfulness 100 times or 1000 times or more. Gradually the law of "development by use" (the inherent power of repetition) will show itself; it works as reliably as the law of "elimination by disuse."

In one minute, one may breathe 15 times (30 inhalations and exhalations). If one is conscious of it, even if only at the beginning, one will have given a definite direction to one's mind 300 times in 10 minutes. If for about 10 minutes no breath has been missed, it is certainly an achievement, though, to a beginner, some fatigue may be noticeable. The simile of the turner ("turning long or short"), given in the 10th Discourse, shows clearly how simply that exercise is meant (long-short, in-out; knowing). Generally spoken, it is the most simple that is truly great and profound. From the foregoing it will become clear how important that simple and easily intelligible exercise is. If patiently sustained, it is bound to result in the calmness and concentration of mind (*samatha*), aspired by you. The Master teaches how to bind a second postulate, a "Must"—mindfulness (*sati*)—to breathing which is the constant companion of man from birth to death. The first "Must" is faithful: man *must* breathe constantly (except in the fourth Absorption). The second "Must" has to be developed from it. In other words, breathing cannot wait; if it is not to escape unnoticed (as it happens in ordinary life), mindfulness (*sati*) must be present and alert. "For one of confused mindfulness, I say, there is no Mindfulness of Breathing."

There are people endowed with outstanding gifts. As soon as they know the method, they will practise with zeal and determination. Perhaps you too will, even after a short time, attain genuine Absorption of mind, will easily leave behind the Sensuous Sphere, and realise one or more stages of meditation. Through those two exercises that degree of *Samatha* (tranquillity) can be achieved only if the five Hindrances are removed, the presence of which is incompatible with Absorption.

But even if, for a long time, the meditator cannot attain to the Absorptions, other gratifying results of *ānāpāna-sati* will become evident. Firstly, the calm and concentration of mind as effected by meditative training in solitude, can now be maintained for increasingly longer periods of time. Calm and concentration will gradually enter into the meditator's innermost being, and will also manifest themselves outwardly in his daily behaviour (in the family, in professional life and towards friends), by a calmer and more composed way of speaking (*santa-vaco,* "quiet of speech"), and by calmer bodily movements (*santa-kāyo*) in going, turning, looking, bending and stretching of limbs. Secondly, what is incomparably more important, there will be a keener insight (*vipassanā*) into the nature of the world, that is, of the five Khandhas, as impermanent, liable to suffering and not-self. A man with keen eyesight will excel in observation. Similarly, greater tranquillity (*samatha*) means deeper insight (*vipassanā*); and, again, strengthened insight into suffering will be an incentive to achieve a greater power of concentration as a means to the end (insight). It is a reciprocal process "No meditative absorption without wisdom: and no wisdom without absorption."

Therefore, after having practised for some time the exercises No. 1 and 2,[9] one may go over to No. 13: "contemplating impermanence, I shall breathe in and out" (Discourse 118 or 62). In doing so, one should keep in mind that what is spoken of here (in the 13th exercise) are phenomena (*dhammā*), objects of thought (i.e., what appears in the mind), pertaining to the fourth Foundation of Mindfulness. The four *Satipaṭṭhānas* may be regarded as stages: 1. at the first stage, one learns to contemplate on the gross material body, as it appears to simple observation (Majjh. 10); 2. in the second *Satipaṭṭhāna,* the feelings, likewise in their simple presentation (as pleasant, unpleasant, etc.); 3. in the third an essential change should follow; the knowledge, gradually prepared and matured by the first three *Satipaṭṭhānas,* that the entire world of plurality is only an object for each subject, a manifestation of thought, hanging only on a single thread: consciousness.

Then the passage in Majjh. 10—"Thus is corporeality, thus is its origin, thus its end," etc.—will appear in a different light, because the proper light has dawned upon the meditator. "Thus is corporeality"; appearances, phenomena, arising in consciousness

9. This refers to the 16 exercises given in Majjh. 118.

with help of the likewise conditioned visual organ (colours) the auditory organ (sound waves), and so on; just as it arises, it disappears again, as a subjective process: appearance, *Aniccā, anattā.* It is similar with the other Khandhas: "Thus is feeling, thus is its origin, thus its end." Here one can learn to understand the whole of existence as an illusion, as not-self (*anattā*); and the Ego-delusion will dissolve quickly. This is so, because all wishing, longing, hating, disliking, fearing, grieving or being excited, in brief all mental afflictions stem from the Atta-idea ("I," "Mine," "my own," self). If that delusion loses its hold, a decisive change takes place, a detachment, a feeling of liberation as never experienced before. The person X is now seen as a temporary combination of ever changing Khandhas (processes of existence); and after sometime this person will disappear from the scene; it has never harboured an eternal self (also Karma can become exhausted).

The idea of *anattā* may get strengthened in us in a way somewhat like this:

> not I (an abiding individuality) breathe, but breathing occurs;
> not I go, but going occurs;
> not I stand, but standing occurs;
> not I sit, but sitting occurs;
> not I lie down, but lying down occurs;
> not I look, but looking occurs;
> not I bend, but bending occurs;
> not I eat, but eating occurs;
> not I talk, but talking occurs;
> not I feel joy or grief, but a pleasant or unpleasant feeling occurs;
> not I think, but thinking occurs.

By such a contemplation, one will become selfless, all-loving, truly detached. and the words in MN 10 will become clear: "He lives independent, and does not cling to anything in the world."

By the power of thinking sharpened and made lucid by the exercises 1 and 2 (of *ānāpāna-sati*), the facts of impermanence and not-self (impersonality) will be visualized more strongly (exercise 13). Therefore I have given here that indication, because it is insight that lastly leads to deliverance. Concentration (*samādhi, samatha*) is only the clarification of mind, which, however, is indispensable; just as in spectacles the glasses are the essential thing, but one can look through them only after removing from them the dirt or moisture.

I have mentioned today only the exercises No. 1, 2 and 13. As you know, talking is here of little avail; doing, practising, is all that matters. After some time you may communicate your experiences, and, if required, ask for further information. You are quite right in saying that, without explanation, one cannot do much with the 16 brief instructions (Discourse 62 or 118), particularly if the translation is unsatisfactory. But in the Canon you will find further elucidations about the single points.

— Sumano

V

Naples
17th October 1906

Dear Friend,

A few words about giving-up. It is better not to have cigars about oneself, on principle. Similarly, he who wishes to wean himself from alcohol will not carry a bottle with him. He who wants to give up desire for women will better not go to places where he will have to face temptation. To be sure of one's steps is important, particularly at a stage of transition. Māra is on the look-out for any possible opening, therefore he must not be given any chance. "Once" is not "never." He who has no cigars about himself *cannot* smoke (and so it is with drinking). No fire can flare up without fuel; for the present, at least, indulgence has been made impossible. Gradually the law of "elimination by disuse" will come into effect. The need and desire for the former enjoyment will weaken and finally cease. If someone says that he has got over smoking, etc., but he carries cigars about him for the sake of a test, then he has not yet fully abandoned *taṇhā* (craving). He who has entirely abolished that craving, will no longer cherish such thoughts; in that respect he is fully at peace, and already thinks further ahead. Thus a disciple who has freed himself from sexual urge will, though immune, not seek temptations. More important things have to be done. No rest before Nibbāna! Besides, if he refrains from testing his power of resistance, this will be more profitable to others in his environment who cannot see into his heart, but observe only his external behaviour; and quite reasonably, their confidence might be shaken by their observations, though they may not talk about it.

Doubtlessly, the struggle against Māra (*taṇhā,* craving) is hard, because for Māra it is actually a question of "to be or not to be," a fight of life or death for his "kingdom of nature." For long, long times we have been his serfs. Now this serfdom is over for us. Nevermore shall we find lasting satisfaction anywhere in this *saṃsāra.* One who has taken the Buddha as his guide and master will understand the nature of "Māra's Realm" so poignantly that he can no longer find full satisfaction in the "Realm of Nature" where everything is impermanent. By seeing the misery of it, we are on the road of escape from it.

What, now, is the principal task for us who already possess a good deal of right understanding, who at least have a knowledge of the doctrine and observe virtue (*sīla*)? *To watch, watch, watch.* To be constantly on guard. In particular: to try to remain mindful. *Samādhi* (concentration, meditation) is the Buddhist practice proper. At the start of the practice the mind is not collected at all, the capacity of concentration is weak. But, as the Master explained, by training, by unceasing training, the little child, first constantly falling, learns to toddle about, till finally as a grown-up man he can walk steadily and continuously for long stretches. If a man possessed of intelligence falls, he has not been watchful, was absent-minded. "Lax mindfulness, produces new taints (*āsava*) and strengthens the old ones; unflinching mindfulness gives no room for new taints and destroys the old ones." For instance, one has seen innumerable times that "all formations are impermanent"; one has also agreed with the Buddha's words: "Whatever corporeality exists, one's own or of others, beautiful or ugly, all corporeality should, with proper understanding, be regarded as it truly is: 'It is not mine...'; thus it will be abandoned, will be rejected." Very often the misery of corporeality has been felt most pungently, and the misery of craving has been understood, yet this or that object will still titillate our senses whenever watchfulness is lacking. But if one remains mindful, and turns at once to an analysis of the perception, one will not be enticed by any material form. One will see that the material form has been made up into an evanescent structure of this or another kind (young or old, beautiful or ugly), by the karmic formations (*saṅkhārā*) which are impermanent in themselves, one will see that material form is put together in a similar way as a potter (himself impermanent) shapes (fragile) pots. Then "his mind, dissecting thus the elements, will become joyful, gladdened, strong and steady."

It is doubtlessly a hard way, but gloriously safe. Truly, in that manner, one can perceptibly detach oneself from the world.

Namo tassa,

Stg.

Appendix I

Reminiscences of Sumano
by Dr. P. Derval

"Fritz Stange, student of natural sciences"—thus my late friend, then a newly registered freshman, was introduced to the academical association to which I belonged. A handsome young man, with smooth, blond hair, and an elegant moustache, with deeply blue and strikingly large eyes, a gentle voice and a mild glance, thus he stood before us. He was a gentle person and a keen student, who, in lonely hours, used to comfort his soul by playing the violin; he was an ardent admirer of Richard Wagner, and, if possible, he did not miss a single performance of Wagner's operas. If anyone had said that a person like he would ever become a Buddhist ascetic, he would have provoked general laughter.

We liked each other from the beginning. Strange became my personal freshman. My other freshman was a great artist in the field of music, and has now become an excellent, though little known, Sanskritist and Vedantist. The three of us, united by bonds of closest friendship, soon met regularly at the sessions of the Theosophical Society which everywhere has prepared the way for the Buddhist movement. Following the wish of his father, Stange had to give up his studies so dear to him and donned the uniform of an official of the Postal Department. For none of us had the student life any special attraction, and Stange himself saw in it only the karmic way by which we came together. As an official, Stange remained a keen Theosophist, lived as a vegetarian, and plunged deeply into the study of those teachings which then we called Buddhism.

Besides he was unusually capable in his profession, and, personally, he was the favourite of all who knew him. When he was a probationer for the higher postal career ("*Oberpostpraktikant*") at Kassel, he began to study the Discourses of the Buddha in Neumann's translation, under the guidance of a friend who was an ardent Buddhist, and soon the resolution matured in him to seek deliverance from the grievous suffering that pervades the life of all beings. He had fully grasped the Truth of Suffering.

But knowledge alone was not sufficient for his fervent, pure, and profound heart. Thus he left, as a true follower of the Blessed One, his home, his property and his relations, in order to enter the Sangha (Buddhist Monkhood) in distant Asia.

"Why does one go to the countries of Buddhism?" he wrote to me once. "Briefly spoken, because there, particularly in Burma, all conditions are cut out for a life in the Sangha. One is relieved of all worldly cares, for eating, drinking, clothing, lodging, etc.; in contrast to Europe, one can live there the holy life, first externally. How one detaches oneself inwardly is everyone's most personal affair." Thus he came to Ceylon. "The reception," he wrote, "was so friendly, the helpful response so strikingly unexpected, that already a fortnight after my arrival in Ceylon, I followed an invitation of the Bhikkhu Jinavaravamsa to stay at Chulla Lanka.[10] There I have spent the holiest time of my life, in meditation, study of Pali, and conversation about the teaching... But this body 'that sickly thing,' did not stand it." On medical advice, Stange decided to return to Europe to cure his lung disease. In summer 1906, he lived first at Wingendorf near Lauban; afterwards, following the invitation of a friendly physician with Buddhist leanings, at Birkfield in Styria (Austria).

On the 11th of October 1906, the ship took him out again, hardly recovered. This time he went soon to the healthy up-country of Ceylon, to Bandarawela. Until his complete recuperation, he took, as preliminary step towards the Sangha, the white dress of an Upasaka, but soon he donned again the yellow robe of a Sāmaṇera (novice). His intention was to return later to Europe, together with Nyanatiloka, for establishing the Sangha there. "The time will come," he wrote in his letter of 7-7-1906, "when a Sangha will be established in Germany by thoroughly trained Bhikkhus, and thereby a firm basis will be formed for the dissemination of the Teaching that brings such unspeakable bliss."

"When illness visits thee, make mindfulness arise.
Illness has come. No time is now for negligence."

(Theragāthā)

10. An island in the sea near the coast of Matara, a town in South Ceylon. The Sinhalese name of the island is Galgodiyana.

How earnest he was in his determination, is confirmed by the following words of his:

"And even if I had not met a single good Bhikkhu, this would not have disconcerted me. 'Rare are Enlightened Ones.' 'Small is the number of those who are gripped by things truly stirring, compared with those who are not gripped by them.' These words of the Enlightened One are of general validity. A perceptive disciple will see in that fact an admonition to make all the quicker an end of suffering. So strongly have I become aware of the truth of this Teaching and of its profundity, that, on the one hand to swerve from that path to another one has become an impossibility; and, on the other hand, even my walking alone on that path would be done without hesitation or surprise."

Now his striving within this present impermanent existence has come to an end. Just as his going forth from home was similar to that of his Lord and Master Gotama, so it was the same illness, dysentery, which had dissolved the body of the Perfect one, that also took away the dear heroic Sāmaṇera Sumano. Death is indeed the lot of everything born and originated.

When Sumano started on his way to Homelessness, he pointed out to his relatives the justification of that step in a beautifully lucid tract, quoting in it, especially, sayings of Jesus of Nazareth. To the public he gave the work published a few weeks ago, "Pabbajjā, Going Forth into Homelessness." Only by absorbing its contents fully, we shall be able to measure the single-minded, pure, noble, and yet firmly rooted work for deliverance done by our friend who is now free from the world of appearance.

Appendix II

From a Letter by the German Bhikkhu Koṇḍañño

"What I have to say about Sumano's death is the following: In autumn last year, Bhikkhu Nyanatiloka, the Burmese monk Silavamsa and myself made a walking tour for a week through the South West of Ceylon, via Adam's Peak, and came also to Bandarawela. First the three of us went to the small mud hut, hardly 3 by 4 metres in size, where Sumano had lived and died. The hut is situated in a very lonely place, outside of the village, in the midst of bare grassy hillocks, so that no sound can be heard from the village, and no human habitation can be seen right around. It is desolate and lonely there, as rarely anywhere else. The second hut which, when Sumano died, was inhabited by Suñño, had already fallen into decay, and the rain had washed away nearly every vestige of it. Afterwards we wanted also to go to the site of the cremation, but we missed the place. Hence I went, without Nyanatiloka, once more there, together with the Thera of the Bandarawela Monastery, and I found there, besides some pieces of molten glass, a few small unburned splinters of bone. I picked them up and handed them over to Nyanatiloka who still keeps them at Dodanduwa as a token.

The site of the cremation is on the top of one of those grassy hillocks, about 10 minutes distance from the hut. Boys planted a Bodhi tree at that spot. A great gathering is said to have been present at the cremation, amongst them hundreds of Christians and Mohammedans who secretly respected the ascetic way of life led by Sumano... After the cremation, the ashes were distributed among the lay people, and many a Christian, Mohammedan, and Hindu took them as gladly as a Buddhist..."

The Light of Asia or The Great Renunciation

(Mahabhinishkramana)

Being the Life and Teaching of Gautama

(As Told in Verse by an Indian Buddhist)

By

Edwin Arnold,
M.A., K.C.I.E., C.S.I.

WHEEL PUBLICATION NO. 29

Publisher's Preface

Considering that in some countries reached by our publications, Edwin Arnold's great poem may not be easily available, we offer here to the readers of "The Wheel" series the last three chapters of *The Light of Asia*. These chapters were chosen for prior publication since they are the culmination of the poem, describing the Buddha's enlightenment, and giving the poet's inspiring rendering of the Teaching.

BUDDHIST PUBLICATION SOCIETY

Book the Sixth

Thou who wouldst see where dawned the light at last,
North-westwards from the "Thousand Gardens" go
By Gunga's valley till thy steps be set
On the green hills where those twin streamlets spring
Nilājan and Mohāna; follow them,
Winding beneath broad-leaved mahūa-trees,
'Mid thickets of the sansār and the bir,
Till on the plain the shining sisters meet
In Phalgū's bed, flowing by rocky banks
To Gāya and the red Barabar hills.
Hard by that river spreads a thorny waste,
Uruwelaya named in ancient days,
With sandhills broken; on its verge a wood
Waves sea-green plumes and tassels 'thwart the sky,
With undergrowth where through a still flood steals,
Dappled with lotus-blossoms, blue and white,
And peopled with quick fish and tortoises.
Near it the village of Senāni reared
Its roofs of grass, nestled amid the palms,
Peaceful with simple folk and pastoral toils.

There in the sylvan solitudes once more
Lord Buddha lived, musing the woes of men,
The ways of fate, the doctrines of the books,
The lessons of the creatures of the brake,
The secrets of the silence whence all come,
The secrets of the gloom whereto all go,
The life which lies between, like that arch flung
From cloud to cloud across the sky, which hath
Mists for its masonry and vapory piers,
Melting to void again which was so fair
With sapphire hues, garnet, and chrysoprase.
Moon after moon our Lord sate in the wood,
So meditating these that he forgot
Oft-times the hour of food, rising from thoughts
Prolonged beyond the sunrise and the noon

To see his bowl unfilled, and eat perforce
Of wild fruit fallen from the boughs o'erhead,
Shaken to earth by chattering ape or plucked
By purple parokeet. Therefore his grace
Faded; his body, worn by stress of soul,
Lost day by day the marks, thirty and two,
Which testify the Buddha. Scarce that leaf,
Fluttering so dry and withered to his feet
From off the sāl-branch, bore less likeliness
Of spring's soft greenery than he of him
Who was the princely flower of all his land.

And once at such a time the o'erwrought Prince
Fell to the earth in deadly swoon, all spent,
Even as one slain, who hath no longer breath
Nor any stir of blood; so wan he was,
So motionless. But there came by that way
A shepherd-boy, who saw Siddārtha lie
With lids fast-closed, and lines of nameless pain
Fixed on his lips—the fiery noonday sun
Beating upon his head—who, plucking boughs
From wild rose-apple trees, knitted them thick
Into a bower to shade the sacred face.
Also he poured upon the Master's lips
Drops of warm milk, pressed from his she-goat's bag,
Lest, being of low caste, he do wrong to one
So high and holy seeming. But the books
Tell how the jambu-branches, planted thus,
Shot with quick life in wealth of leaf and flower
And glowing fruitage interlaced and close,
So that the bower grew like a tent of silk
Pitched for a king at hunting, decked with studs
Of silver-work and bosses of red gold.
And the boy worshipped, deeming him some God;
But our Lord gaining breath, arose and asked
Milk in the shepherd's lota. "Ah, my Lord,
I cannot give thee," quoth the lad, "thou seest
I am a Sudra, and my touch defiles!"
Then the World-honored spake: "Pity and need

Make all flesh kin. There is no caste in blood,
Which runneth of one hue, nor caste in tears,
Which trickle salt with all; neither comes man
To birth with tilka-mark stamped on the brow,
Nor sacred thread on neck. Who doth right deeds
Is twice-born, and who doeth ill deeds vile.
Give me to drink, my brother; when I come
Unto my quest it shall be good for thee."
Thereat the peasant's heart was glad, and gave.

And on another day there passed that road
A band of tinselled girls, the nautch-dancers
Of Indra's temple in the town, with those
Who made their music—one that beat a drum
Set round with peacock feathers, one that blew
The piping bānsuli, and one that twitched
A three-string sitar. Lightly tripped they down
From ledge to ledge and through the chequered paths
To some gay festival, the silver bells
Chiming soft peals about the small brown feet,
Armlets and wrist-rings tattling answer shrill;
While he that bore the sitar thrummed and twanged
His threads of brass, and she beside him sang—

"Fair goes the dancing when the sitar's tuned;
Tune us the sitar neither low nor high,
And we will dance away the hearts of men.

The string overstretched breaks, and the music flies
The string o'erslack is dumb, and music dies;
Tune us the sitar neither low nor high."

So sang the nautch-girl to the pipe and wires,
Fluttering like some vain, painted butterfly
From glade to glade along the forest path,
Nor dreamed her light words echoed on the ear
Of him, that holy man, who sate so rapt
Under the fig-tree by the path. But Buddh
Lifted his great brow as the wantons passed,
And spake: "The foolish ofttimes teach the wise
I strain too much this string of life, belike,

Meaning to make such music as shall save.
Mine eyes are dim now that they see the truth,
My strength is waned now that my need is most;
Would that I had such help as man must have,
For I shall die, whose life was all men's hope."

Now, by that river dwelt a landholder
Pious and rich, master of many herds,
A goodly chief, the friend of all the poor;
And from his house the village drew its name—
"Senāni." Pleasant and in peace he lived,
Having for wife Sujāta, loveliest
Of all the dark-eyed daughters of the plain;
Gentle and true, simple and kind was she,
Noble of mien, with gracious speech to all
And gladsome looks—a pearl of womanhood—
Passing calm years of household happiness
Beside her lord in that still Indian home,
Save that no male child blessed their wedded love.
Wherefore with many prayers she had besought
Lakshmi; and many nights at full-moon gone
Round the great Lingam, nine times nine, with gifts
Of rice and jasmine wreaths and sandal oil,
Praying a boy; also Sujāta vowed—
If this should be—an offering of food
Unto the Wood-God, plenteous, delicate,
Set in a bowl of gold under his tree,
Such as the lips of Devs may taste and take.
And this had been: for there was born to her
A beauteous boy, now three months old, who lay
Between Sujāta's breasts, while she did pace
With grateful foot-steps to the Wood-God's shrine,
One arm clasping her crimson sari close
To wrap the babe, that jewel of her joys,
The other lifted high in comely curve
To steady on her head the bowl and dish
Which held the dainty victuals for the God.

But Radha, sent before to sweep the ground
And tie the scarlet threads around the tree,

Came eager, crying, "Ah, dear Mistress! look!
There is the Wood-God sitting in his place,
Revealed, with folded hands upon his knees.
See how the light shines round about his brow!
How mild and great he seems, with heavenly eyes!
Good fortune is it thus to meet the gods."

So—thinking him divine—Sujāta drew
Tremblingly nigh, and kissed the earth and said,
With sweet face bent "Would that the Holy One
Inhabiting this grove, Giver of good,
Merciful unto me his handmaiden,
Vouchsafing now his presence, might accept
These our poor gifts of snowy curds, fresh-made,
With milk as white as new-carved ivory!"

Therewith into the golden bowl she poured
The curds and milk, and on the hands of Buddh
Dropped attar from a crystal flask—distilled
Out of the hearts of roses: and he ate,
Speaking no word, while the glad mother stood
In reverence apart. But of that meal
So wondrous was the virtue that our Lord
Felt strength and life return as though the nights
Of watching and the days of fast had passed
In dream, as though the spirit with the flesh
Shared that fine meat and plumed its wings anew,
Like some delighted bird at sudden streams
Weary with flight o'er endless wastes of sand,
Which laves the desert dust from neck and crest.
And more Sujāta worshipped, seeing our Lord
Grow fairer and his countenance more bright:
"Art thou indeed the God?" she lowly asked,
And hath my gift found favour?

But Buddh said,
"What is it thou dost bring me?"

"Holy one!"
Answered Sujāta, "from our droves I took
Milk of a hundred mothers, newly-calved,

And with that milk I fed fifty white cows,
And with their milk twenty-and-five, and then
With theirs twelve more, and yet again with theirs
The six noblest and best of all our herds.
That yield I boiled with sandal and fine spice
In silver lotas, adding rice, well grown
From chosen seed, set in new-broken ground,
So picked that every grain was like a pearl.
This did I of true heart, because I vowed
Under thy tree, if I should bear a boy
I would make offering for my joy, and now
I have my son and all my life is bliss!"

Softly our Lord drew down the crimson fold,
And, laying on the little head those hands
Which help the worlds, he said, "Long be thy bliss
And lightly fall on him the load of life!
For thou hast holpen me who am no God,
But one, thy Brother; heretofore a Prince
And now a wanderer, seeking night and day
These six hard years that light which somewhere shines
To lighten all men's darkness, if they knew!
And I shall find the light; yea, now it dawned
Glorious and helpful, when my weak flesh failed
Which this pure food, fair Sister, hath restored,
Drawn manifold through lives to quicken life
As life itself passes by many births
To happier heights and purging off of sins.
Yet dost thou truly find it sweet enough
Only to live? Can life and love suffice?"

Answered Sujāta, "Worshipful! my heart
Is little, and a little rain will fill
The lily's cup which hardly moists the field.
It is enough for me to feel life's sun
Shine in my Lord's grace and my baby's smile,
Making the loving summer of our home.
Pleasant my days pass filled with household cares
From sunrise when I wake to praise the gods,
And give forth grain, and trim the tulsi-plant,

And set my handmaids to their tasks, till noon,
When my Lord lays his head upon my lap
Lulled by soft songs and wavings of the fan;
And so to supper-time at quiet eve,
When by his side I stand and serve the cakes.
Then the stars light their silver lamps for sleep,
After the temple and the talk with friends.
How should I not be happy, blest so much,
And bearing him this boy whose tiny hand
Shall lead his soul to Swerga, if it need?
For holy books teach when a man shall plant
Trees for the travellers' shade, and dig a well
For the folks' comfort, and beget a son,
It shall be good for such after their death;
And what the books say that I humbly take,
Being not wiser than those great of old
Who spake with gods, and knew the hymns and charms,
And all the ways of virtue and of peace.
Also I think that good must come of good
And ill of evil—surely—unto all—
In every place and time—seeing sweet fruit
Groweth from wholesome roots, and bitter things
From poison-stocks; yea, seeing too, how spite
Breeds hate, and kindness friends, and patience peace
Even while we live; and when 'tis willed we die
Shall there not be as good a 'Then' as 'Now'?
Haply much better! since one grain of rice
Shoots a green feather gemmed with fifty pearls,
And all the starry champak's white and gold
Lurks in those little, naked, grey spring-buds.
Ah, Sir! I know there might be woes to bear
Would lay fond Patience with her face in dust;
If this my babe pass first I think my heart
Would break—almost I hope my heart would break!
That I might clasp him dead and wait my Lord—
In whatsoever world holds faithful wives—
Duteous, attending till his hour should come.
But if Death called Senāni, I should mount
The pile and lay that dear head in my lap,

My daily way, rejoicing when the torch
Lit the quick flame and rolled the choking smoke.
For it is written if an Indian wife
Die so, her love shall give her husband's soul
For every hair upon her head a crore
Of years in Swerga. Therefore fear I not.
And therefore, Holy Sir! my life is glad,
Nowise forgetting yet those other lives
Painful and poor, wicked and miserable,
Whereon the gods grant pity! but for me,
What good I see humbly I seek to do,
And live obedient to the law, in trust
That what will come, and must come, shall come well."

Then spake our Lord, "Thou teachest them who teach,
Wiser than wisdom in thy simple lore.
Be thou content to know not, knowing thus
Thy way of right and duty: grow, thou flower!
With thy sweet kind in peaceful shade—the light
Of Truth's high noon is not for tender leaves
Which must spread broad in other suns and lift
In later lives a crowned head to the sky.
Thou who hast worshipped me, I worship thee
Excellent heart! learnéd unknowingly.
As the dove is which flieth home by love.
In thee is seen why there is hope for man
And where we hold the wheel of life at will.
Peace go with thee, and comfort all thy days
As thou accomplishest, may I achieve!
He whom thou thoughtest God bids thee wish this."

"May'st thou achieve," she said, with earnest eyes
Bent on her babe, who reached its tender hands
To Buddh—knowing, belike, as children know,
More than we deem, and reverencing our Lord;
But he arose—made strong with that pure meat—
And bent his footsteps where a great Tree grew,
The Bodhi-tree (thenceforward in all years
Never to fade, and ever to be kept
In homage of the world), beneath whose leaves

It was ordained that Truth should come to Buddh:
Which now the Master knew; wherefore he went
With measured pace, steadfast, majestical,
Unto the Tree of Wisdom. Oh, ye Worlds!
Rejoice! our Lord wended unto the Tree!

Whom—as he passed into its ample shade,
Cloistered with columned dropping stems, and roofed
With vaults of glistening green—the conscious earth
Worshipped with waving grass and sudden flush
Of flowers about his feet. The forest-boughs
Bent down to shade him; from the river sighed
Cool wafts of wind laden with lotus-scents
Breathed by the water-gods. Large wondering eyes
Of woodland creatures—panther, boar, and deer—
At peace that eve, gazed on his face benign
From cave and thicket. From its cold cleft wound
The mottled deadly snake, dancing its hood
In honor of our Lord; bright butterflies
Fluttered their vans, azure and green and gold,
To be his fan-bearers; the fierce kite dropped
Its prey and screamed; the striped palm-squirrel raced
From stem to stem to see; the weaver-bird
Chirped from her swinging nest; the lizard ran;
The koïl sang her hymn; the doves flocked round;
Even the creeping things were 'ware and glad.
Voices of earth and air joined in one song,
Which unto ears that hear said, "Lord and Friend
Lover and Saviour! Thou who hast subdued
Angers and prides, desires and fears and doubts,
Thou that for each and all hast given thyself,
Pass to the Tree! The sad world blesseth thee
Who art the Buddh that shall assuage her woes.
Pass, Hailed and Honored! strive thy last for us,
King and high Conqueror! thine hour is come;
This is the Night the ages waited for!"

Then fell the night even as our Master sate
Under that Tree. But he who is the Prince
Of Darkness, Māra—knowing this was Buddh

Who should deliver men, and now the hour
When he should find the Truth and save the worlds—
Gave unto all his evil powers command.
Wherefore there trooped from every deepest pit
The fiends who war with Wisdom and the Light,
Arati, Trishna, Raga, and their crew
Of passions, horrors, ignorances, lusts,
The brood of gloom and dread; all hating Buddh,
Seeking to shake his mind; nor knoweth one,
Not even the wisest, how those fiends of Hell
Battled that night to keep the Truth from Buddh:
Sometimes with terrors of the tempest, blasts
Of demon-armies clouding all the wind,
With thunder, and with blinding lightning flung
In jagged javelins of purple wrath
From splitting skies; sometimes with wiles and words
Fair-sounding, 'mid hushed leaves and softened airs
From shapes of witching beauty; wanton songs,
Whispers of love; sometimes with royal allures
Of proffered rule; sometimes with mocking doubts.
Making truth vain. But whether these befell
Without and visible, or whether Buddh
Strove with fell spirits in his inmost heart,
Judge ye:—I write what ancient books have writ.

The ten chief Sins came—Māra's mighty ones,
Angels of evil—Attavāda first,
The Sin of Self, who in the Universe
As in a mirror sees her fond face shown,
And crying "I" would have the world say "I,"
And all things perish so if she endure.
"If thou be'st Buddh," she said, "let others grope
Lightless; it is enough that thou art Thou
Changelessly; rise and take the bliss of gods
Who change not, heed not, strive not." But Buddh spake
"The right in thee is base, the wrong a curse;
Cheat such as love themselves." Then came wan Doubt
He that denies—the mocking Sin—and this
Hissed in the Master's ear, "All things are shows,

And vain the knowledge of their vanity;
Thou dost but chase the shadow of thyself;
Rise and go hence, there is no better way
Than patient scorn, nor any help for man,
Nor any staying of his whirling wheel."
But quoth our Lord, "Thou hast no part with me,
False Visikitcha, subtlest of man's foes."
And third came she who gives dark creeds their power,
Sīlabbat-paramāsa, sorceress,
Draped fair in many lands as lowly Faith,
But ever juggling souls with rites and prayers;
The keeper of those keys which lock up Hells
And open Heavens. "Wilt thou dare," she said,
"Put by our sacred books, dethrone our gods,
Unpeople all the temples, shaking down
That law which feeds the priests and props the realms?"
But Buddha answered, "What thou bidd'st me keep
Is form which passes, but the free Truth stands;
Get thee unto thy darkness." Next there drew
Gallantly nigh a braver Tempter, he,
Kama, the King of passions, who hath sway
Over the gods themselves, Lord of all loves,
Ruler of Pleasure's realm. Laughing he came
Unto the Tree, bearing his bow of gold
Wreathed with red blooms, and arrows of desire
Pointed with five-tongued delicate flame which stings
The heart it smites sharper than poisoned barb:
And round him came into that lonely place
Bands of bright shapes with heavenly eyes and lips
Singing in lovely words the praise of Love
To music of invisible sweet chords,
So witching, that it seemed the night stood still
To hear them, and the listening stars and moon
Paused in their orbits while these hymned to Buddh
Of lost delights, and how a mortal man
Findeth nought dearer in the three wide worlds
Than are the yielded loving fragrant breasts
Of Beauty and the rosy breast-blossoms,
Love's rubies; nay, and toucheth nought more high

Than is that dulcet harmony of form
Seen in the fines and charms of loveliness
Unspeakable, yet speaking, soul to soul,
Owned by the bounding blood, worshipped by will
Which leaps to seize it, knowing this is best,
This the true heaven where mortals are like gods,
Makers and Masters, this the gift of gifts
Ever renewed and worth a thousand woes.
For who hath grieved when soft arms shut him safe,
And all life melted to a happy sigh,
And all the world was given in one warm kiss?
So sang they with soft float of beckoning hands,
Eyes lighted with love-flames, alluring smiles;
In dainty dance their supple sides and limbs
Revealing and concealing like burst buds
Which tell their color, but hide yet their hearts.
Never so matchless grace delighted eye
As troop by troop these midnight-dancers swept
Nearer the Tree, each daintier than the last,
Murmuring "O great Siddārtha! I am thine,
Taste of my mouth and see if youth is sweet!"
Also, when nothing moved our Master's mind,
Lo! Kama waved his magic bow, and lo!
The band of dancers opened, and a shape
Fairest and stateliest of the throng came forth
Wearing the guise of sweet Yasodhara.
Tender the passion of those dark eyes seemed
Brimming with tears; yearning those outspread arms
Opened towards him; musical that moan
Wherewith the beauteous shadow named his name,
Sighing "My Prince! I die for lack of thee
What heaven hast thou found like that we knew
By bright Rohini in the Pleasure-house,
Where all these weary years I weep for thee?
Return, Siddārtha! ah! return. But touch
My lips again, but let me to thy breast
Once, and these fruitless dreams will end! Ah, look!
Am I not she thou lovedst?" But Buddh said,
"For that sweet sake of her thou playest thus

Fair and false Shadow! is thy playing vain;
I curse thee not who wear'st a form so dear,
Yet as thou art so are all earthly shows.
Melt to thy void again!" Thereat a cry
Thrilled through the grove, and all that comely rout
Faded with flickering wafts of flame, and trail
Of vaporous robes.

Next under darkening skies
And noise of rising storm came fiercer Sins,
The rearmost of the Ten; Patigha—Hate—
With serpents coiled about her waist, which suck
Poisonous milk from both her hanging dugs,
And with her curses mix their angry hiss.
Little wrought she upon that Holy One
Who with his calm eyes dumbed her bitter lips
And made her black snakes writhe to hide their fangs.
Then followed Ruparaga—Lust of days—
That sensual Sin which out of greed for life
Forgets to live; and next him Lust of Fame,
Nobler Aruparaga, she whose spell
Beguiles the wise, mother of daring deeds,
Battles and toils. And haughty Mano came,
The Fiend of Pride; and smooth Self-Righteousness,
Uddhachcha; and—with many a hideous band
Of vile and formless things, which crept and flapped
Toad-like and bat-like—Ignorance, the Dam
Of Fear and Wrong, Avidya, hideous hag,
Whose footsteps left the midnight darker, while
The rooted mountains shook, the wild winds howled,
The broken clouds shed from their caverns streams
Of levin-lighted rain; stars shot from heaven,
The solid earth shuddered as if one laid
Flame to her gaping wounds; the torn black air
Was full of whistling wings, of screams and yells,
Of evil faces peering, of vast fronts
Terrible and majestic, Lords of Hell
Who from a thousand Limbos led their troops
To tempt the Master.

But Buddh heeded not,
Sitting serene, with perfect virtue walled
As is a stronghold by its gates and ramps;
Also the Sacred Tree—the Bodhi-tree—
Amid that tumult stirred not, but each leaf
Glistened as still as when on moonlit eves
No zephyr spills the glittering gems of dew;
For all this clamor raged outside the shade
Spread by those cloistered stems:

In the third watch,
The earth being still, the hellish legions fled,
A soft air breathing from the sinking moon,
Our Lord attained Sammā-sambuddh; he saw
By light which shines beyond our mortal ken
The line of all his lives in all the worlds,
Far back and farther back and farthest yet,
Five hundred lives and fifty. Even as one,
At rest upon a mountain-summit, marks
His path wind up by precipice and crag,
Past thick-set woods shrunk to a patch; through bogs,
Glittering false-green; down hollows where he toiled
Breathless; on dizzy ridges where his feet
Had well-nigh slipped; beyond the sunny lawns,
The cataract and the cavern and the pool,
Backward to those dim flats wherefrom he sprang
To reach the blue; thus Buddha did behold
Life's upward steps long-linked, from levels low
Where breath is base, to higher slopes and higher
Whereon the ten great Virtues wait to lead
The climber skyward. Also, Buddha saw
How new life reaps what the old life did sow:
How where its march breaks off its march begins;
Holding the gain and answering for the loss;
And how in each life good begets more good,
Evil fresh evil; Death but casting up
Debit or credit, whereupon th' account
In merits or demerits stamps itself
By sure arithmic—where no tittle drops—

Certain and just, on some new-springing life
Wherein are packed and scored past thoughts and deeds,
Strivings and triumphs, memories and marks
Of lives foregone:

And in the middle watch
Our Lord attained *Abhidjna*—insight vast
Ranging beyond this sphere to spheres unnamed,
System on system, countless worlds and suns
Moving in splendid measures, band by band
Linked in division, one yet separate,
The silver islands of a sapphire sea
Shoreless unfathomed, undiminished, stirred
With waves which roll in restless tides of change.
He saw those Lords of Light who hold their worlds
By bonds invisible, how they themselves
Circle obedient round mightier orbs
Which serve profounder splendors, star to star
Flashing the ceaseless radiance of life
From centres ever shifting unto cirques
Knowing no uttermost. These he beheld
With unsealed vision, and of all those worlds,
Cycle on epicycle, all their tale
Of Kalpas, Mahakalpas—terms of time
Which no man grasps, yea, though he knew to count
The drops in Gunga from her springs to the sea,
Measureless unto speech—whereby these wax
And wane; whereby each of this heavenly host
Fulfils its shining life and darkling dies.
Sakwal by Sakwal, depths and heights he passed
Transported through the blue infinitudes,
Marking—behind all modes, above all spheres,
Beyond the burning impulse of each orb—
That fixed decree at silent work which wills
Evolve the dark to light, the dead to life,
To fulness void, to form the yet unformed,
Good unto better, better unto best,
By wordless edict; having none to bid,
None to forbid; for this is past all gods

Immutable, unspeakable, supreme,
A Power which builds, unbuilds, and builds again,
Ruling all things accordant to the rule
Of virtue, which is beauty, truth, and use.
So that all things do well which serve the Power,
And ill which hinder; nay, the worm does well
Obedient to its kind; the hawk does well
Which carries bleeding quarries to its young;
The dewdrop and the star shine sisterly,
Globing together in the common work;
And man who lives to die, dies to live well
So if he guide his ways by blamelessness
And earnest will to hinder not but help
All things both great and small which suffer life.
These did our Lord see in the middle watch.

But when the fourth watch came the secret came
Of Sorrow, which with evil mars the law,
As damp and dross hold back the goldsmith's fire.
Then was the Dukha-satya opened him
First of the "Noble Truths;" how Sorrow is
Shadow to life, moving where life doth move;
Not to be laid aside until one lays
Living aside, with all its changing states,
Birth, growth, decay, love, hatred, pleasure, pain
Being and doing. How that none strips off
These sad delights and pleasant griefs who lacks
Knowledge to know them snares; but he who knows
Avidya—Delusion—sets those snares,
Loves life no longer but ensues escape.
The eyes of such a one are wide, he sees
Delusion breeds Sankhāra, Tendency
Perverse: Tendency Energy—Vidnnān—
Whereby comes Namarûpa, local form
And name and bodiment, bringing the man
With senses naked to the sensible,
A helpless mirror of all shows which pass
Across his heart; and so Vedanā grows—
'Sense-life'—false in its gladness, fell in sadness,

But sad or glad, the Mother of Desire,
Trishna, that thirst which makes the living drink
Deeper and deeper of the false salt waves
Whereon they float, pleasures, ambitions, wealth,
Praise, fame, or domination, conquest, love;
Rich meats and robes, and fair abodes, and pride
Of ancient lines, and lust of days, and strife
To live, and sins that flow from strife, some sweet,
Some bitter. Thus Life's thirst quenches itself
With draughts which double thirst, but who is wise
Tears from his soul this Trishna, feeds his sense
No longer on false shows, files his firm mind
To seek not, strive not, wrong not; bearing meek
All ills which flow from foregone wrongfulness,
And so constraining passions that they die
Famished; till all the sum of ended life—
The Karma—all that total of a soul
Which is the things it did, the thoughts it had,
The 'Self' it wove—with woof of viewless time,
Crossed on the warp invisible of acts—
The outcome of him on the Universe,
Grows pure and sinless; either never more
Needing to find a body and a place,
Or so informing what fresh frame it takes
In new existence that the new toils prove
Lighter and lighter not to be at all,
Thus "finishing the Path"; free from Earth's cheats;
Broken from ties—from Upādānas—saved
From whirling on the wheel; aroused and sane
As is a man wakened from hateful dreams.
Until—greater than Kings, than Gods more glad!—
The aching craze to live ends, and life glides—
Lifeless—to nameless quiet, nameless joy,
Blessed Nirvāna—sinless, stirless rest—
That change which never changes!

Lo! the Dawn
Sprang with Buddh's Victory! lo! in the East
Flamed the first fires of beauteous day, poured forth

Through fleeting folds of Night's black drapery.
High in the widening blue the herald-star
Faded to paler silver as there shot
Brighter and brightest bars of rosy gleam
Across the grey. Far off the shadowy hills
Saw the great Sun, before the world was 'ware,
And donned their crowns of crimson; flower by flower
Felt the warm breath of Mom and 'gan unfold
Their tender lids. Over the spangled grass
Swept the swift footsteps of the lovely Light,
Turning the tears of Night to joyous gems,
Decking the earth with radiance 'broidering.
The sinking storm-clouds with a golden fringe,
Gilding the feathers of the palms, which waved
Glad salutation; darting beams of gold
Into the glades; touching with magic wand
The stream to rippled ruby; in the brake
Finding the mild eyes of the antelopes
And saying "it is day"; in nested sleep
Touching the small heads under many a wing
And whispering, "Children, praise the light of day!"
Whereat there piped anthems of all the birds,
The Köil's fluted song, the Bulbul's hymn,
The "morning, morning" of the painted thrush,
The twitter of the sunbirds starting forth
To find the honey ere the bees be out
The grey crow's caw, the parrot's scream, the strokes
Of the green hammersmith, the myna's chirp,
The never finished love-talk of the doves:
Yea! and so holy was the influence
Of that high Dawn which came with victory
That, far and near, in homes of men there spread
An unknown peace. The slayer hid his knife;
The robber laid his plunder back; the shroff
Counted full tale of coins; all evil hearts
Grew gentle, kind hearts gentler, as the balm
Of that divinest Daybreak lightened Earth.
Kings at fierce war called truce; the sick men leaped
Laughing from beds of pain; the dying smiled

As though they knew that happy Morn was sprung
From fountains farther than the utmost East;
And o'er the heart of sad Yasodhara,
Sitting forlorn at Prince Siddārtha's bed,
Came sudden bliss, as if love should not fail
Nor such vast sorrow miss to end in joy.
So glad the World was—though it wist not why
That over desolate wastes went swooning songs
Of mirth, the voice of bodiless Prets and Bhuts
Foreseeing Buddh; and Devas in the air
Cried "It is finished, finished!" and the priests
Stood with the wondering people in the streets
Watching those golden splendors flood the sky
And saying "There hath happed some mighty thing."
Also in Ran and Jungle grew that day
Friendship amongst the creatures; spotted deer
Browsed fearless where the tigress fed her cubs,
And cheetahs lapped the pool beside the bucks;
Under the eagle's rock the brown hares scoured
While his fierce beak but preened an idle wing;
The snake sunned all his jewels in the beam
With deadly fangs in sheath; the shrike let pass
The nestling-finch; the emerald halcyons
Sate dreaming while the fishes played beneath,
Nor hawked the merops, though the butterflies—
Crimson and blue and amber—flitted thick
Around his perch; the Spirit of our Lord
Lay potent upon man and bird and beast,
Even while he mused under that Bodhi-tree,
Glorified with the Conquest gained for all
And lightened by a Light greater than Day's.

Then he arose—radiant, rejoicing, strong—
Beneath the Tree, and lifting high his voice
Spake this, in hearing of all Times and Worlds:—

Anékajātisangsārang
Sandhdwissang anibhisang
Gahakārakangawesanto
Dukkhājātipunappunang.

Gahakārakadithosi;
Punagehang nakāhasi;
Sabhātephāsukhābhaggā,
Gahakūtangwisang khitang;
Wisangkhāragatang chittang;
Janhānangkhayamajhagā.

Many a house of life
Hath held me—seeking ever him who wrought
These prisons of the senses, sorrow-fraught;
Sore was my ceaseless strife!

But now,
Thou builder of this tabernacle—thou!
I know thee! Never shalt thou build again
These walls of pain,
Nor raise the roof-tree of deceits, nor lay
Fresh rafters on the clay;
Broken thy house is, and the ridge-pole split!
Delusion fashioned it!
Safe pass i thence—deliverance to obtain.

Book the Seventh

Sorrowful dwelt the King Suddhodana
All those long years among the Sākya Lords
Lacking the speech and presence of his Son;
Sorrowful sate the sweet Yasodhara
All those long years, knowing no joy of life,
Widowed of him her living Liege and Prince
And ever, on the news of some recluse
Seen far away by pasturing camel-men
Or traders threading devious paths for gain,
Messengers from the King had gone and come
Bringing account of many a holy sage
Lonely and lost to home; but nought of him
The crown of white Kapilavastu's line,
The glory of her monarch and his hope,
The heart's content of sweet Yasodhara,
Far-wandered now, forgetful, changed, or dead.

But on a day in the Wasanta-time,
When silver sprays swing on the mango-trees
And all the earth is clad with garb of spring,
The Princess sate by that bright garden-stream
Whose gliding glass, bordered with lotus-cups,
Mirrored so often in the bliss gone by
Their clinging hands and meeting lips. Her lids
Were wan with tears, her tender cheeks had thinned
Her lips' delicious curves were drawn with grief;
The lustrous glory of her hair was hid—
Close-bound as widows use; no ornament
She wore, nor any jewel clasped the cloth—
Coarse, and of mourning-white—crossed on her breast.
Slow moved and painfully those small fine feet
Which had the roe's gait and the rose-leaf's fall
In old years at the loving voice of him.
Her eyes, those lamps of love, which were as if
Sunlight should shine from out the deepest dark,
Illumining Night's peace with Daytime's glow

Unlighted now, and roving aimlessly,
Scarce marked the clustering signs of coming Spring
So the silk lashes drooped over their orbs.
In one hand was a girdle thick with pearls,
Siddārtha's—treasured since that night he fled—
(Ah, bitter Night! mother of weeping days
When was fond Love so pitiless to love
Save that this scorned to limit love by life?)
The other led her little son, a boy
Divinely fair, the pledge Siddārtha left—
Named Rahula—now seven years old, who tripped
Gladsome beside his mother, light of heart
To see the spring-blooms burgeon o'er the world.

So while they lingered by the lotus-pools
And, lightly laughing, Rahula flung rice
To feed the blue and purple fish; and she
With sad eyes watched the swiftly-flying cranes,
Sighing, "Oh! creatures of the wandering wing,
If I ye shall light where my dear Lord is hid,
Say that Yasodhara lives nigh to death
For one word of his mouth, one touch of him!"
So, as they played and sighed—mother and child—
Came some among the damsels of the Court
Saying, "Great Princess! there have entered in
At the south gate merchants of Hastinpûr
Tripusha called and Bhalluk, men of worth,
Long travelled from the loud sea's edge, who bring
Marvellous lovely webs pictured with gold,
Waved blades of gilded steel, wrought bowls in brass,
Cut ivories, spice, simples, and unknown birds,
Treasures of far-off peoples; but they bring
That which doth beggar these, for He is seen
Thy Lord—our Lord—the hope of all the land
Siddārtha! they have seen him face to face,
Yea, and have worshipped him with knees and brows,
And offered offerings; for he is become
All which was shown, a teacher of the wise,
World-honored, holy, wonderful; a Buddh

Who doth deliver men and save all flesh
By sweetest speech and pity vast as Heaven:
And, lo! he journeyeth hither these do say."

Then—while the glad blood bounded in her veins
As Gunga leaps when first the mountain snows
Melt at her springs—uprose Yasodhara
And clapped her palms, and laughed, with brimming tears
Beading her lashes. "Oh! call quick," she cried,
"These merchants to my purdah, for mine ears
Thirst like parched throats to drink their blessed news.
Go bring them in—but if their tale be true,
Say I will fill their girdles with much gold,
With gems that Kings shall envy: come ye too,
My girls, for ye shall have guerdon of this
If there be gifts to speak my grateful heart."

So went those merchants to the Pleasure-House,
Full softly pacing through its golden ways
With naked feet, amid the peering maids,
Much wondering at the glories of the Court.
Whom, when they came without the purdah's folds,
A voice, tender and eager, filled and charmed
With trembling music, saying, "Ye are come
From far, fair Sirs! and ye have seen my Lord
Yea, worshipped—for he is become a Buddh,
World-honored, holy, and delivers men,
And journeyeth hither. Speak! for, if this be,
Friends are ye of my House, welcome and dear."

Then answer made Tripusha, "We have seen
That sacred Master, Princess! we have bowed
Before his feet; for who was lost a Prince
Is found a greater than the King of kings.
Under the Bodhi-tree by Phalgū's bank
That which shall save the world hath late been wrought
By him—the Friend of all, the Prince of all—
Thine most, High Lady! from whose tears men win
The comfort of this Word the Master speaks.
Lo! he is well, as one beyond all ills,

Uplifted as a god from earthly woes,
Shining with risen Truth, golden and clear.
Moreover as he entereth town by town,
Preaching those noble ways which lead to peace,
The hearts of men follow his path as leaves
Troop to wind or sheep draw after one
Who knows the pastures. We ourselves have heard
By Gaya in the green Tchīrnika grove
Those wondrous lips and done them reverence:
He cometh hither ere the first rains fall."

Thus spake he, and Yasodhara, for joy,
Scarce mastered breath to answer, "Be it well
Now and at all times with ye, worthy friends!
Who bring good tidings; but of this great thing
Wist ye how it befell?"

Then Bhalluk told
Such as the people of the valleys knew
Of that dread night of conflict, when the air
Darkened with fiendish shadows, and the earth
Quaked, and the waters swelled with Māra's wrath.
Also how gloriously that morning broke
Radiant with rising hopes for man, and how
The Lord was found rejoicing 'neath his Tree.
But many days the burden of release—
To be escaped beyond all storms of doubt,
Safe on Truth's shore—lay, spake he, on that heart
A golden load; for how shall men—Buddh mused—
Who love their sins and cleave to cheats of sense,
And drink of error from a thousand springs—
Having no mind to see, nor strength to break
The fleshly snare which binds them—how should such
Receive the Twelve Nidānas and the Law
Redeeming all, yet strange to profit by,
As the caged bird oft shuns its opened door?
So had we missed the helpful victory
If, in this earth without a refuge, Buddh
Winning the way, had deemed it all too hard
For mortal feet, and passed, none following him.

Yet pondered the compassion of our Lord,
But in that hour there rang a voice as sharp
As cry of travail, so as if the earth
Moaned in birth-throe "*Nasyami aham bhû*
Nasyati lṇka!" SURELY I AM LOST,
I AND MY CREATURES: then a pause, and next
A pleading sigh borne on the western wind,
"*Sruyatām dharma, Bhagwat*!" OH, SUPREME!
LET THY GREAT LAW BE UTTERED! Whereupon
The Master cast his vision forth on flesh,
Saw who should hear and who must wait to hear,
As the keen Sun gilding the lotus-lakes
Seeth which buds will open to his beams
And which are not yet risen from their roots
Then spake, divinely smiling, "Yea! I preach!
Whoso will listen let him learn the Law."

Afterwards passed he, said they, by the hills
Unto Benares, where he taught the Five,
Showing how birth and death should be destroyed,
And how man hath no fate except past deeds,
No Hell but what he makes, no Heaven too high
For those to reach whose passions sleep subdued.
This was the fifteenth day of Vaishya
Mid-afternoon and that night was full moon.

But, of the Rishis, first Kaundinya
Owned the Four Truths and entered on the Paths;
And after him Bhadraka, Asvajit,
Basava, Mahanāma; also there
Within the Deer-park, at the feet of Buddh,
Yasad the Prince with nobles fifty-four
Hearing the blessed word our Master spake
Worshipped and followed; for there sprang up peace
And knowledge of a new time come for men
In all who heard, as spring the flowers and grass
When water sparkles through a sandy plain.

These sixty—said they—did our Lord send forth,
Made perfect in restraint and passion-free,

To teach the Way; but the World-honored turned
South from the Deer-park and Isipatan
To Yashti and King Bimbasāra's realm,
Where many days he taught; and after these
King Bimbasāra and his folk believed,
Learning the law of love and ordered life.
Also he gave the Master, of free gift,
Pouring forth water on the hands of Buddh
The Bamboo-Garden, named Wéluvana,
Wherein are streams and caves and lovely glades;
And the King set a stone there, carved with this:

Yé dharma hetuppabhawā
Yesan hétun Tathāgato;
Aha yesan cha yo nirodho
Ewan wadi Maha samano.

"What life's course and cause sustain
These Tathāgato made plain;
What delivers from life's woe
That our Lord hath made us know."

And, in that Garden—said they—there was held
A high Assembly, where the Teacher spake
Wisdom and power, winning all souls which heard,
So that nine hundred took the yellow robe—
Such as the Master wears—and spread his Law
And this the gāthā was wherewith he closed:

Sabba pāpassa akaranan;
Kusalassa upasampadā;
Sa chitta pariyodapanan
Etan Budhānusāsanan.

"Evil swells the debts to pay,
Good delivers and acquits;
Shun evil, follow good; hold sway
Over thyself. This is the Way."

Whom, when they ended, speaking so of him,
With gifts, and thanks which made the jewels dull,
The Princess recompensed. "But by what road

Wendeth my Lord?" she asked: the merchants said,
"Yojans threescore stretch from the city-walls
To Rājagriha , whence the easy path
Passeth by Sona hither and the hills.
Our oxen, treading eight slow koss a day,
Came in one moon."

Then the King hearing word,
Sent nobles of the Court—well-mounted lords—
Nine separate messengers, each embassy
Bidden to say, "The King Suddhodana—
Nearer the pyre by seven long years of lack,
Wherethrough he hath not ceased to seek for thee
Prays of his son to come unto his own,
The Throne and people of this longing Realm,
Lest he shall die and see thy face no more."
Also nine horsemen sent Yasodhara
Bidden to say, "The Princess of thy House—
Rahula's mother—craves to see thy face
As the night-blowing moon-flower's swelling heart
Pines for the moon, as pale asoka-buds
Wait for a woman's foot: if thou hast found
More than was lost, she prays her part in this,
Rahula's part, but most of all thyself."
So sped the Sākya Lords, but it befell
That each one, with the message in his mouth,
Entered the Bamboo-Garden in that hour
When Buddha taught his Law; and—hearing—each
Forgot to speak, lost thought of King and quest,
Of the sad Princess even; only gazed
Eye-rapt upon the Master; only hung
Heart-caught upon the speech, compassionate,
Commanding, perfect, pure, enlightening all,
Poured from those sacred lips. Look! like a bee
Winged for the hive, who sees the mogras spread
And scents their utter sweetness on the air,
If he be honey-filled, it matters not;
If night be nigh, or rain, he will not heed;
Needs must he light on those delicious blooms

And drain their nectar; so these messengers
One with another, hearing Buddha's words,
Let go the purpose of their speed, and mixed,
Heedless of all, amid the Master's train.
Wherefore the King bade that Udayi go—
Chiefest in all the Court, and faithfullest,
Siddārtha's playmate in the happier days—
Who, as he drew anear the garden, plucked
Blown tufts of tree-wool from the grove and sealed
The entrance of his hearing; thus he came
Safe through the lofty peril of the place
And told the message of the King, and her's.

Then meekly bowed his head and spake our Lord
Before the people, "Surely I shall go!
It is my duty as it was my will;
Let no man miss to render reverence
To those who lend him life, whereby come means
To live and die no more, but safe attain
Blissful Nirvāna, if ye keep the Law,
Purging past wrongs and adding nought thereto,
Complete in love and lovely charities.
Let the King know and let the Princess hear
I take the way forthwith." This told, the folk
Of white Kapilavastu and its fields
Made ready for the entrance of their Prince.
At the south gate a bright pavilion rose
With flower-wreathed pillars and the walls of silk
Wrought on their red and green with woven gold.
Also the roads were laid with scented boughs
Of neem and mango, and full mussuks shed
Sandal and jasmine on the dust, and flags
Fluttered; and on the day when he should come
It was ordained how many elephants—
With silver howdahs and their tusks gold-tipped
Should wait beyond the ford, and where the drums
Should boom "Siddārtha cometh" where the lords
Should light and worship, and the dancing-girls
Where they should strew their flowers with dance and son,

So that the steed he rode might tramp knee-deep
In rose and balsam, and the ways be fair;
While the town rang with music and high joy.
This was ordained, and all men's ears were pricked
Dawn after dawn to catch the first drum's beat
Announcing, "Now he cometh!"

But it fell—
Eager to be before—Yasodhara
Rode in her litter to the city-walls
Where soared the bright pavilion. All around
A beauteous garden smiled—Nigrodha named
Shaded with bel-trees and the green-plumed dates,
New-trimmed and gay with winding walks and banks
Of fruits and flowers; for the southern road
Skirted its lawns, on this hand leaf and bloom,
On that the suburb-huts where base-borns dwelt
Outside the gates, a patient folk and poor,
Whose touch for Kshatriya and priest of Brahm
Were sore defilement. Yet those, too, were quick
With expectation, rising ere the dawn
To peer along the road, to climb the trees
At far-off trumpet of some elephant,
Or stir of temple-drum; and when none came,
Busied with lowly chares to please the Prince;
Sweeping their door-stones, setting forth their flags,
Stringing the fluted fig-leaves into chains,
New furbishing the Lingam, decking new
Yesterday's faded arch of boughs, but aye
Questioning wayfarers if any noise
Be on the road of great Siddārtha. These
The Princess marked with lovely languid eyes,
Watching, as they, the southward plain, and bent
Like them to listen if the passers gave
News of the path. So fell it she beheld
One slow approaching with his head close shorn,
A yellow cloth over his shoulder cast,
Girt as the hermits are, and in his hand
An earthen bowl, shaped melonwise, the which

Meekly at each hut-door he held a space,
Taking the granted dole with gentle thanks
And all as gently passing where none gave.
Two followed him wearing the yellow robe,
But he who bore the bowl so lordly seemed,
So reverend, and with such a passage moved,
With so commanding presence filled the air,
With such sweet eyes of holiness smote all,
That, as they reached him alms the givers gazed
Awestruck upon his face, and some bent down
In worship, and some ran to fetch fresh gifts
Grieved to be poor; till slowly, group by group,
Children and men and women drew behind
Into his steps, whispering with covered lips,
"Who is he? who? when looked a Rishi thus?"
But as he came with quiet footfall on
Nigh the pavilion, lo! the silken door
Lifted, and, all unveiled, Yasodhara
Stood in his path crying, "Siddārtha! Lord!"
With wide eyes streaming and with close-clasped hands,
Then sobbing fell upon his feet, and lay.

Afterwards, when this weeping lady passed
Into the Noble Paths, and one had prayed
Answer from Buddha wherefore—being vowed
Quit of all mortal passion and the touch,
Flower-soft and conquering, of a woman's hands—
He suffered such embrace, the Master said:
"The greater beareth with the lesser love
So it may raise it unto easier heights.
Take heed that no man, being 'scaped from bonds,
Vexeth bound souls with boasts of liberty.
Free are ye rather that your freedom spread
By patient winning and sweet wisdom's skill.
Three eras of long toil bring Bodhisats
Who will be guides and help this darkling world
Unto deliverance, and the first is named
Of deep 'Resolve,' the second of 'Attempt,'
The third of 'Nomination.' Lo! I lived

In era of Resolve, desiring good,
Searching for wisdom, but mine eyes were sealed.
Count the grey seeds on yonder castor-clump,
So many rains it is since I was Ram,
A merchant of the coast which looketh south
To Lanka and the hiding-place of pearls.
Also in that far time Yasodhara
Dwelt with me in our village by the sea,
Tender as now, and Lakshmi was her name.
And I remember how I journeyed thence
Seeking our gain, for poor the household was
And lowly. Not the less with wistful tears
She prayed me that I should not part, nor tempt
Perils by land and water. 'How could love
Leave what it loved?' she wailed; yet, venturing, I
Passed to the Straits, and after storm and toil
And deadly strife with creatures of the deep,
And woes beneath the midnight and the noon,
Searching the wave I won therefrom a pearl
Moonlike and glorious, such as Kings might buy
Emptying their treasury. Then came I glad
Unto mine hills, but over all that land
Famine spread sore; ill was I stead to live
In journey home, and hardly reached my door
Aching for food—with that white wealth of the sea
Tied in my girdle. Yet no food was there;
And on the threshold she for whom I toiled—
More than myself—lay with her speechless lips
Nigh unto death for one small gift of grain
Then cried I, 'If there be who hath of grain,
Here is a kingdom's ransom for one life:
Give Lakshmi bread and take my moonlight pearl.'
Whereat one brought the last of all his hoard,
Millet—three seers—and clutched the beauteous thing.
But Lakshmi lived and sighed with gathered life,
'Lo! thou didst love indeed!' I spent my pearl
Well in that life to comfort heart and mind
Else quite uncomforted, but these pure pearls,
My last large gain, won from a deeper wave—

The Twelve Nidānas and the Law of Good—
Cannot be spent, nor dimmed, and most fulfil
Their perfect beauty being freeliest given.
For like as is to Meru yonder hill
Heaped by the little ants, and like as dew
Dropped in the footmark of a bounding roe
Unto the shoreless seas, so was that gift
Unto my present giving; and so love—
Vaster in being free from toils of sense—
Was wisest stooping to the weaker heart;
And so the feet of sweet Yasodhara
Passed into peace and bliss, being softly led."

But when the King heard how Siddhārtha came
Shorn, with the mendicant's sad-colored cloth,
And stretching out a bowl to gather orts
From base-borns' leavings, wrathful sorrow drove
Love from his heart. Thrice on the ground he spat,
Plucked at his silvered beard, and strode straight forth
Lackeyed by trembling lords. Frowning he clomb
Upon his war-horse, drove the spurs, and dashed,
Angered, through wondering streets and lanes of folk,
Scarce finding breath to say, "The King! bow down!"
Ere the loud cavalcade had clattered by:
Which—at the turning by the Temple-wall
Where the south gate was seen—encountered full
A mighty crowd; to every edge of it
Poured fast more people, till the roads were lost,
Blotted by that huge company which thronged
And grew, close following him whose look serene
Met the old King's. Nor lived the father's wrath
Longer than while the gentle eyes of Buddh
Lingered in worship on his troubled brows,
Then downcast sank, with his true knee, to earth
In proud humility. So dear it seemed
To see the Prince, to know him whole, to mark
That glory greater than of earthly state
Crowning his head, that majesty which brought
All men, so awed and silent, in his steps.

Nathless the King broke forth, "Ends it in this
That great Siddārtha steals into his realm,
Wrapped in a clout, shorn, sandalled, craving food
Of low-borns, he whose life was as a God's?
My son! heir of this spacious power, and heir
Of Kings who did but clap their palms to have
What earth could give or eager service bring?
Thou should'st have come apparelled in thy rank,
With shining spears and tramp of horse and foot.
Lo! all my soldiers camped upon the road,
And all my city waited at the gates;
Where hast thou sojourned through these evil years
Whilst thy crowned fattier mourned? and she, too, there
Lived as the widows use, foregoing joys;
Never once hearing sound of song or string.
Nor wearing once the festal robe, till now
When in her cloth of gold she welcomes home,
A beggar spouse in yellow remnants clad.
Son! why is this?"

"My Father!" came reply,
"It is the custom of my race."

"Thy race,"
Answered the King "counteth a hundred thrones
From Maha Sammāt, but no deed like this."

"Not of a mortal line," the Master said,
"I spake, but of descent invisible,
The Buddhas who have been and who shall be:
Of these am I, and what they did I do,
And this which now befalls so fell before
That at his gate a King in warrior-mail
Should meet his son, a Prince in hermit-weeds
And that, by love and self-control, being more
Than mightiest Kings in all their puissance,
The appointed Helper of the Worlds should bow—
As now do I—and with all lowly love
Proffer, where it is owed for tender debts,
The first-fruits of the treasure he hath brought
Which now I proffer."

Then the King amazed
Inquired "What treasure?" and the Teacher took
Meekly the royal palm, and while they paced
Through worshipping streets—the Princess and the King
On either side—he told the things which make
For peace and pureness, those Four noble Truths
Which hold all wisdom as shores shut the seas,
Those eight right Rules whereby who will may walk—
Monarch or slave—upon the perfect Path
That hath its Stages Four and Precepts Eight,
Whereby whoso will live—mighty or mean
Wise or unlearned, man, woman, young or old
Shall soon or late break from the wheels of life
Attaining blest Nirvāna. So they came
Into the Palace-porch, Suddhodana
With brows unknit drinking the mighty words,
And in his own hand carrying Buddha's bowl,
Whilst a new light brightened the lovely eyes
Of sweet Yasodhara and sunned her tears;
And that night entered they the Way of Peace.

Book the Eighth

A broad mead spreads by swift Kohāna's bank
At Nagara; five days shall bring a man
In ox-wain thither from Benares' shrines
Eastward and northward journeying. The horns
Of white Himāla look upon the place,
Which all the year is glad with blooms and girt
By groves made green from that bright streamlet's wave.
Soft are its slopes and cool its fragrant shades,
And holy all the spirit of the spot
Unto this time: the breath of eve comes hushed
Over the tangled thickets, and high heaps
Of carved red stones cloven by root and stem
Of creeping fig, and clad with waving veil
Of leaf and grass. The still snake glistens forth
From crumbled work of lac and cedar-beams
To coil his folds there on deep-graven slabs;
The lizard dwells and darts o'er painted floors
Where Kings have paced; the grey fox litters safe
Under the broken thrones; only the peaks,
And stream, and sloping lawns, and gentle air
Abide unchanged. All else, like all fair shows
Of life, are fled—for this is where it stood,
The city of Suddhodana, the hill
Whereon, upon an eve of gold and blue
At sinking sun Lord Buddha set himself
To teach the Law in hearing of his own.

Lo! ye shall read it in the Sacred Books
How, being met in that glad pleasaunce-place—
A garden in old days with hanging walks,
Fountains, and tanks, and rose-banked terraces
Girdled by gay pavilions and the sweep
Of stately palace-fronts—the Master sate
Eminent, worshipped, all the earnest throng
Catching the opening of his lips to learn
That wisdom which hath made our Asia mild;

Whereto four hundred crores of living souls
Witness this day. Upon the King's right hand
He sate, and round were ranged the Sākya Lords
Ananda, Devadatta—all the Court.
Behind stood Seriyut and Mugallan, chiefs
Of the calm brethren in the yellow garb,
A goodly company. Between his knees
Rahula smiled with wondering childish eyes
Bent on the awful face, while at his feet
Sate sweet Yasodhara, her heartaches gone,
Foreseeing that fair love which doth not feed
On fleeting sense, that life which knows no age,
That blessed last of deaths when Death is dead,
His victory and hers. Wherefore she laid
Her hand upon his hands, folding around
Her silver shoulder-cloth his yellow robe,
Nearest in all the world to him whose words
The Three Worlds waited for. I cannot tell
A small part of the splendid lore which broke
From Buddha's lips: I am a late-come scribe
Who love the Master and his love of men,
And tell this legend, knowing he was wise,
But have not wit to speak beyond the books
And time hath blurred their script and ancient sense,
Which once was new and mighty, moving all.
A little of that large discourse I know
Which Buddha spake on the soft Indian eve.
Also I know it writ that they who heard
Were more—lakhs more—crores more—than could be seen,
For all the Devas and the Dead thronged there,
Till Heaven was emptied to the seventh zone
And uttermost dark Hells opened their bars
Also the daylight lingered past its time
In rose-leaf radiance on the watching peaks,
So that it seemed Night listened in the glens
And Noon upon the mountains; yea! they write,
The evening stood between them like some maid
Celestial, love-struck, rapt; the smooth-rolled clouds
Her braided hair; the studded stars the pearls

And diamonds of her coronal; the moon
Her forehead-jewel, and the deepening dark
Her woven garments. 'Twas her close-held breath
Which came in scented sighs across the lawns
While our Lord taught, and, while he taught, who heard—
Though he were stranger in the land, or slave,
High caste or low, come of the Aryan blood,
Or Mlech or Jungle-dweller—seemed to hear
What tongue his fellows talked. Nay, outside those
Who crowded by the river, great and small,
The birds and beasts and creeping things—'tis writ—
Had sense of Buddha's vast embracing love
And took the promise of his piteous speech;
So that their lives—prisoned in shape of ape,
Tiger, or deer, shagged bear, jackal, or wolf,
Foul-feeding kite, pearled dove, or peacock gemmed.
Squat toad, or speckled serpent, lizard, bat;
Yea, or of fish fanning the river-waves—
Touched meekly at the skirts of brotherhood
With man who hath less innocence than these;
And in mute gladness knew their bondage broke
Whilst Buddha spake these things before the King:—

Om, AMITAYA! measure not with words
Th' Immeasurable: nor sink the string of thought
Into the Fathomless. Who asks doth err,
Who answers, errs. Say nought!

The Books teach Darkness was, at first of all,
And Brahm, sole meditating in that Night:
Look not for Brahm and the Beginning there!
Nor him, nor any light

Shall any gazer see with mortal eyes,
Or any searcher know by mortal mind,
Veil after veil will lift—but there must be
Veil upon veil behind.

Stars sweep and question not. This is enough
That life and death and joy and woe abide;

And cause and sequence, and the course of time,
And Being's ceaseless tide,

Which, ever-changing, runs, linked like a river
By ripples following ripples, fast or slow—
The same yet not the same—from far-off fountain
To where its waters flow

Into the seas. These, steaming to the Sun,
Give the lost wavelets back in cloudy fleece
To trickle down the hills, and glide again;
Having no pause or peace.

This is enough to know, the phantasms are;
The Heavens, Earths, Worlds, and changes changing them
A mighty whirling wheel of strife and stress
Which none can stay or stem.

Pray not! the Darkness will not brighten! Ask
Nought from the Silence, for it cannot speak!
Vex not your mournful minds with pious pains!
Ah! Brothers, Sisters! seek

Nought from the helpless gods by gift and hymn,
Nor bribe with blood, nor feed with fruit and cakes;
Within yourselves deliverance must be sought;
Each man his prison makes.

Each hath such lordship as the loftiest ones;
Nay, for with Powers above, around, below,
As with all flesh and whatsoever lives,
Act maketh joy and woe.

What hath been bringeth what shall be, and is,
Worse—better—last for first and first for last;
The Angels in the Heavens of Gladness reap
Fruits of a holy past.

The devils in the underworlds wear out
Deeds that were wicked in an age gone by.
Nothing endures: fair virtues waste with time,
Foul sins grow purged thereby.

Who toiled a slave may come anew a Prince
For gentle worthiness and merit won;
Who ruled a King may wander earth in rags
For things done and undone.

Higher than Indra's ye may lift your lot,
And sink it lower than the worm or gnat;
The end of many myriad lives is this,
The end of myriads that.

Only, while turns this wheel invisible,
No pause, no peace, no staying-place can be;
Who mounts will fall, who falls may mount; the spokes
Go round unceasingly!

* * * *

If ye lay bound upon the wheel of change,
And no way were of breaking from the chain,
The Heart of boundless Being is a curse,
The Soul of Things fell Pain.

Ye are not bound! the Soul of Things is sweet,
The Heart of Being is celestial rest;
Stronger than woe is will: that which was Good
Doth pass to Better—Best.

I, Buddh, who wept with all my brothers' tears,
Whose heart was broken by a whole world's woe,
Laugh and am glad, for there is Liberty!
Ho! ye who suffer! know

Ye suffer from yourselves. None else compels,
None other holds you that ye live and die,
And whirl upon the wheel, and hug and kiss
Its spokes of agony,

Its tire of tears, its nave of nothingness.
Behold, I show you Truth! Lower than hell,
Higher than heaven, outside the utmost stars,
Farther than Brahm doth dwell,

Before beginning, and without an end,
As space eternal and as surety sure,
Is fixed a Power divine which moves to good,
Only its laws endure.

This is its touch upon the blossomed rose,
The fashion of its hand shaped lotus-leaves;
In dark soil and the silence of the seeds
The robe of Spring it weaves;

That is its painting on the glorious clouds,
And these its emeralds on the peacock's train;
It hath its stations in the stars; its slaves
In lightning, wind, and rain.

Out of the dark it wrought the heart of man,
Out of dull shells the pheasant's pencilled neck;
Ever at toil, it brings to loveliness
All ancient wrath and wreck.

The grey eggs in the golden sun-bird's nest
Its treasures are, the bees' six-sided cell
Its honey-pot; the ant wots of its ways,
The white doves know them well.

It spreadeth forth for flight the eagle's wings
What time she beareth home her prey; it sends
The she-wolf to her cubs; for unloved things
It findeth food and friends.

It is not marred nor stayed in any use,
All liketh it; the sweet white milk it brings
To mothers' breasts; it brings the white drops, too,
Wherewith the young snake stings.

The ordered music of the marching orbs
It makes in viewless canopy of sky;
In deep abyss of earth it hides up gold,
Sards, sapphires, lazuli.

Ever and ever bringing secrets forth,
It sitteth in the green of forest-glades

Nursing strange seedlings at the cedar's root,
Devising leaves, blooms, blades.

It slayeth and it saveth, nowise moved
Except unto the working out of doom;
Its threads are Love and Life; and Death and Pain
The shuttles of its loom.

It maketh and unmaketh, mending all;
What it hath wrought is better than hath been;
Slow grows the splendid pattern that it plans
Its wistful hands between.

This is its work upon the things ye see,
The unseen things are more; men's hearts and minds,
The thoughts of peoples and their ways and wills,
Those, too, the great Law binds.

Unseen it helpeth ye with faithful hands,
Unheard it speaketh stronger than the storm.
Pity and Love are man's because long stress
Moulded blind mass to form.

It will not be contemned of any one;
Who thwarts it loses, and who serves it gains;
The hidden good it pays with peace and bliss,
The hidden ill with pains.

It seeth everywhere and marketh all:
Do right—it recompenseth! do one wrong—
The equal retribution must be made,
Though DHARMA tarry long.

It knows not wrath nor pardon; utter-true
Its measures mete, its faultless balance weighs;
Times are as nought, to-morrow it will judge,
Or after many days.

By this the slayer's knife did stab himself;
The unjust judge hath lost his own defender;
The false tongue dooms its lie; the creeping thief
And spoiler rob, to render.

Such is the Law which moves to righteousness,
Which none at last can turn aside or stay;
The heart of it is Love, the end of it
Is Peace and Consummation sweet. Obey!

* * *

The Books say well, my Brothers! each man's life
The outcome of his former living is;
The bygone wrongs bring forth sorrows and woes
The bygone right breeds bliss.

That which ye sow ye reap. See yonder fields!
The sesamum was sesamum, the corn
Was corn. The Silence and the Darkness knew!
So is a man's fate born.

He cometh, reaper of the things he sowed,
Sesamum, corn, so much cast in past birth;
And so much weed and poison-stuff, which mar
Him and the aching earth.

If he shall labor rightly, rooting these,
And planting wholesome seedlings where they grew,
Fruitful and fair and clean the ground shall be,
And rich the harvest due.

If he who liveth, learning whence woe springs,
Endureth patiently, striving to pay
His utmost debt for ancient evils done
In Love and Truth alway;

If making none to lack, he throughly purge
The lie and lust of self forth from his blood;
Suffering all meekly, rendering for offence
Nothing but grace and good:

If he shall day by day dwell merciful,
Holy and just and kind and true; and rend
Desire from where it clings with bleeding roots,
Till love of life have end:

He—dying—leaveth as the sum of him
A life-count closed, whose ills are dead and quit,
Whose good is quick and mighty, far and near,
So that fruits follow it.

No need hath such to live as ye name life;
That which began in him when he began
Is finished: he hath wrought the purpose through
Of what did make him Man.

Never shall yearnings torture him, nor sins
Stain him, nor ache of earthly joys and woes
Invade his safe eternal peace; nor deaths
And lives recur. He goes

Unto Nirvāna. He is one with Life
Yet lives not. He is blest, ceasing to be.
OM, MANI PADME, OM! the Dewdrop slips
Into the shining sea!

* * *

This is the doctrine of the KARMA. Learn!
Only when all the dross of sin is quit,
Only when life dies like a white flame spent
Death dies along with it.

Say not "I am," "I was," or "I shall be,"
Think not ye pass from house to house of flesh
Like travellers who remember and forget,
Ill-lodged or well-lodged. Fresh

Issues upon the Universe that sum
Which is the lattermost of lives. It makes
Its habitation as the worm spins silk
And dwells therein. It takes

Function and substance as the snake's egg hatched
Takes scale and fang; as feathered reed-seeds fly
O'er rock and loam and sand, until they find
Their marsh and multiply.

Also it issues forth to help or hurt.
When Death the bitter murderer doth smite,
Red roams the unpurged fragment of him, driven
On wings of plague and blight.

But when the mild and just die, sweet airs breathe;
The world grows richer, as if desert-stream
Should sink away to sparkle up again
Purer, with broader gleam.

So merit won winneth the happier age
Which by demerit halteth short of end;
Yet must this Law of Love reign King of all
Before the Kalpas end.

What lets?—Brothers! the Darkness lets! which breeds
Ignorance, mazed whereby ye take these shows
For true, and thirst to have, and, having, cling
To lusts which work you woes.

Ye that will tread the Middle Road, whose course
Bright Reason traces and soft Quiet smoothes;
Ye who will take the high Nirvāna-way
List the Four Noble Truths.

The First Truth is of *Sorrow*. Be not mocked!
Life which ye prize is long-drawn agony:
Only its pains abide; its pleasures are
As birds which light and fly.

Ache of the birth, ache of the helpless days,
Ache of hot youth and ache of manhood's prime;
Ache of the chill grey years and choking death,
These fill your piteous time.

Sweet is fond Love, but funeral-flames must kiss
The breasts which pillow and the lips which cling;
Gallant is warlike Might, but vultures pick
The joints of chief and King.

Beauteous is Earth, but all its forest-broods
Plot mutual slaughter, hungering to live;

Of sapphire are the skies, but when men cry
Famished, no drops they give.

Ask of the sick, the mourners, ask of him
Who tottereth on his staff, lone and forlorn,
"Liketh thee life?"—these say the babe is wise
That weepeth, being born.

The Second Truth is *Sorrow's Cause.* What grief
Springs of itself and springs not of Desire?
Senses and things perceived mingle and light
Passion's quick spark of fire:

So flameth Trishna, lust and thirst of things.
Eager ye cleave to shadows, dote on dreams;
A false Self in the midst ye plant, and make
A world around which seems;

Blind to the height beyond, deaf to the sound
Of sweet airs breathed from far past Indra's sky;
Dumb to the summons of the true life kept
For him who false puts by.

So grow the strifes and lusts which make earth's war,
So grieve poor cheated hearts and flow salt tears;
So wax the passions, envies, angers, hates;
So years chase blood-stained years

With wild red feet. So, where the grain should grow,
Spreads the birãn-weed with its evil root
And poisonous blossoms; hardly good seeds find
Soil where to fall and shoot;

And drugged with poisonous drink the soul departs,
And fierce with thirst to drink Karma returns;
Sense-struck again the sodden self begins,
And new deceits it earns.

The Third is *Sorrow's Ceasing.* This is peace
To conquer love of self and lust of life,
To tear deep-rooted passion from the breast,
To still the inward strife;

For love to clasp Eternal Beauty close;
For glory to be Lord of self, for pleasure
To live beyond the gods; for countless wealth
To lay up lasting treasure

Of perfect service rendered, duties done
In charity, soft speech, and stainless days:
These riches shall not fade away in life,
Nor any death dispraise.

Then Sorrow ends, for Life and Death have ceased;
How should lamps flicker when their oil is spent?
The old sad count is clear, the new is clean;
Thus hath a man content.

* * *

The Fourth Truth is *The Way.* It openeth wide,
Plain for all feet to tread, easy and near,
The *Noble Eightfold Path*; it goeth straight
To peace and refuge. Hear!

Manifold tracks lead to yon sister-peaks
Around whose snows the gilded clouds are curled;
By steep or gentle slopes the climber comes
Where breaks that other world.

Strong limbs may dare the rugged road which storms,
Soaring and perilous, the mountain's breast;
The weak must wind from slower ledge to ledge
With many a place of rest.

So is the Eightfold Path which brings to peace;
By lower or by upper heights it goes.
The firm soul hastes, the feeble tarries. All
Will reach the sunlit snows.

The First good Level is *Right Doctrine.* Walk
In fear of Dharma, shunning all offence;
In heed of Karma, which doth make man's fate;
In lordship over sense.

The Second is *Right Purpose.* Have good-will
To all that lives, letting unkindness die
And greed and wrath; so that your lives be made
Like soft airs passing by.

The Third is *Right Discourse.* Govern the lips
As they were palace-doors, the King within;
Tranquil and fair and courteous be all words
Which from that presence win.

The Fourth is *Right Behavior.* Let each act
Assoil a fault or help a merit grow:
Like threads of silver seen through crystal beads
Let love through good deeds show.

Four higher roadways be. Only those feet
May tread them which have done with earthly things;
Right Purity, Right Thought, Right Loneliness,
Right Rapture. Spread no wings

For sunward flight, thou soul with unplumed vans!
Sweet is the lower air and safe, and known
The homely levels: only strong ones leave
The nest each makes his own.

Dear is the love, I know, of Wife and Child;
Pleasant the friends and pastimes of your years;
Fruitful of good Life's gentle charities;
False, though firm-set, its fears.

Live—ye who must—such lives as live on these
Make golden stair-ways of your weakness; rise
By daily sojourn with those phantasies
To lovelier verities.

So shall ye pass to clearer heights and find
Easier ascents and lighter loads of sins,
And larger will to burst the bonds of sense,
Entering the Path. Who wins

To such commencement hath the *First Stage* touched;
He knows the Noble Truths, the Eightfold Road;

By few or many steps such shall attain
Nirvāna's blest abode.

Who standeth at the *Second Stage*, made free
From doubts, delusions, and the inward strife,
Lord of all lusts, quit of the priests and books,
Shall live but one more life.

Yet onward lies the *Third Stage*: purged and pure
Hath grown the stately spirit here, hath risen
To love all living things in perfect peace.
His life at end, life's prison

Is broken. Nay, there are who surely pass
Living and visible to utmost goal
By *Fourth Stage* of the Holy ones—the Buddhs—
And they of stainless soul.

Lo! like fierce foes slain by some warrior,
Ten sins along these Stages lie in dust,
The Love of Self, False Faith, and Doubt are three,
Two more, Hatred and Lust.

Who of these Five is conqueror hath trod
Three stages out of Four: yet there abide
The Love of Life on earth, Desire for Heaven,
Self-Praise, Error, and Pride.

As one who stands on yonder snowy horn
Having nought o'er him but the boundless blue,
So, these sins being slain, the man is come
Nirvāna's verge unto.

Him the Gods envy from their lower seats;
Him the Three Worlds in ruin should not shake;
All life is lived for him, all deaths are dead;
Karma will no more make

New houses. Seeking nothing, he gains all;
Foregoing self, the Universe grows "I":
If any teach Nirvāna is to cease,
Say unto such they lie.

If any teach Nirvāna is to live,
Say unto such they err; not knowing this,
Nor what light shines beyond their broken lamps,
Nor lifeless, timeless bliss.

Enter the Path! There is no grief like Hate!
No pains like passions, no deceit like sense!
Enter the Path far hath he gone whose foot
Treads down one fond offence.

Enter the Path! There spring the healing streams
Quenching all thirst! there bloom th' immortal flowers
Carpeting all the way with joy! there throng
Swiftest and sweetest hours!

* * *

More is the treasure of the Law than gems;
Sweeter than comb its sweetness; its delights
Delightful past compare. Thereby to live
Hear the *Five Rules* aright:—

Kill not—for Pity's sake—and lest ye slay
The meanest thing upon its upward way.

Give freely and receive, but take from none
By greed, or force or fraud, what is his own.

Bear not false witness, slander not, nor lie;
Truth is the speech of inward purity.

Shun drugs and drinks which work the wit abuse;
Clear minds, clean bodies, need no Soma juice.

Touch not thy neighbor's wife, neither commit
Sins of the flesh unlawful and unfit.

These words the Master spake of duties due
To father, mother, children, fellows, friends;
Teaching how such as may not swiftly break
The clinging chains of sense—whose feet are weak
To tread the higher road—should order so
This life of flesh that all their hither days
Pass blameless in discharge of charities

And first true footfalls in the Eightfold Path;
Living pure, reverent, patient, pitiful,
Loving all things which live even as themselves;
Because what falls for ill is fruit of ill
Wrought in the past, and what falls well of good;
And that by howsomuch the householder
Purgeth himself of self and helps the world,
By so much happier comes he to next stage,
In so much bettered being. This he spake,
As also long before, when our Lord walked
By Rājagriha in the bamboo-grove:
For on a dawn he walked there and beheld
The householder Singāla, newly bathed,
Bowing himself with bare head to the earth,
To Heaven, and all four quarters; while he threw
Rice, red and white, from both hands. "Wherefore thus
Bowest thou, Brother?" said the Lord; and he,
"It is the way, Great Sir! our fathers taught
At every dawn, before the toil begins,
To hold off evil from the sky above
And earth beneath, and all the winds which blow."
Then the World-honored spake: "Scatter not rice,
But offer loving thoughts and acts to all.
To parents as the East where rises light;
To teachers as the South whence rich gifts come;
To wife and children as the West where gleam
Colors of love and calm, and all days end;
To friends and kinsmen and all men as North;
To humblest living things beneath, to Saints
And Angels and the blessed Dead above:
So shall all evil be shut off, and so
The six main quarters will be safely kept."

But to his own, them of the yellow robe—
They who, as wakened eagles, soar with scorn
From life's low vale, and wing towards the Sun—
To these he taught the Ten Observances
The *Dasa-Sīl*, and how a mendicant
Must know the *Three Doors* and the *Triple Thoughts*;

The *Sixfold States of Mind*; the *Fivefold Powers*;
The *Eight High Gates of Purity*; the *Modes*
Of Understanding; *Iddhi*; *Upekshā*
The *Five Great Meditations,* which are food
Sweeter than Amrit for the holy soul;
The *Jhāna's* and the *Three Chief Refuges.*
Also he taught his own how they should dwell;
How live, free from the snares of love and wealth;
What eat and drink and carry—three plain cloths,—
Yellow, of stitched stuff, worn with shoulder bare—
A girdle, almsbowl, strainer. Thus he laid
The great foundations of our Sangha well,
That noble Order of the Yellow Robe
Which to this day standeth to help the World.

So all that night he spake, teaching the Law:
And on no eyes fell sleep—for they who heard
Rejoiced with tireless joy. Also the King,
When this was finished, rose upon his throne
And with bared feet bowed low before his Son
Kissing his hem; and said, "Take me, O Son!
Lowest and least of all thy Company."
And sweet Yasodhara, all happy now,—
Cried "Give to Rahula—thou Blessed One!
The Treasure of the Kingdom of thy Word
For his inheritance." Thus passed these Three
Into the Path

* * *

Here endeth what I write
Who love the Master for his love of us.
A little knowing, little have I told
Touching the Teacher and the Ways of Peace.
Forty-five rains thereafter showed he those
In many lands and many tongues and gave
Our Asia light, that still is beautiful,
Conquering the world with spirit of strong grace:
All which is written in the holy Books,
And where he passed and what proud Emperors

Carved his sweet words upon the rocks and caves:
And how—in fulness of the times—it fell
The Buddha died, the great Tathāgato,
Even as a man 'mongst men, fulfilling all:
And how a thousand thousand crores since then
Have trod the Path which leads whither he went
Unto Nirvāna where the Silence lives.

* * *

Ah! Blessed lord! Oh, high deliverer!
Forgive this feeble script, which doth thee wrong.
Measuring with little wit thy lofty love.
Ah! Lover! Brother! Guide! Lamp of the law!
I take my refuge in thy name and thee!
I take my refuge in thy Law of Good!
I take my refuge in thy Order! *Om!*
The dew is on the lotus!—rise great sun!
And lift my leaf and mix me with the wave.
Om mani padme hum, the sunrise comes!
The dewdrop slips into the shining sea!

Women in Early Buddhist Literature

A Talk to the All-Ceylon Buddhist Women's Association
Colombo, 18 January 1961

by

I. B. Horner

WHEEL PUBLICATION NO. 30

Women in Early Buddhist Literature

Following a true tradition of Buddhist teaching, more will have to be left unsaid here than can possibly be said. The subject of women is large; and the contents of the Pali Canon on which this article is based are vast. One can make therefore only a relatively small selection of matters that I hope may prove to be of some interest.

Women are often the main upholders and supporters of a religion or faith or movement. This was certainly so with Buddhism when it was at its beginnings, and hence we are able to find a good deal about them in those portions of the Pali Canon known as the Vinaya-piṭaka and the Sutta-piṭaka. The Vinaya, which comprises the rules and regulations for monastic discipline, contains two sections: the Bhikkhunī-vibhaṅga and the Bhikkhunī-khandhaka, both of which deal with the conduct nuns, or bhikkhunīs, and female probationers should observe, and with the legislation that was laid down for the proper management of their Order—now unfortunately extinct. In the Buddha's times, however, it seems that quantities of women became nuns, so as to seek for peace, inner and outer, self-mastery, the light of knowledge, and so on, and perhaps especially for various forms of that freedom which lies at the very heart and center of the Buddha's Teaching: "As this great ocean has but one taste, that of salt, so has this Dhamma but one taste, that of freedom." The ardour and the energy of these early nuns, whether they were active in preaching the Word of the Buddha or were absorbed in contemplation and meditation, come through to us in three portions of the Suttapiṭaka that are specially devoted to the verses such nuns are held to have uttered, mostly at the time they attained arahantship or won a vision of nibbāna. There is, first and most important and unique in any literature, the Therīgāthā, consisting entirely of sets of verses of varying length attributed to seventy-three women who became Therīs or Elder nuns. Then there is the Bhikkhunī-saṃyutta, a part of the Saṃyutta-nikāya, where other verses are collected that are ascribed to ten of these women Elders; and thirdly there are in the Apadāna biographies in verse of forty nuns said to have been contemporary with the Buddha—as against 547 biographies of monks and to most of whom verses are attributed also in the Therīgāthā.

One cannot say therefore that nuns have been neglected in early Buddhist literature. With the exception of the Suttanipāta, I think they are mentioned in every Pali canonical work, even in the Theragāthā (verse 1257), the Anthology of verses attributed to monks who were Elders. Against this, nowhere in the great Nikāyas of the Suttapiṭaka: the Dīgha, Majjhima, Saṃyutta, or Aṅguttara, is it possible to find any large section where lay-women devotees are the central figures. It is true that there are records of long conversations held between the Buddha and this or that woman lay-follower. For example, with Visākha, the most eminent and generous benefactor and supporter of the Order of monks and nuns (A I 2), to whom the Buddha granted eight boons: that as long as she lived she might be allowed to give robes to the members of the Order for the rainy season; food for monks coming into the town of Sāvatthī; food for those leaving it; food for the sick; food for those that wait on the sick; medicines for the sick; a constant supply of rice-gruel for any needing it; and bathing robes for the nuns (Vin I 290ff.). Then, too, there was Queen Mallikā, chief consort of King Pasenadi of Kosala, with whom the Buddha converses now and again; and Nakulamātā, the pious and devoted wife of Nakulapita. And this is typical: such records exist but they are scattered through the Vinaya and the Nikāyas. These, then, have to be searched and carefully sifted in order to build up any reliable picture of the position held by lay-women at the time and the place to which this literature purports to refer.

And, broadly speaking, this refers to India in the 6th century B.C. where the Buddha Gotama was living during the forty-five years that he was propounding his Teaching on suffering and the escape from it, which then, and for all the centuries since, has so deeply affected the lives of millions of people down to the present day.

What with the nuns and the monks, the women lay-devotees and the men-devotees, it is not possible in speaking of women in early Buddhist literature to keep separate these component parts of the fourfold community that grew up around the Buddha, because they were not separate in life. The sexes were not segregated, and though naturally nuns had their quarters apart from those of the monks, they had yet to carry out some of their official acts, such as ordination, in conjunction with an Order of monks. Nor was the cloister cut off from the world. On the contrary, there was much intermingling. The laity gave alms-food to the monks and nuns, and often to the other sectarians who abounded in India at that date, either at the doors of their houses or they invited them to come in for their one meal a day. In return, the monks and the nuns, both of whom could claim some great preachers, taught Dhamma to the laity, thus giving them the gift that excels all others. This freedom of movement enjoyed by the nuns has a parallel with and is perhaps connected with the freedom of movement that was the happy lot of the lay-women who knew not the cramping and enervating system of *purdah*, though their life might contain other disadvantages.

In India, as I see it, at the time when the Buddha was living and teaching there, women were emerging into a relatively free state after they had suffered a certain amount, but perhaps an over-estimated amount, of ignominy, of obedience and subservience to men, and exclusion from this or that worldly occupation or religious education or observance, all of which is generally made out to have been their portion in pre-Buddhist Indian epochs. We have to be a little on our guard against such statements. For example, there is no evidence that women were debarred from taking part in the great debates on philosophical matter that were a feature of Indian life at that time. Famous in the Bṛhadāraṇyaka Upaniṣad, for example, is the lady Gargī who pushed a debate with Yājñavalkya to a point beyond which, as he told her, no further questions should be asked, for they hardly admitted of an answer (III 6)—a distinction no male questioner achieved. A somewhat comparable discussion or "minor catechism" is recorded in the Pali Majjhima-Nikāya (M I 304/MN 44), but here it is the man, the lay-devotee Visākha, who, when he asked his former wife, who had become the nun Dhammadinnā, what is the counterpart of Nibbāna, was told by her that this question goes too far and is beyond the scope of an answer. Dhammadinnā knew very well what she was talking about and was outstanding as the most eminent among the Buddhist nuns who were speakers on Dhamma (A I 25). We too have to believe her.

Leaving the realms of high philosophy, we must now look at what was regarded as woman's proper sphere, namely the home. We have to remember that in India women as mothers had always commanded much veneration and gratitude. By bearing a son she had done what she could and what had been expected of her to ensure the continuance of the family line, and had provided for the due performance of the "rites of the ancestors." Only a son could carry these out; they were thought to be very necessary for bringing peace and serenity to the father, and the grandfather too, after they had died, and so to prevent them from returning as ghosts to harry the family. If a woman had no son, she might be superseded by a second and a third wife or even turned out of the house.

But with the coming of Buddhism, the traditional structure and functions of society undoubtedly underwent some alterations. So numerous were the followers of this new Teaching and so rapidly did it spread, that they may be held responsible for various not unimportant social changes, such as a reduction in size and frequency of the vast animal sacrifices the brahmins had already engaged in for centuries—though even now these have not been abolished entirely from India. Buddhism teaches that sacrifice is internal: a composure of mind to be gained by abandoning all ideas that anything in the world is "mine" or "I" or my self. For, "by things without, none is made pure, so the wise say" (S I 169). So the old-time sacrifices came to be derided and debased:

The sacrifices called The Horse, The Man,
The "Throwing of the Peg," the "Drinking Rite,"
The "House Unbarred"; with all their cruelty
Have little fruit. Where goats and sheep and kine
Of diverse sorts are sacrificed, go not
Those sages great who've traveled the right way.

But sacrifices free from cruelty
Which men keep up for the profit of the clan,
Where goats and sheep and kine of diverse sorts
Are never sacrificed—to such as these
Go sages great who've traveled the right way.

(A II 42; S I 76)

The noble lady, Queen Mallikā, took a very strong line and on one occasion was able to dissuade her husband, King Pasenadi, from holding a great animal sacrifice which had been recommended to him by a brahmin as a means for saving his life. She was horrified, and exclaimed: "Where did you ever hear of the saving of life for one by the death of another? Just because a stupid brahmin told you to, why must you plunge the whole populace into suffering?" (Dhp-a II 8; cf. J-a I 335). For not only would the animals be slain and lost to their owners thereby endangering their means of livelihood; but from a Buddhist point of view such a contravention of true Dhamma and its first moral injunction, *pāṇātipātā veramaṇi*, would prolong the sacrificer's bondage to the wheel of *saṃsāra*: "Long is saṃsāra for fools who do not know true Dhamma" (Dhp 60).

The mention of saṃsāra brings us almost inevitably to kamma, that inexorable impersonal force by which beings are bound to the ever-rolling wheel of saṃsāra. Not that kamma was a new concept introduced by Buddhism. It was age-old, but Buddhism made it very central and illuminated it particularly in relation to "this long, long faring-on and circling" of beings born only to die and be born again and yet again so long as "ignorance," the root cause of all suffering and anguish, persists. It is held that after the dissolution of his body here the so-called "being" will be followed by a new birth and again new ones after that, all according to kamma; that is according to what the "being" has done, whether of good or bad, both in this last birth and in anterior ones, until all the effects of his volitional deeds of body, speech, and thought have worn to their karmic end. The effects of good deeds and bad deeds work in independent series, and are not to be weighed or balanced against one another, or wiped out the one by the other: "As is the seed that is sown, so is the fruit that is gathered. The doer of good (gathers) good, of evil, evil" (S I 227). Or again, to take another quotation by random, and one that is as much Upaniṣadic as Buddhist in sentiment: "The uprising of a being is from what has come to be; by what he has done, by that he uprises" (M I 390/ MN 57). In a word, he, "the being," is responsible for his own saṃsāra—not his mother or his father or brother or sister, or his friends and acquaintances. So it is he himself who will experience the ripening of the deed he himself did.

All this implies that, for women, there was a lessening, an easing of the pious hope that a child could be got by prayers offered to some divinity such as the moon, or by circumambulating a tree. For the workings of kamma will not be affected by such devices. This is a reason why Buddhism had no truck with rites at all. They are a fetter, to be avoided and feared, and useless against the tremendous force of kamma, whether their aim were to give a women a child or purify a person of his wrong-doings. As the nun Puṇṇā so succinctly observed, if bathing and ablution in rivers and wells could purify a person, then fishes and crocodiles, turtles and water snakes would be purified and go straight to heaven (Thī 241).

So, the insistence on impersonal kamma spelt a decrease in a wife's anxiety to give birth to a son, because it was no longer held that the future state of the father or grandfather depended on the obsequies for the departed ancestors that had devolved formerly on the sons. Rather, their future state was now shown to depend solely on the volitional acts they themselves had done. Therefore, as a performer of funeral or ancestral rites a son no longer had a part to play. Nor, apparently—and this was another innovation—would it be any great catastrophe if the family lineage were vested in a woman, at any rate for the time being. On the Western Coast of India there exists even today a very old class of brahmins called Nairs according to whose traditions the inheritance always passes through the female. At all events, the idea, however novel, that after all sons were not a vital necessity but that a daughter might be every whit as acceptable and could also carry on the family line, was early recognized, and perhaps even introduced by, the Buddha. The following words are ascribed to him when he was trying to comfort his friend King Pasenadi, wretched and disappointed on hearing that his Queen Mallikā, had just given birth to a daughter:

A woman-child, O Lord of men, may prove
Even a better offspring than a male.
For she may grow up wise and virtuous,
Her husband's mother rev'rencing, true wife.
The child she may bear may do great deeds,
And rule great realms, yea such a son
Of noble wife becomes his country's guide.

(S I 86)

Not that I think in pre-Buddhist India there had been any consistent ill-treatment of little girls or injustice shown to them for the very reason that they were not boys. Female infanticide, if it obtained at all, must have been extremely rare. It had not the support of custom or tradition, MacDonnell and Keith going so far as to say: "There is no proof that the Vedic Indians (roughly 2000 B.C.) practiced exposure of female children."[1] Besides, the teaching of *ahiṃsā*—non-harming, non-injury, so ancient that its beginnings are lost in the mists of time—held sway, even if in moderation, over the whole of India. It was a teaching much accentuated by the Jains who were precursors of the Buddha and also contemporary with him. Though they were among his greatest rivals, he would not have wished to go against them on such a point or thought a different teaching possible. And they had the backing of public opinion. *Ahiṃsā* certainly would not have tolerated the murder of a defenseless human being. From this teaching the first of the five *sīla*, or precepts for ethical conduct, drew its strength for Jain and Buddhist alike: the abstention from killing or harming any living creature was binding on monks and nuns during the whole of their monastic careers—and on the laity, too. Moreover, the economic conditions prevailing in India from the 7th to the 4th centuries B.C. would appear to have been quite flourishing enough to allow for the survival of little girls. And finally, as the Buddha spoke out strongly against blood-sacrifice, so he would not have permitted the sacrifice of children—boys or girls—though indeed for the purposes of infant-sacrifice boys were apparently usually the victims in non-Buddhist India. Even as late as towards the end of last century some little boys were immured in the stonework of the new bridge over the Hooghly river near Calcutta as an offering to the gods to protect the bridge, and the human beings using it.

If sons were born to courtesans they did however run a certain risk of being murdered. For example, Sālavatī had been established as the courtesan of Rājagaha by the urban council. When she gave birth to a son, she told her slave woman to put him in a winnowing-basket and throw him away on a rubbish heap (Vin I 269). On the other hand, the courtesan Ambapāli, who was to become famous as one of the most loyal and generous supporters of Buddhist monks

1. *Vedic Index of Names and Subjects*, II 114.

(D II 88; DN 16), and the lady known as Abhaya's mother each had a son who became a monk. When this latter lady had heard her son preach she left the world and entered the Buddhist Order of nuns. Daughters born to courtesans do not appear to have been regarded as a disaster, and we hear of at least two who followed the same calling as their mothers, though later they became nuns and gained arahantship (Thī 39; Sn-a 244).

In those days it was customary for at all events a brahmin to embark on the final or "forest" stage of his life only when he was fairly well advanced in years. He would then leave his wife as mother-in-law in his eldest son's house. Women must have been prepared for this eventuality. But, with the coming of Buddhism, there was no longer need for a man to wait to "make his soul" until he was approaching the end of his life, then to seek the solitude of the forest. For once the Order of Buddhist monks had been established, and that was very early in the Buddha's teaching life, it was ruled that a man as young as 20 years, but not less, could be fully ordained, and at the age of fifteen he could leave his home and go into monastic homelessness as a novice. In both cases he had to have the consent of his mother and father—sometimes given very reluctantly. In a way, then, the establishment of the Order of monks no less than that of nuns might be regarded as a new menace to the happiness of women. For now there was nothing to stop their sons and daughters from taking up the "religious life" while they were still quite young.

At the beginning of his career the Buddha had been accused of being a breaker of homes, of turning wives into widows and rendering mothers childless. For this new menace, if we may thus speak of the twofold Order, did not merely swallow up children. A woman might now lose a young husband to the monks, but generally only after he had obtained her consent. Yet, how often, one may ask, was this withheld? And how often did not women, like Cāpā, the daughter of a trapper, hope that the son to whom she had given birth would save her from desertion by her husband:

And this child blossom, O my husband, see
Thy gift to me—now surely thou wilt not
Forsake her who hath borne a son to thee?

(Thī 300)

I think it was perhaps a sign of the changing times that if a husband, no longer dependent on a son for his funeral obsequies since they no longer mattered, felt a strong enough pull to leave the world and become a monk, nothing could restrain him, even as nothing had restrained the Bodhisatta Siddhattha who became the Buddha Gotama from leaving his home and wife and child at the age of twenty-nine to seek for the cause of *dukkha*—anguish or suffering—and the escape from it.

In the same way, neither the thought of his son nor of Cāpā's beauty could keep back her husband Upaka from going forth to find the Lord, though it is true he was a Naked Ascetic and not a typical householder. He was adamant on the point. His may have been a case of a husband's exerting his authority, *issariya*, against which not all the five powers of which a woman may be possessed can prevail: beauty (which Cāpā had), wealth, relations (her father was still alive), a son (which she had), and ethical conduct, sīla. It is said that a woman endowed with these five powers may dwell with confidence as mistress of the house, get the better of her husband and keep him under her thumb (S IV 246), but that if she is lacking in these powers the family may not let her stay in the house, but may drive her forth and expel her (S IV 248), a fate from which only the possession of moral habit could in theory save her.

On the expulsion of the wife, it may be assumed that the husband was then free to take another wife, even as kings, whether or not they were followers of the Buddha's Teaching, might have a number of consorts. Certainly women too could remarry, as is seen from the strange history of Isidāsī who married at least four husbands one after the other and for some reason was displeasing to them all—a reason she attributed to an evil deed she did seven births ago. She then entered the Order of nuns.

Another fear that a woman may have felt on marrying was that of a co-wife, one who may or may not have been installed in the house already. Isidāsī had such an experience with her last husband:

> *...Another wife he had,*
> *A virtuous dame of parts and of repute,*
> *Enamored of her mate. And thus I brought*
> *Discord and enmity within that house.*
>
> (Thī 446)

Thus both wives suffered.

Kisāgotamī too, one of the most widely known of all the Therīs, was a woman who had endured much sorrow:

Woeful is woman's lot, hath he declared,
Charioteer of men to be tamed:
Woeful when sharing home with hostile wives,
Woeful when giving birth in bitter pain,
Some seeking death or e'er they suffer twice,
Piercing the throat, the delicate poison take.

(Thī 216–217)

But the risk of marriage had to be run, and was still the most normal career open to a young woman. As it is said: "A woman's goal is a man, her ambition is for adornment, her resolve is for a child, her desire is to be without a rival, her fulfillment is authority" (A III 363).

We have seen that a husband might desert his wife or throw her out of the house. Further, her relations, even against her will, might take away a wife from the husband she was fond of and give her to another man (M II 109/MN 87). A drastic case is recorded where a husband cut his wife in two rather than let her suffer this fate. He then committed suicide. This is one of several episodes brought together to show that in the Buddhist view grief and suffering, rather than happiness and joy, are born of affection.

Owing to a woman's rather uncertain position after her marriage, though, except for the co-wives perhaps no more uncertain than in our own days, it behooved a girl to reflect well before her marriage on what her duties would be afterwards. An interesting statement of these, ascribed to the Buddha himself, has fortunately survived, and may be regarded as an indication that he liked marriages to be happy:

"Therefore, girls, train yourselves thus: 'To whatever husband our parents shall give us, for him we will rise up early, be the last to retire, be willing workers, order all things sweetly and speak affectionately.' Train yourselves thus, girls.

"And in this way too, girls: 'We will honor and respect all whom our husband honors and respects, whether mother or father, recluse or brahmin, and on their arrival will offer them water and a seat.' Train yourselves thus, girls.

"And in this way too, girls: 'We will be deft and nimble at our husband's home-crafts, whether they be of wool or cotton, making it our business to understand the work so as to do it and get it done.' Train yourselves thus, girls.

"And in this way too, girls: 'Whatever our husband's household consists of—servants and messengers and work-people—we will know the work of each one of them by what has been done, and their remissness by what has not been done; we will know the strength and the weakness of the sick; we will portion out the soft food and the solid food to each according to his share.' Train yourselves thus, girls.

"And this way too, girls: 'The treasure, grain, silver, and gold that our husband brings home we will keep safely, acting as no robber or spendthrift in regard to it.' Train yourselves thus, girls." (A III 37–38/AN 4:265)

If all goes well, then the wife is called the "comrade supreme" (S I 37). A number of devoted couples are mentioned in the Pali canon, such as Queen Mallikā and King Pasenadi, Nakulamātā and Nakulapita, and Dhammadinnā and Visākha.

Nakulamātā and Nakulapita were considered by the Buddha to be the most eminent among his lay-disciples for their close companionship with one another (A I 26). And they were matched in their faith in his Teaching, their self-control, and the affectionate way in which they spoke to one another (A II 62/AN 4:55). A commentary (A-a I 400) asserts that for 500 births they had been parents or relatives of the Buddha, or more strictly speaking of the Bodhisatta: "Him of the ten powers" is the term the Commentary uses to avoid this awkwardness—and so in this life they treated him like a son. Nakulamātā, as was the custom for brides, was taken to Nakulapita's home and, as they tell the Buddha, ever since that time, when he was still a mere lad and she only a girl, neither is aware of having transgressed against the other in thought, much less in person, and each expresses the longing to be together not only here and now but in a future state also. The Buddha reassures them on this point, and gives as his reason that both of them are on the same level in regard to their belief, their ethical conduct, their generosity and wisdom (A II 61f./AN 4:55). In these respects therefore a woman may be the equal of a man.

Another record relates how Nakulamātā once comforted her husband when he was dangerously ill and worrying about what would happen to her and the children should he die. "Do not fret," she said, "I am deft at spinning cotton and carding wool and so would be able, were you to die, to support the children and run the household. Nor would I go to another man. Even greater than when you were alive would be my desire to see the Blessed One and the Order of monks. As long as the Blessed One has female disciples, clad in white, I shall be one of them, fulfilling the precepts of ethical behavior, and gaining inward tranquility of mind. I shall live confident, without doubt or questioning, following the Teacher's instruction. So do not die, householder, while you are fretting, for so to die is anguish" (A III 295ff.). Since restlessness and worry are one of the five hindrances to gaining mind-control, and since to die with an anxious heart works against happiness in the life to come, it is important to develop serenity of mind and impassibility of body.

Husbands might be prevented from crooked dealing if their wives were upholders of the Buddhist way of life. For example, the brahmin Dhānañjāni was not being diligent. "Under the king's patronage he plundered brahmin householders, and under their patronage he plundered the king. His wife, who had had faith in the Buddhist Teaching and had come from a family having faith had died, and he married another woman. But she had no faith herself and came from a family lacking in faith" (M II 185). Here the first wife is clearly thought of as able to keep her husband straight, while the second one at all events seems to countenance his double dealings even if she does nothing herself to aid and abet him actively.

Equally with a man a woman might bring a family to prosperity: "All families that have attained great possessions have done so for one or other of the following reasons: they search for what is lost; repair what is dilapidated; eat and drink in moderation; and place in authority, *issariya*, a virtuous woman or man" (A II 249; AN 4.255).

In pre-Buddhist days a woman had been looked down on if she did not marry—growing old at home, she was called "one who sits with her father." But in early Buddhist times an unmarried girl might go unabused, contented, and adequately occupied in caring for her parents and younger brothers and sisters. Hers would have been a domestic life. Or she might become the mistress of great possessions, of slaves, villages, and rich fields, as did Subhā, the goldsmith's daughter. But once Dhamma had been taught to her, by Mahāpajāpati, who had been the Buddha's foster mother and then became the first nun, she found that "all worldly pleasures irk me sore," that " silver and gold lead neither to peace nor to enlightenment," so she entered the Order of Buddhist nuns. And truly, this was a great boon to the unmarried woman. It gave her, and the married woman too, the means of escaping from some crushing sorrow, from difficult worldly circumstances, or from the ceaseless round of menial tasks that have to be performed in the home. Isidāsī's verses contain a whole catalogue of these (Isidāsī was the one who had at least four husbands in succession; Thī 407ff.). Muttā sums up her domestic drudgery more succinctly:

O free indeed, O gloriously free
Am I in freedom from three crooked things:
From quern, from mortar, and my crooked lord.

(Thī 11)

And then, rejoicingly,

Free am I from birth and dying,
Becoming's cord removed.

I hope to have shown that, in spite of her many trials and tribulations, a virtuous woman could have power in her home, bear the children she wanted, and enjoy the love and respect of her husband and family circle. Again, in the home, there were the serving women, whether themselves unmarried or not I cannot say, the foster mothers, brought in for the occasion, and the women musicians and dancers, for the most part, of course, in the homes of the well-to-do. Outside the home, it would seem that a woman's powers and opportunities were limited. Though they worked in the fields, apparently they did not become doctors, or even nurses, judges, or lawyers nor, apart from looking after their own possessions, did they engage in business (A II 82). The only profession really open to them was the oldest one in the world. The Buddha neither scorned nor rebuked courtesans, but tried to help them by making them realize the impermanence of all conditioned things, including the many forms of beauty. The Order of Nuns was as open to them as it was to any other women who qualified for the higher ordination.

And indeed it was to the Order of Nuns that a woman could go merely if she felt the nagging worries of domestic life to be unendurable, but also if she had a positive vocation for spiritual endeavor. In principle, there was nothing very novel in women leaving the world for the houseless state. The Jain Order of Nuns was in being already, and there were women "wanderers" and freelance debaters, all seeking for Truth and philosophical understanding. An example of a fine woman disputant is Bhaddā Kuṇḍalakesī. Formerly a follower of the Jains, she now toured the country seeking for knowledge among other learned persons. She would stick a rose-apple bough into a heap of sand as a sign that she would debate with anyone who would debate with her.[2] One day Sāriputta, one of the two chief disciples of the Buddha, took up her challenge. But he answered all the questions she put to him, and then overthrew her in the debate by asking the single question: "The one—what is it?" Leaving aside the intricate literary material that surrounds this question and the deep significance of the correct answer that "All beings subsist by food," we can do no more here than notice some of the main results of the debate as they affected Bhaddā. First, she was taken by Sāriputta to the Buddha and after she had heard him speak, she gained arahantship. Secondly, she entered the Order of Nuns as one who was already an arahant; this was unusual. Thirdly, the Buddha himself admitted her with the words: "Come, Bhaddā," and that was her ordination. Great importance came to be attached to this case of a woman being ordained by the Buddha himself, and Dhammapāla ends his commentary on the Verses of the Women Elders, the Therīgāthā, with a note on it.

Another Bhaddā, Bhaddā Kāpilanī (Thī 63ff.), is also noteworthy for providing the only case to be recorded (or the record of which has survived) of a woman going forth into homelessness at the same time as her husband (Th 1051ff.). We need not however regard this as an isolated incident. Both of them

2. See the Commentary to psalm XLVI (Thī 5.9) in *Psalms of the Sisters*, translated by Mrs. C.A.F. Rhys Davids (Oxford: Pali Text Society, 1909, 1989).

felt a positive call to the homeless life, acted in mutual agreement, helped one another to put on the yellow robes of a recluse, to shave off the hair and sling the begging-bowl from the shoulders. Then they set out together, but only to part quite soon and go to the Buddha by different ways for fear people should say that even in their new state they could not do without one another. For then, as Bhaddā and her husband Kassapa realized, such people would run the risk of rebirth in sorrowful states as a result of the false accusations they had made. It is said that, owing to the power of such virtue, the great earth trembled (Th-a III 133). Indeed the second of the eight reasons why earthquakes (D II 107f./DN 16) occur is that a person has attained to mastery over his mind and then develops perception of a minute portion of the earth—and these two had earnestly discussed which route each of them would take, thereby intimating their mastery over mind—over desire, too, perhaps.

Another woman who felt a true vocation was Dhammadinnā, whom I have mentioned earlier. Though happily married to Visākha, a devout citizen of Rājagaha, she yet asked for his consent to go forth into homelessness, for apparently, as with Bhaddā Kāpilanī and her husband Kassapa, the pull of religion was stronger than any earthly tie. Visākha at once sent her to a nunnery in a golden palanquin,[3] but unlike Kassapa, seems to have felt no desire himself to enter the Order of monks. Dhammadinnā gained arahantship, and then returned to Rājagaha where she was eagerly questioned by her former husband on matters pertaining to Dhamma. If the questions showed a deep insight, the answers showed a deeper. Thus, as a result of this dialogue between a nun and a layman, recorded in the Cūlavedalla Sutta (MN 44), the Buddha ranked the nun Dhammadinnā foremost among those nuns who could preach—and these were not lacking in number; and he also endorsed all she had said, declaring that he would have answered all Visākha's questions exactly as she had done. According to the commentary (M-a II 371), this Discourse may therefore be taken as the Conqueror's speech rather than the disciple's. It thus becomes *Buddhavacana*, the word of the Buddha, in virtue of its having won his approval in these terms.

3. See the Commentary to psalm XII (Thī 1.6) in *Psalms of the Sisters*.

There is another occasion when a nun's discourse may be regarded as *Buddhavacana*. This was when the Buddha commended the unnamed nun of Kajaṅgalā for her interpretation of the answers to the Ten Great Questions which begin with the question Sāriputta asked Bhaddā Kuṇḍalakesī: "The one—what is it?" Though the nun says she had not learned the answers she would give either from the Buddha or from any monks who were developing their minds, and though her answers to four of the questions do in fact differ from those found in the Khuddakapāṭha, the *locus classicus* for these Ten Great Questions and their answers, yet the Lord approved of all of them (A V 54ff.), again stating that he would have answered precisely as the nun had done. Therefore we again get a discourse which may be regarded as *Buddhavacana*.

In conclusion, I hope to have presented you with some material for thinking that in the Buddha's time women were not despised and looked down on but, on the contrary, were respected and had a place of honor in the home. The difficulties they had to face and overcome were no more than normal for women in any time or country, even if their life was, at the worldly level, more restricted than it has come to be in the last decades as women go in more and more for public work and hold professional posts. At the higher, more spiritual level however, they had the great advantage and great joy of entering the Order of Nuns either because they wanted to get free of worldly sufferings or, more positively, and above everything else, because they wanted to find the way to the peace and bliss of Nibbāna, all their former craving for sense-pleasures rooted out, tranquil and cool. Many of the women I have mentioned here, whether they have been nuns or lay-devotees, by their response to the majesty of the Buddha's Teaching, have made an imponderable contribution to its strength, vitality, expansion, and longevity. It is as well to survey again from time to time the lives of these ardent contemporaries of the Buddha. Indeed the Buddhist world owes them a large debt of gratitude.

ABOUT PARIYATTI

Pariyatti is dedicated to providing affordable access to authentic teachings of the Buddha about the Dhamma theory (*pariyatti*) and practice (*paṭipatti*) of Vipassana meditation. A 501(c)(3) nonprofit charitable organization since 2002, Pariyatti is sustained by contributions from individuals who appreciate and want to share the incalculable value of the Dhamma teachings. We invite you to visit www.pariyatti.org to learn about our programs, services, and ways to support publishing and other undertakings.

Pariyatti Publishing Imprints

Vipassana Research Publications (focus on Vipassana as taught by S.N. Goenka in the tradition of Sayagyi U Ba Khin)

BPS Pariyatti Editions (selected titles from the Buddhist Publication Society, copublished by Pariyatti)

MPA Pariyatti Editions (selected titles from the Myanmar Pitaka Association, copublished by Pariyatti)

Pariyatti Digital Editions (audio and video titles, including discourses)

Pariyatti Press (classic titles returned to print and inspirational writing by contemporary authors)

Pariyatti enriches the world by

- disseminating the words of the Buddha,
- providing sustenance for the seeker's journey,
- illuminating the meditator's path.

www.ingramcontent.com/pod-product-compliance
Lightning Source LLC
Chambersburg PA
CBHW020346170426
43200CB00005B/63
9781681721286